W9-AIN-709

W Petersen
12 July 1989
Zürich

OCl.

45.40
R

THE ILLUSTRATED

MACAULAY'S HISTORY OF ENGLAND

THE ILLUSTRATED MACAULAY'S HISTORY OF ENGLAND

The Magnificent Journey of the British People from Serfdom to Parliamentary Government

Edited by

JOHN CANNING

Introduced by

LORD HOME OF THE HIRSEL K.T.

WEIDENFELD AND NICOLSON · LONDON

This edition and abridgement © John Canning 1988
Introduction © Lord Home of the Hirsel 1988
Published in Great Britain by
George Weidenfeld & Nicolson Limited
91 Clapham High Street
London SW4 7TA

All rights reserved.

ISBN 0-297-79292-x

Designed by Gaye Allen

Printed in Great Britain by
The Bath Press, Avon

Contents

Editors Note

Thomas Babington Macaulay was accustomed to instant success. His first essay in the *Edinburgh Review*, on Milton, won widespread praise and marked him out as a man to watch. His first speech in the House of Commons was acclaimed by both parties. The *Lays of Ancient Rome*, a first foray into poetry, gained him a mass readership. Even his relatively short residence in India as a member of the Supreme Council was reckoned a brilliant administrative *tour-de-force* and achieved results which have lasted down to the present day.

However, he considered his *History* to be the main achievement and memorial of his life. When the first two volumes were published in 1848, they followed the customary Macaulay formula and became instant best-sellers. On publication day carriages carrying eager readers choked Ludgate Hill up to his publisher's premises in the environs of St Pauls. Volumes 3 and 4 were equally successful. Volume 5 was published in 1861 by his sister Lady Trevelyan after his death.

The History of England took its place almost immediately as the classic 'Whig' account of history. David Hume's great work, giving the alternative conservative version, had up till then held the field. Macaulay eclipsed him completely.

Today the pendulum has partially swung back again; and Macaulay has been criticised for being unfair to certain people, particularly the Quaker Penn and Marlborough.

It is true that Macaulay had strong preconceived ideas, and that he was probably unfair to certain individuals. 'I wish I was as cocksure of anything as Tom Macaulay is of everything,' Lord Melbourne once tartly observed. But this very definiteness imparts to his writing an immense cogency; he never dithers or equivocates. Also, he writes beautifully. He was a great admirer of the novelist's art, particularly of Sir Walter Scott, and considered that history should be as interesting as a fine novel. A good historian, he said, should 'intersperse the details which are the charm of historical romances'. This Macaulay does, and singularly successfully.

The main achievement of the *History* is to describe the events leading up to the bloodless Revolution of 1688, and to put this great turning-point in the history of Britain and Europe into its historical and constitutional perspectives. No historian, before or since, has dealt with this episode in such magisterial detail. Every historian, of whatever historiographical persuasion, is deeply in his debt and is always likely to remain so.

The supremacy of Parliament, which the Revolution brought in train, with the monarchy playing a subordinate rôle, ran against the dominant political philosophy of the Continent, and was at first regarded by Louis

XIV as a situation of national weakness. This impression was gradually dispelled by Britain's growing commercial and financial strength, and by the stunning victories of Marlborough. A parliamentary government was seen to be generating greater economic and moral strength than its autocratic rivals. British institutions were to become the admired exemplars of the French philosophers and encyclopedists of the eighteenth century.

Macaulay had originally intended to bring his story down to a period within living memory; but he died when he had reached a point far short of this – the death of William III. The *History* is nevertheless a complete work, covering a vital segment of history.

We thought it fitting to commemorate on its tercentenary the outstanding constitutional achievement of the year 1688 and Macaulay's magnificent work by producing an illustrated volume with the essential text. Macaulay's singularly felicitous prose has enabled the editor to use the author's own words throughout whilst condensing him to a fraction of his original length – a task which would have been infinitely more difficult if not impossible with most other writers.

I have concluded the narrative on an upbeat note with the Battle of La Hogue. The remainder of the 1690s, with their many campaigns ending with the ultimately indecisive Treaty of Ryswick before the great Marlborough took the field, do not command quite the same compulsive interest as the preceding decades.

We hope that this smaller compass will bring Macaulay to the attention of a new generation of readers perhaps inhibited by the size of the original from embarking on an exciting and unforgettable journey.

A word on spellings: I have retained these as Macaulay has them in the original. The number of words differently spelt in his time is few, and mainly those such as 'sate', 'gripe', 'develope' where the final 'e' has become redundant.

I would like to express my thanks to Stan Remington for his shrewd advice so generously given in the early stages of the project; to Colin Gumbrell and Jane Blackett for most valuable editorial assistance; to Tom Gráves for illustration research; and to the imperturbable David Roberts, ever helpful at all stages of the book's gestation.

JOHN CANNING

Introduction

by Lord Home of the Hirsel K.T.

Time, in these days, is a commodity in short supply, and few can spare enough of it to read the large volumes of history in which our ancestors used to rejoice. As a result, we miss a lot. So the editor of this single volume of Macaulay's History of England has done the modern reader a real service in the abridged version, and he has done so without any loss of style or of the lucidity with which Macaulay told a tale.

And it is some story, for it tells of the early education of the people of England to the truth that the essence of a democratic state is restraint in the use of power. When the people who had to be taught that lesson were Kings, the elements of high drama were there.

The book is well illustrated, and the portraits, prints and drawings integrated with the text will help the young to recognise that, although the characters are clothed in period dress, they were in reality people who were very like us.

The Normans, for instance, are brought alive as a virile proud lot, ready to lead and accustomed to homage. William was well-named the Conqueror, for conquest was the Normans' business and a thorough job they made of it. The English, tribal and disorganised, responded to firm government, and after a century and a half were, with the invaders, pressing the weak King John to recognise their 'rights'. Macaulay marks Magna Carta as the first sign of the 'birth of a nation'.

The Plantagenet Kings were colourful and attractive personalities. They demonstrated courage, won their wars, earned respect, and strengthened the sense of loyalty to the office of Kingship. Under the great Angevins the foundations of liberty were gradually strengthened and extended. It was a process which owed much to the mutual respect of rulers and ruled.

The Tudors too, though assertive and autocratic and holding strongly to the view that 'rights' were also due to Kings, were always shrewd enough to recognise the limits of their power. Henry VIII was an athlete of Olympian proportions, and a compelling personality. Under his rule England grew steadily more prosperous economically, and added to her prestige in Europe. Elizabeth I was careful and politically calculating, and victorious over one of Britain's most powerful enemies – the King of Spain. At the sea-battle which destroyed his Armada she identified her person with the interests of the nation as perceived by the ordinary people who enjoyed a reflected glory. She personified monarchy, and was well-advised politically, especially by the Cecil family. She presided over an England which had emerged as a first-class power.

There was, however, trouble looming, partly because the succession went to the House of Stuart, the first of which – James I – was a feeble man, and partly because the new ideas which we now recognise as the Reformation were circulating and questioning the hitherto accepted religious doctrine as universally practised by the Church of Rome.

The absolutism of the Pope appealed greatly to James, who claimed that a prince of the Royal blood could do no wrong, and that, accordingly, not even an elected Parliament could question the King's actions. The interplay between politics and religion demanded finesse of a high order, but unhappily with the new King statecraft and churchcraft went out of the window.

The scene was full of complications and contradictions. James had, by his succession, united the crowns of Scotland and England, but the Scots were passionate Puritans. The Irish were strongly in favour of Roman Catholicism and looked upon the English King's support for an independent Church of England with disfavour and as treachery to the Church of Rome. There were therefore two internal tensions running concurrently: the political concerned with the King's attempt to dominate Parliament; and the religious which had to do with the King's leaning towards the Episcopal establishment and thereby upsetting the Puritans.

Macaulay dismissed James contemptuously as unmanly – trembling at the sight of a drawn sword, and as 'talking in the style alternately of a buffoon and of a pedagogue'. Certainly he went out of his way to pinprick and to insult Parliament. With the membership he established a relationship of antagonism, both in relation to his claim to act by Divine Right, and by his policy of leniency towards his Catholic subjects. In Church matters he left a legacy of friction which was growing fast and spreading wide.

No one could say that Charles I was unmanly. He had a fine presence, and the education and manners of a gentleman, but he held views on the prerogative of Kings much like his father, while, if he had to choose between a Presbyterian and a Papist he would denounce both, but lean towards Rome. He was aided and abetted by two bad advisers – the Earl of Strafford and Archbishop Laud, and two special Courts – the Star Chamber and the High Commission; the first political and the second religious were used to persecute objectors and dissidents.

Strafford's policy of Thorough was intended to make Charles an absolute monarch, and the necessary instrument for this was a standing army. However the people were shrewd; they had seen the Kings of France and Spain use their standing armies not only against the foreign enemy, but against civil liberties in their own countries. They sensed that England as an island had not been in similar danger – until now.

Macaulay analyses the King's character and concludes that his fault was an infinite capacity for 'faithlessness'. To extract 'supply' from the House of Commons he would make any promise and as light-heartedly go back on it, repeating the process with such frequency that he spread around him a total lack of trust. At last, so despairing was the House that some of its members refused to accept from the King's hand the tax of 'ship-money', which was necessary to the building of a standing army. So much a man of action was Charles that he went in person to try and arrest them in Parliament. He failed, and with that fiasco the point had been reached when the claim to rule had to be settled. Who was to exercise the supreme authority? – the King or Parliament? There could be only one answer, but the argument could not be settled before an appeal to force.

The British people were loyal to the office of monarchy, but still more wedded to the concept of the rule of law. The challenge to law was an offence which had to be met by a trial of strength. The King fled from London to Oxford. The Cavaliers rallied to his standard while the Roundheads' eventually victorious army was recruited and trained by Cromwell.

The Civil War was fought keenly and hard. Happily, however, as Macaulay reports: 'The majority of those who fought for Royalty were averse to despotism, and the great majority of those of the champions of popular rights were against anarchy'! Typically English!

Nevertheless the King had committed the crime of seeking to overthrow Parliament by force, and there was no penalty which was appropriate short of death. In the minds of Parliamentarians the office of King was separated from the individual who occupied it. Charles was executed in public in Whitehall in the capital city of his realm. At his death he revealed all those qualities of courage and chivalry which the English have always held dear, and so moved the nation that the miracle of the restoration of Kingship came within the realm of possibility.

In order to win the war and take over the nation Cromwell, whose personality had forced him to the head of the Parliamentarians, had to raise a standing army. He produced a finely trained, dedicated and efficient force, and deployed it to sustain the elected Parliament. He annihilated the opposition of the Scots, and conquered the Irish; while his foreign policy, stemming from strength, increased English prestige on the Continent of Europe.

He was not however a prince of the Royal blood, and although he wielded great authority he believed that he would not have the support of his army should he declare himself to be King. He became, with the assent of Parliament, Lord Protector of England, Scotland and Ireland, but beyond that imposing title he did not dare to go.

Macaulay paints a vivid picture of how, in Westminster Hall, he was clothed in a purple robe and presented with a Bible, and was allowed to name his successor. All that but no crown. The English people's instinct against a standing army was proved to be right. The soldiers became too big for their boots and in the end the people all over the country rebelled against their abuse of power.

General Monk, no fanatic but a lover of law and order, marched on London with the purpose of restoring the throne to the young King who was in exile in Holland. Monk had rightly calculated the public mood, and the return of the royal line of the Stuarts was greeted by the whole nation with unrestrained acclaim.

With the record and fate of his predecessor so recent it was reasonable to assume that the new King would adapt himself to constitutional rule, and pursue a policy of calculated moderation in Church affairs; but such behaviour was not in the character of Charles II. He gave himself over to a life of pleasure, self-indulgence and dissipation, and laid himself wide open to flattery by beautiful women, and to persuasion by advisers who dealt in duplicity and intrigue. He thought that he could mould Parliament to his ways, and induce them to agree to his financial demands by persuading the King of France to pay him large subsidies which he would use to make himself independent of Parliament.

In undercover negotiations, however, Charles was no match for Louis XIV who supplied him with enough to keep him on a string, but not enough to secure him independence. Charles was caught. He was persuaded to change his foreign policy and support the French King in a war against the Netherlands. Privately he promised to become a Roman Catholic. The French Ambassador was a constant influence in the Court of St. James, and a French woman whom Macaulay described as 'handsome but licentious and crafty' was inserted into the Household by the King of France, and was created Duchess of Portsmouth by the King of England for services given.

The scandals multiplied and became public property, and the people became more and more apprehensive. The King leaned further towards Roman Catholicism, and with the Duke of York already of that persuasion the prospect opened up of a line of heirs under the influence of Rome.

Two calamities added to popular forebodings – the Great Plague and the Fire of London. Charles might plead that he was badly advised, for his Ministers were the notorious five – known as the 'Cabal'; but too many knew that they were self-seeking and corrupt and advanced the kind of advice which the King liked to receive. When Charles died Macaulay records 'there was scarcely a housemaid in London who had not contrived to secure some fragment of crêpe in honour of King Charles'. There is always sympathy for human weakness, but it was scarcely the epitaph for a King.

During the latter years of Charles's reign a rumour had been started and swept the country, that a plot was being hatched by the Pope for Roman Catholics to take over all the main ministerial offices in the government of England. With public opinion on edge the rumour spread like wild-fire, and was fanned by a Church of England clergyman – Titus Oates. He was a disgrace to his cloth, and Macaulay states in unflattering terms that he had a 'face on which villainy seemed to have been written by the hand of God'.

James II, the last of the Stuart Kings, tried actively to reverse the trend of feeling against Catholics, but did so without either sense or sensibility. He packed his own councils with Catholics, actively favoured the claims of his co-religionists for public office, pursued a vengeful course of action against the Puritan sects aided by the infamous Chief Justice Jeffries, and finally made a direct assault on the position of the Established Church.

Reasonable men decided that enough was enough and concluded that the only course of action was to look for rescue to William of Orange and his wife Mary who was at least of the legitimate royal line.

Not unnaturally William had misgivings, but he was a Protestant with a strong sense of duty, and he was persuaded to intervene. Good men played their part; Churchill, later to become Duke of Marlborough, and Halifax, who, in the House of Lords, swayed the debate. Ever since then the British people have boasted that 1688 was the year in which the foundations of our constitutional monarchy were laid, and Parliament was acknowledged to be supreme.

This is an exciting and dramatic tale told in classic English and in impeccable style.

PART 1 From the Conquest to the Restoration

Plantagenets and Tudors

The battle of Hastings, and the events which followed it, not only placed a Duke of Normandy on the English throne, but gave up the whole population of England to the tyranny of the Norman race. During the century and a half which followed the Conquest, there is, to speak strictly, no English history. The French Kings of England rose, indeed, to an eminence which was the wonder and dread of all neighbouring nations. They conquered Ireland. They received the homage of Scotland. By their valour, by their policy, by their fortunate matrimonial alliances, they became far more powerful on the Continent than their liege lords the Kings of France.

Had the Plantagenets, as at one time seemed likely, succeeded in uniting all France under their government, it is probable that England would never have had an independent existence. Her princes, her lords, her prelates, would have been men differing in race and language from the artisans and the tillers of the earth. No man of English extraction would have risen to eminence, except by becoming in speech and habits a Frenchman.

England owes her escape from such calamities to an event which her historians have generally represented as disastrous. Her interest was so directly opposed to the interest of her rulers that she had no hope but in their errors and misfortunes. The talents and even the virtues of her first six French Kings were a curse to her. The follies and vices of the seventh were her salvation. Had John inherited the great qualities of his father, of Henry Beauclerc, or of the Conqueror, nay, had he even possessed the martial courage of Stephen or of Richard, and had the King of France at the same time been as incapable as all the other successors of Hugh Capet had been, the House of Plantagenet must have risen to unrivalled ascendency in Europe. But, just at this conjuncture, France, for the first time since the death of Charlemagne, was governed by a prince of great firmness and ability. On the other hand England, which, since the battle of Hastings, had been ruled generally by wise statesmen, always by brave soldiers, fell under the dominion of a trifler and a coward. From that moment her prospects brightened. John was driven from Normandy. The Norman nobles were compelled to make their election between the island and the Continent. Shut up by the sea with the people whom they had hitherto oppressed and despised, they gradually came to regard England as their country, and the English as their countrymen. The two races, so long hostile, soon found that they had common interests and common enemies. Both were alike aggrieved by the tyranny of a bad king. Both were alike indignant at the favour shown by the court to the natives of Poitou and Aquitaine. The great-grandsons of those who had fought under William and the great-grandsons of those who had fought under Harold began to

Details from the Bayeux Tapestry showing (above) William the Conqueror dining with Bishop Odon and his barons before the battle of Hastings, and (below) in the heat of the battle raising his helmet to let his troops see that he has not been killed.

draw near to each other in friendship; and the first pledge of their reconciliation was the Great Charter, won by their united exertions, and framed for their common benefit.

Here commences the history of the English nation. The history of the preceding events is the history of wrongs inflicted and sustained by various tribes, which indeed all dwelt on English ground, but which regarded each other with aversion such as has scarcely ever existed between communities separated by physical barriers. For even the mutual animosity of countries at war with each other is languid when compared with the animosity of nations which, morally separated, are yet locally intermingled. In no country has the enmity of race been carried farther than in England. In no country has that enmity been more completely effaced. The stages of the process by which the hostile elements were melted down into one homogeneous mass are not accurately known to us. But it is certain that, when John became King, the distinction between Saxons and Normans was strongly marked, and that before the end of the reign of his grandson it had almost disappeared.

Early in the fourteenth century the amalgamation of the races was all but complete; and it was soon made manifest, by signs not to be mistaken, that a people inferior to none existing in the world had been formed by the mixture of three branches of the great Teutonic family with each other, and with the aboriginal Britons. There was, indeed, scarcely anything in common between the England to which John had been chased by Philip Augustus, and the England from which the armies of Edward III went forth to conquer France.

A period of more than a hundred years followed, during which the chief object of the English was to establish, by force of arms, a great empire on the Continent. The claim of Edward to the inheritance occupied by the House of Valois was a claim in which it might seem that his subjects were little interested. But the passion for conquest spread fast from the prince to the people. The war differed widely from the wars which the Plantagenets of the twelfth century had waged against the descendants of Hugh Capet. For the success of Henry II, or of Richard I, would have made England a province of France. The effect of the success of Edward III and Henry V was to make France, for a time, a province of England. The disdain with which, in the twelfth century, the conquerors from the Continent had regarded the islanders, was now retorted by the islanders on the people of the Continent. Every yeoman from Kent to Northumberland valued himself as one of a race born for victory and dominion, and looked down with scorn on the nation before which his ancestors had trembled. The most splendid victories recorded in the history of the middle ages were gained at this time, against great odds, by the English armies. A French King was brought prisoner to London. An English King was crowned at Paris. The banner of Saint George was carried far beyond the Pyrenees and the Alps.

Nor were the arts of peace neglected by our fathers during that stirring period. While France was wasted by war, till she at length found in her own desolation a miserable defence against invaders, the English gathered in their harvests, adorned their cities, pleaded, traded, and studied in security. Many of our noblest architectural monuments belong to that age. Then rose the fair chapels of New College and of Saint George, the nave of Winchester and the choir of York, the spire of Salisbury and the majestic towers of Lincoln. A copious and forcible language, formed by an infusion of French into German, was now the common property of the aristocracy and of the people. Nor was it long before genius began to apply that admirable machine to worthy purposes. While English warriors, leaving behind them the devastated provinces of France, entered Valladolid in triumph, and spread terror to the gates of Florence, English poets depicted in vivid tints all the wide variety of human manner and fortunes, and

HERTFORDSCIRE.

ad preccore 7 libatore iussu epi baioc. qd ei libauit p excabio
In Anestei ten pagan de hard dim hid. de Sutterehele.
Tra. e. i. car 7 dim. 7 ibi sunt cu. iiii. bord. 7 iii. cot. 7 uno
seruo. prat dim car. pasta ad pecun. Silua. xii. porc.
H tra ual. xx. sol. qdo recep. x. sol. T.R.E. xx. sol.
hanc tenuit Aluuard ho Algari. 7 uende potuit.
Ipse hard ten Berchehastede. In Hertford hund.
p. v. hid se defd. Tra. e. viii. car. In dnio. iii. hide. 7 ibi
sunt. ii. car. 7 tcia pot fieri. Ibi. vi. uilli cu. v. bord. hnt
iii. car. 7 v. pot fieri. Ibi. vi. cot. 7 i. seruus. prat. iii. car.
Silua. l. porc. In totis ualent ual. c. sol. X do recep.
l. sol. T.R.E. c. sol. De hoc m tenuit Semar. ii. hid. 7 qda
uidua Leuefa. ii. hid. 7 Wluric. i. hid. he tre fuer de ele
mosina. R.E. 7 omiu regu antecessor suor. ut scira testat.
m Ipse harduin ten Brandefelle. p. v. hid se defd. Tra e
vi. car. In dnio. iii. hide. 7 ibi e. i. car 7 dim. 7 dim pot fieri.
Ibi. x. uilli hnt. ii. car 7 dim. 7 adhuc. i. car 7 dim pot fieri.
Ibi. i. seruus. prat. i. car. pastura ad pec. Silua. c. porc.
7 xii. den de ea. In totis ualent ual. iii. lib. X do recep.
xl. sol. T.R.E. c. sol. hoc m tenuit Achi teign heraldi.
In Briceuuolde ten Balduin de hard uende pot.
iii. uirg. Tra. e. ii. car. Ibi. e una. 7 alia poss fieri. Ibi. ii.
uilli. 7 iii. bord. prat. iii. bob. Silua. xv. porc. H tra ual
v. sol. X do recep. x. sol. 7 tntd T.R.E.
xxxviii. TERRA EDGARI ADELING. In Edwinestreu hd.
EDGARUS Adeling 7 Goduin de eo ten in Berchewei
. i. hid 7 dim. Tra. e. ii. car. In dnio. e una. 7 iii. bord
cu. iiii. cot hnt. i. car. Ibi. i. seruus. pasta ad pecun. Silua
xv. porc. H tra ual. xl. sol. X do recep. x. sol. T.R.E. xl. sol.
hanc tenuer. ii. sochi hoes Algari. 7 uende potuer.
m Isde Goduin ten de Edgaro Horemede. p. vi. hid 7 iii.
uirg se defd. Tra. e. x. car. In dnio sunt. iii. 7 v. pot fieri.
Ibi. vi. uilli cu. xv. bord. hnt. v. car. Ibi. ii. cot 7 vi. serui.
prat. i. car. pasta ad pecun. Silua. xxiiii. porc. In totis ua
lent ual. viii. lib. X do recep. vi. lib. T.R.E. xii. lib.
De hoc m tenuit Alnod teign Stig arch. i. hid dim p. i. m.
7 Aluuin ho Algari. i. hida. 7 Aluuard ho Almar de belint
. i. hida. 7 vii. sochi. R.E. tenuer. iii. hid 7 i. uirg. 7 uicecomiti
xiii. denar p annu reddider. Oms hi tra sua uende potuer.
Hos. vii. sochos 7 Aluuin 7 Aluuard apposuit Ilbt uicec
huic m tepore. R.W. qui nfuer ibi T.R.E. ut hund testat.
xxxix. TERRA MANNON BRITONIS. In Redunge hund.
MAINO Brito ten in Deneslai tcia part de dim hida.
Tra e uno boui. Val 7 ualuit sep. xii. den. hanc tra te
nuit Engelri T.R.E. 7 iacuit in Tredinge 7 est de. vii. hid
qual com morit assupsit.
. xl. TERRA GISLEBERTI filii SALOMON.
GISLEBERTUS fili Salom ten Mapleshale. p. iii.
hid 7 una uirg se defd. Ibi sunt. iii. uilli 7 iii. cot.
H tra. e appciata in Bedefordscyre cu alia tra.
hanc tra tenuit Leuuin teign. R.E.
. xli. TERRA SIGAR DE CIOCHES. In Odesei hundret.
SIGAR de Cioches ten Risendene. p. v. hid se defd.
Tra. e. viii. car. In dnio. iii. hide. 7 ibi sunt. ii. car. 7 tcia
pot fieri. Ibi. viii. uilli cu. iii. bord. hnt. v. car. Ibi un
sochs. 7 iii. cot 7 iii. serui. prat dim car. pasta ad pecun.

Silua. l. porc. In totis ualent ual 7 ualuit. c. x. sol. T.R.E.
x. sol. hoc m tenuer. ii. sochi hoes Stig archiepi. 7 uende
In Bradefelle ten Sigar. i. hid 7 iii. partes potuer.
uni uirg. Tra. e. ii. car. Ibi. e una. 7 alia pot fieri. Ibi. iiii.
uilli cu. ii. bord. prat dim car. pastura ad pecun. Silua. l.
porc. In totis ual 7 ualuit. xxx. sol. T.R.E. lx. sol. hanc
tra tenuit Ansgot ho Stig archiepi. 7 uende potuit.
. xlii. TERRA TAINORU REGIS. In Bradewatre hund.
DERMAN 7 ALWARD ten de rege Wodtone. p. v.
hid se defd. Tra. e. vii. car. In dnio. iii. hide 7 dim.
7 ibi sunt. ii. car. 7 adhuc dim pot fieri. Ibi. x. uilli cu. iiij.
bord hnt. iii. car 7 dim. Ibi. iiii. serui. 7 i. molin de xii.
solid. 7 iii. den. prat. i. car. pastura ad pecun. Silua
c. porc. In totis ual 7 ualuit. c. sol. T.R.E. vii. lib.
hanc tra tenuit Aluuin horne teign. R.E. 7 uende pot.
m Ipse Derman ten Walchra. p. x. hid se defd. Tra e
xii. car. In dnio v. hide. 7 ibi sunt. ii. car 7 aliae duae
possunt fieri. Ibi. xiiii. uilli cu pbro 7 vi. bord hnt
viii. car. Ibi. viii. cot 7 iii. serui. pastura ad pecun.
Silua. cc. porc. In totis ualent ual. x. lib. X do recep.
viii. lib. T.R.E. xvi. lib. hoc m tenuit Aluuin horne
teign. R.E. 7 uende potuit.
In Sutterehele. ten Derman. iii. uirg. Tra. e. i. car.
s; n est ibi car. H tra. e appciata in Watone m Derman.
In ead uilla ten Derman. iii. ac. Val 7 ualuer sep. iii. den.
In Sueuechap ten Derman dim uirg. Tra. e. ii. bob.
Val 7 ualuit sep. xii. den. hanc tra 7 alias superores
tenuit Aluuin horne teign. R.E. 7 uende potuit.
In Hertford hund.
In Wermelai. ten Aluuin Dodesone. ii. hid 7 dim de
rege. Tra. e. ii. car. 7 ibi sunt cu. vi. uillis 7 uno seruo.
prat. ii. car. pastura ad pecun. Silua. cl. porc. In totis
ual. xl. sol. X do recep. l. sol. T.R.E. lx. sol. Hoc m
tenuit Wluuard ho Algari stalr. 7 uende potuit.
hoc m fuit uenditu. iii. mark auri. p aduent regis Willi.
Petrus qda burgensis ten. ii. hid de rege in Dodesdone.
Tra. e. i. car 7 dim. 7 ibi sunt cu. i. uillo. 7 iii. cot
7 ii. seruis. prat. ii. car. pasta ad pecun. Silua. x. porc.
In totis ual. xx. sol. X do recep. x. sol. T.R.E. xxx. sol.
hoc m tenuit Goda ho Eddid regine. 7 uende potuit.
Balduin qda seruiens regis ten. iii. uirg in Brichedone.
Tra. e. i. car. 7 ibi. e. Silua. xl. porc. H tra ual 7 ualuit
x. sol. T.R.E. xv. sol. hanc tra tenuer. iii. frs. 7 uende
In Briceuuolde ten qda pbr 7 soror ei potuer.
de rege. iii. uirg. Tra. e. ii. car. Ibi. e una. 7 alia pot
fieri. Ibi. i. uills 7 i. cot. prat. iii. bob. Silua. xv. porc. H tra
ual. v. sol. X do recep. x. sol. 7 tntd T.R.E. Istimet tenuer
T.R.E. de soca ei. 7 uende potuer.
In Thepecape ten qda pbr de elemosina regis dim hida.
Tra. e. i. car. 7 ibi. e cu. ii. seruis. prat. i. car. 7 i. molin de. xii.
den. H tra ual 7 ualuit. xx. sol. T.R.E. xx. sol. Istimet
tenuit. T.R.E. 7 adhuc ten in demosina. In Bradewatre hd.
In Welge ten qda pbr. i. hid in demosina de rege. Tra. e
. iii. car. In dnio. e una. 7 alia pot fieri. Ibi. vi. bord hnt
. i. car. Ibi. ii. cot. prat. i. car. pastura ad pecun. Silua. l. porc.
In totis ual 7 ualuit sep. xxv. sol. Istimet tenuit de rege. E.

Magna Carta, sealed in 1215, was a document dealing essentially with the privileges of Norman barons. In the course of time however these privileges were extended to a growing body of citizens and came to be regarded as part of the nation's constitutional rights.

English thinkers aspired to know, or dared to doubt, where bigots had been content to wonder and to believe. The same age which produced the Black Prince and Derby, Chandos and Hawkwood, produced also Geoffrey Chaucer and John Wycliffe.

In so splendid and imperial a manner did the English people, properly so called, take first place among the nations of the world. But the spirit of the French was at last aroused: they began to oppose a vigorous national resistance to the foreign conquerors; and from that time the skill of the English captains and the courage of the English soldiers were, happily for mankind, exerted in vain. After many desperate struggles, and with many bitter regrets, our ancestors gave up the contest. Since that age no British government has ever seriously and steadily pursued the design of making great conquests on the Continent. The people, indeed, continued to cherish with pride the recollection of Cressy, of Poitiers, and of Agincourt. Even after the lapse of many years it was easy to fire their blood and to draw forth their subsidies by promising them an expedition for the conquest of France. But happily the energies of our country have been directed to better objects; and she now occupies in the history of mankind a place far more glorious than if she had, as at one time seemed not improbable, acquired by the sword an ascendency similar to that which formerly belonged to the Roman republic.

A page from the great Domesday Book, commissioned in 1086 to enumerate the wealth of the country and make possible a system of taxation.

Cooped up once more within the limits of the island, the warlike people employed in civil strife those arms which had been the terror of Europe. Two aristocratical factions, headed by two branches of the royal family, engaged in a long and fierce struggle for supremacy. As the animosity of

Art burgeoned with constitutional progress. The spire of Salisbury Cathedral rose in the 13th century, the period that Macaulay considered the seed time of the English Parliamentary system and of the Common Law.

those factions did not really arise from the dispute about the succession, it lasted long after all ground of dispute about the succession was removed. The party of the Red Rose survived the last prince who claimed the crown in right of Henry IV. The party of the White Rose survived the marriage of Richmond and Elizabeth. Left without chiefs who had any decent show of right, the adherents of Lancaster rallied round a line of bastards, and the adherents of York set up a succession of impostors. When, at length, many aspiring nobles had perished on the field of battle or by the hands of the executioner, when many illustrious houses had disappeared for ever from history, when those great families which remained had been exhausted and sobered by calamities, it was universally acknowledged that the claims of all the contending Plantagenets were united in the house of Tudor.

Meanwhile a change was proceeding infinitely more momentous than the acquisition or loss of any province, than the rise or fall of any dynasty. Slavery and the evils by which slavery is everywhere accompanied were fast disappearing.

It is remarkable that the two greatest and most salutary social revolutions which have taken place in England, that revolution which, in the thirteenth century, put an end to the tyranny of nation over nation, and that revolution which, a few generations later, put an end to the property of man in man, were silently and imperceptibly effected. Moral causes noiselessly effaced first the distinction between Norman and Saxon, and then the distinction between master and slave.

There can be no doubt that, when these two great revolutions had been effected, our forefathers were by far the best governed people in Europe. During three hundred years the social system had been in a constant course of improvement. Under the first Plantagenets there had been barons able to bid defiance to the sovereign, and peasants degraded to the level of the swine and oxen which they tended. The exorbitant power of the baron had been gradually reduced. The condition of the peasant had been gradually elevated. Between the aristocracy and the working people had sprung up a middle class, agricultural and commercial. There was still, it may be, more inequality than is favourable to the happiness and virtue of our species: but no man was altogether above the restraints of law; and no man was altogether below its protection.

After the wars of York and Lancaster, the links which connected the nobility and the commonalty became closer and more numerous than ever. The constitution of the House of Commons tended greatly to promote the salutary intermixture of classes. The knight of the shire was the connecting link between the baron and the shopkeeper. On the same benches on which sate the goldsmiths, drapers, and grocers, who had been returned to Parliament by the commercial towns, sate also members who, in any other country, would have been called noblemen, hereditary lords of manors, entitled to hold courts and to bear coat armour, and able to trace back an honourable descent through many generations. Some of them were younger sons and brothers of lords. Others could boast of even royal blood. Thus our democracy was, from an early period, the most aristocratic, and our aristocracy the most democratic in the world.

The government of Henry VII, of his son, and of his grandchildren was, on the whole, more arbitrary than that of the Plantagenets. Personal character may in some degree explain the difference; for courage and force of will were common to all the men and women of the House of Tudor.

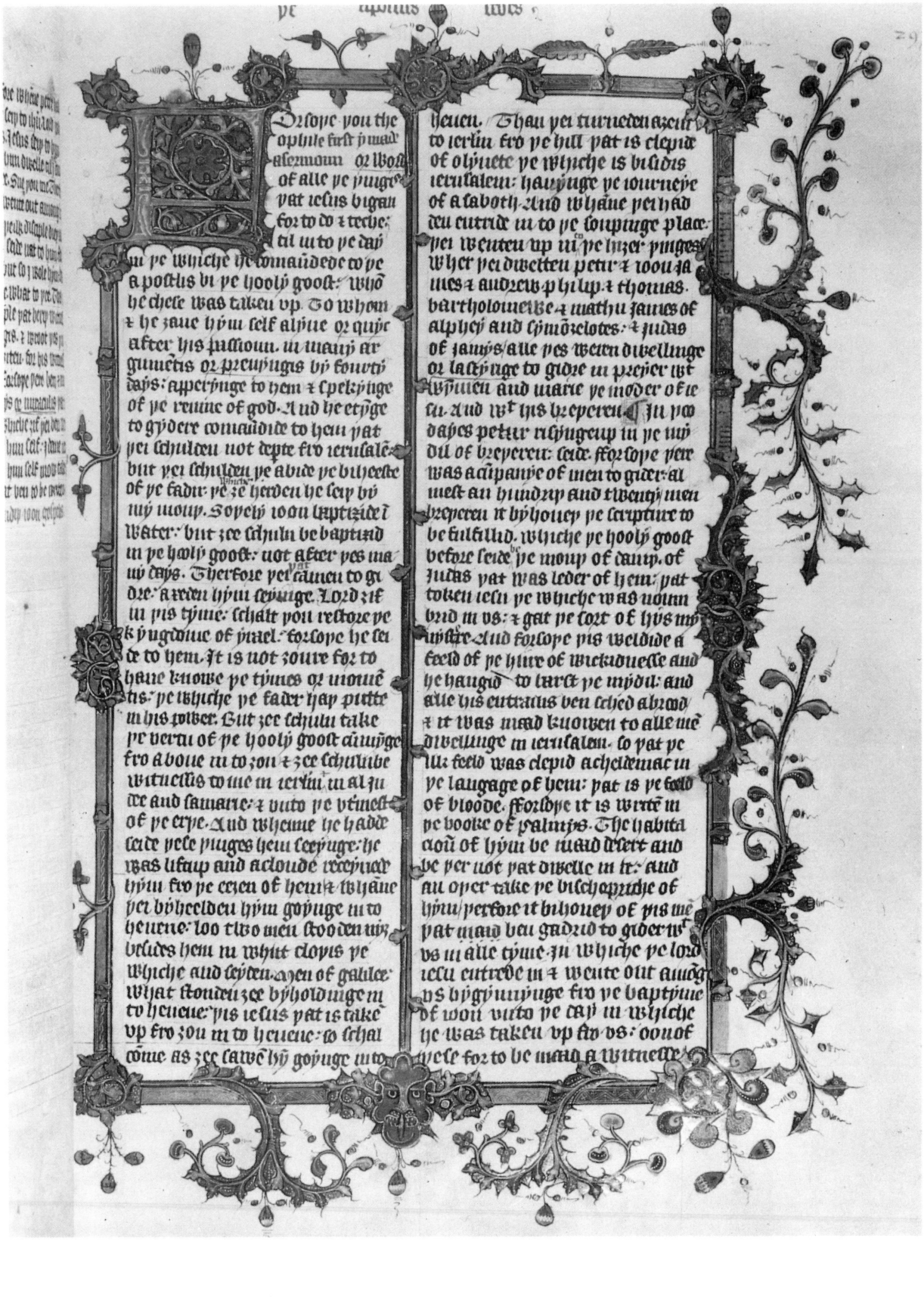

þe apostlis dedis

Forsoþe þou theofile first y made sermoun of alle þe þingis þat iesus bigan for to do & teche: til in to þe dai in þe whiche he comaundide to þe apostlis bi þe hooly goost: whom he chese was taken up. To whom & he zaue hym self alyue or quyk after his passioun. in many argumentis or preuyngis by fourti days: apperynge to hem & spekynge of þe rewme of god. And he etynge to gidere comaundide to hem þat þei schulden not depte fro ierusalem: but þei schulden abide þe biheeste of þe fadir: þe whiche ze herden he seiþ by my mouþ. Forsoþe ioon baptizide in water: but ze schuln be baptized in þe hooly goost: not after þes many days. Therfore þei þat camen to gidere axiden hym seiynge. Lord zif in þis tyme: schalt þou restore þe kyngdome of israel: forsoþe he seide to hem. It is not zoure for to haue knowe þe tymes or momentis: þe whiche þe fadir haþ putte in his power. But ze schuln take þe vertu of þe hooly goost cummynge fro aboue in to zou & ze schuln be witnessis to me in ierusalem in al iudee and samarie: & unto þe utmest of þe erþe. And whanne he hadde seide þese þingis hem seeynge: he was lift up and a cloude receyuede hym fro þe eyen of hem. & whanne þei biheelden hym goynge in to heuene: loo two men stooden nyz bisidis hem in whit cloþis þe whiche and seiden. men of galilee: what stonden ze byholdinge in to heuene: þis iesus þat is taken up fro zou in to heuene: so schal come as ze sawen hym goynge in to heuen.

Than þei turneden azein to ierusalem fro þe hill þat is clepid of olyuete þe whiche is bisidis ierusalem: hauynge þe iourneye of a saboth. And whanne þei hadden entride in to þe soupinge place: þei wenten up in to þe hizer þingis wher þei dwelten petir & ioon iames & andrew philip & thomas. bartholomew & mathu iames of alphey and symound zelotes: & iudas of iamys. alle þes weren dwellinge or lastynge to gidre in preier wiþ wymmen and marie þe moder of iesu. and wiþ his breþeren. In þo dayes petir risynge up in þe myddil of breþeren: seide. forsoþe þer was a cumpanye of men to gidere: almest an hundryþ and twenti men. Breþeren it byhoueþ þe scripture to be fulfillid. whiche þe hooly goost bifore seide bi þe mouþ of dauiþ. of iudas þat was leder of hem: þat token iesu þe whiche was noumbrid in us: & gat þe lot of þis mynystrie. And forsoþe þis weldide a feeld of þe hire of wickidnesse and he hangid to brast þe myddil: and alle his entrailis ben sched abrood & it was maad knowen to alle men dwellinge in ierusalem. so þat þe ilk feeld was clepid acheldemac in þe langage of hem: þat is þe feeld of bloode. fforsoþe it is writen in þe booke of salmys. The habitacioun of hym be maad desert and be þer not þat dwelle in it: and an oþer take þe bischopriche of hym. þerfore it bihoueþ of þis men þat ben gadrid to gider wiþ us in alle tyme. in which þe lord iesu entrede in & wente out among us bigynnynge fro þe baptyme of ioon unto þe day in which he was taken up fro us: oon of þese for to be maad a witnesse

Macaulay remarks that the same age that produced the Black Prince produced also Geoffrey Chaucer and John Wycliffe. An early rebel against the system of papal rule, Wycliffe produced the first complete version of the Bible in English. A page from the late fourteenth-century Wycliffe Bible.

They exercised their power during a period of a hundred and twenty years, always with vigour, often with violence, sometimes with cruelty. It was, however, impossible for the Tudors to carry oppression beyond a certain point: for they had no armed force, and they were surrounded by an armed people. Their palace was guarded by a few domestics, whom the array of a single shire, or of a single ward of London, could with ease have overpowered. These haughty princes were therefore under a restraint stronger than any which mere law can impose, under a restraint which did not, indeed, prevent them from sometimes treating an individual in an arbitrary and even in a barbarous manner, but which effectually secured the nation against general and long continued oppression. Henry VIII, for example, encountered no opposition when he wished to send Buckingham and Surrey, Anne Boleyn and Lady Salisbury, to the scaffold. But when, without the consent of Parliament, he demanded of his subjects a contribution amounting to one sixth of their goods, he soon found it necessary to

Print of an original MS of the Parliament of Edward I showing the King seated between King Alexander of Scotland and Llewellen, Prince of Wales. This is one of the earliest representations of the King in Parliament.

retract. The cry of hundreds of thousands was that they were English and not French, freemen and not slaves. Henry, proud and selfwilled as he was, shrank, not without reason, from a conflict with the roused spirit of the nation. He had before his eyes the fate of his predecessors who had perished at Berkeley and Pomfret. He not only cancelled his illegal commissions; he not only granted a general pardon to all the malecontents; but he publicly and solemnly apologised for his infraction of the laws.

His conduct, on this occasion, well illustrates the whole policy of his house. The temper of the princes of that line was hot, and their spirit high: but they understood the character of the nation which they governed, and never once, like some of their predecessors, and some of their successors, carried obstinacy to a fatal point. The discretion of the Tudors was such, that their power, though it was often resisted, was never subverted.

Thus, from the age of Henry III to the age of Elizabeth, England grew and flourished under a polity which contained the germ of our present institutions, and which, though not very exactly defined, or very exactly observed, was yet effectually prevented from degenerating into despotism, by the awe in which the governors stood of the spirit and strength of the governed.

But such a polity is suited only to a particular stage in the progress of society. The same causes which produce a division of labour in the peaceful arts must at length make war a distinct science and a distinct trade. A time arrives when the use of arms begins to occupy the entire attention of a separate class. It soon appears that peasants and burghers, however brave, are unable to stand their ground against veteran soldiers, whose whole life is a preparation for the day of battle. It is found that the defence of nations can no longer be safely entrusted to warriors taken from the plough or the loom for a campaign of forty days. If any state forms a great regular army, the bordering states must imitate the example, or must submit to a foreign yoke. But, where a great regular army exists, limited monarchy, such as it was in the middle ages, can exist no longer. The sovereign is at once emancipated from what had been the chief restraint on his power; and he inevitably becomes absolute, unless he is subjected to checks such as would be superfluous in a society where all are soldiers occasionally, and none permanently.

With the danger came also the means of escape. In the monarchies of the middle ages the power of the sword belonged to the prince; but the power of the purse belonged to the nation; and the progress of civilisation, as it made the sword of the prince more and more formidable to the nation, made the purse of the nation more and more necessary to the prince. It was utterly impossible that, without a regular and extensive system of taxation, he could keep in constant efficiency a great body of disciplined troops. The policy which the parliamentary assemblies of Europe ought to have adopted was to take their stand firmly on their constitutional right to give or withhold money, and resolutely to refuse funds for the support of armies, till ample securities had been provided against despotism.

This wise policy was followed in our country alone. In the neighbouring kingdoms great military establishments were formed; no new safeguards for public liberty were devised; and the consequence was, that the old parliamentary institutions everywhere ceased to exist. In France, where they had always been feeble, they languished, and at length died of mere weakness. In Spain, where they had been as strong as in any part of Europe, they struggled fiercely for life, but struggled too late.

The Great Seal of Henry VIII.

King Henry VIII by Holbein.

In England events took a different course. This singular felicity she owed chiefly to her insular situation. Before the end of the fifteenth century great military establishments were indispensable to the dignity, and even to the safety, of the French and Castilian monarchies. If either of those two powers had disarmed, it would soon have been compelled to submit to the dictation of the other. But England, protected by the sea against invasion, and rarely engaged in warlike operations on the Continent, was not, as yet, under the necessity of employing regular troops. The sixteenth century, the seventeenth century, found her still without a standing army. At the commencement of the seventeenth century political science had made considerable progress. The fate of the Spanish Cortes and of the French States General had given solemn warning to our Parliaments; and our Parliaments, fully aware of the nature and magnitude of the danger, adopted, in good time, a system of tactics which, after a contest protracted through three generations, was at length successful.

It seems certain that, had none but political causes been at work, the seventeenth century would not have passed away without a fierce conflict between our Kings and their Parliaments. But other causes of perhaps greater potency contributed to produce the same effect. While the government of the Tudors was in its highest vigour an event took place which has coloured the destinies of all Christian nations, and in an especial manner the destinies of England. That great change emphatically called the Reformation began.

Foundation of the Church of England

It is difficult to say whether England owes more to the Roman Catholic religion or to the Reformation. For the amalgamation of races and for the abolition of villenage, she is chiefly indebted to the influence which the priesthood in the middle ages exercised over the laity. For political and intellectual freedom, and for all the blessings which political and intellectual freedom have brought in their train, she is chiefly indebted to the great rebellion of the laity against the priesthood.

The struggle between the old and the new theology in our country was long, and the event sometimes seemed doubtful. There were two extreme parties, prepared to act with violence or to suffer with stubborn resolution. Between them lay, during a considerable time, a middle party, which blended, very illogically, but by no means unnaturally, lessons learned in the nursery with the sermons of the modern evangelists, and, while clinging with fondness to old observances, yet detested abuses with which those observances were closely connected. Men in such a frame of mind were willing to obey, almost with thankfulness, the dictation of an able ruler who spared them the trouble of judging for themselves, and, raising a firm and commanding voice above the uproar of controversy, told them how to worship and what to believe. It is not strange, therefore, that the Tudors should have been able to exercise a great influence on ecclesiastical affairs; nor is it strange that their influence should, for the most part, have been exercised with a view to their own interest.

Henry VIII attempted to constitute an Anglican Church differing from the Roman Catholic Church on the point of the supremacy, and on that point alone. His success in this attempt was extraordinary. The force of his character, the singularly favourable situation in which he stood with respect to foreign powers, the immense wealth which the spoliation of the abbeys placed at his disposal, and the support of that class which still halted between two opinions, enabled him to bid defiance to both the extreme parties, to burn as heretics those who avowed the tenets of the Reformers, and to hang as traitors those who owned the authority of the Pope. But Henry's system died with him.

The ministers who held the royal prerogatives in trust for his infant son could not venture to persist in so hazardous a policy; nor could Elizabeth venture to return to it. It was necessary to make a choice. The government must either submit to Rome, or must obtain the aid of the Protestants. The government and the Protestants had only one thing in common, hatred of the Papal power. The English Reformers were eager to go as far as their brethren on the Continent. They unanimously condemned as Antichristian numerous dogmas and practices to which Henry had stubbornly adhered, and which Elizabeth reluctantly abandoned. Many felt a strong repugnance even to things indifferent which had formed part of the polity or ritual of the mystical Babylon. Thus Bishop Hooper, who died manfully at Gloucester for his religion, long refused to wear the episcopal vestments. Bishop Ridley, a martyr of still greater renown, pulled down the ancient altars of his diocese, and ordered the Eucharist to be administered in the middle of churches, at tables which the Papists irreverently termed oyster boards. Bishop Ponet was of opinion that the word bishop should be abandoned to the Papists, and that the chief officers of the purified church should be called superintendents. When it is considered that none of these prelates belonged to the extreme section of the Protestant party, it cannot be doubted that, if the general sense of that party had been followed, the work of reform would have been carried on as unsparingly in England as in Scotland.

But, as the government needed the support of the Protestants, so the Protestants needed the protection of the government. Much was therefore given up on both sides: a union was effected; and the fruit of that union was the Church of England.

To the peculiarities of this great institution, and to the strong passions which it has called forth in the minds both of friends and of enemies, are to be attributed many of the most important events which have, since the Reformation, taken place in our country.

The man who took the chief part in settling the conditions of the alliance which produced the Anglican church was Archbishop Cranmer. He was the representative of both parties which, at that time, needed each other's assistance. He was at once a divine and a courtier. In his character of divine he was perfectly ready to go as far in the way of change as any Swiss or Scottish Reformer. In his character of courtier he was desirous to preserve that organisation which had, during many ages, admirably served the purposes of the Bishops of Rome, and might be expected now to serve equally well the purposes of the English Kings and of their ministers. His temper and his understanding eminently fitted him to act as mediator. Saintly in his professions, unscrupulous in his dealings, zealous for nothing, bold in speculation, a coward and a timeserver in action, a placable enemy and a lukewarm friend, he was in every way qualified to arrange the terms of the coalition between the religious and the worldly enemies of Popery.

The Church of Rome held that episcopacy was of divine institution, and

Thomas Cranmer carried out a policy which has associated his name more closely than that of any other ecclesiastic with the Reformation in England. He set practically no limits to the ecclesiastical authority of Kings. Church and State to him were one.

that certain supernatural graces of a high order had been transmitted by the imposition of hands through fifty generations, from the Eleven who received their commission on the Galilean mount, to the bishops who met at Trent. A large body of Protestants, on the other hand, regarded prelacy as positively unlawful, and persuaded themselves that they found a very different form of ecclesiastical government prescribed in Scripture. The founders of the Anglican Church took a middle course. They retained episcopacy; but they did not declare it to be an institution essential to the welfare of a Christian society, or to the efficacy of the sacraments.

Among the Presbyterians, the conduct of public worship is, to a great extent, left to the minister. Their prayers, therefore, are not exactly the

The seating for the opening of Parliament in the House of Lords, 1523. The plan shows the justices (centre, seated on woolsacks), bishops and abbots (left) and peers (right). The Commons, headed by the Speaker, who stands at the bar of the House, appear at the bottom of the page. At the back the court crowds in behind the King; on his left sit the Archbishop of Canterbury and Cardinal Wolsey, the chief minister.

same in any two assemblies on the same day, or on any two days in the same assembly. The priests of the Roman Catholic Church, on the other hand, have, during many generations, daily chaunted the same ancient confessions, supplications, and thanksgivings, in India and Lithuania, in Ireland and Peru. The service, being in a dead language, is intelligible only to the learned; and the great majority of the congregation may be said to assist as spectators rather than auditors. Here, again, the Church of England took a middle course. She copied the Roman Catholic forms of prayer, but translated them into the vulgar tongue, and invited the illiterate multitude to join its voice to that of the minister.

In every part of her system the same policy may be traced. Utterly rejecting the doctrine of transubstantiation, and condemning as idolatrous all adoration paid to the sacramental bread and wine, she yet, to the disgust of the Puritan, required her children to receive the memorials of divine love, meekly kneeling upon their knees. Discarding many rich vestments which surrounded the altars of the ancient faith, she yet retained, to the horror of weak minds, a robe of white linen, typical of the purity which belonged to her as the mystical spouse of Christ. Shrift was no part of her system. Yet she gently invited the dying penitent to confess his sins to a divine, and empowered her ministers to soothe the departing soul by an absolution which breathes the very spirit of the old religion. In general it may be said that she appeals more to the understanding, and less to the senses and the imagination, than the Church of Rome, and that she appeals less to the understanding, and more to the senses and imagination, than the Protestant Churches of Scotland, France and Switzerland.

Nothing, however, so strongly distinguished the Church of England from other Churches as the relation in which she stood to the monarchy. The King was her head. The limits of the authority which he possessed, as such, were not traced with precision. For the founders of the English Church wrote and acted in an age of violent intellectual fermentation, and of constant action and reaction. They therefore often contradicted each other, and sometimes contradicted themselves. That the King was, under Christ, sole head of the Church, was a doctrine which they all with one voice affirmed: but those words had very different significations in different mouths, and in the same mouth at different conjunctures. What Henry and his favourite counsellors meant, at one time, by the supremacy, was certainly nothing less than the whole power of the keys. The King was to be the Pope of his kingdom, the vicar of God, the expositor of Catholic verity, the channel of sacramental graces. According to this system, as expounded by Cranmer, the King was the spiritual as well as the temporal chief of the nation. In both capacities His Highness must have lieutenants. As he appointed civil officers to keep his seal, to collect his revenues, and to dispense justice in his name, so he appointed divines of various ranks to preach the gospel, and to administer the sacraments. It was unnecessary that there should be any imposition of hands. The King – such was the opinion of Cranmer given in the plainest words – might, in virtue of authority derived from God, make a priest; and the priest so made needed no ordination whatever.

These high pretensions gave scandal to Protestants as well as to Catholics; and the scandal was greatly increased when the supremacy, which Mary had resigned back to the Pope, was again annexed to the crown, on the accession of Elizabeth. It seemed monstrous that a woman should be the chief bishop of a Church in which an apostle had forbidden her even to let her voice be heard. The Queen, therefore, found it necessary expressly to disclaim that sacerdotal character which her father had assumed, and which, according to Cranmer, had been inseparably joined, by divine ordinance, to the regal function. When the Anglican confession of faith was revised in her reign, the supremacy was explained in a manner somewhat different from that which had been fashionable at the court of Henry. Cranmer had declared, in emphatic terms, that God had immediately committed to Christian princes the whole cure of all their subjects, as well concerning the administration of God's word for the cure of souls, as concerning the administration of things political. The thirty-seventh article of religion, framed under Elizabeth, declares, in terms as emphatic, that the ministering of God's word does not belong to princes. The Queen, however, still had over the Church a visitatorial power of vast and undefined extent.

Nor did the Church grudge this extensive power to our princes. By them she had been called into existence, nursed through a feeble infancy, guarded from Papists on one side and from Puritans on the other, protected against Parliaments which bore her no good will, and avenged on literary assailants whom she found it hard to answer. Thus gratitude, hope, fear, common attachments, common enmities, bound her to the throne. Loyalty became a point of professional honour among her clergy, the peculiar badge which distinguished them at once from Calvinists and

Coronation portrait of Elizabeth I.

from Papists. Both Calvinists and Papists maintained that subjects might justifiably draw the sword against ungodly rulers. In France Calvinists resisted Charles IX: Papists resisted Henry IV: both Papists and Calvinists resisted Henry III. In Scotland Calvinists led Mary captive. On the north of the Trent Papists took arms against the English throne. The Church of England meantime condemned both Calvinists and Papists, and loudly boasted that no duty was more constantly or earnesly inculcated by her than that of submission to princes.

The advantages which the Crown derived from this close alliance with the Established Church were great; but they were not without serious drawbacks. The compromise arranged by Cranmer had from the first been considered by a large body of Protestants as a scheme for serving two masters, as an attempt to unite the worship of the Lord with the worship of Baal. In the days of Edward VI the scruples of this party had repeatedly thrown great difficulties in the way of the government. When Elizabeth came to the throne, those difficulties were much increased. Violence naturally engenders violence. The spirit of Protestantism was therefore far fiercer and more intolerant after the cruelties of Mary than before them. Many persons who were warmly attached to the new opinions had, during the evil days, taken refuge in Switzerland and Germany. These men returned to their country, convinced that the reform which had been effected under King Edward had been far less searching and extensive than the interests of pure religion required. But it was in vain that they attempted to obtain any concession from Elizabeth. Indeed her system, wherever it differed from her brother's, seemed to them to differ for the worse. They were little disposed to submit, in matters of faith, to any human authority. Long accustomed to regard the Pope as the successor of the chief of the apostles, as the bearer of the keys of earth and heaven, they had learned to regard him as the Beast, the Antichrist, the Man of Sin. It was not to be expected that they would immediately transfer to an upstart authority the homage which they had withdrawn from the Vatican; that they would submit their private judgment to the authority of a Church founded on private judgment alone; that they would be afraid to dissent from teachers who themselves dissented from what had lately been the universal faith of western Christendom.

Since these men could not be convinced, it was determined that they should be persecuted. Persecution produced its natural effect on them. It found them a sect: it made them a faction. To their hatred of the Church was now added hatred of the Crown. The two sentiments were intermingled; and each embittered the other.

Thus, as the priest of the Established Church was, from interest, from principle, and from passion, zealous for the royal prerogatives, the Puritan was, from interest, from principle, and from passion, hostile to them. The power of the discontented sectaries was great. They were found in every rank; but they were strongest among the mercantile classes in the towns, and among the small proprietors in the country. Early in the reign of Elizabeth they began to return a majority of the House of Commons. And doubtless, had our ancestors been then at liberty to fix their attention entirely on domestic questions, the strife between the Crown and the Parliament would instantly have commenced. But that was no season for internal dissensions. Roman Catholic Europe and reformed Europe were struggling for death or life. France, divided against herself, had, for a time, ceased to be of any account in Christendom. The English government was at the head of the Protestant interest, and, while persecuting Presbyterians at home, extended a powerful protection to Presbyterian Churches abroad. At the head of the opposite party was the mightiest prince of the age, a prince who ruled Spain, Portugal, Italy, the Netherlands, the East and the West Indies, whose armies repeatedly marched to Paris, and whose fleets kept the coasts of Devonshire and Sussex in alarm. It long seemed probable that Englishmen would have to fight desperately on English ground for their religion and independence.

Whatever might be the faults of Elizabeth, it was plain that, to speak humanly, the fate of the realm and of all reformed Churches was staked on the security of her person and on the success of her administration. To strengthen her hands was, therefore, the first duty of a patriot and a Protestant; and that duty was well performed. The Puritans, even in the depths of the prisons to which she had sent them, prayed, and with no simulated fervour, that she might be kept from the dagger of the assassin, that rebellion might be put down under her feet, and that her arms might be victorious by sea and land. One of the most stubborn of the stubborn sect, immediately after his hand had been lopped off for an offence into which he had been hurried by his intemperate zeal, waved his hat with the hand which was still left him, and shouted 'God save the Queen!'

During the greater part of her reign, therefore, the Puritans in the House of Commons, though sometimes mutinous, felt no disposition to array themselves in systematic opposition to the government. But, when the defeat of the Armada, the successful resistance of the United Provinces to the Spanish power, the firm establishment of Henry IV on the throne of France, and the death of Philip II, had secured the State and the Church against all danger from abroad, an obstinate struggle, destined to last during several generations, instantly began at home.

English fire-ships attacking the Spanish Armada. The defeat of the Armada gave England security from foreign assault, and provided the climax of Elizabeth's reign.

The Court of Chancery c 1450. The Court had concurrent jurisdiction when the common law did not give adequate relief. Not being bound by legal precedent and providing remedies not available under common law, the powers and work load of the Court increased dramatically during the fifteenth century.

The Reign of James I

In the year 1603 the great Queen died. That year is, on many accounts, one of the most important epochs in our history. It was then that both Scotland and Ireland became parts of the same empire with England. Both Scotland and Ireland, indeed, had been subjugated by the Plantagenets; but neither country had been patient under the yoke. Scotland had, with heroic energy, vindicated her independence, had, from the time of Robert Bruce, been a separate kingdom, and was now joined to the southern part of the island in a manner which rather gratified than wounded her national pride. Ireland had never, since the days of Henry II, been able to expel the foreign invaders; but she had struggled against them long and fiercely. At length, a few weeks before the death of Elizabeth, the conquest, which had been begun more than four hundred years before by Strongbow, was completed by Mountjoy. Scarcely had James I mounted the English throne when the last O'Donnel and O'Neil who have held the rank of independent princes kissed his hand at Whitehall. Thenceforward his writs ran and his judges held assizes in every part of Ireland; and the English law superseded the customs which had prevailed among the aboriginal tribes.

In extent Scotland and Ireland were nearly equal to each other, and were together nearly equal to England, but were much less thickly peopled than England, and were very far behind England in wealth and civilisation. Scotland had been kept back by the sterility of her soil; and, in the midst of light, the thick darkness of the middle ages still rested on Ireland.

Scotland, in becoming part of the British monarchy, preserved her dignity. Having, during many generations, courageously withstood the English arms, she was now joined to her stronger neighbour on the most honourable terms. She gave a King instead of receiving one. She retained her own constitution and laws. Her tribunals and Parliaments remained entirely independent of the tribunals and Parliaments which sate at Westminster. Nevertheless Scotland by no means escaped the fate ordained for every country which is connected, but not incorporated, with another country of greater resources. Though in name an independent kingdom, she was, during more than a century, really treated, in many respects, as a subject province.

Ireland was undisguisedly governed as a dependency won by the sword. Her rude national institutions had perished. The English colonists submitted to the dictation of the mother country, without whose support they could not exist, and indemnified themselves by trampling on the people among whom they had settled. The Parliaments which met at Dublin could pass no law which had not been previously approved by the English Privy Council. The authority of the English legislature extended over Ireland. The executive administration was entrusted to men taken either from England or from the English pale, and, in either case, regarded as foreigners, and even as enemies, by the Celtic population.

But the circumstance which, more than any other, has made Ireland to differ from Scotland remains to be noticed. Scotland was Protestant. In no part of Europe had the movement of the popular mind against the Roman Catholic Church been so rapid and violent. The Reformers had vanquished, deposed, and imprisoned their idolatrous sovereign. They would not endure even such a compromise as had been effected in England. Unfortunately for Scotland, the prince whom she sent to govern a fairer inheritance had been so much annoyed by the pertinacity with which her theologians had asserted against him the privileges of the synod and the pulpit that he hated the ecclesiastical polity to which she was fondly attached as much as it was in his effeminate nature to hate anything, and had no sooner mounted the English throne than he began to show an intolerant zeal for the government and ritual of the English Church.

The Irish were the only people of northern Europe who had remained true to the old religion. The object of their animosity was not Rome, but England; and they had especial reason to abhor those English sovereigns who had been the chiefs of the great schism, Henry VIII and Elizabeth. During the vain struggle which two generations of Milesian princes maintained against the Tudors, religious enthusiasm and national enthusiasm became inseparably blended in the minds of the vanquished race. The new feud of Protestant and Papist inflamed the old feud of Saxon and Celt. The English conquerors, meanwhile, neglected all legitimate means of conversion. No care was taken to provide the vanquished nation with instructors capable of making themselves understood. No translation of the Bible was put forth in the Irish language. The government contended itself with setting up a vast hierarchy of Protestant archbishops, bishops, and rectors, who did nothing, and who, for doing nothing, were paid out of the spoils of a Church loved and revered by the great body of the people.

There was much in the state both of Scotland and of Ireland which might well excite the painful apprehensions of a farsighted statesman. As yet, however, there was the appearance of tranquillity. For the first time all the British isles were peaceably united under one sceptre.

It should seem that the weight of England among European nations ought, from this epoch, to have greatly increased. The territory which her new King governed was, in extent, nearly double that which Elizabeth had inherited. His empire was the most complete within itself and the most secure from attack that was to be found in the world. It might not unreasonably be expected that England, Scotland, and Ireland combined would form a state second to none that then existed.

All such expectations were strangely disappointed. On the day of the accession of James I England descended from the rank which she had hitherto held, and began to be regarded as a power hardly of the second

The Gunpowder Plot, 5 November 1665. A Dutch engraving of the conspirators and the terrible deaths they suffered. The Plot was the reaction of a group of Catholic gentlemen to the disappointment of failing to obtain relief from anti-Catholic laws.

order. During many years the great British monarchy, under four successive princes of the House of Stuart, was scarcely a more important member of the European system than the little kingdom of Scotland had previously been. This, however, is little to be regretted. Of James I, as of John, it may be said that, if his administration had been able and splendid, it would probably have been fatal to our country, and that we owe more to his weakness and meanness than to the wisdom and courage of much better sovereigns. He came to the throne at a critical moment. The time was fast approaching when either the King must become absolute, or the Parliament must control the whole executive administration. Had James been, like Henry IV, like Maurice of Nassau, or like Gustavus Adolphus, a valiant, active, and politic ruler, had he put himself at the head of the Protestants of Europe, and had he found himself, after great achievements, at the head of fifty thousand troops, brave, well disciplined, and devotedly attached to his person, the English Parliament would soon have been nothing more than a name. Happily he was not a man to play such a part. He began his administration by putting an end to the war which had raged during many years between England and Spain; and from that time he shunned hostilities with a caution which was proof against the insults of his neighbours and the clamours of his subjects. The effect of his pacific policy was that, in his time, no regular troops were needed, and that, while France, Spain, Italy, Belgium, and Germany swarmed with mercenary soldiers, the defence of our island was still confided to the militia.

As the King had no standing army, and did not even attempt to form one, it would have been wise in him to avoid any conflict with his people. But such was his indiscretion that, while he altogether neglected the means which alone could make him really absolute, he constantly put forward, in the most offensive form, claims of which none of his predecessors had ever dreamed. It was gravely maintained that the Supreme Being regarded hereditary monarchy, as opposed to other forms of government, with peculiar favour; that the rule of succession in order of primogeniture was a divine institution, anterior to the Christian, and even to the Mosaic dispensation; that no human power, not even that of the whole legislature, no length of adverse possession, though it extended to ten centuries, could deprive a legitimate prince of his rights; that the authority of such a prince was necessarily always despotic; that the laws, by which, in England and in other countries, the prerogative was limited, were to be regarded merely as concessions which the sovereign had freely made and might at his pleasure resume; and that any treaty which a King might conclude with his people was merely a declaration of his present intentions, and not a contract of which the performance could be demanded.

Regarded by the English as an alien, and excluded from the throne by the testament of Henry VIII, the King of Scots was yet the undoubted heir of William the Conqueror and of Egbert. He had, therefore, an obvious interest in inculcating the superstitious notion that birth confers rights anterior to law, and unalterable by law. It was a notion, moreover, well suited to his intellect and temper. It soon found many advocates among those who aspired to his favour, and made rapid progress among the clergy of the Established Church.

Thus, at the very moment at which a republican spirit began to manifest itself strongly in the Parliament and in the country, the claims of the monarch took a monstrous form which would have disgusted the proudest and most arbitrary of those who had preceded him on the throne.

James was always boasting of his skill in what he called kingcraft; and yet it is hardly possible even to imagine a course more directly opposed to all the rules of kingcraft than that which he followed. He enraged and alarmed his Parliament by constantly telling them that they held their privileges merely during his pleasure, and that they had no more business to inquire what he might lawfully do than what the Deity might lawfully do. Yet he quailed before them, abandoned minister after minister to their vengeance, and suffered them to tease him into acts directly opposed to his strongest inclinations. Thus the indignation excited by his claims and the scorn excited by his concessions went on growing together. By his fondness for worthless minions, and by the sanction which he gave to their tyranny and rapacity, he kept discontent constantly alive. His cowardice, his childishness, his pedantry, his ungainly person and manners, his provincial accent, made him an object of derision. During two hundred years all the sovereigns who had ruled England, with the single exception of the unfortunate Henry VI, had been strongminded, highspirited, courageous, and of princely bearing. Almost all had possessed abilities above the ordinary level. It was no light thing that, on the very eve of the decisive struggle between our Kings and their Parliaments, royalty should be exhibited to the world stammering, slobbering, shedding unmanly tears, trembling at a drawn sword, and talking in the style alternately of a buffoon and of a pedagogue.

In the meantime the religious dissensions, by which, from the days of Edward VI, the Protestant body had been distracted, had become more formidable than ever. While the recollection of Mary's cruelties was still fresh, while the power of the Roman Catholic party still inspired apprehension, while Spain still retained ascendency and aspired to universal dominion, all the reformed sects knew that they had a strong common interest and a deadly common enemy. The animosity which they felt towards each other was languid when compared with the animosity which they all felt towards Rome. Conformists and nonconformists had heartily joined in enacting penal laws of extreme severity against the Papists. But when more than half a century of undisturbed possession had given confidence to the Established Church, when nine tenths of the nation had become heartily Protestant, when England was at peace with all the world, a change took place in the feeling of the Anglican clergy. Their hostility to the Roman Catholic doctrine and discipline was considerably mitigated. Their dislike of the Puritans, on the other hand, increased daily. The controversies which had from the beginning divided the Protestant party took such a form as made reconciliation hopeless; and new controversies of still greater importance were added to the old subjects of dispute.

The founders of the Anglican Church had retained episcopacy as an ancient, a decent, and a convenient ecclesiastical polity, but had not declared that form of Church government to be of divine institution. But a new race of divines was already rising in the Church of England. In their view the episcopal office was essential to the welfare of a Christian society and to the efficacy of the most solemn ordinances of religion. To that office belonged certain high and sacred privileges, which no human power could give or take away.

In the days of Edward VI and of Elizabeth, the defenders of the Anglican ritual had generally contented themselves with saying that it might be used

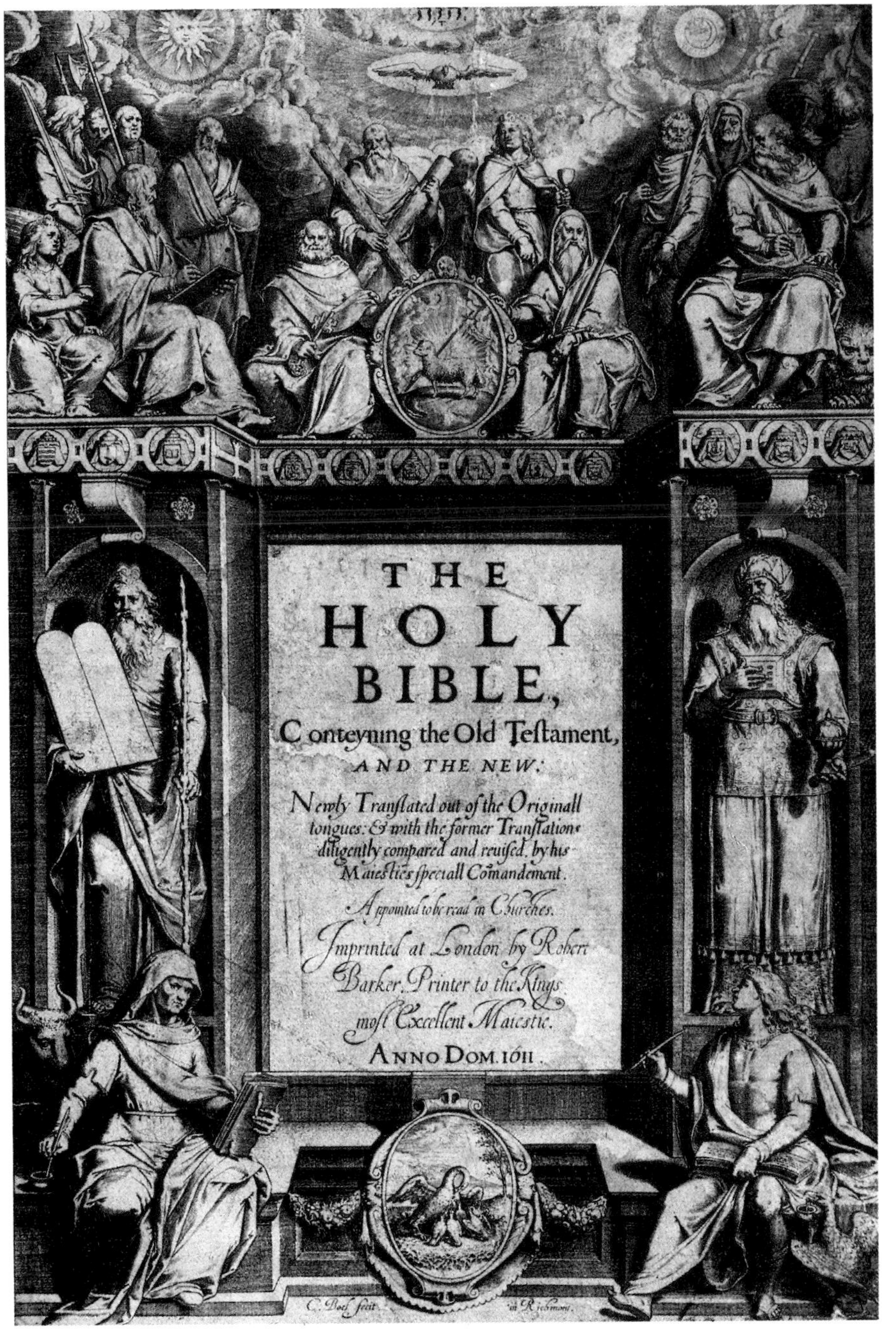
THE
HOLY
BIBLE,
Conteyning the Old Teſtament,
AND THE NEW:
Newly Tranſlated out of the Originall
tongues: & with the former Tranſlations
diligently compared and reuiſed, by his
Maieſties ſpeciall Comandement.
Appointed to be read in Churches.
Imprinted at London by Robert
Barker, Printer to the Kings
moſt Excellent Maieſtie.
ANNO DOM. 1611.

The title page of the Authorised version of the Bible, 1611. This translation is perhaps James I's main claim to the gratitude of later generations.

without sin, and that, therefore, none but a perverse and undutiful subject would refuse to use it when enjoined to do so by the magistrate. Now, however, that rising party which claimed for the polity of the Church a celestial origin began to ascribe to her services a new dignity and importance. It was hinted that, if the established worship had any fault, that fault was extreme simplicity, and that the Reformers had, in the heat of their quarrel with Rome, abolished many ancient ceremonies which might with advantage have been retained.

While the majority of the Anglican clergy quitted, in one direction, the position which they had originally occupied, the majority of the Puritan

An early seventeenth-century drawing of Westminster Hall with the Courts of Chancery and King's Bench in session, the former hearing cases of equity, the latter adjudicating on common law. The judges are sitting under the canopies.

body departed, in a direction diametrically opposite, from the principles and practices of their fathers. The persecution which the separatists had undergone had been severe enough to irritate, but not severe enough to destroy. They had been, not tamed into submission, but baited into savageness and stubbornness. After the fashion of oppressed sects, they mistook their own vindictive feelings for emotions of piety, encouraged in themselves by reading and meditation a disposition to brood over their wrongs, and, when they had worked themselves up into hating their enemies, imagined that they were only hating the enemies of heaven. In the New Testament there was little indeed which, even when perverted by the most disingenuous exposition, could seem to countenance the indulgence of malevolent passions. But the Old Testament contained the history of a race selected by God to be witnesses of his unity and ministers of his vengeance, and specially commanded by him to do many things which, if done without his special command, would have been atrocious crimes. In such a history it was not difficult for fierce and gloomy spirits to find much that might be distorted to suit their wishes. The extreme Puritans therefore began to feel for the Old Testament a preference, which, perhaps, they did not distinctly avow even to themselves; but which showed itself in all their sentiments and habits.

Morals and manners were subjected to a code resembling that of the synagogue, when the synagogue was in its worst state. The dress, the deportment, the language, the studies, the amusements of the rigid sect were regulated on principles not unlike those of the Pharisees who, proud of their washed hands and broad phylacteries, taunted the Redeemer as a sabbath-breaker and a winebibber. It was a sin to hang garlands on a May-pole, to drink a friend's health, to fly a hawk, to hunt a stag, to play at chess, to wear lovelocks, to put starch into a ruff, to touch the virginals, to read the Fairy Queen. Half the fine paintings in England were idolatrous, and the other half indecent. The extreme Puritan was at once known from other men by his gait, his garb, his lank hair, the sour solemnity of his face, the upturned white of his eyes, the nasal twang with which he spoke and, above all, by his peculiar dialect. He employed, on every occasion, the imagery and style of Scripture.

Thus the political and religious schism which had originated in the sixteenth century was, during the first quarter of the seventeenth century, constantly widening. Theories tending to Turkish despotism were in fashion at Whitehall. Theories tending to republicanism were in favour with a large portion of the House of Commons. The violent Prelatists who were, to a man, zealous for prerogative, and the violent Puritans who were, to a man, zealous for the privileges of Parliament, regarded each other with animosity more intense than that which, in the preceding generation, had existed between Catholics and Protestants.

While the minds of men were in this state, the country, after a peace of many years, at length engaged in a war which required strenuous exertions. This war hastened the approach of the great constitutional crisis. It was necessary that the King should have a large military force. He could not have such a force without money. He could not legally raise money without the consent of Parliament. It followed, therefore, that he either must administer the government in conformity with the sense of the House of Commons, or must venture on such a violation of the fundamental laws of the land as had been unknown during several centuries. It seemed that the decisive hour was approaching, and that the English Parliament would soon either share the fate of the senates of the Continent, or obtain supreme ascendency in the state.

Charles I

Just at this conjuncture James died. Charles I succeeded to the throne. He had received from nature a far better understanding, a far stronger will, and a far keener and firmer temper than his father's. He had inherited his father's political theories, and was much more disposed than his father to carry them into practice. He was, like his father, a zealous Episcopalian. Though no Papist, he liked a Papist much better than a Puritan. It would be unjust to deny that Charles had some of the qualities of a good, and even of a great prince. He wrote and spoke, not, like his father, with the exactness of a professor, but after the fashion of intelligent and well educated gentlemen. His taste in literature and art was excellent, his manner dignified, though not gracious, his domestic life without blemish. Faithlessness was the chief cause of his disasters, and is the chief stain on his memory. He was, in truth, impelled by an incurable propensity to dark and crooked ways.

He seems to have learned from the theologians whom he most esteemed that between him and his subjects there could be nothing of the nature of mutual contract; that he could not, even if he would, divest himself of his despotic authority; and that, in every promise which he made, there was an implied reservation that such promise might be broken in case of necessity, and that of the necessity he was the sole judge.

Iesuit
One Evins a Welch man was lately comitted to New-gate for saying hee was Christ
Heere's one blasphemously That hee was christ did say Such spirits were foretold To rise ith latter dayes
Arminian
Arian
Adamite
Libertin
Ante Scripturian
Soule Sleeper
Anabaptist
Familist
Seeker
Diuorcer

Varieties of religious belief, from an early seventeenth-century pamphlet. The broad Elizabethan church settlement had encouraged the proliferation of religious sects. Apart from foreign affairs and revenue raising, the principal concern of Charles I during his period of personal government between 1629 and 1640 was the government of the Church and matters of religion.

And now began that hazardous game on which were staked the destinies of the English people. It was played on the side of the House of Commons with keenness, but with admirable dexterity, coolness, and perseverance. Great statesmen who looked far behind them and far before them were at the head of that assembly. They were resolved to place the King in such a situation that he must either conduct the administration in conformity with the wishes of his Parliament, or make outrageous attacks on the most sacred principles of the constitution. They accordingly doled out supplies to him very sparingly. He found that he must govern either in harmony with the House of Commons, or in defiance of all law. His choice was soon made. He dissolved his first Parliament, and levied taxes by his own authority. He convoked a second Parliament, and found it more intractable than the first. He again resorted to the expedient of dissolution, raised fresh taxes without any show of legal right, and threw the chiefs of the opposition into prison. At the same time a new grievance, which the peculiar feelings and habits of the English nation made insupportably painful, and which seemed to all discerning men to be of fearful augury, excited general discontent and alarm. Companies of soldiers were billeted on the people; and martial law was, in some places, substituted for the ancient jurisprudence of the realm.

The King called a third Parliament, and soon perceived that the opposition was stronger and fiercer than ever. He now determined on a change of tactics. Instead of opposing an inflexible resistance to the demands of the Commons, he, after much altercation and many evasions, agreed to a compromise which, if he had faithfully adhered to it, would have averted a long series of calamities. The Parliament granted an ample supply. The King ratified, in the most solemn manner, that celebrated law, which is known by the name of the Petition of Right, and which is the second Great Charter of the liberties of England. By ratifying that law he bound himself never again to raise money without the consent of the Houses, never again to imprison any person, except in due course of law, and never again to subject his people to the jurisdiction of courts martial.

The day on which the royal sanction was, after many delays, solemnly given to this great act, was a day of joy and hope; but within three weeks it became manifest that Charles had no intention of observing the compact into which he had entered. The supply given by the representatives of the nation was collected. The promise by which that supply had been obtained was broken. A violent contest followed. The Parliament was dissolved with every mark of royal displeasure. Some of the most distinguished members were imprisoned; and one of them, Sir John Eliot, after years of suffering, died in confinement.

Charles, however, could not venture to raise, by his own authority, taxes sufficient for carrying on war. He accordingly hastened to make peace with his neighbours, and thenceforth gave his whole mind to British politics.

Now commenced a new era. Many English Kings had occasionally committed unconstitutional acts: but none had ever systematically attempted to make himself a despot, and to reduce the Parliament to a nullity. Such was the end which Charles distinctly proposed to himself. From March 1629 to April 1640, the Houses were not convoked. Never in our history had there been an interval of eleven years between Parliament and Parliament. Only once had there been an interval of even half that length.

It is proved, by the testimony of the King's most strenuous supporters, that, during this part of his reign, the provisions of the Petition of Right were violated by him, not occasionally, but constantly, and on system; that a large part of the revenue was raised without any legal authority; and that persons obnoxious to the government languished for years in prison, without being ever called upon to plead before any tribunal.

For these things history must hold the King himself chiefly responsible. From the time of his third Parliament he was his own prime minister. Several persons, however, whose temper and talents were suited to his purposes, were at the head of different departments of the administration.

Thomas Wentworth, successively created Lord Wentworth and Earl of Strafford, a man of great abilities, eloquence, and courage, but of a cruel and imperious nature, was the counsellor most trusted in political and military affairs. He had been one of the most distinguished members of the opposition, and felt towards those whom he had deserted that peculiar malignity which has, in all ages, been characteristic of apostates. He perfectly understood the feelings, the resources, and the policy of the party to which he had lately belonged, and had formed a vast and deeply meditated scheme which very nearly confounded even the able tactics of the statesmen by whom the House of Commons had been directed. To this scheme, in his confidential correspondence, he gave the expressive name of Thorough. His object was to do in England all, and more than all, that Richelieu was doing in France; to make Charles a monarch as absolute as any on the Continent; to put the estates and the personal liberty of the whole people at the disposal of the Crown; to deprive the courts of law of all independent authority, even in ordinary questions of civil right between man and man; and to punish with merciless rigour all who murmured at the acts of the government, or who applied, even in the most decent and regular manner, to any tribunal for relief against those acts.

This was his end; and he distinctly saw in what manner alone this end could be attained. He saw that there was one instrument, and only one, by which his vast and daring projects could be carried into execution. That instrument was a standing army. To the forming of such an army, therefore, he directed all the energy of his strong mind. In Ireland, where he was viceroy, he actually succeeded in establishing a military despotism, not only over the aboriginal population, but also over the English colonists, and was able to boast that, in that island, the King was as absolute as any prince in the whole world could be.

The ecclesiastical administration was, in the meantime, principally directed by William Laud, Archbishop of Canterbury. Of all the prelates of the Anglican Church, Laud had departed farthest from the principles of the Reformation, and drawn nearest to Rome. He was by nature rash, irritable, quick to feel for his own dignity, slow to sympathise with the sufferings of others, and prone to the error, common in superstitious men, of mistaking his own peevish and malignant moods for emotions of pious zeal. Under his direction every corner of the realm was subjected to a constant and minute inspection. Every little congregation of separatists was tracked out and broken up. Even the devotions of private families could not escape the vigilance of his spies. Such fear did his rigour inspire that the deadly hatred of the Church, which festered in innumerable bosoms, was generally disguised under an outward show of conformity. On the very eve of troubles, fatal to himself and to his order, the bishops of several extensive dioceses were able to report to him that not a single dissenter was to be found within their jurisdiction.

The tribunals afforded no protection to the subject against the civil and ecclesiastical tyranny of that period. The judges of the common law, holding their situations during the pleasure of the King, were scandalously obsequious. Yet, obsequious as they were, they were less ready and less

Canterbury, is here all the dishes, that are provided?
Doct. My *Lord*, there is all : and 'tis enough, wert for a Princes table,
Ther's 24. severall dainty dishes, and all rare.
B, Cant. Are these rare : no, no, they please me not,
Give me a Carbinadoed cheeke, or a tippet of a Cocks combe :
None of all this, here is meate for my Pallet.
Lawyer. My Lord, here is both Cocke and Phesant.

A Puritan satire showing Laud dining off Prynne's ears. Prynne's ears had been cropped because he had dared to criticize the episcopal form of Church government.

Archbishop Laud: a portrait by Van Dyck. 'Of all the prelates of the Anglican Church, Laud had departed farthest from the principles of the Reformation, and had drawn nearest to Rome.'

efficient instruments of arbitrary power than a class of courts, the memory of which is still, after the lapse of more than two centuries, held in deep abhorrence by the nation. Foremost among these courts in power and in infamy were the Star Chamber and the High Commission, the former a political, the latter a religious inquisition. The power which these boards had possessed before the accession of Charles had been extensive and formidable, but had been small indeed when compared with that which they now usurped. Guided chiefly by the violent spirit of the primate, and freed from the control of Parliament, they displayed a rapacity, a violence, a malignant energy, which had been unknown to any former age. The government was able, through their instrumentality, to fine, imprison, pillory, and mutilate without restraint. A separate council which sate at York, under the presidency of Wentworth, was armed, in defiance of law, by a pure act of prerogative, with almost boundless power over the northern counties.

John Hampden. In 1637 Hampden took upon himself the risk and the cost of opposing the King's prerogative in the matter of ship money. He contested the case in the Court of Exchequer, and even the panel of obsequious judges voted against him only by the narrowest of margins. In this as in so many other matters Charles chose to ignore the warning signs of growing public opposition.

The government of England was now, in all points but one, as despotic as that of France. But that one point was all important. There was still no standing army. There was, therefore, no security that the whole fabric of tyranny might not be subverted in a single day; and, if taxes were imposed by the royal authority for the support of an army, it was probable that there would be an immediate and irresistible explosion. This was the difficulty which more than any other perplexed Wentworth. The Lord Keeper Finch, in concert with other lawyers who were employed by the government, recommended an expedient, which was eagerly adopted. The ancient princes of England, as they called on the inhabitants of the counties near Scotland to arm and array themselves for the defence of the border, had sometimes called on the maritime counties to furnish ships for the defence of the coast. In the room of ships money had sometimes been accepted. This old practice it was now determined, after a long interval, not only to revive but to extend. Former princes had raised shipmoney only for the maritime defence of the country: it was now exacted, by the admission of the Royalists themselves, with the object, not of maintaining a navy, but of furnishing the King with supplies which might be increased at his discretion to any amount, and expended at his discretion for any purpose.

The whole nation was alarmed and incensed. John Hampden, an opulent and well born gentleman of Buckinghamshire, highly considered in his own neighbourhood, but as yet little known to the kingdom generally, had the courage to step forward, to confront the whole power of the government, and take on himself the cost and the risk of disputing the prerogative to which the King laid claim. The case was argued before the judges in the Exchequer Chamber. So strong were the arguments against the pretensions of the Crown that, dependent and servile as the judges were, the majority against Hampden was the smallest possible. Still there was a majority. The interpreters of the law had pronounced that one great and productive tax might be imposed by the royal authority. Wentworth justly observed that it was impossible to vindicate their judgment except by reasons directly leading to a conclusion which they had not ventured to draw. If money might legally be raised without the consent of Parliament for the support of a fleet, it was not easy to deny that money might, without consent of Parliament, be legally raised for the support of an army.

And now Wentworth exulted in the near prospect of Thorough. A few years might probably suffice for the execution of his great design. If strict economy were observed, if all collision with foreign powers were carefully avoided, the debts of the crown would be cleared off: there would be funds available for the support of a large military force; and that force would soon break the refractory spirit of the nation.

At this crisis an act of insane bigotry suddenly changed the whole face of public affairs. Had the King been wise, he would have pursued a cautious and soothing policy towards Scotland till he was master in the south. For Scotland was of all his kingdoms that in which there was the greatest risk that a spark might produce a flame, and that a flame might become a conflagration. Constitutional opposition, indeed, such as he had encountered at Westminster, he had not to apprehend at Edinburgh. But, though the Scottish Parliament was obsequious, the Scottish people had always been singularly turbulent and ungovernable. Whatever loyalty the nation had anciently felt to the Stuarts had cooled during their long absence. All orders of men complained that their country, that country

Charles's blindness to public feeling was shown again when he moved to bring the Scottish Church into line with the Church of England. The imposition of a new Prayer Book excited a riot in St Giles Cathedral at Edinburgh, during which a foot-stool was thrown at the priest.

which had, with so much glory, defended her independence against the ablest and bravest Plantagenets, had, though the instrumentality of her native princes, become in effect, through not in name, a province of England. In no part of Europe had the Calvinistic doctrine and discipline taken so strong a hold on the public mind. The Church of Rome was regarded by the great body of the people with a hatred which might justly be called ferocious; and the Church of England, which seemed to be every day becoming more and more like the Church of Rome, was an object of scarcely less aversion.

The government had long wished to extend the Anglican system over the whole island, and had already, with this view, made several changes highly distasteful to every Presbyterian. One innovation, however, the most hazardous of all, because it was directly cognisable by the senses of the common people, had not yet been attempted. The public worship of God was still conducted in the manner acceptable to the nation. Now, however, Charles and Laud determined to force on the Scots the English liturgy, or rather a liturgy which, wherever it differed from that of England, differed, in the judgment of all rigid Protestants, for the worse.

To this step, taken in the mere wantonness of tyranny, and in criminal ignorance or more criminal contempt of public feeling, our country owes her freedom. The first performance of the foreign ceremonies produced a riot. The riot rapidly became a revolution. Ambition, patriotism, fanaticism, were mingled in one headlong torrent. The whole nation was in arms. An attempt was made to put down the insurrection by the sword: but the King's military means and military talents were unequal to the task. To impose fresh taxes on England in defiance of law would, at this conjuncture, have been madness. No resource was left but a Parliament; and in the spring of 1640 a Parliament was convoked.

The nation had been put into good humour by the prospect of seeing constitutional government restored, and grievances redressed. The new House of Commons was more temperate and more respectful to the throne than any which had sate since the death of Elizabeth. The moderation of this assembly has been highly extolled by the most distinguished Royalists, and seems to have caused no small vexation and disappointment to the chiefs of the opposition: but it was the uniform practice of Charles, a practice equally impolitic and ungenerous, to refuse all compliance with the desires of his people, till those desires were expressed in a menacing tone. As soon as the Commons showed a disposition to take into consideration the grievances under which the country had suffered during eleven years, the King dissolved the Parliament with every mark of displeasure.

Everything now depended on the event of the King's military operations against the Scots. Among his troops there was little of that feeling which separates professional soldiers from the mass of a nation, and attaches them to their leaders. His army, composed for the most part of recruits, who regretted the plough from which they had been violently taken, and who were imbued with the religious and political sentiments then prevalent throughout the country, was more formidable to himself than to the enemy. The Scots, encouraged by the heads of the English opposition, and feebly resisted by the English forces, marched across the Tweed and the Tyne, and encamped on the borders of Yorkshire. And now the murmurs of discontent swelled into an uproar by which all spirits save one were overawed. But the voice of Strafford was still for Thorough; and he, even in this extremity, showed a nature so cruel and despotic, that his own pikemen were ready to tear him in pieces.

There was yet one last expedient which, as the King flattered himself, might save him from the misery of facing another House of Commons. To the House of Lords he was less averse. The bishops were devoted to him; and, though the temporal peers were generally dissatisfied with his administration, they were, as a class, so deeply interested in the maintenance of order, and in the stability of ancient institutions, that they were not likely to call for extensive reforms. Departing from the uninterrupted practice of centuries, he called a Great Council consisting of lords alone. But the Lords were too prudent to assume the unconstitutional functions with which he wished to invest them. Without money, without credit, without authority even in his own camp, he yielded to the pressure of necessity. The Houses were convoked; and the elections proved that, since the spring, the distrust and hatred with which the government was regarded had made fearful progress.

In November 1640 met that renowned Parliament which, in spite of many errors and disasters, is justly entitled to the reverence and gratitude of all who, in any part of the world, enjoy the blessings of constitutional government.

During the year which followed, no very important division of opinion appeared in the Houses. It was enacted that no interval of more than three years should ever elapse between Parliament and Parliament, and that, if writs under the Great Seal were not issued at the proper time, the returning officers should, without such writs, call the constituent bodies together for the choice of representatives. The Star Chamber, the High Commission, the Council of York were swept away. Men who, after suffering cruel mutilations, had been confined in remote dungeons, regained their liberty. On the chief ministers of the crown the vengeance of the nation was unsparingly wreaked. The Lord Keeper, the Primate, the Lord Lieutenant were

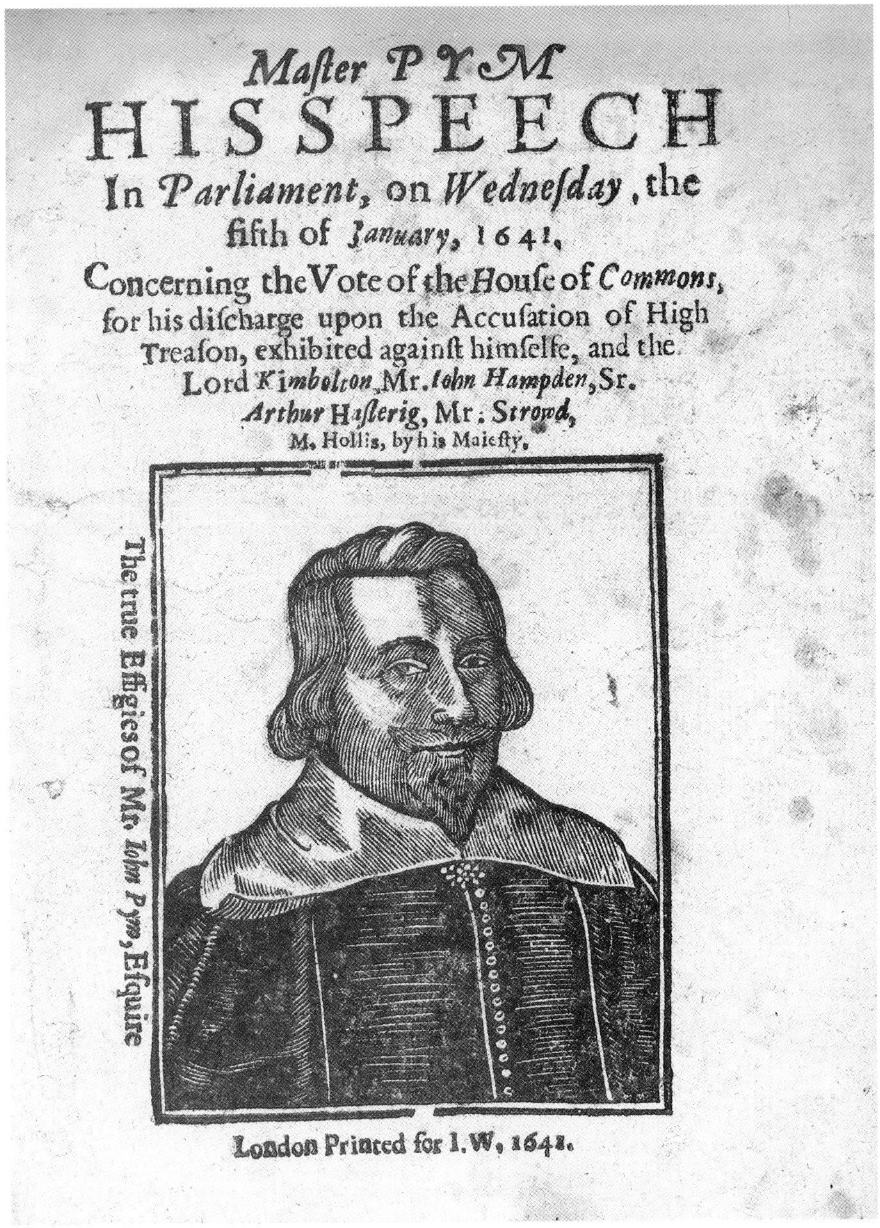
Maſter PYM
HIS SPEECH
In Parliament, on Wedneſday, the
fifth of January, 1641,
Concerning the Vote of the Houſe of Commons,
for his diſcharge upon the Accuſation of High
Treaſon, exhibited againſt himſelfe, and the
Lord Kimbolton, Mr. Iohn Hampden, Sr.
Arthur Haſlerig, Mr. Strowd,
M. Hollis, by his Maieſty,

The true Effigies of Mr Iohn Pym, Eſquire

London Printed for I. W, 1641.

John Pym, master tactician and leader of the Parliamentary opposition to the King. The first twelve months of the Long Parliament saw the nadir of royal influence in the House.

impeached. Finch saved himself by flight. Laud was flung into the Tower. Strafford was put to death by act of attainder. On the day on which this act passed, the King gave his assent to a law by which he bound himself not to adjourn, prorogue, or dissolve the existing Parliament without its own consent.

After ten months of assiduous toil, the Houses, in September 1641, adjourned for a short vacation; and the King visited Scotland. He with difficulty pacified that kingdom by consenting, not only to relinquish his plans of ecclesiastical reform, but even to pass, with a very bad grace, an act declaring that episcopacy was contrary to the word of God.

The recess of the English Parliament lasted six weeks. The day on which the Houses met again is one of the most remarkable epochs in our history. From that day dates the corporate existence of the two great parties which

Thomas Wentworth, Earl of Strafford, by Van Dyck. Strafford's policy of 'Thorough' had as its object the concentration of all power in the hands of the Crown, and was an important factor in bringing to a critical pitch the tension between King and Parliament.

have ever since alternately governed the country. In one sense, indeed, the distinction which then became obvious had always existed, and always must exist. For it has its origin in diversities of temper, of understanding, and of interest, which are found in all societies, and which will be found till the human mind ceases to be drawn in opposite directions by the charm of habit and by the charm of novelty. Everywhere there is a class of men who cling with fondness to whatever is ancient, and who, even when convinced by overpowering reasons that innovation would be beneficial, consent to it with many misgivings and forebodings. We find also everywhere another class of men, sanguine in hope, bold in speculation, always pressing forward, quick to discern the imperfections of whatever exists, disposed to think lightly of the risks and inconveniences which attend improvements, and disposed to give every change credit for being an improvement. In the sentiments of both classes there is something to approve. But of both the best specimens will be found not far from the common frontier.

There can be no doubt that in our very first Parliaments might have been discerned a body of members anxious to preserve, and a body eager to reform. But, while the sessions of the legislature were short, these bodies did not take definite and permanent forms, array themselves under recognised leaders, or assume distinguishing names, badges, and war cries. During the first months of the Long Parliament, the indignation excited by many years of lawless oppression was so strong and general that the House of Commons acted as one man. Not till the law attainting Strafford was proposed did the signs of serious disunion become visible. Even against that law, a law which nothing but extreme necessity could justify, only about sixty members of the House of Commons voted. Even the few who entertained a scruple about inflicting death by a retrospective enactment thought it necessary to express the utmost abhorrence of Strafford's character and administration.

But under this apparent concord a great schism was latent; and when, in October 1641, the Parliament reassembled after a short recess, two hostile parties, essentially the same with those which, under different names, have ever since contended for the direction of public affairs, appeared confronting each other. During some years they were designated as Cavaliers and Roundheads. They were subsequently called Tories and Whigs; nor does it seem that these appellations are likely soon to become obsolete.

The difference between the two great sections of English politicians has always been a difference rather of degree than of principle. There were certain limits on the right and on the left, which were very rarely overstepped. A few enthusiasts on one side were ready to lay all our laws and franchises at the feet of our Kings. A few enthusiasts on the other side were bent on pursuing, through endless civil troubles, their darling phantom of a republic. But the great majority of those who fought for the Crown were averse to despotism; and the great majority of the champions of popular rights were averse to anarchy. Twice, in the course of the seventeenth century, the two parties suspended their dissensions, and united their strength in a common cause. Their first coalition restored hereditary monarchy. Their second coalition rescued constitutional freedom.

It is also to be noted that these two parties have never been the whole nation, nay, that they have never, taken together, made up a majority of the nation. Between them has always been a great mass, which has not

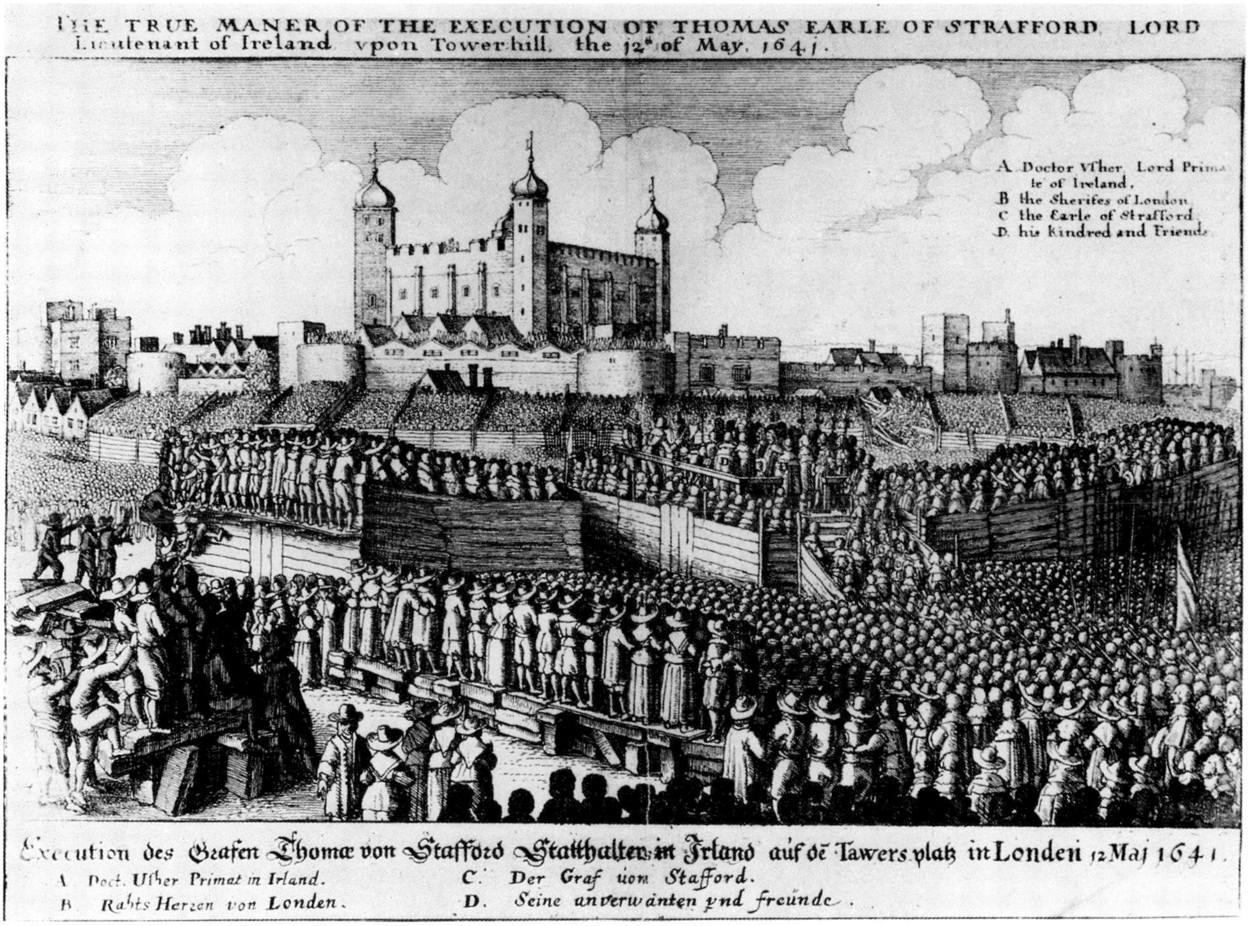

The execution of Strafford on Tower Hill. Strafford was condemned by act of attainder, and after much agonising Charles signed the bill. He never forgave himself however and declared on the scaffold that his own execution was God's punishment for this crime.

steadfastly adhered to either, which has sometimes remained inertly neutral, and which has sometimes oscillated to and fro. That mass has more than once passed in a few years from one extreme to the other, and back again. Sometimes it has changed sides, merely because it was tired of supporting the same men, sometimes because it was dismayed by its own excesses, sometimes because it had expected impossibilities, and had been disappointed. But, whenever it has leaned with its whole weight in either direction, that weight has, for the time, been irresistible.

When the rival parties first appeared in a distinct form, they seemed to be not unequally matched. On the side of the government was a large majority of the nobles, and of those opulent and well descended gentlemen to whom nothing was wanting of nobility but the name. On the same side were the great body of the clergy, both the universities, and all those laymen who were strongly attached to episcopal government and to the Anglican ritual. These respectable classes found themselves in the company of some allies much less decorous than themselves. The Puritan austerity drove to the King's faction all who made pleasure their business, who affected gallantry, splendour of dress, or taste in the lighter arts. With these went all who live by amusing the leisure of others, from the painter and the comic poet, down to the ropedancer and the Merry Andrew. In the same interest were the Roman Catholics to a man. The Queen, a daughter of France, was of their own faith. Her husband was known to be strongly attached to her, and not a little in awe of her. Though undoubtedly a Protestant on conviction, he regarded the professors of the old religion with no ill will, and would gladly have granted them a much larger toleration than he was disposed to concede to the Presbyterians. If the opposition obtained the mastery, it was probable that the sanguinary laws enacted against Papists, in the reign of Elizabeth, would be severely enforced. The Roman Catholics were therefore induced by the strongest motives to espouse the cause of the court.

The main strength of the opposition lay among the small freeholders in the country, and among the merchants and shopkeepers of the towns. But these were headed by a formidable minority of the aristocracy, a minority which included the rich and powerful Earls of Northumberland, Bedford, Warwick, Stamford, and Essex, and several other Lords of great wealth and influence. In the same ranks was found the whole body of Protestant Nonconformists, and most of those members of the Established Church who still adhered to the Calvinistic opinions which, forty years before, had been generally held by the prelates and clergy. The municipal corporations took, with few exceptions, the same side. In the House of Commons the opposition preponderated, but not very decidedly.

The two parties were still regarding each other with cautious hostility, and had not yet measured their strength, when news arrived which inflamed the passions and confirmed the opinions of both. The great chieftains of Ulster, who, at the time of the accession of James, had, after a long struggle, submitted to the royal authority, had not long brooked the humiliation of dependence. They had conspired against the English government, and had been attainted of treason. Their immense domains had been forfeited to the Crown, and had soon been peopled by thousands of English and Scotch emigrants. The new settlers were, in civilisation and intelligence, far superior to the native population, and sometimes abused their superiority. The animosity produced by difference of race was increased by difference of religion. Under the iron rule of Wentworth, scarcely a murmur was heard: but, when that strong pressure was withdrawn, when Scotland had set the example of successful resistance, when England was distracted by internal quarrels, the smothered rage of the Irish broke forth into acts of fearful violence. A war, to which national and theological hatred gave a character of peculiar ferocity, desolated Ulster, and spread to the neighbouring provinces. The castle of Dublin was scarcely thought secure.

These evil tidings roused to the height the zeal of both the great parties which were marshalled against each other at Westminster. The Royalists maintained that it was the first duty of every good Englishman and Protestant, at such a crisis, to strengthen the hands of the sovereign. To the opposition it seemed that there were now stronger reasons than ever for thwarting and restraining him. That the commonwealth was in danger was undoubtedly a good reason for giving large powers to a trustworthy magistrate: but it was a good reason for taking away powers from a magistrate who was at heart a public enemy. To raise a great army had always been the King's first object. A great army must now be raised. It was to be feared that, unless some new securities were devised, the forces levied for the reduction of Ireland would be employed against the liberties of England.

After some weeks of prelude, the first great parliamentary conflict between the parties took place on the 22nd of November 1641. It was

It became clear by the end of 1641 that the difference between King and Commons could only be resolved by an appeal to force. This woodcut from a broadside of 1642 shows the royalist standard being raised at Nottingham.

moved by the opposition, that the House of Commons should present to the King a Remonstrance, enumerating the faults of his administration from the time of his accession, and expressing the distrust with which his policy was still regarded by his people. That assembly, which a few months before had been unanimous in calling for the reform of abuses, was now divided into two fierce and eager factions of nearly equal strength. After a hot debate of many hours, the Remonstrance was carried by only eleven votes.

The result of this struggle was highly favourable to the conservative party. It could not be doubted that only some great indiscretion could prevent them from shortly obtaining the predominance in the Lower House. The Upper House was already their own. Nothing was wanting to insure their success, but that the King should, in all his conduct, show respect for the laws and scrupulous good faith towards his subjects.

His first measures promised well. He had, it seemed, at last discovered that an entire change of system was necessary, and had wisely made up his mind to what could no longer be avoided. He declared his determination to govern in harmony with the Commons, and, for that end, to call to his councils men in whose talents and character the Commons might place confidence. Nor was the selection ill made. Falkland, Hyde and Colepepper, all three distinguished by the part which they had taken in reforming abuses and in punishing evil ministers, were invited to become the confidential advisers of the Crown, and were solemnly assured by Charles that he would take no step in any way affecting the Lower House of Parliament without their privity.

Had he kept this promise, it cannot be doubted that the reaction which was already in progress would very soon have become quite as strong as the most respectable Royalists would have desired. That the fair prospects which had begun to open before the King were suddenly overcast, that his life was darkened by adversity, and at length shortened by violence, is to be attributed to his own faithlessness and contempt of law.

The Civil War

The truth seems to be that he detested both the parties into which the House of Commons was divided: nor is this strange; for in both those parties the love of liberty and the love of order were mingled, though in different proportions. The advisers whom necessity had compelled him to call round him were by no means men after his own heart. They had joined in condemning his tyranny, in abridging his power, and in punishing his instruments. They were now indeed prepared to defend in a strictly legal way his strictly legal prerogative; but they would have recoiled with horror from the thought of reviving Wentworth's projects of Thorough. They were, therefore, in the King's opinion, traitors, who differed only in the degree of their seditious malignity from Pym and Hampden.

He accordingly, a few days after he had promised the chiefs of the constitutional Royalists that no step of importance should be taken without their knowledge, formed a resolution the most momentous of his whole life, carefully concealed that resolution from them, and executed it in a manner which overwhelmed them with shame and dismay. He sent the Attorney General to impeach Pym, Hollis, Hampden, and other members of the House of Commons of high treason at the bar of the House of Lords. Not content with this flagrant violation of the Great Charter and of the uninterrupted practice of centuries, he went in person, accompanied by armed men, to seize the leaders of the opposition within the walls of Parliament.

The attempt failed. The accused members had left the House a short time before Charles entered it. A sudden and violent revulsion of feeling, both in the Parliament and in the country, followed. Those who had the chief sway in the Lower House now felt that not only their power and popularity, but their lands and their necks, were staked on the event of the struggle in which they were engaged. The flagging zeal of the party opposed to the court revived in an instant. During the night which followed the outrage the whole city of London was in arms. In a few hours the roads leading to the capital were covered with multitudes of yeomen spurring hard to Westminster with the badges of the parliamentary cause in their hats. In the House of Commons the opposition became at once irresistible, and carried, by more than two votes to one, resolutions of unprecedented violence. Strong bodies of the trainbands, regularly relieved, mounted guard round Westminster Hall. The gates of the King's palace were daily besieged by a furious multitude whose taunts and execrations were heard even in the presence chamber, and who could scarcely be kept out of the royal apartments by the gentlemen of the household. Had Charles remained much longer in his stormy capital, it is probable that the Commons would have found a plea for making him, under outward forms of respect, a State prisoner.

He quitted London, never to return till the day of a terrible and memorable reckoning had arrived. A negotiation began which occupied many months. Accusations and recriminations passed backward and forward between the contending parties. All accommodation had become impossible. The sure punishment which waits on habitual perfidy had at length overtaken the King. It was to no purpose that he now pawned his royal word, and invoked heaven to witness the sincerity of his professions. The distrust with which his adversaries regarded him was not to be removed by oaths or treaties. They were convinced that they could be safe only when he was utterly helpless. Their demand, therefore, was, that he should surrender, not only those prerogatives which he had usurped in violation of ancient laws and of his own recent promises, but also other prerogatives which the English kings had possessed from time immemorial. No minister must be appointed, no peer created, without the consent of the Houses. Above all, the sovereign must resign that supreme military authority which, from time beyond all memory, had appertained to the regal office.

The change which the Houses proposed to make in our institutions, though it seems exorbitant, when distinctly set forth and digested into articles of capitulation, really amounts to little more than the change which, in the next generation, was effected by the revolution. In fact, the leaders of the Roundhead party in 1642, and the statesmen who, about half a century later, effected the revolution, had exactly the same object in view. That object was to terminate the contest between the Crown and the Parliament, by giving to the Parliament a supreme control over the executive administration. The statesmen of the revolution effected this indirectly by changing the dynasty. The Roundheads of 1642, being unable to change the dynasty, were compelled to take a direct course towards their end.

In October 1642 the first pitched battle of the war was fought at Edgehill. Though the result was indecisive, the quality of the Royalist troops at this stage was superior. Cromwell remarked to Hampden afterwards: 'Your troopers are most of them old decayed servingmen and tapsters; and their troopers [the Royalists] are gentlemen's sons . . .'

We cannot, however, wonder that the demands of the opposition, importing as they did a complete and formal transfer to the Parliament of powers which had always belonged to the Crown, should have shocked that great party of which the characteristics are respect for constituted authority and dread of violent innovation. The constitutional Royalists were forced to make their choice between two dangers; and they thought it their duty rather to rally round a prince whose past conduct they condemned, and whose word inspired them with little confidence, than to suffer the regal office to be degraded, and the polity of the realm to be entirely remodelled. With such feelings, many men whose virtues and abilities would have done honour to any cause ranged themselves on the side of the King.

In August 1642 the sword was at length drawn; and soon, in almost every shire of the kingdom, two hostile factions appeared in arms against each other. It is not easy to say which of the contending parties was at first the more formidable. The Houses commanded London and the counties round London, the fleet, the navigation of the Thames, and most of the large towns and seaports. They had at their disposal almost all the military stores of the kingdom, and were able to raise duties, both on goods imported from foreign countries, and on some important products of domestic industry. The King was ill provided with artillery and ammunition. The taxes which he laid on the rural districts occupied by his troops produced, it is probable, a sum far less than that which the Parliament drew from the city of London alone. He relied, indeed, chiefly, for pecuniary aid, on the munificence of his opulent adherents. Many of these mortgaged their land, pawned their jewels, and broke up their silver chargers and christening bowls, in order to assist him.

Charles had one advantage, which, if he used it well, would have more than compensated for the want of stores and money, and which, notwithstanding his mismanagement, gave him, during some months, a superiority in the war. His troops at first fought much better than those of the Parliament. Both armies, it is true, were almost entirely composed of men who had never seen a field of battle. Nevertheless, the difference was great. The parliamentary ranks were filled with hirelings whom want and idleness had induced to enlist. Hampden's regiment was regarded as one of the best; and even Hampden's regiment was described by Cromwell as a mere rabble of tapsters and serving men out of place. The royal army, on the other hand, consisted in great part of gentlemen, high spirited, ardent, accustomed to consider dishonour as more terrible than death, accustomed to fencing, to the use of fire arms, to bold riding, and to manly and perilous sport. Such gentlemen, mounted on their favourite horses, and commanding little bands, composed of their younger brothers, grooms, gamekeepers, and huntsmen, were, from the very first day on which they took the field, qualified to play their part with credit in a skirmish. The steadiness, the prompt obedience, the mechanical precision of movement, which are characteristic of the regular soldier, these gallant volunteers never attained. But they were at first opposed to enemies as undisciplined as themselves, and far less active, athletic, and daring. For a time, therefore, the Cavaliers were successful in almost every encounter.

The Houses had also been unfortunate in the choice of a general. The rank and wealth of the Earl of Essex made him one of the most important members of the parliamentary party. He had borne arms on the Continent with credit, and, when the war began, had as high a military reputation as any man in the country. But it soon appeared that he was unfit for the post of commander in chief. He had little energy and no originality. The methodical tactics which he had learned in the war of the Palatinate did not save him from the disgrace of being surprised and baffled by such a captain as Rupert, who could claim no higher fame than that of an enterprising partisan.

When the war had lasted a year, the advantage was decidedly with the Royalists. They were victorious, both in the western and in the northern counties. They had wrested Bristol, the second city in the kingdom, from the Parliament. They had won several battles and had not sustained a single serious or ignominious defeat. Among the Roundheads adversity had begun to produce dissension and discontent. It was thought necessary to fortify London against the royal army, and to hang some disaffected citizens at their own doors. Several of the most distinguished peers who had hitherto remained at Westminster fled to the court at Oxford; nor can it be doubted that, if the operations of the Cavaliers had, at this season, been directed by a sagacious and powerful mind, Charles would soon have marched in triumph to Whitehall.

But the King suffered the auspicious moment to pass away; and it never returned. In August 1643 he sate down before the city of Gloucester. That city was defended by the inhabitants and by the garrison, with a determination such as had not, since the commencement of the war, been shown by the adherents of the Parliament. The emulation of London was excited. The trainbands of the City volunteered to march wherever their services might be required. A great force was speedily collected, and began to move westward. The siege of Gloucester was raised: the Royalists in every part of the kingdom were disheartened: the spirit of the parliamentary party revived; and the apostate Lords, who had lately fled from Westminster to Oxford, hastened back from Oxford to Westminster.

And now a new and alarming class of symptoms began to appear in the distempered body politic. There had been, from the first, in the parliamentary party, some men whose minds were set on objects from which the majority of that party would have shrunk with horror. These men were, in religion, Independents. They conceived that every Christian congregation had, under Christ, supreme jurisdiction in things spiritual; that appeals to provincial and national synods were scarcely less unscriptural than appeals to the Court of Arches, or to the Vatican; and that Popery, Prelacy, and Presbyterianism were merely three forms of one great apostasy. In politics the Independents were, to use the phrase of their time, root and branch men, or, to use the kindred phrase of our own time, radicals. Not content with limiting the power of the monarch, they were desirous to erect a commonwealth on the ruins of the old English polity. At first they had been inconsiderable, both in numbers and in weight; but before the war had lasted two years they became, not indeed the largest, but the most powerful faction in the country. Some of the old parliamentary leaders had been removed by death; and others had forfeited the public confidence. Pym had been borne, with princely honours, to a grave among the Plantagenets. Hampden had fallen, as became him, while vainly endeavouring, by his heroic example, to inspire his followers with courage to face the fiery cavalry of Rupert. Essex and his lieutenants had shown little vigour and ability in the conduct of military operations. At such a conjuncture it was that the Independent party, ardent, resolute, and uncompromising, began to raise its head, both in the camp and in the House of Commons.

The soul of the party was Oliver Cromwell. Bred to peaceful occupations, he had, at more than forty years of age, accepted a commission in the parliamentary army. No sooner had he become a soldier than he discerned, with the keen glance of genius, what Essex and men like Essex, with all their experience, were unable to perceive. He saw precisely where the strength of the Royalists lay, and by what means alone that strength could be overpowered. He saw that it was necessary to reconstruct the army of the Parliament. He saw also that there were abundant and excellent materials for the purpose, materials less showy, indeed, but more solid, than those of which the gallant squadrons of the King were composed. It was necessary to look for recruits who were not mere mercenaries, for recruits of decent station and grave character, fearing God and zealous for public liberty. With such men he filled his own regiment, and, while he subjected them to a discipline more rigid than had ever before been known in England, he administered to their intellectual and moral nature stimulants of fearful potency.

The events of the year 1644 fully proved the superiority of his abilities. In the south, where Essex held the command, the parliamentary forces underwent a succession of shameful disasters; but in the north the victory of Marston Moor fully compensated for all that had been lost elsewhere. That victory was not a more serious blow to the Royalists than to the party which had hitherto been dominant at Westminster; for it was notorious that the day, disgracefully lost by the Presbyterians, had been retrieved by the energy of Cromwell, and by the steady valour of the warriors whom he had trained.

These events produced the Selfdenying Ordinance and the new model of the army. Under decorous pretexts, and with every mark of respect, Essex and most of those who had held high posts under him were removed; and the conduct of the war was intrusted to very different hands. Fairfax, a brave soldier, but of mean understanding and irresolute temper, was the nominal Lord General of the forces; but Cromwell was their real head.

Cromwell made haste to organise the whole army on the same principles on which he had organised his own regiment. As soon as this process was complete, the event of the war was decided. The Cavaliers had now to encounter natural courage equal to their own, enthusiasm stronger than their own, and discipline such as was utterly wanting to them. At Naseby took place the first great encounter between the Royalists and the remodelled army of the Houses. The victory of the Roundheads was complete and decisive. It was followed by other triumphs in rapid succession. In a few months the authority of the Parliament was fully established over the whole kingdom. Charles fled to the Scots, and was by them, in a manner which did not much exalt their national character, delivered up to his English subjects.

While the event of the war was still doubtful, the Houses had put the Primate to death, had interdicted, within the sphere of their authority, the use of the liturgy, and had required all men to subscribe that renowned instrument known by the name of the Solemn League and Covenant. Covenanting work, as it was called, went on fast. Hundreds of thousands affixed their names to the rolls, and, with hands lifted up towards heaven,

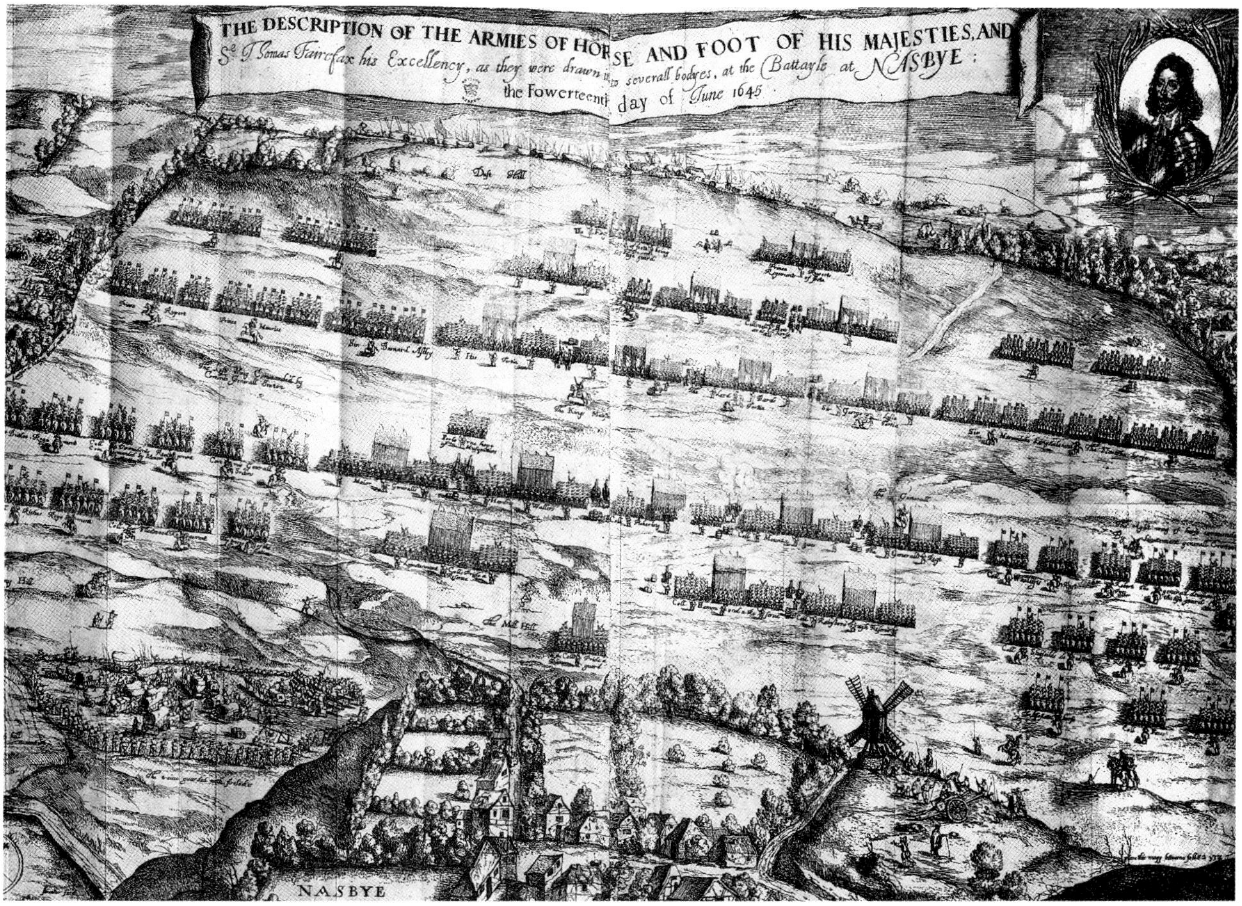
THE DESCRIPTION OF THE ARMIES OF HORSE AND FOOT OF HIS MAJESTIES, AND
Sr. Thomas Fairfax his Excellency, as they were drawn into severall bodyes, at the Battayle at NASBYE:
the Fowerteenth day of June 1645
NASBYE

The opposing armies at the battle of Naseby in 1645: an engraving by John Sprigge in Anglia Rediviva. *Cromwell's remodelled army had by 1645 established a clear superiority on the battlefield, and at Naseby inflicted a crushing defeat on the Royalists. Apart from a few sporadic skirmishes the Civil War was over.*

swore to endeavour, without respect of persons, the extirpation of Popery and Prelacy, heresy and schism, and to bring to public trial and condign punishment all who should hinder the reformation of religion. When the struggle was over, the work of innovation and revenge was pushed on with increased ardour. The ecclesiastical polity of the kingdom was remodelled. Most of the old clergy were ejected from their benefices. Fines, often of ruinous amount, were laid on the Royalists, already impoverished by large aids furnished to the King. Many estates were confiscated. In consequence of these spoliations, a great part of the soil of England was at once offered for sale. As money was scarce, as the market was glutted, as the title was insecure, and as the awe inspired by powerful bidders prevented free competition, the prices were often merely nominal. Thus many old and honourable families disappeared and were heard of no more; and many new men rose rapidly to affluence.

But, while the Houses were employing their authority thus, it suddenly passed out of their hands. It had been obtained by calling into existence a power which could not be controlled. In the summer of 1647, about twelve months after the last fortress of the Cavaliers had submitted to the Parliament, the Parliament was compelled to submit to its own soldiers.

Thirteen years followed, during which England was, under various names and forms, really governed by the sword. Never before that time, or since that time, was the civil power in our country subjected to military dictation.

On 27 April 1646 Charles escaped from Oxford through the surrounding Parliamentary forces and surrendered to the Scots. This contemporary print, possibly used in a broadside, shows the King escaping in disguise.

England Under Cromwell

The army of the Long Parliament was raised for home service. The pay of the private soldier was much above the wages earned by the great body of the people; and, if he distinguished himself by intelligence and courage, he might hope to attain high commands. The ranks were accordingly composed of persons superior in station and education to the multitude. These persons, sober, moral, diligent, and accustomed to reflect, had been induced to take up arms, not by the pressure of want, not by the love of novelty and license, not by the arts of recruiting officers, but by religious and political zeal, mingled with the desire of distinction and promotion. The boast of the soldiers, as we find it recorded in their solemn resolutions, was that they had not been forced into the service, nor had enlisted chiefly for the sake of lucre, that they were no janissaries, but freeborn Englishmen, who had, of their own accord, put their lives in jeopardy for the liberties and religion of England, and whose right and duty it was to watch over the welfare of the nation which they had saved.

In war this strange force was irresistible. The stubborn courage characteristic of the English people was, by the system of Cromwell, at once regulated and stimulated. Other leaders have maintained order as strict. Other leaders have inspired their followers with zeal as ardent. But in his camp alone the most rigid discipline was found in company with the fiercest enthusiasm. His troops moved to victory with the precision of machines, while burning with the wildest fanaticism of Crusaders. From the time when the army was remodelled to the time when it was disbanded, it never found, either in the British islands or on the Continent, an enemy who could stand its onset. In England, Scotland, Ireland, Flanders, the Puritan warriors, often surrounded by difficulties, sometimes contending against threefold odds, not only never failed to conquer, but never failed to destroy and break in pieces whatever force was opposed to them. They at length came to regard the day of battle as a day of certain triumph, and marched against the most renowned battalions of Europe with disdainful confidence.

Oliver Cromwell, the miniature by Samuel Cooper painted when he was in his early fifties. A man of immense moral stature and iron courage, he evoked even from his enemy Clarendon the tribute that he achieved those [things] in which none but a valiant and great man could have succeeded.

To keep down the English people was no light task even for that army. No sooner was the first pressure of military tyranny felt, than the nation, unbroken to such servitude, began to struggle fiercely. Insurrections broke out even in those counties which, during the recent war, had been the most submissive to the Parliament. Indeed, the Parliament itself abhorred its old defenders more than its old enemies, and was desirous to come to terms of accommodation with Charles at the expense of the troops. In Scotland, at the same time, a coalition was formed between the Royalists and a large body of Presbyterians who regarded the doctrines of the Independents with detestation. At length the storm burst. There were risings in Norfolk, Suffolk, Essex, Kent, Wales. The fleet in the Thames suddenly hoisted the royal colours, stood out to sea, and menaced the southern coast. A great Scottish force crossed the frontier and advanced into Lancashire.

But the yoke of the army was not to be so shaken off. While Fairfax suppressed the risings in the neighbourhood of the capital, Oliver routed the Welsh insurgents, and, leaving their castles in ruins, marched against the Scots. His troops were few, when compared with the invaders; but he was little in the habit of counting his enemies. The Scottish army was utterly destroyed. A change in the Scottish government followed. An administration, hostile to the King, was formed at Edinburgh; and Cromwell, more than ever the darling of his soldiers, returned in triumph to London.

And now a design, to which, at the commencement of the civil war, no man would have dared to allude, and which was not less inconsistent with the Solemn League and Covenant than with the old law of England, began to take a distinct form. The austere warriors who ruled the nation had, during some months, meditated a fearful vengeance on the captive King. When and how the scheme originated; whether it spread from the general to the ranks, or from the ranks to the general; whether it is to be ascribed to policy using fanaticism as a tool, or to fanaticism bearing down policy with headlong impulse, are questions which, even at this day, cannot be answered with perfect confidence. It seems, however, on the whole, probable that he who seemed to lead was really forced to follow, and that he sacrificed his own judgment and his own inclinations to the wishes of the army. The truth is that Cromwell had, at one time, meant to mediate between the throne and the Parliament, and to reorganise the distracted State by the power of the sword, under the sanction of the royal name. In this design he persisted till he was compelled to abandon it by the refractory temper of the soldiers, and by the incurable duplicity of the King.

The vices of Charles had grown upon him. They were, indeed, vices which difficulties and perplexities generally bring out in the strongest light. Cunning is the natural defence of the weak. A prince, therefore, who is habitually a deceiver when at the height of power, is not likely to learn frankness in the midst of embarrassments and distresses. Charles was not only a most unscrupulous but a most unlucky dissembler. There never was a politician to whom so many frauds and falsehoods were brought home by undeniable evidence. He publicly recognised the Houses at Westminster as a legal Parliament, and, at the same time, made a private minute in council declaring the recognition null. He publicly disclaimed all thought of calling in foreign aid against his people: he privately solicited aid from France, from Denmark, and from Loraine. He publicly denied that he employed Papists: at the same time he privately sent to his generals directions to employ every Papist that would serve. To such an extent, indeed, had insincerity now tainted the King's whole nature, that his most devoted friends could not refrain from complaining to each other, with bitter grief and shame, of his crooked politics. His defeats, they said, gave them less pain than his intrigues. Since he had been a prisoner, there was no section of the victorious party which had not been the object both of his flatteries and of his machinations: but never was he more unfortunate than when he attempted at once to cajole and to undermine Cromwell.

Cromwell had to determine whether he would put to hazard the attachment of his party, the attachment of his army, his own greatness, nay his own life, in an attempt, which would probably have been vain, to save a prince whom no engagement could bind. With many struggles and misgivings, the decision was made. Charles was left to his fate. The military saints resolved that, in defiance of the old laws of the realm, and of the almost universal sentiment of the nation, the King should expiate his crimes with his blood. He for a time expected a death like that of his unhappy predecessors, Edward II and Richard II. But he was in no danger of such treason. Those who had him in their gripe were not midnight stabbers. What they did they did in order that it might be a spectacle to heaven and earth, and that it might be held in everlasting remembrance. They enjoyed keenly the very scandal which they gave. That the ancient constitution and the public opinion of England were directly opposed to regicide made regicide seem strangely fascinating to a party bent on effecting a complete political and social revolution. In order to accomplish their purpose, it was necessary that they should first break in pieces every part of the machinery of the government; and this necessity was rather agreeable than painful to them. The Commons passed a vote tending to accommodation with the King. The soldiers excluded the majority by force. The Lords unanimously rejected the proposition that the King should be brought to trial. Their house was instantly closed. No court, known to the law, would take on itself the office of judging the fountain of justice. A revolutionary tribunal was created. That tribunal pronounced Charles a tyrant, a traitor, a murderer, and a public enemy; and his head was severed from his shoulders, before thousands of spectators, in front of the banqueting hall of his own palace.

In no long time it became manifest that those political and religious zealots, to whom this deed is to be ascribed, had committed, not only a crime, but an error. They had given to a prince, hitherto known to his people chiefly by his faults, an opportunity of displaying, on a great theatre, before the eyes of all nations and all ages, some qualities which irresistibly call forth the admiration and love of mankind, the high spirit of a gallant gentleman, the patience and meekness of a penitent Christian. Nay, they had so contrived their revenge that the very man whose life had been a series of attacks on the liberties of England now seemed to die a martyr in the cause of those liberties. No demagogue ever produced such an impression on the public mind as the captive King, who, retaining in that extremity all his regal dignity, and confronting death with dauntless courage, gave utterance to the feelings of his oppressed people, manfully refused to plead before a court unknown to the law, appealed from military violence to the principles of the constitution, asked by what right the House of Commons had been purged of its most respectable members and the House of Lords deprived of its legislative functions, and told his weeping hearers that he was defending, not only his own cause, but theirs. His long misgovernment, his innumerable perfidies, were forgotten. From that day began a reaction in favour of monarchy and of the exiled house, a reaction which never ceased till the throne had again been set up in all its old dignity.

At first, however, the slayers of the King seemed to have derived new energy from that sacrament of blood by which they had bound themselves closely together, and separated themselves for ever from the great body of their countrymen. England was declared a commonwealth. The House of Commons, reduced to a small number of members, was nominally the supreme power in the state. In fact, the army and its great chief governed everything. Oliver had made his choice. He had kept the hearts of his soldiers, and had broken with almost every other class of his fellow citizens. Beyond the limits of his camps and fortresses he could scarcely be said to have a party. Those elements of force which, when the civil war broke out, had appeared arrayed against each other, were combined against him; all the Cavaliers, the great majority of the Roundheads, the Anglican Church, the Presbyterian Church, the Roman Catholic Church,

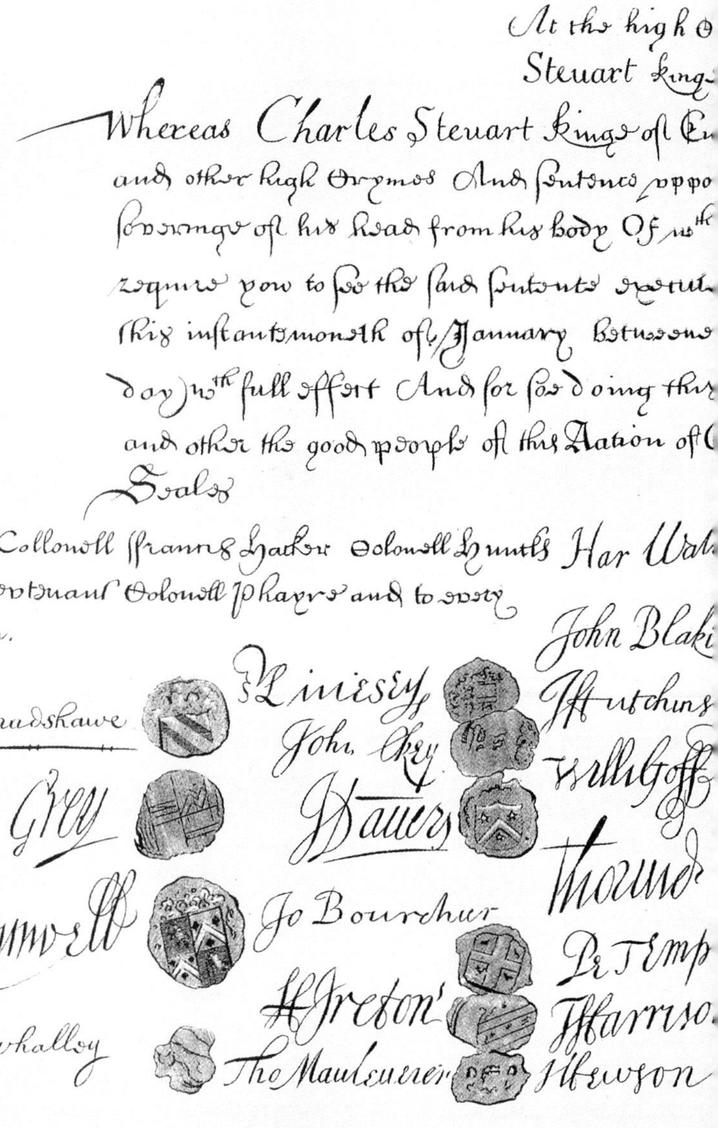
Whereas Charles Steuart Kinge of E[ngland]
Jo. Bradshawe
Tho: Grey
O Cromwell
Edw. Whalley
Jo Bourchier
H Ireton
Tho Maulever
John Blak[iston]
Harrison
Hewson

The death warrant of Charles I. The first signature is that of John Bradshaw, the president of the court which tried Charles; the third signature is that of Cromwell.

England, Scotland, Ireland. Yet such was his genius and resolution that he was able to overpower and crush everything that crossed his path, to make himself more absolute master of his country than any of her legitimate Kings had been, and to make his country more dreaded and respected than she had been during many generations under the rule of her legitimate Kings.

Everything yielded to the vigour and ability of Cromwell. In a few months he subjugated Ireland, as Ireland had never been subjugated during the five centuries of slaughter which had elapsed since the landing of the first Norman settlers. He resolved to put an end to that conflict of races and religions which had so long distracted the island, by making the English and Protestant population decidedly predominant. For this end he gave the rein to the fierce enthusiasm of his followers, waged war resembling that which Israel waged on the Canaanites, smote the idolaters with the edge of the sword, so that great cities were left without inhabitants,

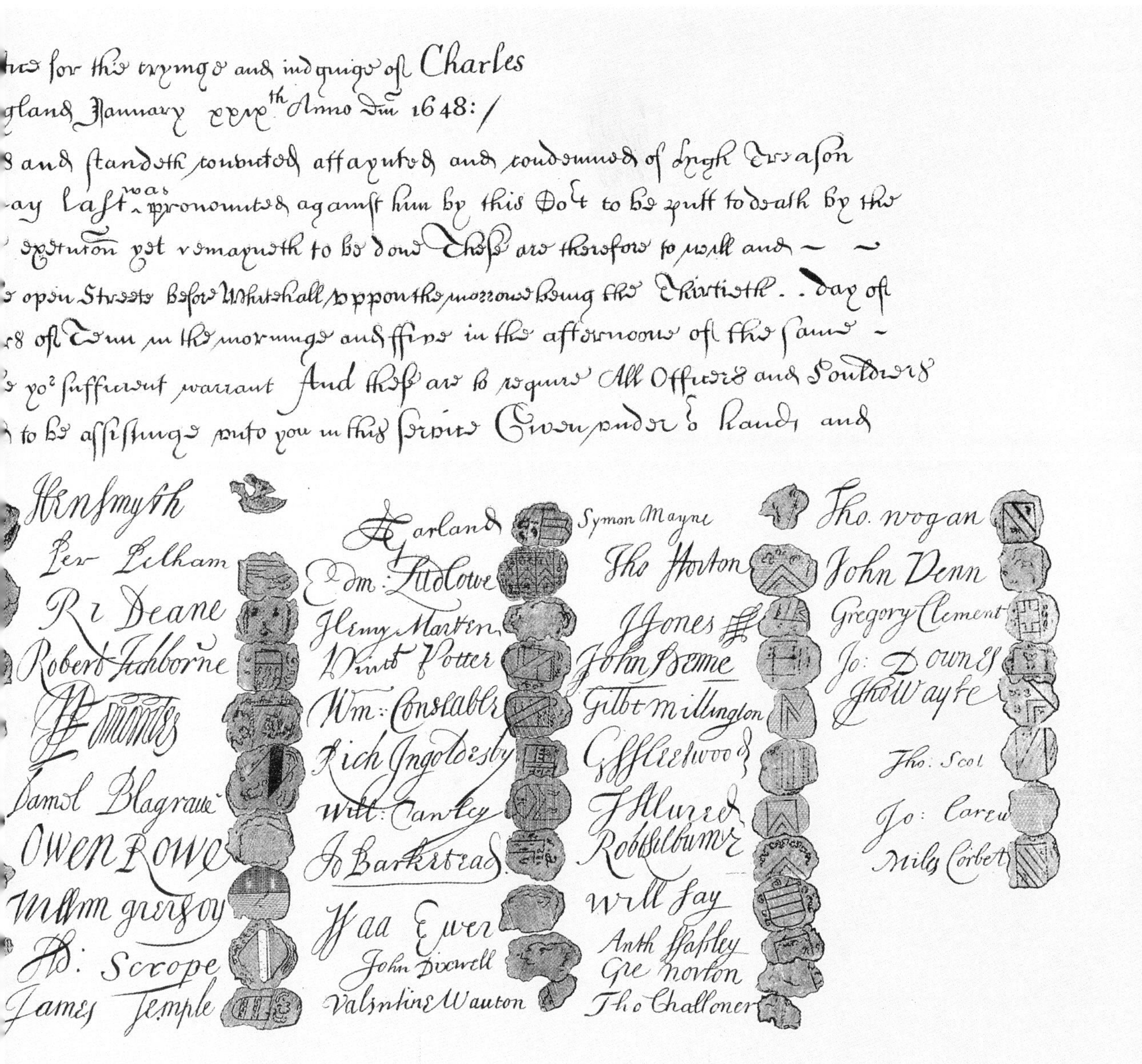
...re for the tryinge and judginge of Charles
...gland January xxix th Anno Dni 1648:/
...and standeth convicted attainted and condemned of High Treason
...ay last was pronounced against him by this Court to be putt to death by the
...execution yet remaineth to be done These are therefore to will and ~ ~
...open Streete before Whitehall uppon the morrowe being the Thirtieth . . day of
...8 of Clocke in the morninge and Five in the afternoone of the same ~
...your sufficient warrant And these are to require All Officers and Souldiers
...to be assisting unto you in this Service Given under our hands and

Hen Smyth
Per Pelham
Ri Deane
Robert Tichborne
H Edwardes
Daniel Blagrave
Owen Rowe
William Purefoy
Ad: Scrope
James Temple
A Garland
Edm: Ludlowe
Henry Marten
Vinct Potter
Wm: Constable
Rich Ingoldesby
Will: Cawley
Jo Barkstead
Isaa Ewer
John Dixwell
Valentine Wauton
Symon Mayne
Tho Horton
J Jones
John Downe
Gilbt Millington
G Fleetwood
J Alured
Robt Lilburne
Will Say
Anth Stapley
Gre Norton
Tho Challoner
Tho Wogan
John Venn
Gregory Clement
Jo: Downes
Tho Wayte
Tho: Scot
Jo: Carew
Miles Corbet

drove many thousands to the Continent, shipped off many thousands to the West Indies, and supplied the void thus made by pouring in numerous colonists, of Saxon blood, and of Calvinistic faith.

From Ireland the victorious chief, who was now in name, as he had long been in reality, Lord General of the armies of the commonwealth, turned to Scotland. The young King was there. He had consented to profess himself a Presbyterian, and to subscribe the Covenant; and, in return for these concessions, the austere Puritans who bore sway at Edinburgh had permitted him to assume the crown, and to hold, under their inspection and control, a solemn and melancholy court. This mock royalty was of short duration. In two great battles Cromwell annihilated the military force of Scotland. Charles fled for his life, and, with extreme difficulty, escaped the fate of his father. The ancient kingdom of the Stuarts was reduced, for the first time, to profound submission.

Thus far there had been at least the semblance of harmony between the warriors who had subjugated Ireland and Scotland and the politicians who sate at Westminster: but the alliance which had been cemented by danger was dissolved by victory. The Parliament forgot that it was but the creature of the army. The army was less disposed than ever to submit to the dictation of the Parliament. Indeed the few members who made up what was contemptuously called the Rump of the House of Commons had no more claim than the military chiefs to be esteemed the representatives of the nation. The dispute was soon brought to a decisive issue. Cromwell filled the House with armed men. The Speaker was pulled out of his chair, the mace taken from the table, the room cleared, and the door locked.

King, Lords, and Commons, had now in turn been vanquished and destroyed; and Cromwell seemed to be left the sole heir of the powers of all three. Yet were certain limitations still imposed on him by the very army to which he owed his immense authority. The object of the warlike saints who surrounded Cromwell was the settlement of a free and pious commonwealth. For that end they were ready to employ, without scruple, any means, however violent and lawless. It was not impossible, therefore, to establish by their aid a dictatorship such as no King had ever exercised: but it was probable that their aid would be at once withdrawn from a ruler who, even under strict constitutional restraints, should venture to assume the kingly name and dignity.

The sentiments of Cromwell were widely different. He was not what he had been; nor would it be just to consider the change which his views had undergone as the effect merely of selfish ambition. He had, when he came up to the Long Parliament, brought with him from his rural retreat little knowledge of books, no experience of great affairs, and a temper galled by the long tyranny of the government and of the hierarchy. He had, during the thirteen years which followed, gone through a political education of no common kind. It would have been strange indeed if his notions had been still the same as in the days when his mind was principally occupied by his fields and his religion, and when the greatest events which diversified the course of his life were a cattle fair or a prayer meeting at Huntingdon. He saw that some schemes of innovation for which he had once been zealous, whether good or bad in themselves, were opposed to the general feeling of the country, and that, if he persevered in those schemes, he had nothing before him but constant troubles, which must be suppressed by the constant use of the sword. He therefore wished to restore, in all essentials, that ancient constitution which the majority of the people had always loved, and for which they now pined. The course afterwards taken by Monk was not open to Cromwell. The memory of one terrible day separated the great regicide for ever from the House of Stuart. What remained was that he should mount the ancient English throne, and reign according to the ancient English polity. If he could effect this, he might hope that the wounds of the lacerated State would heal fast. Great numbers of honest and quiet men would speedily rally round him. Those Royalists whose attachment was rather to institutions than to persons, to the kingly office than to King Charles I or King Charles II, would soon kiss the hand of King Oliver. A sentiment of loyalty would gradually bind the people to the new dynasty; and, on the decease of the founder of that dynasty, the royal dignity might descend with general acquiescence to his posterity.

The ablest Royalists were of opinion that these views were correct, and

Charles I at his trial, by Edward Bower. The King, when he was allowed to speak, made a skilful and eloquent presentation of his case.

that, if Cromwell had been permitted to follow his own judgment, the exiled line would never have been restored. But his plan was directly opposed to the feelings of the only class which he dared not offend. The name of King was hateful to the soldiers. Some of them were indeed unwilling to see the administration in the hands of any single person. The great majority, however, were disposed to support their general, as elective first magistrate of a commonwealth, against all factions which might resist his authority: but they would not consent that he should assume the regal title, or that the dignity, which was the just reward of his personal merit, should be declared hereditary in his family. All that was left to him was to give to the new republic a constitution as like the constitution of the old monarchy as the army would bear. That his elevation to power might not seem to be merely his own act, he convoked a council, composed partly of persons on whose support he could depend, and partly of persons whose opposition he might safely defy. This assembly, which he called a Parliament, and which the populace nicknamed, from one of the most conspicuous members, Barebone's Parliament, after exposing itself during a short time to the public contempt, surrendered back to the general the powers which it had received from him, and left him at liberty to frame a plan of government.

His plan bore, from the first, a considerable resemblance to the old English constitution: but, in a few years, he thought it safe to proceed further, and to restore almost every part of the ancient system under new names and forms. The title of King was not revived: but the kingly prerogatives were intrusted to a Lord High Protector. The sovereign was called not His Majesty, but His Highness. He was not crowned and anointed in Westminster Abbey, but was solemnly enthroned, girt with a sword of State, clad in a robe of purple, and presented with a rich Bible, in Westminster Hall. His office was not declared hereditary: but he was permitted to name his successor; and none could doubt that he would name his son.

His wish seems to have been to govern constitutionally, and to substitute the empire of the laws for that of the sword. But he soon found that, hated as he was, both by Royalists and Presbyterians, he could be safe only by being absolute. The first House of Commons which the people elected by his command, questioned his authority, and was dissolved without having passed a single act. His second House of Commons, though it recognised him as Protector, and would gladly have made him King, obstinately refused to acknowledge his new Lords. He had no course left but to dissolve the Parliament. 'God', he exclaimed, at parting, 'be judge between you and me!'

Had he been a cruel, licentious, and rapacious prince, the nation might have found courage in despair, and might have made a convulsive effort to free itself from military domination. But the grievances which the country suffered, though such as excited serious discontent, were by no means such as impel great masses of men to stake their lives, their fortunes, and the welfare of their families against fearful odds. The taxation, though heavier than it had been under the Stuarts, was not heavy when compared with that of the neighbouring states and with the resources of England. Property was secure. Even the Cavalier, who refrained from giving disturbance to the new settlement, enjoyed in peace whatever the civil troubles had left him.

The Protector's foreign policy at the same time extorted the ungracious approbation of those who most detested him. The Cavaliers could scarcely refrain from wishing that one who had done so much to raise the fame of the nation had been a legitimate King; and the Republicans were forced to own that the tyrant suffered none but himself to wrong his country, and that, if he had robbed her of liberty, he had at least given her glory in exchange. After half a century during which England had been of scarcely more weight in European politics than Venice or Saxony, she at once became the most formidable power in the world, dictated terms of peace to the United Provinces, avenged the common injuries of Christendom on the pirates of Barbary, vanquished the Spaniards by land and sea, seized one of the finest West Indian islands, and acquired on the Flemish coast a fortress which consoled the national pride for the loss of Calais. She was supreme on the ocean. She was the head of the Protestant interest. All the reformed

Churches scattered over Roman Catholic kingdoms acknowledged Cromwell as their guardian.

While he lived his power stood firm, an object of mingled aversion, admiration, and dread to his subjects. It has often been affirmed, but with little reason, that Oliver died at a time fortunate for his renown, and that, if his life had been prolonged, it would probably have closed amidst disgraces and disasters. It is certain that he was, to the last, honoured by his soldiers, obeyed by the whole population of the British islands, and dreaded by all foreign powers, that he was laid among the ancient sovereigns of England with funeral pomp such as London had never before seen, and that he was succeeded by his son Richard as quietly as any King had ever been succeeded by any Prince of Wales.

During five months, the administration of Richard Cromwell went on so tranquilly and regularly that all Europe believed him to be firmly established on the chair of State. In truth his situation was in some respects much more advantageous than that of his father. The young man had made no enemy. His hands were unstained by civil blood. His humanity, ingenuousness, and modesty, the mediocrity of his abilities, and the docility with which he submitted to the guidance of persons wiser than himself, admirably qualified him to be the head of a limited monarchy.

For a time it seemed highly probable that he would, under the direction of able advisers, effect what his father had attempted in vain. A Parliament was called, and the writs were directed after the old fashion. Had the Protector and the Parliament been suffered to proceed undisturbed, there can be little doubt that an order of things similar to that which was afterwards established under the House of Hanover would have been established under the House of Cromwell. But there was in the State a power more than sufficient to deal with Protector and Parliament together. Over the soldiers Richard had no authority except that which he derived from the great name which he had inherited. The officers who had the principal influence among the troops stationed near London were not his friends. They were men distinguished by valour and conduct in the field, but destitute of the wisdom and civil courage which had been conspicuous in their deceased leader. Some of them were honest, but fanatical, Independents and Republicans. Others were impatient to be what Oliver had been. They were as well born as he, and as well educated: they could not understand why they were not as worthy to wear the purple robe, and to wield the sword of state; and they pursued the objects of their wild ambition, not, like him, with patience, vigilance, sagacity, and determination, but with the restlessness and irresolution characteristic of aspiring mediocrity. Among these feeble copies of a great original the most conspicuous was Lambert.

On the very day of Richard's accession the officers began to conspire against their new master. The good understanding which existed between him and his Parliament hastened the crisis. Alarm and resentment spread through the camp. A coalition was formed between the military malecontents and the republican minority of the House of Commons. It may well be doubted whether Richard could have triumphed over that coalition, even if he had inherited his father's clear judgment and iron courage. It is certain that simplicity and meekness like his were not the qualities which the conjuncture required. He fell ingloriously, and without a struggle. He was used by the army as an instrument for the purpose of dissolving the Parliament, and was then contemptuously thrown aside. The officers gratified their republican allies by declaring that the expulsion of the Rump had been illegal, and by inviting that assembly to resume its functions. The old Speaker and a quorum of the old members came together, and were proclaimed, amidst the scarcely stifled derision and execration of the whole nation, the supreme power in the commonwealth. It was at the same time expressly declared that there should be no first magistrate, and no House of Lords.

But this state of things could not last. On the day on which the Long Parliament revived, revived also its old quarrel with the army. Again the Rump forgot that it owed its existence to the pleasure of the soldiers, and began to treat them as subjects. Again the doors of the House of Commons were closed by military violence; and a provisional government, named by the officers, assumed the direction of affairs.

Meanwhile the sense of great evils, and the strong apprehension of still greater evils close at hand, had at length produced an alliance between the Cavaliers and the Presbyterians. Some Presbyterians had, indeed, been disposed to such an alliance even before the death of Charles I: but it was not till after the fall of Richard Cromwell that the whole party became eager for the restoration of the royal house. There was no longer any reasonable hope that the old constitution could be reestablished under a new dynasty. One choice only was left, the Stuarts or the army. Anything was preferable to the yoke of a succession of incapable and inglorious tyrants, raised to power, like the Deys of Barbary, by military revolutions recurring at short intervals. If the Presbyterians obstinately stood aloof from the Royalists, the state was lost; and men might well doubt whether, by the combined exertions of Presbyterians and Royalists, it could be saved.

While the soldiers remained united, all the plots and risings of the malecontents were ineffectual. But a few days after the second expulsion of the Rump, came tidings which gladdened the hearts of all who were attached either to monarchy or to liberty. That mighty force which had, during many years, acted as one man, and which, while so acting, had been found irresistible, was at length divided against itself. There appears to have been less fanaticism among the troops stationed in Scotland than in any other part of the army; and their general, George Monk, was himself the very opposite of a zealot. He had, at the commencement of the civil war, borne arms for the King, had been made prisoner by the Roundheads, had then accepted a commission from the Parliament, and, with very slender pretensions to saintship, had raised himself to high commands by his courage and professional skill. He seems to have been impelled to attack the new rulers of the Commonwealth less by the hope that, if he overthrew them, he should become great, than by the fear that, if he submitted to them, he should not even be secure. Whatever were his motives, he declared himself the champion of the oppressed civil power, refused to acknowledge the usurped authority of the provisional government, and, at the head of seven thousand veterans, marched into England.

This step was the signal for a general explosion. The people everywhere refused to pay taxes. The apprentices of the City assembled by thousands and clamoured for a free Parliament. The fleet sailed up the Thames, and declared against the tyranny of the soldiers. The soldiers, no longer under the control of one commanding mind, separated into factions. Every regiment, afraid lest it should be left alone a mark for the vengeance of the

A Dutch engraving of Cromwell's dissolution of the Rump of the Long Parliament in April 1653. 'King, Lords and Commons had now in turn been vanquished and destroyed; and Cromwell seemed to be left the sole heir of the powers of all three.'

oppressed nation, hastened to make a separate peace. Lambert, who had hastened northward to encounter the army of Scotland, was abandoned by his troops, and became a prisoner. The Rump, generally hated and despised, but still the only body in the country which had any show of legal authority, returned again to the house from which it had been twice ignominiously expelled.

In the meantime Monk was advancing towards London. Wherever he came, the gentry flocked round him, imploring him to use his power for the purpose of restoring peace and liberty to the distracted nation. The general, coldblooded, taciturn, zealous for no polity and for no religion, maintained an impenetrable reserve. It was probably not till he had been some days in the capital that he made up his mind. The cry of the whole people was for a free Parliament; and there could be no doubt that a Parliament really free would instantly restore the exiled family. During a short time, the dissimulation or irresolution of Monk kept all parties in a state of painful suspense. At length he broke silence, and declared for a free Parliament.

As soon as his declaration was known, the whole nation was wild with delight. Wherever he appeared thousands thronged round him, shouting and blessing his name. The bells of all England rang joyously: the gutters ran with ale; and, night after night, the sky five miles round London was reddened by innumerable bonfires. Temporary provision was made for the government: writs were issued for a general election; and then that memorable Parliament, which had, in the course of twenty eventful years, experienced every variety of fortune, which had triumphed over its sovereign, which had been enslaved and degraded by its servants, which had been twice ejected and twice restored, solemnly decreed its own dissolution.

The result of the elections was such as might have been expected from the temper of the nation. The new House of Commons consisted, with few exceptions, of persons friendly to the royal family. The Presbyterians formed the majority.

The new Parliament, which, having been called without the royal writ, is more accurately described as a Convention, met at Westminster. The Lords repaired to the hall, from which they had, during more than eleven years, been excluded by force. Both Houses instantly invited the King to return to his country. He was proclaimed with pomp never before known. A gallant fleet convoyed him from Holland to the coast of Kent. When he landed, the cliffs of Dover were covered by thousands of gazers, among whom scarcely one could be found who was not weeping with delight. The journey to London was a continued triumph. The whole road from Rochester was bordered by booths and tents, and looked like an interminable fair. Everywhere flags were flying, bells and music sounding, wine and ale flowing in rivers to the health of him whose return was the return of peace, of law, and of freedom. But in the midst of the general joy, one spot presented a dark and threatening aspect. On Blackheath the army was drawn up to welcome the sovereign. He smiled, bowed, and extended his hand graciously to the lips of the colonels and majors. But all his courtesy was vain. The countenances of the soldiers were sad and lowering; and, had they given way to their feelings, the festive pageant of which they reluctantly made a part would have had a mournful and bloody end. But there was no concert among them. Discord and defection had left them no confidence in their chiefs or in each other. The whole array of the City of London was under arms. Numerous companies of militia had assembled from various parts of the realm, under the command of loyal noblemen and gentlemen, to welcome the King. The great day closed in peace; and the restored wanderer reposed safe in the palace of his ancestors.

PART 2 The Reign of Charles II

Persecution of the Puritans

The troops were now to be disbanded. Fifty thousand men, accustomed to the profession of arms, were at once thrown on the world: and experience seemed to warrant the belief that this change would produce much misery and crime, that the discharged veterans would be seen begging in every street, or that they would be driven by hunger to pillage. But no such result followed. In a few months there remained not a trace indicating that the most formidable army in the world had just been absorbed into the mass of the community. The Royalists themselves confessed that, in every department of honest industry, the discarded warriors prospered beyond other men, and that, if a baker, a mason or a waggoner attracted notice by his diligence and sobriety, he was in all probability one of Oliver's soldiers.

Charles II during his period of exile. The engraving by Abraham Bosse shows the King dancing at a ball at the Hague.

The military tyranny had passed away; but it had left deep and enduring traces in the public mind. The name of standing army was long held in abhorrence. That instrument by which alone the monarchy could be made absolute became an object of peculiar horror and disgust to the monarchical party, and long continued to be inseparably associated in the imagination of Royalists and Prelatists with regicide and field preaching.

The coalition which had restored the King terminated with the danger from which it had sprung; and two hostile parties again appeared ready for conflict.

The restored King was at this time more loved by the people than any of his predecessors had been. The calamities of his house, the heroic death of his father, his own long sufferings and romantic adventures, made him an object of tender interest. His return had delivered the country from an intolerable bondage. Recalled by the voice of both the contending factions, he was in a position which enabled him to arbitrate between them; and in some respects he was well qualified for the task. He had received from nature excellent parts and a happy temper. His education had been such as might have been expected to develope his understanding and to form him to the practice of every public and private virtue. He had passed through all varieties of fortune, and had seen both sides of human nature. He had been taught by bitter experience how much baseness, perfidy, and ingratitude may lie hid under the obsequious demeanour of courtiers. He had found, on the other hand, in the huts of the poorest, true nobility of soul.

From such a school it might have been expected that a young man who wanted neither abilities nor amiable qualities would have come forth a great and good King. Charles came forth from that school with social habits, with polite and engaging manners, and with some talent for lively conversation, addicted beyond measure to sensual indulgence, fond of sauntering and of frivolous amusements, incapable of self-denial and of exertion, without faith in human virtue or in human attachment, without desire of renown, and without sensibility to reproach. According to him, every person was to be bought: but some people haggled more about their price than others; and when this haggling was very obstinate and very skilful it was called by some fine name. The chief trick by which clever men kept up the price of their abilities was called integrity. The chief trick by which handsome women kept up the price of their beauty was called modesty. The love of God, the love of country, the love of family, the love of friends, were phrases of the same sort, delicate and convenient synonyms for the love of self. Thinking thus of mankind, Charles naturally cared very little what they thought of him. Honour and shame were scarcely more to him than light and darkness to the blind.

It is creditable to Charles's temper that, ill as he thought of his species, he never became a misanthrope. He saw little in men but what was hateful. Yet he did not hate them. Nay, he was so far humane that it was highly disagreeable to him to see their sufferings or to hear their complaints. Worthless men and women, to the very bottom of whose hearts he saw, and whom he knew to be destitute of affection for him and undeserving of his confidence, could easily wheedle him out of titles, places, domains, State secrets and pardons. The consequence was that his bounty generally went, not to those who deserved it best, nor even to those whom he liked best, but to the most shameless and importunate suitor who could obtain an audience.

In 1650 the exiled King set sail for Scotland, having signed, very reluctantly and in bad faith, a declaration approving the Solemn League and Covenant and undertaking to establish Presbyterianism throughout his dominions. The illustration shrewdly comments on the King's subsequent invidious situation.

The motives which governed the political conduct of Charles II differed widely from those by which his predecessor and his successor were actuated. He was not a man to be imposed upon by the patriarchal theory of government and the doctrine of divine right. He was utterly without ambition. He detested business, and would sooner have abdicated his Crown than have undergone the trouble of really directing the administration. He wished merely to be a King such as Louis XV of France afterwards was; a King who could draw without limit on the treasury for the gratification of his private tastes, who could hire with wealth and honours persons capable of assisting him to kill the time, and who, even when the State was brought by maladministration to the depths of humiliation and to the brink of ruin, could still exclude unwelcome truth from the purlieus of his own seraglio, and refuse to see and hear whatever might disturb his luxurious repose. For these ends, and these ends alone, he wished to obtain arbitrary power, if it could be obtained without risk of trouble. In the religious disputes which divided his Protestant subjects his conscience was not at all interested. For his opinions oscillated in contented suspense between infidelity and Popery. But, though his conscience was neutral in the quarrel between the Episcopalians and the Presbyterians, his taste was by no means so. His favourite vices were precisely those to which the Puritans were least indulgent. He could not get through one day without the help of diversions which the Puritans regarded as sinful. As a man eminently well bred, and keenly sensible of the ridiculous, he was moved to contemptuous mirth by the Puritan oddities. Under the influence of such feelings as these Charles was desirous to depress the party which had resisted his father.

Charles was crowned with due ceremony and display at Scone on 1 January 1651, but not before a special day of humiliation had been observed for the sins of the royal family.

The King's brother, James Duke of York, took the same side. Though a libertine, James was diligent, methodical, and fond of authority and business. His understanding was singularly slow and narrow, and his temper obstinate, harsh and unforgiving. That such a prince should have looked with no good will on the free institutions of England, and on the party which was peculiarly zealous for those institutions, can excite no surprise. As yet the duke professed himself a member of the Anglican Church: but he had already shown inclinations which had seriously alarmed good Protestants.

The person on whom devolved at this time the greatest part of the labour of governing was Edward Hyde, Chancellor of the realm, who was soon created Earl of Clarendon. He had, during the first year of the Long Parliament, been honourably distinguished among the senators who laboured to redress the grievances of the nation. When the great schism took place, when the reforming party and the conservative party first appeared marshalled against each other, he, with many wise and good men, took the conservative side. He thenceforward followed the fortunes of the court, enjoyed as large a share of the confidence of Charles I as the reserved nature and tortuous policy of that prince allowed to any minister, and subsequently shared the exile and directed the political conduct of Charles II. At the Restoration Hyde became chief minister. In a few months it was announced that he was closely related by affinity to the royal house. His daughter had become, by a secret marriage, Duchess of York. His grandchildren might perhaps wear the crown. He was raised by this illustrious connection over the heads of the old nobility of the land, and was for a time supposed to be all powerful.

In some respects he was well fitted for his great place. No man spoke with more weight and dignity in Council and in Parliament. No man observed the varieties of character with a more discriminating eye. It must be added that he had a strong sense of moral and religious obligation, a sincere reverence for the laws of his country, and a conscientious regard for the honour and interest of the Crown. But his temper was sour, arrogant, and impatient of opposition. Above all, he had been long an exile; and this circumstance alone would have completely disqualified him for the supreme direction of affairs. From 1646 to 1660 he had lived beyond sea, looking on all that passed at home from a great distance, and through a false medium. His notions of public affairs were necessarily derived from the reports of plotters, many of whom were ruined and desperate men. Events naturally seemed to him auspicious, not in proportion as they increased the prosperity and glory of the nation, but in proportion as they tended to hasten the hour of his own return. To him England was still the England of his youth; and he sternly frowned down every theory and every practice which had sprung up during his own exile. His zeal for Episcopacy and for the Book of Common Prayer was now more ardent than ever, and was mingled with a vindictive hatred of the Puritans, which did him little honour either as a statesman or as a Christian.

While the House of Commons which had recalled the royal family was sitting, it was impossible to effect the reestablishment of the old ecclesiastical system. Not only were the intentions of the court strictly concealed, but assurances which quieted the minds of the moderate Presbyterians were given by the King in the most solemn manner. He had promised, before his restoration, that he would grant liberty of conscience to his subjects. He now repeated that promise, and added a promise to use his best endeavours for the purpose of effecting a compromise between the contending sects. When the King had thus laid asleep the vigilance of those whom he most feared, he dissolved the Parliament. He had already given his assent to an act by which an amnesty was granted, with few exceptions, to all who, during the late troubles, had been guilty of political offences.

Early in 1661 took place a general election. The people were mad with loyal enthusiasm. The capital was excited by preparations for the most splendid coronation that had ever been known. The result was that a body of representatives was returned, such as England had never yet seen. A large proportion of the successful candidates were men who had fought for the Crown and the Church, and whose minds had been exasperated by many injuries and insults suffered at the hands of the Roundheads. When

A contemporary print depicting the adventures of Charles II after the battle of Worcester in August 1651. At top Charles's Scottish army is scattering before the onslaught of the English. Next he is shown hiding with Major Careless from Cromwell's soldiers in the Boscobel oak; travelling in disguise to Bristol as Jane Lane's servant; and finally escaping by sea from Brighton.

The Declaration of Breda issued in 1660 by Charles was drafted by Edward Hyde, the King's Chancellor in exile soon to be rewarded with the Earldom of Clarendon. It was a carefully worded document in which the King promised to leave all difficult problems for Parliament to settle, and extended assurances of protection to Nonconformists.

the members met, the passions which animated each individually acquired new strength from sympathy. The House of Commons was, during some years, more zealous for royalty than the King, more zealous for episcopacy than the bishops. Charles and Clarendon were almost terrified at the completeness of their own success. Even if the King had been desirous to fulfil the promises which he had made to the Presbyterians, it would have been out of his power to do so. It was indeed only by the strong exertion of his influence that he could prevent the victorious Cavaliers from rescinding the act of indemnity, and retaliating without mercy all that they had suffered.

The Commons began by resolving that every member should, on pain of expulsion, take the sacrament according to the form prescribed by the old liturgy, and that the Covenant should be burned by the hangman in Palace Yard. An act was passed, which not only acknowledged the power of the sword to be solely in the King, but declared that in no extremity whatever could the two Houses be justified in withstanding him by force. The bishops were restored to their seats in the Upper House. The old ecclesiastical polity and the old liturgy were revived without any modification which had any tendency to conciliate even the most reasonable Presbyterians.

Then came penal statutes against Nonconformists, statutes for which

Charles II: a portrait which captures the heavy, dark features of the King.

precedents might too easily be found in the Puritan legislation, but to which the King could not give his assent without a breach of promises publicly made, in the most important crisis of his life, to those on whom his fate depended. The Presbyterians, in extreme distress and terror, fled to the foot of the throne, and pleaded their recent services and the royal faith solemnly and repeatedly plighted. The King wavered. His temper was not that of a persecutor. He disliked the Puritans indeed; but in him dislike was a languid feeling, very little resembling the energetic hatred which had burned in the heart of Laud. He made a feeble attempt to restrain the intolerant zeal of the House of Commons; but that House was under the influence of far deeper convictions and far stronger passions than his own. After a faint struggle he yielded, and passed, with the show of alacrity, a series of odious acts against the separatists. It was made a crime to attend a dissenting place of worship. A single justice of the peace might convict without a jury, and might, for the third offence, pass sentence of transportation beyond sea for seven years. A new and most unreasonable test was imposed on divines who had been deprived of their benefices for nonconformity; and all who refused to take that test were prohibited from coming within five miles of any town which was governed by a corporation, or of any town which was represented in Parliament, or of any town where they had themselves resided as ministers. The gaols were therefore soon crowded with dissenters; and, among the sufferers, were some of whose genius and virtue any Christian society might well be proud.

The Church of England was not ungrateful for the protection which she received from the government. She accordingly magnified in fulsome phrase that prerogative which was constantly employed to defend and to aggrandise her, and reprobated, much at her ease, the depravity of those whom oppression, from which she was exempt, had goaded to rebellion. Her favourite theme was the doctrine of nonresistance. That doctrine she taught without any qualification, and followed out to all its extreme consequences. Her disciples were never weary of repeating that in no conceivable case, not even if England were cursed with a King who, in defiance of law, and without the pretence of justice, should daily doom hundreds of innocent victims to torture and death, would all the estates of the realm united be justified in withstanding his tyranny by physical force.

While these changes were in progress, a change still more important took place in the morals and manners of the community. Those passions and tastes which, under the rule of the Puritans, had been sternly repressed, and, if gratified at all, had been gratified by stealth, broke forth with ungovernable violence as soon as the check was withdrawn. Men flew to frivolous amusements and to criminal pleasures with the greediness which long and enforced abstinence naturally produces. There was no excess which was not encouraged by the ostentatious profligacy of the King and of his favourite courtiers.

All the lighter kinds of literature were deeply tainted by the prevailing licentiousness. Poetry stooped to be the pandar of every low desire. The restored Church contended indeed against the prevailing immorality, but contended feebly and with half a heart. Her attention was elsewhere engaged. Her whole soul was in the work of crushing the Puritans, and of teaching her disciples to give unto Caesar the things which were Caesar's. The ribaldry of Etherege and Wycherley was, in the presence and under the special sanction of the head of the Church, publicly recited by female lips in female ears, while the author of the *Pilgrim's Progress* languished in a dungeon for the crime of proclaiming the gospel to the poor.

The Triple Alliance: The Treaty of Dover

Had the administration been faultless, the enthusiasm with which the return of the King and the termination of the military tyranny had been hailed could not have been permanent. For it is the law of our nature that such fits of excitement shall always be followed by remissions. The manner in which the court abused its victory made the remission speedy and complete. Every moderate man was shocked by the insolence, cruelty, and perfidy with which the Nonconformists were treated. These feelings became stronger when it was noised abroad that the court was not disposed to treat Papists with the same rigour which had been shown to Presbyterians. A vague suspicion that the King and the duke were not sincere Protestants sprang up and gathered strength. Many persons too who had been disgusted by the austerity and hypocrisy of the Saints of the Commonwealth began to be still more disgusted by the open profligacy of the court and of the Cavaliers, and were disposed to doubt whether the sullen preciseness of Praise God Barebone might not be preferable to the outrageous profaneness and licentiousness of the Buckinghams and Sedleys.

A large body of Royalists joined in these complaints, and added many sharp reflections on the King's ingratitude. They justly said that one half of

Catharine of Braganza: a miniature by Samuel Cooper. On seeing a portrait of her Charles remarked, 'that person cannot be unhandsome'.

what His Majesty squandered on concubines and buffoons would gladden the hearts of hundreds of old Cavaliers who, after cutting down their oaks and melting their plate to help his father, now wandered about in threadbare suits, and did not know where to turn for a meal.

The minds of men were now in such a temper that every public act excited discontent. Charles had taken to wife Catharine Princess of Portugal. The marriage was generally disliked; and the murmurs became loud when it appeared that the King was not likely to have any legitimate posterity. Dunkirk, won by Oliver from Spain, was sold to Louis XIV, King of France. This bargain excited general indignation. Englishmen were already beginning to observe with uneasiness the progress of the French power, and to regard the House of Bourbon with the same feeling with which their grandfathers had regarded the House of Austria. The public discontent was heightened, when it was found that, while Dunkirk was abandoned on the plea of economy, the fortress of Tangier, which was part of the dower of Queen Catharine, was repaired and kept up at an enormous charge.

But the murmurs excited by these errors were faint, when compared with the clamours which soon broke forth. The government engaged in war with the United Provinces. The House of Commons readily voted sums unexampled in our history, sums exceeding those which had supported the fleets and armies of Cromwell at the time when his power was the terror of all the world. But such was the extravagance, dishonesty, and

THE KING'S MISTRESSES

Above: *A portrait by Lely of Barbara Palmer, Countess of Castelmaine, the King's mistress at the time of the Restoration.*

Right: *A miniature by Samuel Cooper of Frances Stewart, Duchess of Richmond. Her favours were said to have been denied to the King until after she was married.*

incapacity of those who had succeeded to his authority, that this liberality proved worse than useless. The sycophants of the court, ill qualified to contend against the great men who then directed the arms of Holland, against such a statesman as De Witt, and such a commander as De Ruyter, made fortunes rapidly, while the sailors mutinied from very hunger, while the dockyards were unguarded, while the ships were leaky and without rigging. The Dutch fleet sailed up the Thames, and burned the ships of war which lay at Chatham. It was said that, on the very day of that great humiliation, the King feasted with the ladies of his seraglio, and amused himself with hunting a moth about the supper room. Soon the capital began to feel the miseries of a blockade. Fuel was scarcely to be procured. Tilbury Fort, the place where Elizabeth had, with manly spirit, hurled foul scorn at Parma and Spain, was insulted by the invaders. The roar of foreign guns was heard, for the first and last time, by the citizens of London. The houses and carriages of the ministers were attacked by the populace; and it seemed likely that the government would have to deal at once with an invasion and with an insurrection. The extreme danger, it is true, soon passed by. A treaty was concluded, very different from the treaties which Oliver had been in the habit of signing; and the nation was once more at peace, but was in a mood scarcely less fierce and sullen than in the days of shipmoney.

The discontent engendered by maladministration was heightened by calamities which the best administration could not have averted. While the ignominious war with Holland was raging, London suffered two great disasters, such as never, in so short a space of time, befell one city. A pestilence, surpassing in horror any that during three centuries had visited

Above: *Louise de Querouaille, Duchess of Portsmouth, by Henri Gascar. Sent to London by Louis XIV, 'Madam Carwell' as she was called by the English, soon became Charles's dominant mistress.*

Right: *Eleanor (Nell) Gwynn, by Lely. Though the bawdiness and lewdness of the actress at times shocked even Charles's debauched court, her undoubted charm and vivacity ensured that she remained a favourite of the King.*

the island, swept away, in six months, more than a hundred thousand human beings. And scarcely had the dead cart ceased to go its rounds, when a fire, such as had not been known in Europe since the conflagration of Rome under Nero, laid in ruins the whole city, from the Tower to the Temple, and from the river to the purlieus of Smithfield.

The Parliament was still the Cavalier Parliament, chosen in the transport of loyalty which had followed the Restoration. Nevertheless it soon became evident that no English legislature, however loyal, would now consent to be merely what the legislature had been under the Tudors. The great English revolution of the seventeenth century, that is to say, the transfer of the supreme control of the executive administration from the Crown to the House of Commons, was, through the whole long existence of this Parliament, proceeding noiselessly, but rapidly and steadily. Charles, kept poor by his follies and vices, wanted money. The Commons alone could legally grant him money. The price which they put on their grants was this, that they should be allowed to interfere with every one of the King's prerogatives, to wring from him his consent to laws which he disliked, to break up cabinets, to dictate the course of foreign policy, and even to direct the administration of war. To the royal office, and the royal person, they loudly and sincerely professed the strongest attachment. But to Clarendon they owed no allegiance; and they fell on him as furiously as their predecessors had fallen on Strafford. He was the ostensible head of the administration, and was therefore held responsible even for those acts which he had strongly, but vainly, opposed in Council. He fell with a great ruin. The seal was taken from him: the Commons impeached him: his head was not safe: he fled from the country: an act was passed which doomed him to perpetual exile; and those who had assailed and undermined him began to struggle for the fragments of his power.

We have now reached a point at which the history of the great English revolution begins to be complicated with the history of foreign politics. The power of Spain had, during many years, been declining. France was now, beyond all doubt, the greatest power in Europe. The State implicitly obeyed the direction of a single mind. The great fiefs which, three hundred years before, had been, in all but name, independent principalities, had been annexed to the Crown. Only a few old men could remember the last meeting of the States General. The resistance which the Huguenots, the nobles, and the parliaments had offered to the kingly power, had been put down by the two great cardinals who had ruled the nation during forty years. The government was now a despotism, but, at least in its dealings with the upper classes, a mild and generous despotism, tempered by courteous manners and chivalrous sentiments. The means at the disposal of the sovereign were, for that age, truly formidable. His army, excellently disciplined, and commanded by the greatest generals then living, already consisted of more than a hundred and twenty thousand men. Such an array of regular troops had not been seen in Europe since the downfall of the Roman empire.

The personal qualities of the French King added to the respect inspired by the power and importance of his kingdom. No sovereign has ever represented the majesty of a great State with more dignity and grace. He was his own prime minister, and performed the duties of a prime minister with an ability and an industry which could not be reasonably expected from one who had in infancy succeeded to a crown, and who had been surrounded by flatterers before he could speak. In his dealings with foreign powers he had some generosity, but no justice. To unhappy allies who threw themselves at his feet, and had no hope but in his compassion, he extended his protection with a romantic disinterestedness, which seemed better suited to a knight errant than to a statesman. But he broke through the most sacred ties of public faith without scruple or shame, whenever they interfered with his interest, or with what he called his glory. His perfidy and violence, however, excited less enmity than the insolence with which he constantly reminded his neighbours of his own greatness and of their littleness. He was as licentious, though by no means as frivolous and indolent, as his brother of England. But he was a sincere Roman Catholic; and both his conscience and his vanity impelled him to use his power for the defence and propagation of the true faith, after the example of his renowned predecessors, Clovis, Charlemagne, and Saint Louis.

Our ancestors naturally looked with serious alarm on the growing power of France. This feeling, in itself perfectly reasonable, was mingled with other feelings less praiseworthy. France was our old enemy. The title of King of France was still borne by our sovereigns. The lilies of France still appeared, mingled with our own lions, on the shield of the House of Stuart. In the sixteenth century the dread inspired by Spain had suspended the animosity of which France had anciently been the object. But the dread inspired by Spain had given place to contemptuous compassion; and France was again regarded as our national foe.

One of the chief objects of the policy of Louis throughout his life was to extend his dominions towards the Rhine. For this end he had engaged in war with Spain, and he was now in the full career of conquest. The United

Provinces saw with anxiety the progress of his arms. That renowned federation had reached the height of power, prosperity, and glory. The Batavian territory, conquered from the waves and defended against them by human art, was in extent little superior to the principality of Wales. But all that narrow space was a busy and populous hive, in which new wealth was every day created, and in which vast masses of old wealth were hoarded. Rich, however, as the Republic was, and highly considered in Europe, she was no match for the power of Louis. She apprehended, not without good cause, that his kingdom might soon be extended to her frontiers; and she might well dread the immediate vicinity of a monarch so great, so ambitious, and so unscrupulous. Yet it was not easy to devise any expedient which might avert the danger. The Dutch alone could not turn the scale

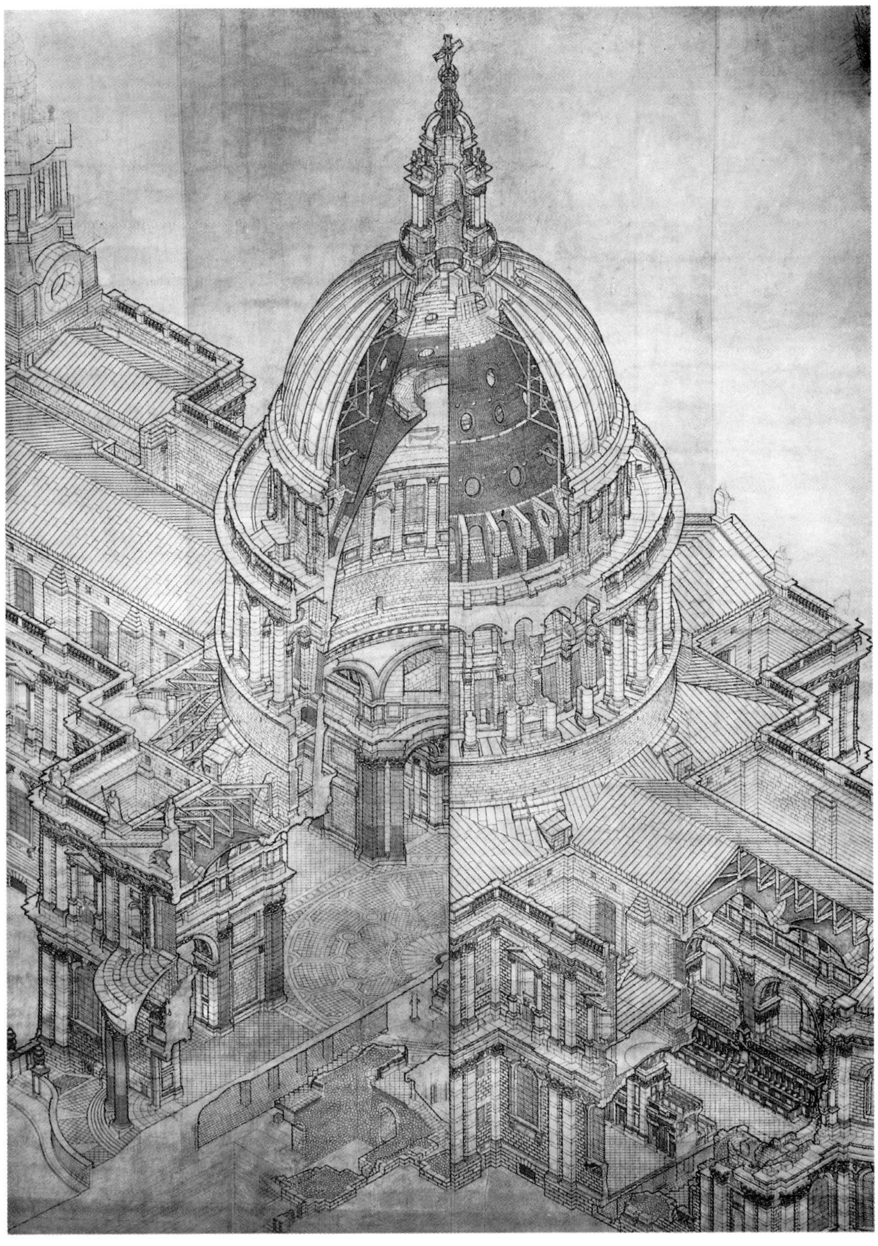

St Paul's Cathedral: an isometric view of the dome and crossing. Sir Christopher Wren's masterpiece, the new St Paul's symbolised the resurrection of London from the ashes of the Great Fire of 1666.

The Sheldonian Theatre, Oxford. An early (1663) example of Wren's genius.

against France. On the side of the Rhine no help was to be expected. England was separated from the United Provinces by the recollection of cruel injuries recently inflicted and endured; and her policy had, since the Restoration, been so devoid of wisdom and spirit, that it was scarcely possible to expect from her any valuable assistance.

But the fate of Clarendon and the growing ill humour of the Parliament determined the advisers of Charles to adopt on a sudden a policy which amazed and delighted the nation.

The English resident at Brussels, Sir William Temple, one of the most expert diplomatists and most pleasing writers of that age, had already represented to his court that it was both desirable and practicable to enter into engagements with the States General for the purpose of checking the progress of France. For a time his suggestions had been slighted; but it was now thought expedient to act on them. He was commissioned to negotiate with the States General. He proceeded to the Hague, and soon came to an understanding with John De Witt, then the chief minister of Holland. Sweden, small as her resources were, had, forty years before, been raised by the genius of Gustavus Adolphus to a high rank among European powers, and had not yet descended to her natural position. She was induced to join on this occasion with England and the States. Thus was formed that coalition known as the Triple Alliance. Louis did not think it politic to draw on himself the hostility of such a confederacy in addition to that of Spain. He consented, therefore, to relinquish a large part of the territory which his armies had occupied. Peace was restored to Europe; and the English government, lately an object of general contempt, was, during a few months, regarded by foreign powers with respect scarcely less than that which the Protector had inspired.

At home the Triple Alliance was popular in the highest degree. It gratified alike national animosity and national pride. The House of Commons loudly applauded the treaty; and some uncourtly grumblers described it as the only good thing that had been done since the King came in.

The King, however, cared little for the approbation of his Parliament or of his people. The Triple Alliance he regarded merely as a temporary expedient for quieting discontents which had seemed likely to become serious. He had begun to find constitutional restraints galling. Already had been formed in the Parliament a strong connection known by the name of the Country Party. That party included all the public men who leaned towards Puritanism and Republicanism, and many who, though attached to the Church and to hereditary monarchy, had been driven into opposition by dread of Popery, by dread of France, and by disgust at the extravagance, dissoluteness, and faithlessness of the court. The power of this band of politicians was constantly growing. Charles did not think himself a King while an assembly of subjects could call for his accounts before paying his debts, and could insist on knowing which of his mistresses or boon companions had intercepted the money destined for the equipping and manning of the fleet. But, impatient as he was of constitutional restraints, how was he to emancipate himself from them? He could make himself despotic only by the help of a great standing army; and such an army was not in existence. His revenues did indeed enable him to keep up some regular troops: but those troops were scarcely numerous enough to protect Whitehall and the Tower against a rising of the mob of London.

Since the King was bent on emancipating himself from the control of Parliament, and since, in such an enterprise, he could not hope for effectual aid at home, it followed that he must look for aid abroad. The power and wealth of the King of France might be equal to the arduous task of establishing absolute monarchy in England. Such an ally would undoubtedly expect substantial proofs of gratitude for such a service. Charles must descend to the rank of a great vassal, and must make peace and war according to the directions of the government which protected him. Such a life would be insupportable to a man of high spirit and of powerful understanding. But to Charles, destitute alike of all patriotism and of all sense of personal dignity, the prospect had nothing unpleasing.

That the Duke of York should have concurred in the design of degrading that crown which it was probable that he would himself one day wear may seem more extraordinary. For his nature was haughty and imperious; and, indeed, he continued to the very last to show, by occasional starts and struggles, his impatience of the French yoke. But he was almost as much debased by superstition as his brother by indolence and vice. James was now a Roman Catholic. Religious bigotry had become the dominant sentiment of his narrow and stubborn mind, and had so mingled itself with his love of rule, that the two passions could hardly be distinguished from each other. It seemed highly improbable that, without foreign aid, he would be able to obtain ascendency, or even toleration, for his own faith:

and he was in a temper to see nothing humiliating in any step which might promote the interests of the true Church.

A negotiation was opened which lasted during several months. The chief agent between the English and French courts was the beautiful, graceful, and intelligent Henrietta, Duchess of Orleans, sister of Charles, sister in law of Louis, and a favourite with both. The King of England offered to declare himself a Roman Catholic, to dissolve the Triple Alliance, and to join with France against Holland, if France would engage to lend him such military and pecuniary aid as might make him independent of his Parliament. Louis at first affected to receive these propositions coolly, and at length agreed to them with the air of a man who is conferring a great favour: but in truth, the course which he had resolved to take was one by which he might gain and could not lose.

He already meditated gigantic designs, which were destined to keep Europe in constant fermentation during more than forty years. He wished to humble the United Provinces, and to annex Belgium, Franche Comté, and Loraine to his dominions. Nor was this all. The King of Spain was a sickly child. It was likely that he would die without issue. His eldest sister was Queen of France. A day would almost certainly come, and might come

LOUYS loopt KAREL achter na,
En roept; O Koning, sta, eÿ sta,
Rent zo niet na de Vrede:
Ik heb noch menig zak met gelt,
K Zal Hollant dwingen door gewelt,
En gantsch tot puÿn vertreden.
Maar, Koning, Looje mÿ verlaat,
Ik ben dan zonder moet en raat;
Mÿn kusten die staan open.
De RUYTER met zyn honte paart,
En TROMP daar elk is voor vervaart
Zal al den bras af loopen.

A Dutch political satire showing Louis XIV pursuing Charles II with a handful of gold to buy his support. In fact, it was the British monarch who took the initiative in making himself a pensioner of France.

very soon, when the House of Bourbon might lay claim to that vast empire on which the sun never set. The union of two great monarchies under one head would doubtless be opposed by a continental coalition. But for any continental coalition France singlehanded was a match. England could turn the scale. On the course which, in such a crisis, England might pursue, the destinies of the world would depend; and it was notorious that the English Parliament and nation were strongly attached to the policy which had dictated the Triple Alliance. Nothing, therefore, could be more gratifying to Louis than to learn that the princes of the House of Stuart needed his help, and were willing to purchase that help by unbounded subserviency. He determined to profit by the opportunity, and laid down for himself a plan to which, without deviation, he adhered, till the revolution of 1688 disconcerted all his politics. He professed himself desirous to promote the designs of the English court. He promised large aid. He from time to time doled out such aid as might serve to keep hope alive, and as he could without risk or inconvenience spare. In this way, at an expense very much less than that which he incurred in building and decorating Versailles or Marli, he succeeded in making England, during nearly twenty years, almost as insignificant a member of the political system of Europe as the republic of San Marino.

His object was not to destroy our constitution, but to keep the various elements of which it was composed in a perpetual state of conflict, and to set irreconcilable enmity between those who had the power of the purse and those who had the power of the sword. With this view he bribed and stimulated both parties in turn, encouraged the court to withstand the seditious encroachments of the Parliament, and conveyed to the Parliament intimations of the arbitrary designs of the court.

One of the devices to which he resorted for the purpose of obtaining an ascendency in the English counsels deserves especial notice. Charles, though incapable of love in the highest sense of the word, was the slave of any woman whose person excited his desires, and whose airs and prattle amused his leisure. He had patiently endured the termagant passions of Barbara Palmer and the pert vivacity of Eleanor Gwynn. Louis thought that the most useful envoy who could be sent to London, would be a handsome, licentious, and crafty Frenchwoman. Such a woman was Louisa, a lady of the House of Querouaille, whom our rude ancestors called Madam Carwell. She was soon triumphant over all his rivals, was created Duchess of Portsmouth, was loaded with wealth, and obtained a dominion which ended only with the life of Charles.

The most important conditions of the alliance between the Crowns were digested into a secret treaty which was signed at Dover in May 1670, just ten years after the day on which Charles had landed at that very port amidst the acclamations and joyful tears of a too confiding people.

By this treaty Charles bound himself to make public profession of the Roman Catholic religion, to join his arms to those of Louis for the purpose of destroying the power of the United Provinces, and to employ the whole strength of England, by land and sea, in support of the rights of the House of Bourbon to the vast monarchy of Spain. Louis, on the other hand, engaged to pay a large subsidy, and promised that, if any insurrection should break out in England, he would send an army at his own charge to support his ally.

The Duke of York, too dull to apprehend danger, or too fanatical to care

Sir Peter Lely's portrait of Edward Hyde, Earl of Clarendon. At the Restoration Hyde became Charles II's chief minister, and his daughter married the Duke of York. He was however dismissed in humiliating circumstances in 1667, and wrote the great History of the Rebellion *during his years of exile.*

about it, was impatient to see the article touching the Roman Catholic religion carried into immediate execution: but Louis had the wisdom to perceive that, if this course were taken, there would be such an explosion in England as would probably frustrate those parts of the plan which he had most at heart. It was therefore determined that Charles should still call himself a Protestant, and should still, at high festivals, receive the sacrament according to the ritual of the Church of England. His more scrupulous brother ceased to appear in the royal chapel.

About this time died the Duchess of York, daughter of the banished Earl of Clarendon. She had been, during some years, a concealed Roman Catholic. She left two daughters, Mary and Anne, afterwards successively Queens of Great Britain. They were bred Protestants by the positive command of the King, who knew that it would be vain for him to profess himself a member of the Church of England, if children who seemed likely to inherit his throne were, by his permission, brought up as members of the Church of Rome.

The Ministers of Charles

Few things in our history are more curious than the origin and growth of the power now possessed by the Cabinet. From an early period the Kings of England had been assisted by a Privy Council to which the law assigned many important functions and duties. By degree its character changed. It became too large for despatch and secrecy. The rank of Privy Councillor was often bestowed as an honorary distinction on persons to whom nothing was confided, and whose opinion was never asked. The sovereign, on the most important occasions, resorted for advice to a small knot of leading ministers. During many years old fashioned politicians continued to regard the Cabinet as an unconstitutional and dangerous board. Nevertheless, it constantly became more and more important. It at length drew to itself the chief executive power, and has now been regarded, during several generations, as an essential part of our polity.

During some years the word Cabal was popularly used as synonymous with Cabinet. But it happened by a whimsical coincidence that, in 1671, the Cabinet consisted of five persons the initial letters of whose names made up the word Cabal; Clifford, Arlington, Buckingham, Ashley, and Lauderdale. These ministers were therefore emphatically called the Cabal; and they soon made that appellation so infamous that it has never since their time been used except as a term of reproach.

Sir Thomas Clifford was a Commissioner of the Treasury, and had greatly distinguished himself in the House of Commons. Of the members of the Cabal he was the most respectable. For, with a fiery and imperious temper, he had a strong though a lamentably perverted sense of duty and honour.

Henry Bennet, Lord Arlington, then Secretary of State, had, since he came to manhood, resided principally on the Continent, and had learned that cosmopolitan indifference to constitutions and religions which is often observable in persons whose life has been passed in vagrant diplomacy. He had learned the art of accommodating his language and deportment to the society in which he found himself. His vivacity in the closet amused the King: his gravity in debates and conferences imposed on the public: and he had succeeded in attaching to himself a considerable number of personal retainers.

Buckingham, Ashley, and Lauderdale were men in whom the immorality which was epidemic among the politicians of that age appeared in its most malignant type, but variously modified by great diversities of temper and understanding. Buckingham was a sated man of pleasure, who had turned to ambition as to a pastime. He had already, rather from fickleness and love of novelty than from any deep design, been faithless to every party.

Ashley, with a far stronger head, and with a far fiercer and more earnest ambition, had been equally versatile. But Ashley's versatility was the effect, not of levity, but of deliberate selfishness. He had served and betrayed a succession of governments. But he had timed all his treacheries so well that, through all revolutions, his fortunes had constantly been rising.

Lauderdale, loud and coarse both in mirth and anger, was perhaps, under the outward show of boisterous frankness, the most dishonest man in the whole Cabal. He had made himself conspicuous among the Scotch insurgents in 1638 by his zeal for the Covenant. He often talked with noisy jocularity of the days when he was a canter and a rebel. He was now the chief instrument employed by the court in the work of forcing episcopacy

CHARLES II'S CABINET

Macaulay writes that 'by a whimsical coincidence' the King's Cabinet consisted of five persons the initial letters of whose names spelled out the word Cabal. The actions of these ministers proved so unpopular that the word Cabal has ever since carried a pejorative connotation.

Sir Thomas Clifford. 'With a fiery and imperious temper, he had a strong though lamentably perverted sense of duty and honour.'

Henry Bennet, Lord Arlington, 'had learned that cosmopolitan indifference to constitutions and religions which is so often observable in persons whose life has been spent in vagrant diplomacy'.

on his reluctant countrymen; nor did he in that cause shrink from the unsparing use of the sword, the halter, and the boot. Yet those who knew him knew that thirty years had made no change in his real sentiments, that he still hated the memory of Charles I, and that he still preferred the Presbyterian form of Church government to every other.

The first object of Charles was to obtain from the Commons supplies which might be employed in executing the secret treaty. The Cabal, holding power at a time when our government was in a state of transition, united in itself two different kinds of vices belonging to two different ages and to two different systems. As those five evil counsellors were among the last English statesmen who seriously thought of destroying the Parliament, so they were the first English statesmen who attempted extensively to corrupt it. They soon perceived, however, that, though the House of Commons was chiefly composed of Cavaliers, and though places and French gold had been lavished on the members, there was no chance that even the least odious parts of the scheme arranged at Dover would be supported by a majority. It was necessary to have recourse to fraud. The King accordingly professed great zeal for the principles of the Triple Alliance, and pretended that, in order to hold the ambition of France in check, it would be necessary to augment the fleet. The Commons fell into the snare, and voted a grant of eight hundred thousand pounds. The Parliament was instantly prorogued; and the court, thus emancipated from control, proceeded to the execution of the great design.

Rapid strides were made towards despotism. Proclamations, dispensing with Acts of Parliament, or enjoining what only Parliament could lawfully enjoin, appeared in rapid succession. Of these edicts the most important was the Declaration of Indulgence. By this instrument the penal laws

Buckingham was 'a sated man of pleasure who had turned to ambition as to a pastime'.

Ashley 'had timed all his treacheries so well that through all revolutions, his fortunes had been constantly rising'.

Lauderdale 'was now the chief instrument employed by the court in the work of forcing episcopacy on his reluctant countrymen'.

against Roman Catholics were set aside; and, that the real object of the measure might not be perceived, the laws against Protestant Nonconformists were also suspended.

A few days after the appearance of the Declaration of Indulgence, war was proclaimed against the United Provinces. By sea the Dutch maintained the struggle with honour; but on land they were at first borne down by irresistible force. A great French army passed the Rhine. Fortress after fortress opened its gates. Three of the seven provinces of the federation were occupied by the invaders. The republic, thus fiercely assailed from without, was torn at the same time by internal dissensions. The government was in the hands of a close oligarchy of powerful burghers. There were numerous self-elected town councils, each of which exercised, within its own sphere, many of the rights of sovereignty. These councils sent delegates to the Provincial states, and the Provincial States again sent delegates to the States General. A hereditary first magistrate was no essential part of this polity. Nevertheless one family, singularly fertile of great men, had gradually obtained a large and somewhat indefinite authority. William, first of the name, Prince of Orange Nassau, and Stadtholder of Holland, had headed the memorable insurrection against Spain. His son Maurice had been captain general and first minister of the States, had raised himself to almost kingly power, and had bequeathed a great part of that power to his family. The influence of the Stadtholders was an object of extreme jealousy to the municipal oligarchy. But the army, and that great body of citizens which was excluded from all share in the government, were as zealous for the House of Orange as the legions and the common people of Rome for the House of Caesar. The Stadtholder commanded the forces of the commonwealth, disposed of all military commands, had a large share of the civil patronage, and was surrounded by pomp almost regal.

Prince William II had been strongly opposed by the oligarchical party. His life had terminated in the year 1650, amidst great civil troubles. He died childless: the adherents of his house were left for a short time without a head; and the powers which he had exercised were divided among the town councils, the Provincial States, and the States General.

But, a few days after William's death, his widow, Mary, daughter of Charles I, King of Great Britain, gave birth to a son, destined to raise the glory and authority of the House of Nassau to the highest point, to save the United Provinces from slavery, to curb the power of France, and to establish the English constitution on a lasting foundation.

This prince, named William Henry, was from his birth an object of serious apprehension to the party now supreme in Holland, and of loyal attachment to the old friends of his line. He enjoyed high consideration as the possessor of a spendid fortune, as the chief of one of the most illustrious houses in Europe, as a magnate of the German empire, as a prince of the blood royal of England, and, above all, as the descendant of the founders of Batavian liberty. But the high office which had once been considered as hereditary in his family, remained in abeyance; and the intention of the aristocratical party was that there should never be another Stadtholder. The want of a first magistrate was, to a great extent, supplied by the Grand Pensionary of the Province of Holland, John de Witt, whose abilities, firmness, and integrity had raised him to unrivalled authority in the councils of the municipal oligarchy.

The French invasion produced a complete change. The suffering and terrified people raged fiercely against the government. In their madness they attacked the bravest captains and the ablest statesmen of the distressed commonwealth. De Ruyter was insulted by the rabble. De Witt was torn in pieces before the gate of the palace of the States General at the Hague. The Prince of Orange, who had no share in the guilt of the murder, became chief of the government without a rival. Young as he was, his ardent and unconquerable spirit, though disguised by a cold and sullen manner, soon roused the courage of his dismayed countrymen. It was in vain that both his uncle and the French King attempted by splendid offers to seduce him from the cause of the republic. The national spirit swelled and rose high. The terms offered by the allies were firmly rejected. The dykes were opened. The whole country was turned into one great lake, from which the cities, with their ramparts and steeples, rose like islands. The invaders were forced to save themselves from destruction by a precipitate retreat. Louis, who greatly preferred a palace to a camp, had already returned to enjoy the adulation of poets and the smiles of ladies in the newly planted alleys of Versailles.

And now the tide turned fast. Alarmed by the vast designs of Louis, both the branches of the great House of Austria sprang to arms. Spain and Holland, divided by the memory of ancient wrongs and humiliations, were reconciled by the nearness of the common danger. From every part of Germany troops poured towards the Rhine. The English government had already expended all the funds which had been obtained by pillaging the public creditor. No loan could be expected from the City. An attempt to raise taxes by the royal authority would have at once produced a rebellion; and Louis, who had now to maintain a contest against half Europe, was in

Willem Schellinks's portrayal of the burning in 1667 of the English fleet in the Medway by the Dutch. It was an example of the disgraceful state to which the affairs of the nation had sunk within a few years.

no condition to furnish the means of coercing the people of England. It was necessary to convoke the Parliament.

In the spring of 1673, therefore, the Houses reassembled after a recess of near two years. Clifford, now a peer and Lord Treasurer, and Ashley, now Earl of Shaftesbury and Lord Chancellor, were the persons on whom the King principally relied as Parliamentary managers. The Country Party instantly began to attack the policy of the Cabal. The Commons at first held out hopes that they would give support to the King's foreign policy, but insisted that he should purchase that support by abandoning his whole system of domestic policy. Their chief object was to obtain the revocation of the Declaration of Indulgence. Of all the many unpopular steps taken by the government the most unpopular was the publishing of this declaration. The most opposite sentiments had been shocked by an act so liberal, done in a manner so despotic. All the enemies of religious freedom, and all the friends of civil freedom, found themselves on the same side; and these two classes made up nineteen twentieths of the nation.

It must in candour be admitted that the constitutional question was then not quite free from obscurity. Our ancient Kings had undoubtedly claimed and exercised the right of suspending the operation of penal laws. The tribunals had recognised that right. Parliaments had suffered it to pass unchallenged. That some such right was inherent in the crown, few even of the Country Party ventured, in the face of precedent and authority, to deny. Yet it was clear that, if this prerogative were without limit, the English government could scarcely be distinguished from a pure des-

Admiral de Ruyter, one of the great naval commanders of the United Provinces during the Dutch wars. Portrait by Bell.

potism. That there was a limit was fully admitted by the King and his ministers. Whether the Declaration of Indulgence lay within or without the limit was the question; and neither party could succeed in tracing any line which would bear examination. The doctrine which seems to have been generally received in the House of Commons was, that the dispensing power was confined to secular matters, and did not extend to laws enacted for the security of the established religion. Yet, as the King was supreme head of the Church, it should seem that, if he possessed the dispensing power at all, he might well possess that power where the Church was concerned.

The truth is that the dispensing power was a great anomaly in politics. It had not been very grossly abused in practice. It had therefore been tolerated, and had gradually acquired a kind of prescription. At length it was employed, after a long interval, in an enlightened age, and at an important conjuncture, to an extent never before known, and for a purpose generally abhorred. It was instantly subjected to a severe scrutiny. Men did not, indeed, at first, venture to pronounce it altogether unconstitutional. But they began to perceive that it was at direct variance with the spirit of the consitution, and would, if left unchecked, turn the English government from a limited into an absolute monarchy.

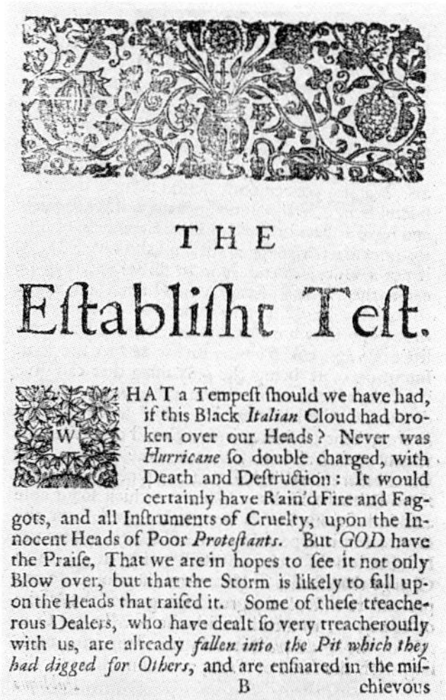
THE

Eſtabliſht Teſt.

WHAT a Tempeſt ſhould we have had, if this Black *Italian* Cloud had broken over our Heads? Never was *Hurricane* ſo double charged, with Death and Deſtruction: It would certainly have Rain'd Fire and Faggots, and all Inſtruments of Cruelty, upon the Innocent Heads of Poor *Proteſtants*. But *GOD* have the Praiſe, That we are in hopes to ſee it not only Blow over, but that the Storm is likely to fall upon the Heads that raiſed it. Some of theſe treacherous Dealers, who have dealt ſo very treacherouſly with us, are already *fallen into the Pit which they had digged for Others*, and are enſnared in the miſ-

B chievous

The Test Act of 1673 required all officials under the Crown to take the oath of allegiance and supremacy, and to publicly receive the sacrament according to Anglican rites. Though aimed against both Roman Catholics and Dissenters, it was chiefly the former whom the Commons feared. The first casualty under the Act was the Duke of York, forced to resign as Lord High Admiral.

Under the influence of such apprehensions, the Commons denied the King's right to dispense, not indeed with all penal statutes, but with penal statutes in matters ecclesiastical, and gave him plainly to understand that, unless he renounced that right, they would grant no supply for the Dutch war. Shaftesbury, with his proverbial sagacity, saw that a violent reaction was at hand, and that all things were tending towards a crisis resembling that of 1640. He was determined that such a crisis should not find him in the situation of Strafford. He therefore turned suddenly round, and acknowledged, in the House of Lords, that the declaration was illegal. The King, thus deserted by his Chancellor, yielded, cancelled the declaration, and solemnly promised that it should never be drawn into precedent.

Even this concession was insufficient. The Commons, not content with having forced their sovereign to annul the Indulgence, next extorted his unwilling assent to a celebrated law, which continued in force to the reign of George IV. This law, known as the Test Act, provided that all persons holding any office, civil or military, should take the oath of supremacy, should subscribe a declaration against transubstantiation, and should publicly receive the sacrament according to the rites of the Church of England. The act was passed; and the Duke of York was consequently under the necessity of resigning the great place of Lord High Admiral.

Hitherto the Commons had not declared against the Dutch war. But, when the King had, in return for money cautiously doled out, relinquished his whole plan of domestic policy, they fell impetuously on his foreign policy. They requested him to dismiss Buckingham and Lauderdale from his councils for ever, and appointed a committee to consider the propriety of impeaching Arlington. In a short time the Cabal was no more. Clifford, who, alone of the five, had any claim to be regarded as an honest man, refused to take the new test, laid down his white staff, and retired to his country seat. Arlington quitted the post of Secretary of State for a quiet and dignified employment in the royal household. Shaftesbury and Buckingham made their peace with the opposition, and appeared at the head of the stormy democracy of the city. Lauderdale, however, still continued to be minister for Scotch affairs, with which the English Parliament could not interfere.

And now the Commons urged the King to make peace with Holland, and expressly declared that no more supplies should be granted for the war, unless it should appear that the enemy obstinately refused to consent to reasonable terms. Temple, who, during the ascendency of the Cabal, had lived in seclusion among his books and flower beds, was called forth from his hermitage. By his instrumentality a separate peace was concluded with the United Provinces; and he again became ambassador at the Hague, where his presence was regarded as a sure pledge for the sincerity of his court.

The chief direction of affairs was now intrusted to Sir Thomas Osborne, a Yorkshire baronet, who had, in the House of Commons, shown eminent talents for business and debate. Osborne became Lord Treasurer, and was soon created Earl of Danby. He was greedy of wealth and honours, corrupt himself, and a corrupter of others. The Cabal had bequeathed to him the art of bribing Parliaments, an art still rude, and giving little promise of the rare perfection to which it was brought in the following century. He improved greatly on the plan of the first inventors. They had merely purchased orators: but every man who had a vote, might sell himself to Danby. Yet

(Above left) Thomas Osborne, Earl of Danby, by Lely. On the break up of the Cabal in 1673, Danby was entrusted with the nation's affairs. With the help of the old Cavalier interest, of the nobles, of the country gentlemen, and of the clergy, he conceived it might be possible to strengthen the royal prerogative.

(Above right) George Savile, Viscount Halifax, was chief of the Trimmers, those politicians who occupied the middle ground between Whigs and Tories. Immensely persuasive in debate and of a towering intellect, Halifax is acknowledged to have been mainly responsible for the rejection by Parliament of the Exclusion Bill – a measure which would have denied the succession to James II.

the new minister must not be confounded with the negotiators of Dover. He was not without the feelings of an Englishman and a Protestant; nor did he, in his solicitude for his own interests, ever wholly forget the interests of his country and of his religion. His opinions touching foreign policy were directly opposed to those of the Cabal, and differed little from those of the Country Party. He bitterly lamented the degraded situation to which England was reduced, and declared, with more energy than politeness, that his dearest wish was to cudgel the French into a proper respect for her.

Thus the sovereign leaned towards one system of foreign politics, and the minister towards a system diametrically opposite. Neither the sovereign nor the minister, indeed, was of a temper to pursue any object with undeviating constancy. Each occasionally yielded to the importunity of the other; and their jarring inclinations and mutual concessions gave to the whole administration a strangely capricious character. Charles sometimes, from levity and indolence, suffered Danby to take steps which Louis resented as mortal injuries. Danby, on the other hand, rather than relinquish his great place, sometimes stooped to compliances which caused him bitter pain and shame. The King was brought to consent to a marriage between the Lady Mary, eldest daughter and presumptive heiress of the

Duke of York, and William of Orange, the deadly enemy of France, and the hereditary champion of the Reformation. The Treasurer, on the other hand, was induced, not only to connive at some scandalous pecuniary transactions which took place between his master and the court of Versailles, but to become, unwillingly indeed and ungraciously, an agent in those transactions.

Meanwhile, the Country Party was driven by two strong feelings in two opposite directions. The popular leaders were afraid of the greatness of Louis, who was not only making head against the whole strength of the continental alliance, but was even gaining ground. Yet they were afraid to entrust their own King with the means of curbing France, lest those means should be used to destroy the liberties of England. The conflict between these apprehensions, both of which were perfectly legitimate, made the policy of the Opposition seem as eccentric and fickle as that of the court. The Commons called for a war with France, till the King, pressed by Danby to comply with their wish, seemed disposed to yield, and began to raise an army. But, as soon as they saw that the recruiting had commenced, their dread of Louis gave place to a nearer dread. They began to fear that the new levies might be employed on a service in which Charles took much more interest than in the defence of Flanders. They therefore refused supplies, and clamoured for disbanding as loudly as they had just before clamoured for arming.

These jealousies were studiously fomented by the French King. He had long kept England passive by promising to support the throne against the Parliament. He now, alarmed at finding that the patriotic counsels of Danby seemed likely to prevail in the closet, began to inflame the Parliament against the throne. Between Louis and the Country Party there was one thing, and one only, in common, profound distrust of Charles. Could the Country Party have been certain that their sovereign meant only to make war on France, they would have been eager to support him. Could Louis have been certain that the new levies were intended only to make war on the constitution of England, he would have made no attempt to stop them. But the unsteadiness and faithlessness of Charles were such that the French Government and the English opposition, agreeing in nothing else, agreed in disbelieving his protestations, and were equally desirous to keep him poor and without an army. Communications were opened between Barillon, the ambassador of Louis, and those English politicians who had always professed, and who indeed sincerely felt, the greatest dread and dislike of the French ascendency. The most upright member of the Country Party, William Lord Russell, son of the Earl of Bedford, did not scruple to concert with a foreign mission schemes for embarrassing his own sovereign. This was the whole extent of Russell's offence. His principles and his fortune alike raised him above all temptations of a sordid kind: but there is too much reason to believe that some of his associates were less scrupulous.

The effect of these intrigues was that England, though she occasionally took a menacing attitude, remained inactive till the continental war, having lasted near seven years, was terminated by the treaty of Nimeguen. The United Provinces, which in 1672 had seemed to be on the verge of utter ruin, obtained honourable and advantageous terms. This narrow escape was generally ascribed to the ability and courage of the young Stadtholder. His fame was great throughout Europe, and especially among the English,

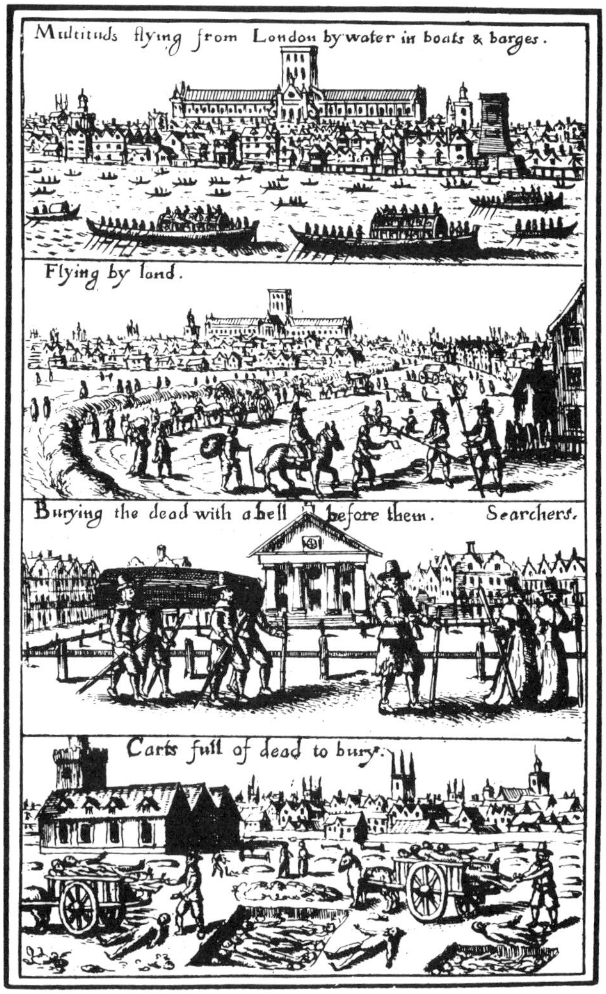

Multituds flying from London by water in boats & barges.
Flying by land.
Burying the dead with a bell before them.
Searchers.
Carts full of dead to bury.

In early June 1665 the Great Plague claimed its first victims in London, and continued to rage throughout the summer and autumn. People fled from the city by any conveyance, and those left behind had the grisly task of burying the dead in mass graves.

The plague had hardly subsided before the Great Fire of 1666 engulfed the city of London. This engraving by Vischer after Schut shows London in flames. An area from the Tower to the Temple, and from a great stretch of the Thames to the environs of Smithfield was laid in ruins.

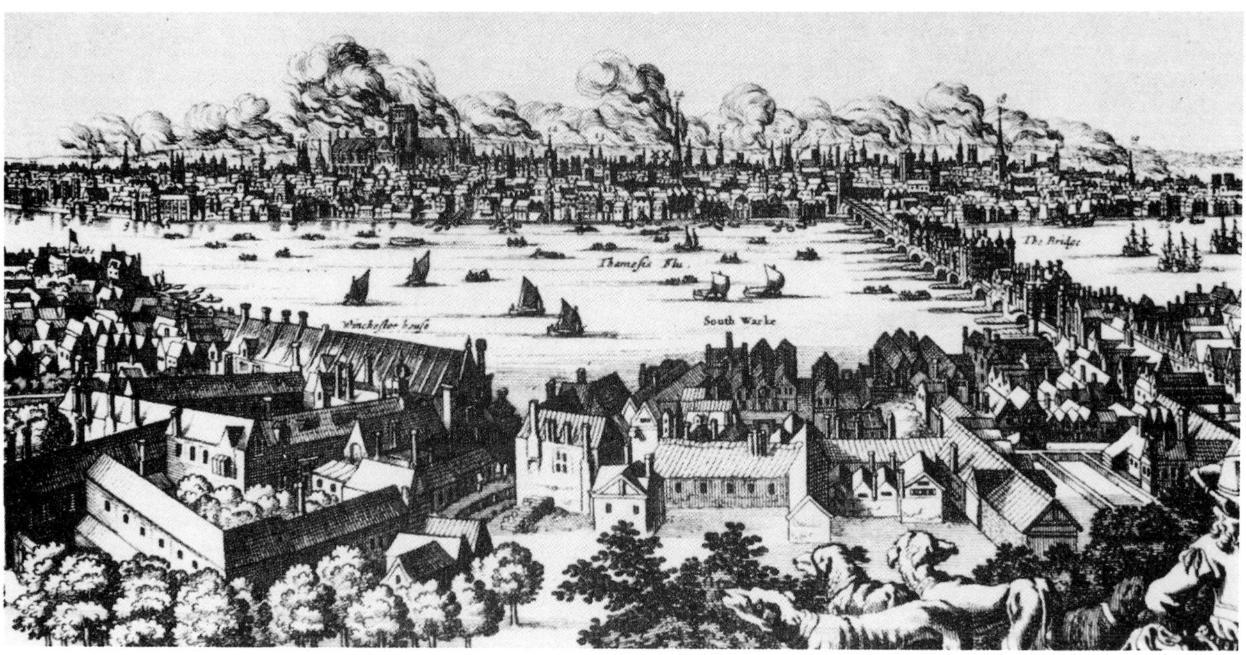

who regarded him as one of their own princes, and rejoiced to see him the husband of their future Queen. France retained many important towns in the Low Countries and the great province of Franche Comté. Almost the whole loss was borne by the decaying monarchy of Spain.

The Popish Plot

A few months after the termination of hostilities on the Continent came a great crisis in English politics. Towards such a crisis things had been tending during eighteen years. The whole stock of popularity, great as it was, with which the King had commenced his administration, had long been expended. To loyal enthusiasm had succeeded profound disaffection. The public mind had now measured back again the space over which it had passed between 1640 and 1660, and was once more in the state in which it had been when the Long Parliament met.

The prevailing discontent was compounded of many feelings. One of these was wounded national pride. That generation had seen England, during a few years, allied on equal terms with France, victorious over Holland and Spain, the mistress of the sea, the terror of Rome, the head of the Protestant interest. Her resources had not diminished; yet she had, in consequence of the imbecility and meanness of her rulers, sunk so low that any German or Italian principality which brought five thousand men into the field was a more important member of the commonwealth of nations.

With the sense of national humiliation was mingled anxiety for civil liberty. Rumours imputed to the court a deliberate design against all the constitutional rights of Englishmen. It had even been whispered that this design was to be carried into effect by the intervention of foreign arms. The thought of such intervention made the blood, even of the Cavaliers, boil in their veins.

But neither national pride nor anxiety for public liberty had so great an influence on the popular mind as hatred of the Roman Catholic religión. That hatred had become one of the ruling passions of the community, and was as strong in the ignorant and profane as in those who were Protestants from conviction. The cruelties of Mary's reign, the conspiracies against Elizabeth, and above all the Gunpowder Plot, had left in the minds of the vulgar a deep and bitter feeling which was kept up by annual commemorations, prayers, bonfires, and processions. The general impression was that a great blow was about to be aimed at the Protestant religion. The King was suspected by many of a leaning towards Rome. His brother and heir presumptive was known to be a bigoted Roman Catholic. The first Duchess of York had died a Roman Catholic. James had then, in defiance of the remonstrances of the House of Commons, taken to wife the Princess Mary of Modena, another Roman Catholic. If there should be sons by this marriage, there was reason to fear that they might be bred Roman Catholics, and that a long succession of princes, hostile to the established faith, might sit on the English throne. Under such circumstances it is not strange that the common people should have been inclined to apprehend a return of the times of her whom they called Bloody Mary.

Thus the nation was in such a temper that the smallest spark might raise a flame. At this conjuncture fire was set in two places at once to the vast mass of combustible matter; and in a moment the whole was in a blaze.

The French court, which knew Danby to be its mortal enemy, artfully contrived to ruin him by making him pass for its friend. Louis, by the instrumentality of Ralph Montague, a faithless and shameless man who had resided in France as minister from England, laid before the House of Commons proofs that the Treasurer had been concerned in an application made by the court of Whitehall to the court of Versailles for a sum of money. This discovery produced its natural effect. The Treasurer was, in truth, exposed to the vengeance of Parliament, not on account of his delinquencies, but on account of his merits; not because he had been an accomplice in a criminal transaction, but because he had been a most unwilling and unserviceable accomplice. But of the circumstances, which have, in the judgment of posterity, greatly extenuated his fault, his contemporaries were ignorant. In their view he was the broker who had sold England to France. It seemed clear that his greatness was at an end, and doubtful whether his head could be saved.

Yet was the ferment excited by this discovery slight, when compared with the commotion which arose when it was noised abroad that a great Popish plot had been detected. One Titus Oates, a clergyman of the Church of England, had, by his disorderly life and heterodox doctrine, drawn on himself the censure of his spiritual superiors, had been compelled to quit his benefice, and had ever since led an infamous and vagrant life. He had once professed himself a Roman Catholic, and had passed some time on the Continent in English colleges of the order of Jesus. In those seminaries he had heard much wild talk about the best means of bringing England back to the true Church. From hints thus furnished he constructed a hideous romance, resembling rather the dream of a sick man than any transaction which ever took place in the real world. The Pope, he said, had entrusted the government of England to the Jesuits. The Jesuits had, by commissions under the seal of their society, appointed Roman Catholic clergymen, noblemen, and gentlemen, to all the highest offices in Church and State. The Papists had burned down London once. They had tried to burn it down again. They were at that moment planning a scheme for setting fire to all the shipping in the Thames. They were to rise at a signal and massacre all their Protestant neighbours. A French army was at the same time to land in Ireland. All the leading statesmen and divines of England were to be murdered. Three or four schemes had been formed for assassinating the King. He was to be stabbed. He was to be poisoned in his medicine. He was to be shot with silver bullets. The public mind was so sore and excitable that these lies readily found credit with the vulgar; and two events which speedily took place led even some reflecting men to suspect that the tale, though evidently distorted and exaggerated, might have some foundation.

Edward Coleman, a very busy, and not very honest, Roman Catholic intriguer, had been among the persons accused. Search was made for his papers. It was found that he had just destroyed the greater part of them. But a few which had escaped contained some passages such as, to minds strongly prepossessed, might seem to confirm the evidence of Oates. It was urged, with some show of reason, that, if papers which had been passed over as unimportant were filled with matter so suspicious, some great mystery of iniquity must have been contained in those documents which had been carefully committed to the flames.

A few days later it was known that Sir Edmund Berry Godfrey, an eminent justice of the peace who had taken the depositions of Oates against Coleman, had disappeared. Search was made; and Godfrey's

The Popish Plot. In 1678 Titus Oates, a disgraced Church of England clergyman who had lived for a time in a Jesuit seminary in France, arrived in England to proclaim the existence of a vast plot for Roman Catholics to take over the country. He claimed it was the brainchild of the Pope and the Society of Jesus. So inflamed had feelings become at the Catholic leanings of the Court and the prospect of a Catholic succession with the Duke of York that he was for a time readily believed. This satire of 1681 shows, below, the infernal conclave of the Pope and his supporters plotting to murder Charles; whilst above, Titus Oates and Charles are represented as the beatified saviours of the nation.

corpse was found in a field near London. It was clear that he had died by violence. It was equally clear that he had not been set upon by robbers. His fate is to this day a secret. Some think that he perished by his own hand; some, that he was slain by a private enemy. The most probable supposition seems, on the whole, to be that some hotheaded Roman Catholic, driven to frenzy by the lies of Oates and by the insults of the multitude, and not nicely distinguishing between the perjured accuser and the innocent magistrate, had taken a revenge of which the history of persecuted sects furnishes but too many examples. If this were so, the assassin must have afterwards bitterly execrated his own wickedness and folly. The capital and the whole nation went mad with hatred and fear. The penal laws, which had begun to lose something of their edge, were sharpened anew. Everywhere justices were busied in searching houses and seizing papers. All the gaols were filled with Papists. London had the aspect of a city in a state of siege. The trainbands were under arms all night. Preparations were made for barricading the great thoroughfares. Patrols marched up and down the streets. Cannon were planted round Whitehall. No citizen thought himself safe unless he carried under his coat a small flail loaded with lead to brain the Popish assassins.

The Houses insisted that a guard should be placed in the vaults over which they sate, in order to secure them against a second Gunpower Plot. All their proceedings were of a piece with this demand. Ever since the reign of Elizabeth the oath of supremacy had been exacted from members of the House of Commons. Some Roman Catholics, however, had contrived so to interpret this oath that they could take it without scruple. A more stringent test was now added: every member of Parliament was required to make the Declaration against Transubstantiation; and thus the Roman Catholic Lords were for the first time excluded from their seats. Strong resolutions were adopted against the Queen. The Commons impeached the Lord Treasurer of high treason. They even attempted to wrest the command of the militia out of the King's hands. To such a temper had eighteen years of misgovernment brought the most loyal Parliament that had ever met in England.

Yet it may seem strange that, even in that extremity, the King should have ventured to appeal to the people; for the people were more excited

An anonymous water-colour print of a coffee-house in 1668. Coffee-houses were much frequented by the country party. Pamphlets were exchanged and discussed; favourite targets were the Duke of York, Popish practices at Court, and the friendship with France.

than their representatives. The Lower House, discontented as it was, contained a larger number of Cavaliers than were likely to find seats again. But it was thought that a dissolution would put a stop to the prosecution of the Lord Treasurer, a prosecution which might probably bring to light all the guilty mysteries of the French alliance, and might thus cause extreme personal annoyance and embarrassment to Charles. Accordingly, in January 1679, the Parliament, which had been in existence ever since the beginning of the year 1661, was dissolved; and writs were issued for a general election.

During some weeks the contention over the whole country was fierce and obstinate beyond example. The tide ran strong against the government. Most of the new members came up to Westminster in a mood little differing from that of their predecessors who had sent Strafford and Laud to the Tower.

Meanwhile the courts of justice were disgraced by wilder passions and fouler corruptions than were to be found even on the hustings. The tale of Oates, though it had sufficed to convulse the whole realm, would not, unless confirmed by other evidence, suffice to destroy the humblest of those whom he had accused. For, by the old law of England, two witnesses are necessary to establish a charge of treason. But the success of the first impostor produced its natural consequences. In a few weeks he had been raised from penury and obscurity to opulence, to power which made him the dread of princes and nobles, and to notoriety such as has for low and bad minds all the attractions of glory. He was not long without coadjutors and rivals. A wretch named Carstairs, who had earned a livelihood in Scotland by going disguised to conventicles and then informing against the preachers, led the way. Bedloe, a noted swindler, followed; and soon, from all the brothels, gambling houses, and spunging houses of London, false witnesses poured forth to swear away the lives of Roman Catholics. One came with a story about an army of thirty thousand men who were to muster in the disguise of pilgrims at Corunna, and to sail thence to Wales. Another had been promised canonisation and five hundred pounds to murder the King. A third had stepped into an eating house in Covent Garden, and had there heard a great Roman Catholic banker vow, in the hearing of all the guests and drawers, to kill the heretical tyrant. Oates, that he might not be eclipsed by his imitators, soon added a large supplement to his original narrative. He had the portentous impudence to affirm, among other things, that he had once stood behind a door which was ajar, and had there overheard the Queen declare that she had resolved to give her consent to the assassination of her husband. The vulgar believed, and the highest magistrates pretended to believe, even such fictions as these.

The leaders of the Country Party encouraged the prevailing delusion. The most respectable among them, indeed, were themselves so far deluded as to believe the greater part of the evidence of the plot to be true. Such men as Shaftesbury and Buckingham doubtless perceived that the whole was a romance. But it was a romance which served their turn; and to their seared consciences the death of an innocent man gave no more uneasiness than the death of a partridge. The juries partook of the feelings then common throughout the nation, and were encouraged by the bench to indulge those feelings without restraint. The multitude applauded Oates and his confederates, hooted and pelted the witnesses who appeared on behalf of the accused, and shouted with joy when the verdict of Guilty was pronounced. It was in vain that the sufferers appealed to the respectability of their past lives: for the public mind was possessed with a belief that the more conscientious a Papist was, the more likely he must be to plot against a Protestant government. It was in vain that, just before the cart passed from under their feet, they resolutely affirmed their innocence: for the general opinion was that a good Papist considered all lies which were serviceable to his Church as not only excusable but meritorious.

While innocent blood was shedding under the forms of justice, the new Parliament met; and such was the violence of the predominant party that even men who remembered the attainder of Strafford, the attempt on the five members, the abolition of the House of Lords, the execution of the King, stood aghast at the aspect of public affairs. The impeachment of Danby was resumed. He pleaded the royal pardon. But the Commons treated the plea with contempt, and insisted that the trial should proceed. Danby, however, was not their chief object. They were convinced that the only effectual way of securing the liberties and religion of the nation was to exclude the Duke of York from the throne.

The King was in great perplexity. He had insisted that his brother, the sight of whom inflamed the populace to madness, should retire for a time to Brussels: but this concession did not seem to have produced any favourable effect. The Roundhead party was now decidedly preponderant. Of the old Cavaliers many participated in the prevailing fear of Popery, and many, bitterly resenting the ingratitude of the prince for whom they had sacrificed so much, looked on his distress as carelessly as he had looked on theirs. Even the Anglican clergy, mortified and alarmed by the apostasy of the Duke of York, so far countenanced the opposition as to join cordially in the outcry against the Roman Catholics.

The King in this extremity had recourse to Sir William Temple. Of all the official men of that age Temple had preserved the fairest character. Of the numerous crimes and blunders of the last eighteen years none could be imputed to him. His private life, though not austere, was decorous: his manners were popular; and he was not to be corrupted either by titles or by money.

The scheme which he proposed showed considerable ingenuity. He seems to have discerned more clearly than most of his contemporaries one cause of the difficulties by which the government was beset. The character of the English polity was gradually changing. The Parliament was slowly, but constantly, gaining ground on the prerogative. The theory of the constitution was that the King might name his own ministers. But the House of Commons had driven Clarendon, the Cabal, and Danby successively from the direction of affairs. The theory of the constitution was that the King was the sole judge of the cases in which it might be proper to pardon offenders. Yet he was so much in dread of the House of Commons that, at that moment, he could not venture to rescue from the gallows men whom he well knew to be the innocent victims of perjury.

Temple, it should seem, was desirous to secure to the legislature its undoubted constitutional powers, and yet to prevent it, if possible, from encroaching further on the province of the executive administration. With this view he determined to interpose between the sovereign and the Parliament a body which might break the shock of their collision. There was a body, ancient, highly honourable, and recognised by the law, which, he thought, might be so remodelled as to serve this purpose. He determined to give to the Privy Council a new character and office in the government. The number of councillors he fixed at thirty. Fifteen of them were to be the chief ministers of State, of law, and of religion. The other fifteen were to be unplaced noblemen and gentlemen of ample fortune and high character. There was to be no interior cabinet. All the thirty were to be entrusted with every political secret, and summoned to every meeting; and the King was to declare that he would, on every occasion, be guided by their advice.

This plan, though in some respects not unworthy of the abilities of its author, was in principle vicious. The new board was half a cabinet and half a Parliament, and, like almost every other contrivance, whether mechanical or political, which is meant to serve two purposes altogether different, failed of accomplishing either. It was too large and too divided to be a good administrative body. It was too closely connected with the Crown to be a good checking body. The plan, therefore, even if it had been fairly tried, could scarcely have succeeded; and it was not fairly tried. The King was fickle and perfidious: the Parliament was excited and unreasonable; and the materials out of which the new Council was made, though perhaps the best which that age afforded, were still bad.

The commencement of the new system was, however, hailed with general delight; for the people were in a temper to think any change an improvement. They were also pleased by some of the new nominations. Shaftesbury, now their favourite, was appointed Lord President. Russell and some other distinguished members of the Country Party were sworn of the Council. But a few days later all was again in confusion. The inconveniences of having so numerous a cabinet were such that Temple himself consented to infringe one of the fundamental rules which he had laid down, and to become one of a small knot which really directed everything. With him were joined three other ministers, Arthur Capel, Earl of Essex, George Savile, Viscount Halifax, and Robert Spencer, Earl of Sunderland.

Of the Earl of Essex, then First Commissioner of the Treasury, it is sufficient to say that he was a man of solid, though not brilliant parts, and of grave and melancholy character, that he had been connected with the Country Party, and that he was honestly desirous to effect a reconciliation between that party and the throne.

Among the statesmen of those times Halifax was, in genius, the first. His intellect was fertile, subtle, and capacious. His polished, luminous, and animated eloquence, set off by the silver tones of his voice, was the delight of the House of Lords. His political tracts well deserve to be studied for their literary merit, and fully entitle him to a place among English classics. To the weight derived from talents so great and various he united all the influence which belongs to rank and ample possessions. Yet those intellectual peculiarities which make his writings valuable frequently impeded him in the contests of active life. For he always saw passing events, not in the point of view in which they commonly appear to one who bears a part in them, but in the point of view in which, after the lapse of many years, they appear to the philosophic historian. With such a turn of mind, he could not long continue to act cordially with any body of men. All the prejudices, all the exaggerations, of both the great parties in the state moved his scorn. He sneered impartially at the bigotry of the Churchman and at the bigotry of the Puritan. In religion he was so far from being a zealot that he was called by the uncharitable an atheist: but this imputation he vehemently repelled.

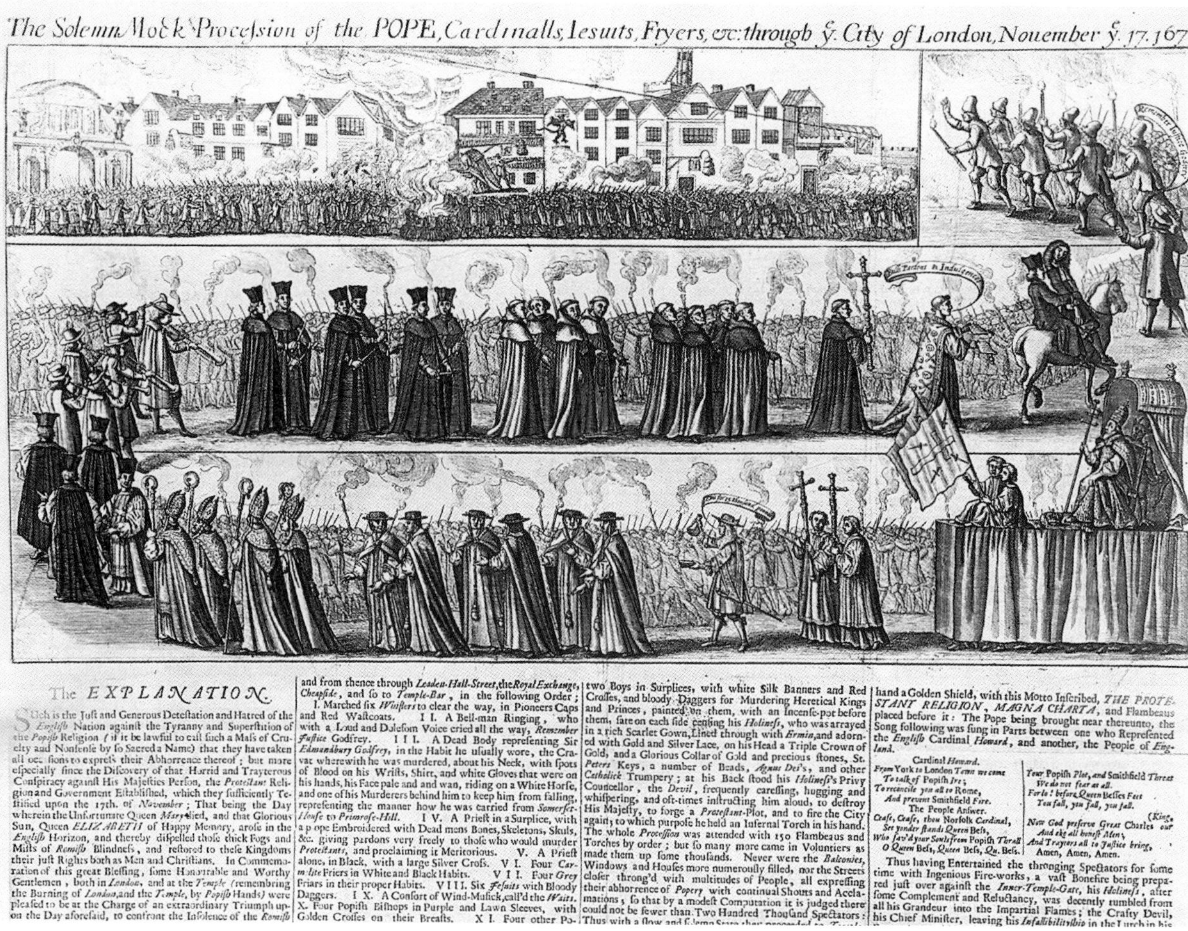

The Solemn Mock Procession of the POPE, Cardinalls, Jesuits, Fryers, &c: through ye City of London, November ye 17. 1679
The EXPLANATION.
Such is the Just and Generous Detestation and Hatred of the English Nation against the Tyranny and Superstition of the Popish Religion (if it be lawful to call such a Mass of Cruelty and Nonsense by so Sacred a Name) that they have taken all occasions to express their Abhorrence thereof; but more especially since the Discovery of that Horrid and Trayterous Conspiracy against His Majesties Person, the Protestant Religion and Government Established, which they sufficiently Testified upon the 17th. of November; That being the Day wherein the Unfortunate Queen Mary died, and that Glorious Sun, Queen ELIZABETH of Happy Memory, arose in the English Horizon, and thereby dispelled those thick Fogs and Mists of Romish Blindness, and restored to these Kingdoms their just Rights both as Men and Christians. In Commemoration of this great Blessing, some Honourable and Worthy Gentlemen, both in London, and at the Temple (remembring the Burning of London, and the Temple, by Popish Hands) were pleased to be at the Charge of an extraordinary Triumph upon the Day aforesaid, to confront the Insolence of the Romish
and from thence through Leaden-Hall-Street, the Royal Exchange, Cheapside, and so to Temple-Bar, in the following Order;
I. Marched six Whistlers to clear the way, in Pioneers Caps and Red Wastcoats. II. A Bell-man Ringing, who with a Loud and Dolesom Voice cried all the way, Remember Justice Godfrey. III. A Dead Body representing Sir Edmundbury Godfrey, in the Habit he usually wore, the Cravat wherewith he was murdered, about his Neck, with spots of Blood on his Wrists, Shirt, and white Gloves that were on his hands, his Face pale and and wan, riding on a White Horse, and one of his Murderers behind him to keep him from falling, representing the manner how he was carried from Somerset-House to Primrose-Hill. IV. A Priest in a Surplice, with a pope Embroidered with Dead mens Bones, Skeletons, Skuls, &c. giving pardons very freely to those who would murder Protestants, and proclaiming it Meritorious. V. A Priest alone, in Black, with a large Silver Cross. VI. Four Carmelite Friers in White and Black Habits. VII. Four Grey Friars in their proper Habits. VIII. Six Jesuits with Bloody Daggers. IX. A Consort of Wind-Musick, call'd the Waits. X. Four Popish Bishops in Purple and Lawn Sleeves, with Golden Crosses on their Breasts. XI. Four other Po-
two Boys in Surplices, with white Silk Banners and Red Crosses, and bloody Daggers for Murdering Heretical Kings and Princes, painted on them, with an Incense-pot before them, sate on each side censing his Holiness, who was arrayed in a rich Scarlet Gown, Lined through with Ermin, and adorned with Gold and Silver Lace, on his Head a Triple Crown of Gold, and a Glorious Collar of Gold and precious stones, St. Peters Keys, a number of Beads, Agnus Dei's, and other Catholick Trumpery; at his Back stood his Holiness's Privy Councellor, the Devil, frequently caressing, hugging and whispering, and oft-times instructing him aloud, to destroy His Majesty, to forge a Protestant-Plot, and to fire the City again; to which purpose he held an Infernal Torch in his hand. The whole Procession was attended with 150 Flambeaus and Torches by order; but so many more came in Voluntiers as made them up some thousands. Never were the Balconies, Windows and Houses more numerously filled, nor the Streets closer throng'd with multitudes of People, all expressing their abhorrence of Popery with continual Shouts and Acclamations; so that by a modest Computation it is judged there could not be fewer than Two Hundred Thousand Spectators:
hand a Golden Shield, with this Motto Inscribed, THE PROTESTANT RELIGION, MAGNA CHARTA, and Flambeaus placed before it: The Pope being brought near thereunto, the Song following was sung in Parts between one who Represented the English Cardinal Howard, and another, the People of England.
Cardinal Howard.
From York to London Town we come
To talk of Popish Ire;
To reconcile you all to Rome,
And prevent Smithfield Fire.
The People Answer.
Cease, Cease, thou Norfolk Cardinal,
See yonder stands Queen Bess,
Who sav'd your Souls from Popish Thrall
O Queen Bess, Queen Bess, Qu. Bess.
Your Popish Plot, and Smithfield Threat
We do not fear at all.
For lo! before Queen Besses Feet
You fall, you fall, you fall.
Now God preserve Great Charles our (King,
And eke all honest Men;
And Traytors all to Justice bring,
Amen, Amen, Amen.
Thus having Entertained the thronging Spectators for some time with Ingenious Fire-works, a vast Bonefire being prepared just over against the Inner-Temple-Gate, his Holiness, after some Complement and Reluctancy, was decently tumbled from all his Grandeur into the Impartial Flames; the Crafty Devil, his Chief Minister, leaving his Infallibilityship in the Lurch in his

On 17 November 1679, the anniversary of the accession of Queen Elizabeth I, Shaftesbury organised a procession through London enacting the alleged Popish Plot. The Pope leads the procession behind the slain Godfrey, and behind him come tonsured priests and Jesuits with daggers unsheathed.

He was the chief of those politicians whom the two great parties contemptuously called Trimmers. Instead of quarrelling with this nickname, he assumed it as a title of honour, and vindicated, with great vivacity, the dignity of the appellation. Everything good, he said, trims between extremes. Virtue is nothing but a just temper between propensities any one of which if indulged to excess, becomes vice. Thus, Halifax was a Trimmer on principle. He was also a Trimmer by the constitution both of his head and of his heart. His place was on the debatable ground between the hostile divisions of the community, and he never wandered far beyond the frontier of either. The party to which he at any moment belonged was the party which, at that moment, he liked least, because it was the party of which at that moment he had the nearest view. He was therefore always severe upon his violent associates, and was always in friendly relations with his moderate opponents.

As soon as he had obtained a footing at court, the charms of his manner and of his conversation made him a favourite. He was seriously alarmed by the violence of the public discontent. He thought that liberty was for the present safe, and that order and legitimate authority were in danger. He therefore, as was his fashion, joined himself to the weaker side.

Sunderland was Secretary of State. In this man the political immorality of his age was personified in the most lively manner. Nature had given him a keen understanding, a restless and mischievous temper, a cold heart, and

Anti-Popery feeling reached a climax with the imprisonment and execution of many leading Catholics condemned on the perjured evidence of Oates and his associates. Edward Coleman, the Duke of York's private secretary, was one of the victims. This woodcut from a contemporary broadsheet shows him being dragged to his execution.

an abject spirit. His mind had undergone a training by which all his vices had been nursed up to the rankest maturity. At his entrance into public life, he had passed several years in diplomatic posts abroad, and had been, during some time, minister in France. The relations between Charles and Louis were such that no English nobleman could long reside in France as envoy, and retain any patriotic or honourable sentiment. Sunderland came forth from the bad school in which he had been brought up, cunning, supple, shameless, free from all prejudices, and destitute of all principles.

Like many other accomplished flatterers and negotiators, he was far more skilful in the art of reading the characters and practising on the weaknesses of individuals, than in the art of discerning the feelings of great masses, and of foreseeing the approach of great revolutions. He was adroit in intrigue; and it was difficult even for shrewd and experienced men who had been amply forewarned of his perfidy to withstand the fascination of his manner, and to refuse credit to his professions of attachment. But he was so intent on observing and courting particular persons, that he often forgot to study the temper of the nation. He therefore miscalculated grossly with respect to some of the most momentous events of his time. More than one important movement and rebound of the public mind took him by surprise; and the world, unable to understand how so clever a man could be blind to what was clearly discerned by the politicians of the coffee houses, sometimes attributed to deep design what were in truth mere blunders.

It was only in private conference that his eminent abilities displayed themselves. In the royal closet, or in a very small circle, he exercised great influence. But at the Council board he was taciturn; and in the House of Lords he never opened his lips.

The Exclusion Bill

The four confidential advisers of the Crown soon found that their position was embarrassing and invidious. The other members of the Council murmured at a distinction inconsistent with the King's promises; and some of them, with Shaftesbury at their head, again betook themselves to strenuous opposition in Parliament. The agitation, which had been suspended by the late changes, speedily became more violent than ever. It was in vain that Charles offered to grant to the Commons any security for the Protestant religion which they could devise, provided only that they would not touch the order of succession. They would hear of no compromise. They would have the Exclusion Bill, and nothing but the Exclusion Bill. The King, therefore, a few weeks after he had publicly promised to take no step without the advice of his new Council, went down to the House of Lords without mentioning his intention in Council, and prorogued the Parliament.

The day of that prorogation, the 26th of May 1679, is a great era in our history. For on that day the Habeas Corpus Act received the royal assent. From the time of the Great Charter, the substantive law respecting the personal liberty of Englishmen had been nearly the same as at present: but it had been inefficacious for want of a stringent system of procedure. What was needed was not a new right, but a prompt and searching remedy; and such a remedy the Habeas Corpus Act supplied. The King would gladly have refused his consent to that measure: but he was about to appeal from his Parliament to his people on the question of the succession, and he could not venture, at so critical a moment, to reject a bill which was in the highest degree popular.

Shortly after the prorogation came a dissolution and another general election. The zeal and strength of the opposition were at the height. The cry for the Exclusion Bill was louder than ever; and with this cry was mingled another cry, which fired the blood of the multitude, but which was heard with regret and alarm by all judicious friends of freedom. Not only the rights of the Duke of York, an avowed Papist, but those of his two daughters, sincere and zealous Protestants, were assailed. It was confidently affirmed that the eldest natural son of the King had been born in wedlock, and was lawful heir to the Crown.

Charles, while a wanderer on the Continent, had fallen in at the Hague with Lucy Walters, a Welsh girl of great beauty, but of weak understanding and dissolute manners. She became his mistress, and presented him with a son. Charles poured forth on little James Crofts, as the boy was then called, an overflowing fondness, such as seemed hardly to belong to that cool and careless nature. Soon after the Restoration, the young favourite, who had learned in France the exercises then considered necessary to a fine gentleman, made his appearance at Whitehall. He was lodged in the palace, attended by pages, and permitted to enjoy several distinctions which had till then been confined to princes of the blood royal. He was married, while still in tender youth, to Anne Scott, heiress of the noble house of Buccleuch. He took her name, and received with her hand possession of her ample domains. Titles, and favours more substantial than titles, were lavished on him. He was made Duke of Monmouth in England, Duke of Buccleuch in Scotland, a Knight of the Garter, Master of the Horse, Commander of the first troop of Life Guards, Chief Justice of Eyre south of Trent, and Chancellor of the University of Cambridge. Nor did he appear to the public unworthy of his high fortunes. His countenance was eminently handsome and engaging, his temper sweet, his manners polite and affable. When Charles and Louis united their forces against Holland, Monmouth commanded the English auxiliaries who were sent to the Continent, and approved himself a gallant soldier and a not unintelligent officer. On his return he found himself the most popular man in the kingdom.

Nothing was withheld from him but the Crown; nor did even the Crown seem to be absolutely beyond his reach.

Charles, even at a ripe age, was devoted to his pleasures and regardless of his dignity. It could hardly be thought incredible that he should at twenty have secretly gone through the form of espousing a lady whose beauty had fascinated him. While Monmouth was still a child, and while the Duke of York still passed for a Protestant, it was rumoured throughout the country, and even in circles which ought to have been well informed, that the King had made Lucy Walters his wife, and that, if every one had his right, her son would be Prince of Wales. When Monmouth had returned from the Low Countries with a high character for valour and conduct, and when the Duke of York was known to be a member of a church detested by the great majority of the nation, this idle story became important. For it there was not the slightest evidence. Against it there was the solemn asseveration of the King, made before his Council, and by his order communicated to his people. But the multitude, always fond of romantic adventures, drank in eagerly the tale of the secret espousals.

The popularity of Monmouth constituted a great part of the strength of the opposition. The elections went against the court: the day fixed for the meeting of the Houses drew near; and it was necessary that the King should determine on some line of conduct. Those who advised him discerned the first faint signs of a change of public feeling, and hoped that, by merely postponing the conflict, he would be able to secure the victory. He therefore, without even asking the opinion of the Council of the Thirty, resolved to prorogue the new Parliament before it entered on business. At the same time the Duke of York, who had returned from Brussels, was ordered to retire to Scotland, and was placed at the head of the administration of that kingdom.

Temple's plan of government was now avowedly abandoned and very soon forgotten. The Privy Council again became what it had been. Shaftesbury and those who were connected with him in politics resigned their seats. Temple himself, as was his wont in unquiet times, retired to his garden and his library. Essex quitted the board of Treasury, and cast in his lot with the opposition. But Halifax, disgusted and alarmed by the violence of his old associates, and Sunderland, who never quitted place while he could hold it, remained in the King's service.

In consequence of the resignations which took place at this conjuncture, the way to greatness was left clear to a new set of aspirants. Two statesmen, who subsequently rose to the highest eminence which a British subject can reach, soon began to attract a large share of the public attention. These were Lawrence Hyde and Sidney Godolphin.

Lawrence Hyde was the second son of the Chancellor Clarendon, and was brother of the first Duchess of York. He had excellent parts, which had been improved by parliamentary and diplomatic experience; but the infirmities of his temper detracted much from the effective strength of his abilities. Negotiator and courtier as he was, he never learned the art of governing or of concealing his emotions. His writings prove that he had many of the qualities of an orator: but his irritability prevented him from doing himself justice in debate: for nothing was easier than to goad him into a passion; and, from the moment when he went into a passion, he was at the mercy of opponents far inferior to him in capacity.

Unlike most of the leading politicians of that generation he was a consistent, dogged, and rancorous party man, a Cavalier of the old school, a zealous champion of the Crown and of the Church, and a hater of Republicans and Nonconformists.

He now succeeded Essex at the Treasury. It is to be observed that the place of First Lord of the Treasury had not then the importance and dignity which now belong to it. When there was a Lord Treasurer, that great officer was generally prime minister: but, when the white staff was in commission, the chief commissioner hardly ranked so high as a Secretary of State. It was not till the time of Walpole that the First Lord of the Treasury became, under a humbler name, all that the Lord High Treasurer had been.

Godolphin had been bred a page at Whitehall, and had early acquired all the flexibility and the selfpossession of a veteran courtier. He was laborious, clearheaded, and profoundly versed in the details of finance. Every government, therefore, found him a useful servant; and there was nothing in his opinions or in his character which could prevent him from serving any government. 'Sidney Godolphin', said Charles, 'is never in the way, and never out of the way.' This pointed remark goes far to explain Godolphin's extraordinary success in life.

Like most men of cautious tempers and prosperous fortunes, he had a strong disposition to support whatever existed. He disliked revolutions. His deportment was remarkably grave and reserved: but his personal tastes were low and frivolous; and most of the time which he could save from public business was spent in racing, cardplaying, and cockfighting. He now sate below Rochester at the Board of Treasury, and distinguished himself there by assiduity and intelligence.

Before the new Parliament was suffered to meet for the despatch of business a whole year elapsed, an eventful year, which has left lasting traces in our manners and language. Never before had political controversy been carried on with so much freedom. The one question of the Exclusion occupied the public mind. All the presses and pulpits of the realm took part in the conflict. On one side it was maintained that the constitution and religion of the State could never be secure under a Popish King; on the other, that the right of James to wear the Crown in his turn was derived from God, and could not be annulled, even by the consent of all the branches of the legislature. Every county, every town, every family, was in agitation. The dearest ties of friendship and of blood were sundered. Even schoolboys were divided into angry parties; and the Duke of York and the Earl of Shaftesbury had zealous adherents on all the forms of Westminster and Eton. The malecontents besieged the throne with petitions, demanding that Parliament might be forthwith convened. The loyalists sent up addresses, expessing the utmost abhorrence of all who presumed to dictate to the sovereign. The citizens of London assembled by tens of thousands to burn the Pope in effigy. The government posted cavalry at Temple Bar, and placed ordnance round Whitehall. In that year our tongue was enriched with two words, Mob and Sham, remarkable memorials of a season of tumult and imposture.

At this time were first heard two nicknames which, though originally given in insult, were soon assumed with pride, which have spread as widely as the English race, and which will last as long as the English literature. It is a curious circumstance that one of these nicknames was of Scotch, and the other of Irish, origin. Both in Scotland and in Ireland, misgovernment had called into existence bands of desperate men whose ferocity was heightened by religious enthusiasm. In Scotland some of the persecuted Covenanters, driven mad by oppression, had lately murdered the primate, had taken arms against the government, had obtained some advantages against the King's forces, and had not been put down till Monmouth, at the head of some troops from England, had routed them at Bothwell Bridge. These zealots were most numerous among the rustics of the western lowlands, who were vulgarly called Whigs. Thus the appellation of Whig was fastened on the Presbyterian zealots of Scotland, and was transferred to those English politicians who showed a disposition to oppose the court, and to treat Protestant Nonconformists with indulgence. The bogs of Ireland, at the same time, afforded a refuge to Popish outlaws, much resembling those who were afterwards known as Whiteboys. These men were then called Tories. The name of Tory was therefore given to Englishmen who refused to concur in excluding a Roman Catholic prince from the throne.

Through all this agitation a discerning eye might have perceived that the public opinion was gradually changing. The persecution of the Roman Catholics went on; but convictions were no longer matters of course. A new brood of false witnesses infested the courts: but the stories of these men, though better constructed than that of Oates, found less credit. Juries were no longer so easy of belief as during the panic which had followed the murder of Godfrey; and judges, who, while the popular frenzy was at the height, had been its most obsequious instruments, now ventured to express some part of what they had from the first thought.

At length, in October 1680, the Parliament met. The Whigs had so great a majority in the Commons that the Exclusion Bill went through all its stages there without difficulty. The King scarcely knew on what members of his own cabinet he could reckon. Hyde had been true to his Tory opinions, and had steadily supported the cause of hereditary monarchy. But Godolphin, anxious for quiet, and believing that quiet could be restored only by concession, wished the bill to pass. Sunderland, ever false, and ever shortsighted, unable to discern the signs of approaching reaction, and anxious to conciliate the party which he believed to be irresistible, determined to vote against the court.

If there were any point on which the King had a scruple of conscience or of honour, it was the question of the succession; but during some days it seemed that he would submit. He wavered, asked what sum the Commons would give him if he yielded, and suffered a negotiation to be opened with the leading Whigs. But a deep mutual distrust which had been many years growing, and which had been carefully nursed by the arts of France, made a treaty impossible. Neither side would place confidence in the other. The whole nation now looked with breathless anxiety to the House of Lords. The assemblage of peers was large. The King himself was present. The debate was long, earnest, and occasionally furious. Shaftesbury and Essex were joined by the treacherous Sunderland. But the genius of Halifax bore down all opposition. Deserted by his most important colleagues, and opposed to a crowd of able antagonists, he defended the cause of the Duke of York, in a succession of speeches which, many years later, were remembered as masterpieces of reasoning, of wit, and of eloquence. It is seldom that oratory changes votes. Yet the attestation of contemporaries leaves no doubt that, on this occasion, votes were changed by the oratory of Halifax. The bishops, true to their doctrines, supported the principle of hereditary right, and the bill was rejected by a great majority.

The party which preponderated in the House of Commons, bitterly mortified by this defeat, found some consolation in shedding the blood of Roman Catholics. William Howard, Viscount Stafford, one of the unhappy men who had been accused of a share in the plot, was impeached; and on the testimony of Oates and of two other false witnesses, Dugdale and Turberville, was found guilty of high treason, and suffered death. But the circumstances of his trial and execution ought to have given an useful warning to the Whig leaders. A large and respectable minority of the House of Lords pronounced the prisoner not guilty. The multitude, which a few months before had received the dying declaration of Oates's victims with mockery and execrations, now loudly expressed a belief that Stafford was a murdered man. When he with his last breath protested his innocence, the cry was, 'God bless you, my lord! We believe you, my lord.'

The King determined to try once more the experiment of a dissolution. A new Parliament was summoned to meet at Oxford, in March 1681. Since the days of the Plantagenets the House had constantly sate at Westminster, except when the plague was raging in the capital: but so extraordinary a conjuncture seemed to require extraordinary precautions. If the Parliament were held in its usual place of assembling, the House of Commons might declare itself permanent, and might call for aid on the magistrates and citizens of London. The trainbands might rise to defend Shaftesbury as they had risen forty years before to defend Pym and Hampden. At Oxford there was no such danger. The university was devoted to the Crown; and the gentry of the neighbourhood were generally Tories. Here, therefore, the opposition had more reason than the King to apprehend violence.

The elections were sharply contested. The Whigs still composed a majority of the House of Commons: but it was plain that the Tory spirit was fast rising throughout the country.

The eventful day arrived. The meeting at Oxford resembled rather that of a Polish Diet than that of an English Parliament. The Whig members were escorted by great numbers of their armed and mounted tenants and serving men, who exchanged looks of defiance with the royal guards. The slightest provocation might, under such circumstances, have produced a civil war; but neither side dared to strike the first blow. The King again offered to consent to anything but the Exclusion Bill. The Commons were determined to accept nothing but the Exclusion Bill. In a few days the Parliament was again dissolved.

The King had triumphed. The reaction, which had begun some months before the meeting of the Houses at Oxford, now went rapidly on. The nation, indeed, was still hostile to Popery: but, when men reviewed the whole history of the plot, they felt that their Protestant zeal had hurried them into folly and crime, and could scarcely believe that they had been induced by nursery tales to clamour for the blood of fellow subjects and fellow Christians. The most loyal, indeed, could not deny that the administration of Charles had often been highly blamable. But men who had not the full information which we possess touching his dealings with France, and who were disgusted by the violence of the Whigs, enumerated the large concessions which, during the last few years, he had made to his Parliaments, and the still larger concessions which he had declared himself willing to make. One thing only had the King denied to his people. He had refused to take away his brother's birthright. And was there not good reason to believe that this refusal was prompted by laudable feelings? What selfish motive could faction itself impute to the royal mind? The Exclusion Bill did not curtail the reigning King's prerogative, or diminish his income. Indeed, by passing it, he might easily have obtained an ample addition to his own revenue. And what was it to him who ruled after him? Nay, if he had personal predilections, they were known to be rather in favour of the Duke of Monmouth than of the Duke of York. The most natural explanation of the King's conduct seemed to be that, careless as was his temper and loose as were his morals, he had, on this occasion, acted from a sense of duty and honour.

Strongly moved by these apprehensions, the majority of the upper and middle classes hastened to rally round the throne. The situation of the King bore, at this time, a great resemblance to that in which his father stood just after the Remonstrance had been voted. But the reaction of 1641 had not been suffered to run its course. Charles I, at the very moment when his people, long estranged, were returning to him with hearts disposed to reconciliation, had, by a perfidious violation of the fundamental laws of the realm, forfeited their confidence for ever. Had Charles II taken a similar course, had he arrested the Whig leaders in an irregular manner, had he impeached them of high treason before a tribunal which had no legal jurisdiction over them, it is highly probable that they would speedily have regained the ascendency which they had lost. Fortunately for himself he was induced, at this crisis, to adopt a policy singularly judicious. He determined to conform to the law, but at the same time to make vigorous and unsparing use of the law against his adversaries. He was not bound to convoke a Parliament till three years should have elapsed. He was not much distressed for money. He had, therefore, ample time and means for a systematic attack on the opposition under the forms of the constitution. The judges were removable at his pleasure: the juries were nominated by the sheriffs; and, in almost all the counties of England, the sheriffs were nominated by himself. Witnesses, of the same class with those who had recently sworn away the lives of Papists, were ready to swear away the lives of Whigs.

Whig Conspiracies

The first victim was College, a noisy and violent demagogue of mean birth and education. He was by trade a joiner, and was celebrated as the inventor of the Protestant flail. He had been at Oxford when the Parliament sate there, and was accused of having planned a rising and an attack on the King's guards. Evidence was given against him by Dugdale and Turberville, the same infamous men who had, a few months earlier, borne false witness against Stafford. College was convicted. The crowd which filled the court house of Oxford received the verdict with a roar of exultation, as barbarous as that which he and his friends had been in the habit of raising when innocent Papists were doomed to the gallows. His execution was the beginning of a new judicial massacre, not less atrocious than that in which he had himself borne a share.

The government, emboldened by this first victory, now aimed a blow at an enemy of a very different class. It was resolved that Shaftesbury should be brought to trial for his life. Evidence was collected which, it was thought, would support a charge of treason. But the facts which it was necessary to prove were alleged to have been committed in London. The

Sheriffs of London, chosen by the citizens, were zealous Whigs. They named a Whig grand jury, which threw out the bill. This defeat, far from discouraging those who advised the King, suggested to them a new and daring scheme. Since the charter of the capital was in their way, that charter must be annulled. It was pretended, therefore, that the City had by some irregularities forfeited its municipal privileges; and proceedings were instituted against the corporation in the Court of the King's Bench. At the same time those laws which had, soon after the Restoration, been enacted against Nonconformists, and which had remained dormant during the ascendency of the Whigs, were enforced all over the kingdom with extreme rigour.

Yet the spirit of the Whigs was not subdued. Though in evil plight, they were still a numerous and powerful party; and, as they mustered strong in the large towns, and especially in the capital, they made a noise and a show more than proportioned to their real force. Unscrupulous and hotheaded chiefs of the party formed and discussed schemes of resistance, and were heard, if not with approbation, yet with the show of acquiescence, by much better men than themselves. It was proposed that there should be simultaneous insurrections in London, in Cheshire, at Bristol, and at Newcastle.

While the leaders of the opposition thus revolved plans of open rebellion, but were still restrained by fears or scruples from taking any decisive step, a design of a very different kind was meditated by some of their accomplices. To fierce spirits, unrestrained by principle, or maddened by fanaticism, it seemed that to waylay and murder the King and his brother was the shortest and surest way of vindicating the Protestant religion and the liberties of England. A place and a time were named; and the details of the butchery were frequently discussed, if not definitely arranged. This scheme was known but to few, and was concealed with especial care from the upright and humane Russell, and from Monmouth, who, though not a man of delicate conscience, would have recoiled with horror from the guilt of parricide. Thus there were two plots, one within the other. The object of the great Whig plot was to raise the nation in arms against the government. The lesser plot, commonly called the Rye House Plot, in which only a few desperate men were concerned, had for its object the assassination of the King and of the heir presumptive.

Both plots were soon discovered. Cowardly traitors hastened to save themselves, by divulging all, and more than all, that had passed in the deliberations of the party. That only a small minority of those who meditated resistance had admitted into their minds the thought of assassination is fully established: but as the two conspiracies ran in to each other, it was not difficult for the government to confound them together. The just indignation excited by the Rye House Plot was extended for a time to the whole Whig body. The King was now at liberty to exact full vengeance for years of restraint and humiliation. Shaftesbury, indeed, had escaped the fate which his manifold perfidy had well deserved. He had seen that the ruin of his party was at hand, had in vain endeavoured to make his peace with the royal brothers, had fled to Holland, and had died there, under the generous protection of a government which he had cruelly wronged. Monmouth threw himself at his father's feet and found mercy, but soon gave new offence, and thought it prudent to go into voluntary exile. Essex perished by his own hand in the Tower. Russell, who appears to have been guilty of no offence falling within the definition of high treason, and Algernon Sidney, of whose guilt no legal evidence could be produced, were beheaded in defiance of law and justice. Russell died with the fortitude of a Christian, Sidney with the fortitude of a Stoic. Some active politicians of meaner rank were sent to the gallows. Many quitted the country.

Actions were brought against persons who had defamed the Duke of York; and damages tantamount to a sentence of perpetual imprisonment were demanded by the plaintiff, and without difficulty obtained. The Court of King's Bench pronounced that the franchises of the City of London were forfeited to the Crown. Flushed with this great victory, the government proceeded to attack the constitutions of other corporations which were governed by Whig officers, and which had been in the habit of returning Whig members to Parliament. Borough after borough was compelled to surrender its privileges; and new charters were granted which gave the ascendency everywhere to the Tories.

These proceedings were accompanied by an act intended to quiet the uneasiness with which many loyal men looked forward to the accession of a Popish sovereign. The Lady Anne, younger daughter of the Duke of York by his first wife, was married to George, a prince of the orthodox House of Denmark. The Tory gentry and clergy might now flatter themselves that the Church of England had been effectually secured without any violation of the order of succession. The King and the heir presumptive were nearly of the same age. Both were approaching the decline of life. The King's health was good. It was therefore probable that James, if he ever came to the throne, would have but a short reign. Beyond his reign there was the gratifying prospect of a long series of Protestant sovereigns.

The King at length ventured to overstep the bounds which he had during some years observed, and to violate the plain letter of the law. The law was that not more than three years should pass between the dissolving of one Parliament and the convoking of another. But, when three years had elapsed after the dissolution of the Parliament which sate at Oxford, no writs were issued for an election.

In a short time the law was again violated in order to gratify the Duke of York. That prince was so unpopular that it had been thought necessary to keep him out of sight while the Exclusion Bill was before Parliament, lest his appearance should give an advantage to the party which was struggling to deprive him of his birthright. He had therefore been sent to govern Scotland, where the savage old tyrant Lauderdale was sinking into the grave. Even Lauderdale was now outdone. The administration of James was marked by odious laws, by barbarous punishments, and by judgments to the iniquity of which even that age furnished no parallel. The Scottish Privy Council had power to put state prisoners to the question. But the sight was so dreadful that, as soon as the boots appeared, even the most servile and hard-hearted courtiers hastened out of the chamber. The board was sometimes quite deserted: and it was at length found necessary to make an order that the members should keep their seats on such occasions. The Duke of York, it was remarked, seemed to take pleasure in the spectacle which some of the worst men then living were unable to contemplate without pity and horror. Thus he employed himself at Edinburgh, till the event of the conflict between the court and the Whigs was no longer doubtful. He then returned to England: but he was still excluded by the Test Act from all public employment; nor did the King at first think it safe to violate a statute which the great majority of his most loyal subjects regarded as one of the chief securities of their religion and of their civil rights. When, however, it appeared, from a succession of trials, that the nation had patience to endure almost anything that the government had courage to do, Charles ventured to dispense with the law in his brother's favour. The duke again took his seat in the Council, and resumed the direction of naval affairs.

These breaches of the constitution were not unanimously approved even by the King's ministers. Halifax in particular, now a Marquess and Lord Privy Seal, had, from the very day on which the Tories had by his help gained the ascendent, begun to turn Whig. As soon as the Exclusion Bill had been thrown out, he had pressed the House of Lords to make provision against the danger to which, in the next reign, the liberties and religion of the nation might be exposed. He now saw with alarm the violence of that reaction which was, in no small measure, his own work. He disapproved of the long intermission of Parliaments. He regretted the severity with which the vanquished party was treated. He who, when the Whigs were predominant, had ventured to pronounce Stafford not guilty, ventured, when they were vanquished and helpless, to intercede for Russell.

The moderate and constitutional counsels of Halifax were timidly and feebly seconded by Francis North, Lord Guildford, who had lately been made Keeper of the Great Seal. The intellect of Guildford was clear, his industry great, his proficiency in letters and science respectable, and his legal learning more than respectable. His faults were selfishness, cowardice, and meanness. Though of noble descent, he rose in his profession by paying ignominious homage to all who possessed influence in the courts. He had at length reached the highest post in the law. But a lawyer, who, after many years devoted to professional labour, engages in politics for the first time at an advanced period of life, seldom distinguishes himself as a statesman; and Guildford was no exception to the general rule. Even on questions relating to his own profession his opinion had less weight at the Council board than that of any man who had ever held the Great Seal. Such as his influence was, however, he used it, as far as he dared, on the side of the laws.

The chief opponent of Halifax was Lawrence Hyde, who had recently been created Earl of Rochester. Of all Tories, Rochester was the most intolerant and uncompromising. The Duke of York, pleased with a spirit which so much resembled his own, supported his brother in law passionately and obstinately.

The attempts of the rival ministers to surmount and supplant each other kept the court in incessant agitation. While the two factions were struggling, Godolphin, cautious, silent, and laborious, observed a neutrality between them. Sunderland, with his usual restless perfidy, intrigued against them both. He had been turned out of office in disgrace for having voted in favour of the Exclusion Bill, but he had made his peace by employing the good offices of the Duchess of Portsmouth and by cringing to the Duke of York, and was once more Secretary of State.

Halifax was not content with standing on the defensive. He openly accused Rochester of malversation. An inquiry took place. It appeared that forty thousand pounds had been lost to the public by the mismanagement of the First Lord of the Treasury. In consequence of this discovery he was

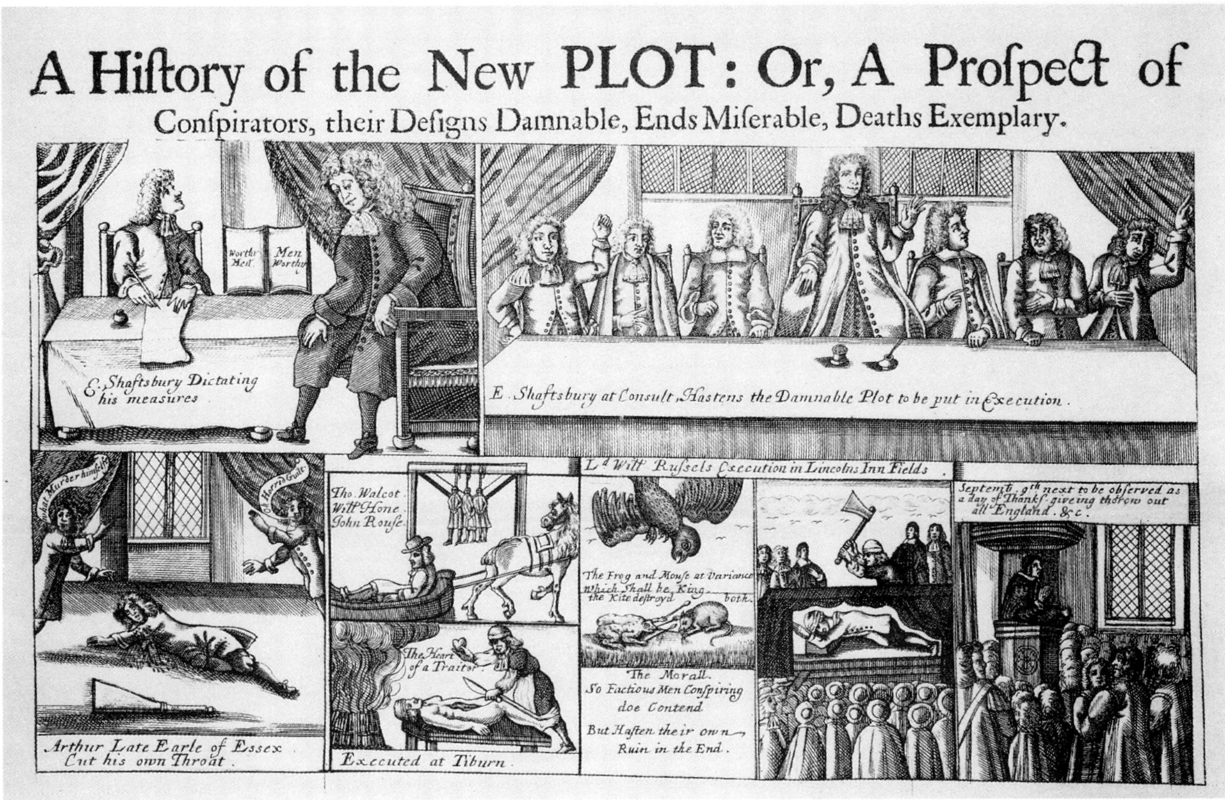

A few desperate men, frustrated by the failure to exclude the Duke of York from the succession, planned to assassinate the King and his brother on their return to London from Newmarket. The plot failed, and many leading Whigs who were ardent exclusionists but knew nothing of the plot were executed. The broadside shows, above, the devious Shaftesbury planning the scheme from Holland; whilst, below, Essex commits suicide and Russell is executed.

not only forced to relinquish his hopes of the white staff, but was removed from the direction of the finances to the more dignified but less lucrative and important post of Lord President. 'I have seen people kicked downstairs,' said Halifax; 'but my Lord Rochester is the first person that I ever saw kicked upstairs.' Godolphin, now a peer, became First Commissioner of the Treasury.

Still, however, the contest continued. The event depended wholly on the will of Charles; and Charles could not come to a decision. In his perplexity he promised everything to everybody. He would stand by France: he would break with France: he would never meet another Parliament: he would order writs for a Parliament to be issued without delay. He assured the Duke of York that Halifax should be dismissed from office, and Halifax that the duke should be sent to Scotland. In public he affected implacable resentment against Monmouth, and in private conveyed to Monmouth assurances of unalterable affection. How long, if the King's life had been protracted, his hesitation would have lasted, and what would have been his resolve, can only be conjectured. Early in the year 1685, while hostile parties were anxiously awaiting his determination, he died, and a new scene opened.

Death of Charles II

The death of King Charles II took the nation by surprise. His frame was naturally strong, and did not appear to have suffered from excess. He had always been mindful of his health even in his pleasures; and his habits were such as promise a long life and a robust old age. Indolent as he was on all occasions which required tension of the mind, he was active and persevering in bodily exercise. He had, when young, been renowned as a tennis player, and was, even in the decline of life, an indefatigable walker. He rose early, and generally passed three or four hours a day in the open air.

Towards the close of the year 1684, he was prevented, by a slight attack of what was supposed to be gout, from rambling as usual. He now spent his mornings in his laboratory, where he amused himself with experiments on the properties of mercury. His temper seemed to have suffered from confinement. His irritation frequently showed itself by looks and words such as could hardly have been expected from a man so eminently distinguished by good humour and good breeding. It was not supposed however that his constitution was seriously impaired.

His palace had seldom presented a gayer or a more scandalous appearance than on the evening of Sunday the 1st of February 1685. Some grave persons who had gone thither, after the fashion of that age, to pay their duty to their sovereign, and who had expected that, on such a day, his court would wear a decent aspect, were struck with astonishment and horror. The great gallery of Whitehall, an admirable relic of the magnificence of the Tudors, was crowded with revellers and gamblers. The King sate there chatting and toying with three women, whose charms were the boast, and whose vices were the disgrace, of three nations. Barbara Palmer, Duchess of Cleveland, was there, no longer young, but still retaining some traces of that superb and voluptuous loveliness which twenty years before overcame the hearts of all men. There too was the Duchess of Portsmouth, whose soft and infantine features were lighted up with the vivacity of France. Hortensia Mancini, Duchess of Mazarin, and niece of the great cardinal, completed the group. A party of twenty courtiers was seated at cards round a large table on which gold was heaped in mountains. Even then the King had complained that he did not feel quite well. He had no appetite for his supper: his rest that night was broken; but on the following morning he rose, as usual, early.

To that morning the contending factions in his council had, during some days, looked forward with anxiety. The struggle between Halifax and Rochester seemed to be approaching a decisive crisis. Halifax, not content with having already driven his rival from the Board of Treasury, had undertaken to prove him guilty of such dishonesty or neglect in the conduct of the finances as ought to be punished by dismission from the public service. It was even whispered that the Lord President would probably be sent to the Tower. The King had promised to enquire into the matter. The 2nd of February had been fixed for the investigation; and several officers of the revenue had been ordered to attend with their books on that day. But a great turn of fortune was at hand.

Scarcely had Charles risen from his bed when his attendants perceived that his utterance was indistinct, and that his thoughts seemed to be wandering. Several men of rank had, as usual, assembled to see their sovereign shaved and dressed. He made an effort to converse with them in his usual gay style; but his ghastly look surprised and alarmed them. Soon his face grew black; his eyes turned in his head; he uttered a cry, staggered, and fell into the arms of one of his lords. A physician who had charge of the royal retorts and crucibles happened to be present. He had no lancet; but he opened a vein with a penknife. The blood flowed freely; but the King was still insensible.

He was laid on his bed, where, during a short time, the Duchess of Portsmouth hung over him with the familiarity of a wife. But the alarm had been given. The Queen and the Duchess of York were hastening to the room. The favourite concubine was forced to retire to her own apartments.

And now the gates of Whitehall, which ordinarily stood open to all comers, were closed. But persons whose faces were known were still permitted to enter. The antechambers and galleries were soon filled to overflowing; and even the sick room was crowded with peers, privy councillors, and foreign ministers. All the medical men of note in London were summoned. The patient was bled largely. Hot iron was applied to his head. A loathsome volatile salt, extracted from human skulls, was forced into his mouth. He recovered his senses; but he was evidently in a situation of extreme danger.

On the morning of Thursday the 5th of February, the *London Gazette* announced that his Majesty was going on well, and was thought by the physicians to be out of danger. The bells of all the churches rang merrily; and preparations for bonfires were made in the streets. But in the evening it was known that a relapse had taken place, and that the medical attendants had given up all hope.

The King was in great pain, and complained that he felt as if a fire was burning within him. Yet he bore up against his sufferings with a fortitude which did not seem to belong to his soft and luxurious nature. The sight of his misery affected his wife so much that she fainted, and was carried senseless to her chamber. The prelates who were in waiting had from the first exhorted him to prepare for his end. They now thought it their duty to address him in a still more urgent manner. William Sancroft, Archbishop of Canterbury, an honest and pious, though narrowminded, man, used great freedom. 'It is time', he said, 'to speak out; for, sir, you are about to appear before a judge who is no respecter of persons.' The King answered not a word.

Thomas Ken, Bishop of Bath and Wells, then tried his powers of persuasion. He was a man of parts and learning, of quick sensibility and stainless virtue. It was to no purpose, however, that the good bishop now put forth all his eloquence. Charles was unmoved. He made no objection indeed when the service for the Visitation of the Sick was read. In reply to the pressing questions of the divines, he said that he was sorry for what he had done amiss; and he suffered the absolution to be pronounced over him according to the forms of the Church of England: but, when he was urged to declare that he died in the communion of that Church, he seemed not to hear what was said; and nothing could induce him to take the Eucharist from the hands of the bishops.

Many attributed this apathy to contempt for divine things, and many to the stupor which often precedes death. But there were in the palace a few persons who knew better. Charles had never been a sincere member of the Established Church. When his health was good and his spirits high, he was a scoffer. In his few serious moments he was a Roman Catholic. The Duke of York was aware of this, but was entirely occupied with the care of his own interests. He had ordered the outports to be closed. He had posted detachments of the guards in different parts of the City. These things occupied the attention of James to such a degree that, though, on ordinary occasions, he was indiscreetly and unseasonably eager to bring over proselytes to his Church, he never reflected that his brother was in danger of dying without the last sacraments. This neglect was the more extraordinary because the Duchess of York had, at the request of the Queen, suggested, on the morning on which the King was taken ill, the propriety of procuring spiritual assistance. For such assistance Charles was at last indebted to an agency very different from that of his pious wife and sister in law. A life of frivolity and vice had not extinguished in the Duchess of Portsmouth all sentiments of religion, or all that kindness which is the glory of her sex. The French ambassador Barillon, who had come to the palace to enquire after the King, paid her a visit. He found her in an agony of sorrow. She took him into a secret room, and poured out her whole heart to him. 'I have', she said, 'a thing of great moment to tell you. The King is really and truly a Catholic; but he will die without being reconciled to the Church. His bedchamber is full of Protestant clergymen. The duke is thinking only of himself. Speak to him. Remind him that there is a soul at stake. He is master now. He can clear the room. Go this instant, or it will be too late.'

Barillon hastened to the bedchamber, took the duke aside, and delivered the message of the mistress. The conscience of James smote him. He started as if roused from sleep, and declared that nothing should prevent him from discharging the sacred duty which had been too long delayed. Several schemes were discussed and rejected. At last the duke commanded the crowd to stand aloof, went to the bed, stooped down, and whispered something which none of the spectators could hear. Charles answered in an audible voice, 'Yes, yes, with all my heart.' None of the bystanders, except the French ambassador, guessed that the King was declaring his wish to be admitted into the bosom of the Church of Rome.

'Shall I bring a priest?' said the duke. 'Do, brother,' replied the sick man. 'For God's sake do, and lose no time. But no; you will get into trouble.' 'If it costs me my life,' said the duke, 'I will fetch a priest.'

To find a priest, however, for such a purpose, at a moment's notice, was not easy. For, as the law then stood, the person who admitted a proselyte into the Roman Catholic Church was guilty of a capital crime. The duke and Barillon were about to send to the Venetian minister for a clergyman, when they heard that a Benedictine monk, named John Huddleston, happened to be at Whitehall. This man had, with great risk to himself, saved the King's life after the battle of Worcester, and had, on that account, been, ever since the Restoration, a privileged person. In the sharpest proclamations which had been put forth against Popish priests, when false witnesses had inflamed the nation to fury, Huddleston had been excepted by name. He readily consented to put his life a second time in peril for his prince; and was brought up the back stairs by Chiffinch, a confidential servant, who, if the satires of that age are to be credited, had often introduced visitors of a very different description by the same entrance. The duke then, in the King's name, commanded all who were present to quit the room, except Lewis Duras, Earl of Feversham, and John Granville, Earl of Bath. Both these lords professed the Protestant religion; but James conceived that he could count on their fidelity. Feversham, a Frenchman of noble birth, and nephew of the great Turenne, held high rank in the English army, and was Chamberlain to the Queen. Bath was Groom of the Stole.

The duke's orders were obeyed; and even the physicians withdrew. The back door was then opened; and Father Huddleston entered. A cloak had been thrown over his sacred vestments; and his shaven crown was concealed by a flowing wig. 'Sir,' said the duke, 'this good man once saved your life. He now comes to save your soul.' Charles faintly answered, 'He is welcome.' Huddleston knelt by the bed, listened to the confession, pronounced the absolution, and administered extreme unction. He asked if the King wished to receive the Lord's Supper, 'Surely,' said Charles, 'if I am not unworthy.' The host was brought in. Charles feebly strove to rise and kneel before it. The priest bade him lie still, and assured him that God would accept the humiliation of the soul, and would not require the humiliation of the body. The King found so much difficulty in swallowing the bread that it was necessary to open the door and to procure a glass of water. This rite ended, the monk held up a crucifix before the penitent, charged him to fix his last thoughts on the sufferings of the Redeemer, and withdrew. The whole ceremony had occupied about three quarters of an hour. The door was at length thrown open, and the crowd again filled the chamber of death.

It was now late in the evening. The King seemed much relieved by what had passed. His natural children were brought to his bedside, the Dukes of Grafton, Southampton, and Northumberland, sons of the Duchess of Cleveland, the Duke of Saint Albans, son of Eleanor Gwynn, and the Duke of Richmond, son of the Duchess of Portsmouth. Charles blessed them all, but spoke with peculiar tenderness to Richmond. One face which should have been there was wanting. The eldest and best beloved child was an exile and a wanderer. His name was not once mentioned by his father.

During the night Charles earnestly recommended the Duchess of Portsmouth and her boy to the care of James; 'And do not', he goodnaturedly added, 'let poor Nelly starve.' The Queen sent excuses for her absence by Halifax. She said that she was too much disordered to resume her post by the couch, and implored pardon for any offence which she might unwittingly have given. 'She ask my pardon, poor woman!' cried Charles; 'I ask hers with all my heart.'

The morning light began to peep through the windows of Whitehall; and Charles desired the attendants to pull aside the curtains, that he might have one more look at the day. He remarked that it was time to wind up a clock which stood near his bed. These little circumstances were long remembered, because they proved beyond dispute that, when he declared himself a Roman Catholic, he was in full possession of his faculties. He apologised to those who had stood round him all night for the trouble which he had caused. He had been, he said, a most unconscionable time dying; but he hoped that they would excuse it. This was the last glimpse of that exquisite urbanity, so often found potent to charm away the resentment of a justly incensed nation. At noon on Friday, the 6th of February, he passed away without a struggle.

When all was over, James retired from the bedside to his closet, where, during a quarter of an hour, he remained alone. Meanwhile the Privy Councillors who were in the palace assembled. The new King came forth, and took his place at the head of the board. He commenced his administration, according to usage, by a speech to the Council. He expressed his regret for the loss which he had just sustained, and he promised to imitate the singular lenity which had distinguished the late reign. He was aware, he said, that he had been accused of a fondness for arbitrary power. But that was not the only falsehood which had been told of him. He was resolved to maintain the established government both in Church and State. The Church of England he knew to be eminently loyal. It should therefore always be his care to support and defend her. The laws of England, he also knew, were sufficient to make him as great a King as he could wish to be. He would not relinquish his own rights; but he would respect the rights of others.

This speech was not, like modern speeches on similar occasions, carefully prepared by the advisers of the sovereign. It was the extemporaneous expression of the new King's feelings at a moment of great excitement. The members of the Council broke forth into clamours of delight and gratitude. The Lord President, Rochester, in the name of his brethren, expressed a hope that His Majesty's most welcome declaration would be made public. The Solicitor General, Heneage Finch, offered to act as clerk.

The King had been exhausted by long watching and by many violent emotions. He now retired to rest. The Privy Councillors, having respectfully accompanied him to his bedchamber, returned to their seats, and issued orders for the ceremony of proclamation. The guards were under arms; the heralds appeared in their gorgeous coats; and the pageant proceeded without any obstruction. Casks of wine were broken up in the streets, and all who passed were invited to drink to the health of the new sovereign. But, though an occasional shout was raised, the people were not in a joyous mood. Tears were seen in many eyes; and it was remarked that there was scarcely a housemaid in London who had not contrived to procure some fragment of black crape in honour of King Charles.

PART 3 The Reign of James II

New Arrangements

The great offices of State had become vacant by the demise of the Crown; and it was necessary for James to determine how they should be filled. Rochester, the only member of the Cabinet who stood high in the favour of the new King, was declared Lord Treasurer, and thus became prime minister. Sunderland exerted so much art and address, and was in possession of so many secrets, that he was suffered to retain his seals. Godolphin was made Chamberlain to the Queen. With these three lords the King took counsel on all important questions.

Halifax was told that he must give up the Privy Seal and accept the Presidency of the Council. The Privy Seal was delivered to Rochester's elder brother, Henry Earl of Clarendon.

Marshal Turenne, Louis XIV's greatest soldier, was tutor to James as to many others in the arts of war.

Anne Hyde, daughter of the Earl of Clarendon, was James's first wife and the mother of two English Queens – Mary and Anne.

The Great Seal was left in Guildford's custody: but a marked indignity was at the same time offered to him. It was determined that another lawyer of more vigour and audacity should be called to assist in the administration. The person selected was Sir George Jeffreys, Chief Justice of the Court of King's Bench.

He was a man of quick and vigorous parts, but constitutionally prone to insolence and to the angry passions. When just emerging from boyhood he had risen into practice at the Old Bailey bar. Here, during many years, his chief business was to examine and cross-examine the most hardened miscreants of a great capital. Daily conflicts with prostitutes and thieves called out and exercised his powers so effectually that he became the most consummate bully ever known in his profession. Impudence and ferocity sate upon his brow. The glare of his eyes had a fascination for the unhappy victim on whom they were fixed. His yell of fury, as was said by one who had often heard it, sounded like the thunder of the judgment day. These qualifications he carried, while still a young man, from the bar to the bench. As a judge at the City sessions he exhibited the same propensities which afterwards, in a higher post, gained for him an unenviable immortality. There was a fiendish exultation in the way in which he pronounced sentence on offenders; and he loved to scare them into fits by dilating with luxuriant amplification on all the details of what they were to suffer.

By this time the heart of Jeffreys had been hardened to that temper which tyrants require in their worst implements. He soon found a patron in the obdurate and revengeful James, but was always regarded with scorn and disgust by Charles. Work was to be done, however, which could be trusted to no man who reverenced law or was sensible of shame; and thus Jeffreys, at an age at which a barrister thinks himself fortunate if he is employed to conduct an important cause, was made Chief Justice of the King's Bench.

His enemies could not deny that he possessed some of the qualities of a great judge. He had one of those happily constituted intellects which, across labyrinths of sophistry, and through masses of immaterial facts, go straight to the true point. Of his intellect, however, he seldom had the full use. Even when he was sober, his violence was sufficiently frightful. But in general his reason was overclouded and his evil passions stimulated by the

At the Restoration James was appointed Lord High Admiral. With the outbreak of the Third Dutch War in 1672 he was entrusted with the command of the English fleet, and fought an action at Sole Bay as savage as any that the participants could remember. In this painting by William van de Velde The Royal James *is seen blowing up after being set on fire by Dutch fireships.*

fumes of intoxication. Respectable Tories lamented the disgrace which the barbarity and indecency of so great a functionary brought upon the administration of justice. But the excesses which filled such men with horror were titles to the esteem of James. Jeffreys, therefore, very soon after the death of Charles, obtained a seat in the cabinet and a peerage.

It was not without many misgivings that James determined to call the estates of his realm together. The moment was, indeed, most auspicious for a general election. But the new sovereign's mind was haunted by an apprehension not to be mentioned without shame and indignation. He was afraid that by summoning his Parliament he might incur the displeasure of the King of France.

Rochester, Godolphin, and Sunderland were consulted by James as to the expediency of convoking the legislature. They acknowledged the importance of keeping Louis in good humour: but it seemed to them that the calling of a Parliament was not a matter of choice. Patient as the nation appeared to be, there were limits to its patience. The King therefore notified to the country his intention of holding a Parliament. But he was painfully anxious to exculpate himself from the guilt of having acted undutifully towards France. He led Barillon into a private room, and there apologised for having dared to take so important a step without the previous sanction of Louis. 'Assure your master', said James, 'of my gratitude and attachment. I hope that he will not take it amiss that I have acted without consulting him. He has a right to be consulted; and it is my wish to consult him about everything. But in this case the delay even of a week might have produced serious consequences.'

These ignominious excuses were, on the following morning, repeated by Rochester. Barillon received them civilly. Rochester, grown bolder, proceeded to ask for money. 'It will be well laid out', he said: 'your master cannot employ his revenues better.'

Barillon hastened to communicate to Louis the wishes of the English government; but Louis had already anticipated them. His first act, after he was apprised of the death of Charles, was to collect bills of exchange on England to the amount of five hundred thousand livres, a sum equivalent to about thirty-seven thousand five hundred pounds sterling. As soon as Barillon received the remittance, he flew to Whitehall, and communicated the welcome news. James was not ashamed to shed, or pretend to shed, tears of delight and gratitude. 'Nobody but your King', he said, 'does such kind, such noble things. I never can be grateful enough. Assure him that my attachment will last to the end of my days.'

It was resolved that an extraordinary embassy should be sent to assure Louis of the gratitude and affection of James. For this mission was selected a man who did not as yet occupy a very eminent position, but whose renown filled at a later period the whole civilised world.

Soon after the Restoration, James had been attracted by Arabella Churchill, one of the maids of honour who waited on his first wife. The young lady was plain: but the taste of James was not nice: and she became his avowed mistress. Her interest was of great use to her relations: but none of them was so fortunate as her eldest brother John, a fine youth, who carried a pair of colours in the foot guards. He rose fast in the court and in the army, and was early distinguished as a man of fashion and of pleasure. His stature was commanding, his face handsome, his address singularly winning; his temper, even in the most vexatious circumstances,

Samuel Pepys, the great diarist of the Restoration, was a civil servant of the highest calibre. In 1660 he was appointed Clerk of the Acts of the Navy, and in that capacity assisted the Lord High Admiral, winning James's complete confidence.

James II as Duke of York during his period of office as Lord High Commissioner for Scotland: portrait by Peter Lely. His face shows a hardness not apparent in earlier portraits.

always under perfect command. His education had been so much neglected that he could not spell the most common words of his own language: but his acute and vigorous understanding amply supplied the place of book learning. His courage was singularly cool and imperturbable.

Unhappily the splendid qualities of John Churchill were mingled with alloy of the most sordid kind. He was thrifty in his very vices, and levied ample contributions on ladies enriched by the spoils of more liberal lovers. Already his private drawer contained a hoard of broad pieces which, fifty years later, when he was a duke, a prince of the empire, and the richest subject in Europe, remained untouched.

He had been attached to the household of the Duke of York, had accompanied his patron to the Low Countries and to Edinburgh, and had been rewarded for his services with a Scotch peerage and with the command of the only regiment of dragoons which was then on the English establishment. His wife had a post in the family of James's younger daughter, the Princess of Denmark.

Lord Churchill was now sent as ambassador extraordinary to Versailles. He had it in charge to express the warm gratitude of the English government for the money which had been so generously bestowed. He was directed to confine himself to thanks for what was past, and to say nothing about the future. In a very few weeks, however, Barillon received from Versailles fifteen hundred thousand livres more. This sum, equivalent to about a hundred and twelve thousand pounds sterling, he was instructed to dole out cautiously. He was authorised to furnish the English government with thirty thousand pounds, for the purpose of corrupting members of the new House of Commons. The rest he was directed to keep in reserve for some extraordinary emergency, such as a dissolution or an insurrection.

James became the slave of France: but it would be incorrect to represent

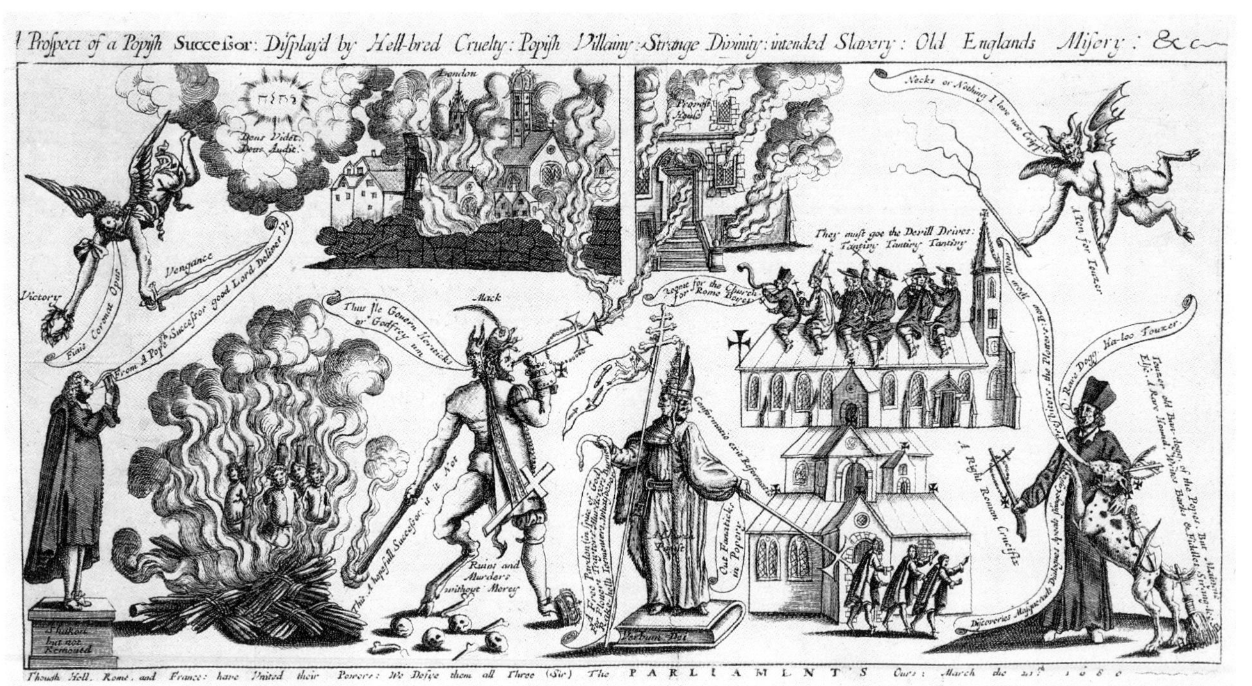

Satire of 1680, at the height of the Exclusion Bill crisis, illustrating the dire consequences of a Popish succession.

DVKE OF YORK

him as a contented slave. It galled his soul to think that the kingdom which he ruled was of far less account in the world than many states which possessed smaller natural advantages; and he listened eagerly to foreign ministers when they urged him to assert the dignity of his rank, to become the protector of injured nations, and to tame the pride of that power which held the Continent in awe. But a vigorous foreign policy necessarily implied a conciliatory domestic policy. It was impossible at once to confront the might of France and to trample on the liberties of England. Thus James found that the two things which he most desired could not be enjoyed together. His second wish was to be feared and respected abroad. But his first wish was to be absolute master at home.

By this time England had recovered from the sadness and anxiety caused by the death of the good-natured Charles. The Tories were loud in professions of attachment to their new master. The hatred of the Whigs was kept down by fear. That great mass which is not steadily Whig or Tory was still on the Tory side. The reaction which had followed the dissolution of the Oxford parliament had not yet spent its force.

The King early put the loyalty of his Protestant friends to the proof. Passion week came; and he determined to hear mass with the same pomp with which his predecessors had been surrounded when they repaired to the temples of the established religion. On Easter Sunday, the rites of the Church of Rome were once more, after an interval of a hundred and twenty-seven years, performed at Westminster with regal splendour.

Within a week after this ceremony James made a far greater sacrifice of his own religious prejudices than he had yet called on any of his Protestant subjects to make. He was crowned on the 23rd of April, the feast of the patron saint of the realm. He had ordered Sancroft to abridge the ritual. The reason publicly assigned was that the day was too short for all that was to be done. But the real object was to remove some things highly offensive to the religious feelings of a zealous Roman Catholic. What remained, however, after all this curtailment, might well have raised scruples in the mind of a man who sincerely believed the Church of England to be a heretical society. The King made an oblation on the altar. He appeared to join in the petitions of the litany which was chaunted by the bishops. He received from those false prophets the unction typical of a divine influence, and knelt with the semblance of devotion while they called down upon him that Holy Spirit of which they were, in his estimation, the malignant and obdurate foes. Such are the inconsistencies of human nature that this man, who, from a fanatical zeal for his religion, threw away three kingdoms, yet chose to commit what was little short of an act of apostasy, rather than forego the childish pleasure of being invested with the gewgaws symbolical of kingly power.

Meanwhile the writs for the new Parliament had gone forth, and the country was agitated by the tumult of a general election. The result exceeded the most sanguine expectations of the court. James said that, with the exception of about forty members, the House of Commons was just such as he should himself have named. And this House of Commons it was in his power, as the law then stood, to keep to the end of his reign.

Secure of parliamentary support, he might now indulge in the luxury of revenge. A short time before his accession, he had instituted a civil suit against Oates for defamatory words; and a jury had given damages to the enormous amount of a hundred thousand pounds. The defendant was

Mary of Modena, by Wissing. James married his second wife in November 1673, and the nation was appalled that the now self-confessed Papist had married the rumoured daughter of the Pope.

lying in prison as a debtor, without hope of release. Two bills of indictment against him for perjury had been found by the grand jury of Middlesex, a few weeks before the death of Charles. Soon after the close of the elections the trial came on.

On the day in which Titus was brought to the bar, Westminster Hall was crowded with spectators. A few years earlier his short neck, his legs uneven, the vulgar said, as those of a badger, his forehead low as that of a baboon, his purple cheeks, and his monstrous length of chin, had been familiar to all who frequented the courts of law. He had then been the idol of the nation. Times had now changed; and many, who had formerly regarded him as the deliverer of his country, shuddered at the sight of those hideous features on which villainy seemed to be written by the hand of God.

It was proved, beyond all possibility of doubt, that this man had, by false testimony, deliberately murdered several guiltless persons. He was sentenced to be stripped of his clerical habit, to be pilloried in Palace Yard, to

Mary of Modena with her confessor, Edward Petre; a pointed commentary on the thinly veiled intentions of the Jesuits to subvert the established Church with the aid of the Court.

be led round Westminster Hall with an inscription declaring his infamy over his head, to be pilloried again in front of the Royal Exchange, to be whipped from Aldgate to Newgate, and, after an interval of two days, to be whipped from Newgate to Tyburn. If he should happen to survive this horrible infliction, he was to be kept close prisoner during life.

The rigorous sentence was rigorously executed. On the day on which Oates was pilloried in Palace Yard, he was mercilessly pelted and ran some risk of being pulled in pieces. On the following morning he was brought forth to undergo his first flogging. The hangman laid on the lash with such unusual severity as showed that he had received special instructions. For a time the criminal showed a strange constancy: but at last his stubborn fortitude gave way. His bellowings were frightful to hear. He swooned several times; but the scourge still continued to descend. James was entreated to remit the second flogging. His answer was short and clear: 'He shall go through with it, if he has breath in his body.' After an interval of only forty-eight hours, Oates was again brought out of his dungeon. He was unable to stand, and it was necessary to drag him to Tyburn on a sledge. A person who counted the stripes on the second day said that they were seventeen hundred. The bad man escaped with life, but so narrowly that his ignorant and bigoted admirers thought his recovery miraculous, and appealed to it as a proof of his innocence. The doors of the prison closed upon him.

The Coronation of James II and Mary of Modena: 23 April 1685. Macaulay comments on the inconsistency of the King who was prepared to throw away three kingdoms for his faith and yet 'chose to commit what was little short of an act of apostasy, rather than forego the childish pleasure of being invested with the geegaws of kingly power'.

R.P. ANTONIUS TURNER PRIESTER DER SOCIETEYT IESV. GEHANGEN EN GEVIERENDEELT BUYTEN LONDEN. 30 Iunii 1679.
R.P. IOANNES FENWYCK PRIESTER DER SOCIETEYT IESV. GEHANGEN EN GEVIERENDEELT BUYTEN LONDE. 30 Iunii 1679.
R.P. IOANNES GAVIN PRIESTER DER SOCIETEYT IESV. GEHANGEN EN GEVIERENDEELT BUYTEN LONDEN den 30 Iunii 1679.
R.P. GVLIELMVS WARING VANDE SOCIETEYT IESV. GEHANGEN EN GEVIERENDEELT BVYTEN LONDEN 30 Iunii 1679.
R.P. THOMAS HARCOVRT VANDE SOCIETEYT IESV. GEHANGEN EN GEVIERENDEELT BVYTEN LONDEN. den 30 Iunii 1679.
R. P. CAROLUS BAKER PRIESTER DER SOCIETEYT IESV. GEHANGEN EN GEVIERENDEELT BUYTEN LONDEN 6 Sept. 1679.
R.P. PHILIPPVS EVAN PRIESTER DER SOCIETEYT IESV. GEHANGEN EN GEVIERENDEELT BUYTEN LONDE. 1. Aug. 1679.
TITUS OATES OP VOLLE BLYCKINGHE
OVERWONNEN VAN VALSCHE GHETUYGHEN
TITUS OATES
TITUS OATES WORT OP DEFERENTE RYSEN VREESELYCK GEGEESELT OM VELE VALSCHE GETUYGEN GEDAEN TEGEN DESE SEVEN BOVEN STAENDE PATERS DER SOCIETEYT IESV. EN ANDERE CATHOLIICKEN TOT LONDEN DEN. 26 MEY 1685.

When James became King it was inevitable that Titus Oates would be brought to account. He was sentenced to be pilloried in front of the Royal Exchange, and to a sentence of whipping which would have killed most other men. This Dutch print shows him in the stocks surrounded by seven of the men he had sent to their deaths through his lies and perjured evidence.

The King hated the Puritan sects with a manifold hatred, theological and political, hereditary and personal. The fiery persecution, which had raged when he ruled Scotland as vicegerent, waxed hotter than ever from the day on which he became sovereign. Those shires in which the Covenanters were most numerous were given up to the license of the army. With the army was mingled a militia, composed of the most violent and profligate of those who called themselves Episcopalians. Preeminent among the bands which oppressed and wasted these unhappy districts were the dragoons commanded by John Graham of Claverhouse, a soldier of distinguished courage and professional skill, but rapacious and profane, of violent temper and obdurate heart.

In England the King's authority, though great, was circumscribed by ancient and noble laws which even the Tories would not patiently have seen him infringe. Yet even in England he continued to persecute the Puritans as far as his power extended, till events which will hereafter be related induced him to form the design of uniting Puritans and Papists in a coalition for the humiliation and spoliation of the Established Church.

And now the time had arrived when the English Parliament was to meet. On the 19th of May the session was opened. The benches of the Commons presented a singular spectacle. That great party, which, in the last three Parliaments, had been predominant, had now dwindled to a pitiable minority, and was indeed little more than a fifteenth part of the House. Of the five hundred and thirteen knights and burgesses only a hundred and thirty five had ever sate in that place before.

On the 22nd of May the Commons were summoned to the bar of the Lords; and the King, seated on his throne, made a speech to both Houses. He declared himself resolved to maintain the established government in Church and State. But he weakened the effect of this declaration by addressing an extraordinary admonition to the Commons. He was apprehensive, he said, that they might be inclined to dole out money to him, from time to time, in the hope that they should thus force him to call them frequently together. But he must warn them that he was not to be so dealt with, and that, if they wished him to meet them often, they must use him well. As it was evident that without money the government could not be carried on, these expressions plainly implied that, if they did not give him as much money as he wished, he would take it. Strange to say, this harangue was received with loud cheers by the Tory gentlemen at the bar. The Commons returned to their own chamber, went into committee without delay, and voted to the King, for life, the whole revenue enjoyed by his brother.

Monmouth's Rebellion

Towards the close of the reign of Charles II, some Whigs who had been deeply implicated in the plot so fatal to their party, and who knew themselves to be marked out for destruction, had sought an asylum in the Low Countries. One of the most conspicuous among them was Ford Grey, Lord Grey of Wark. He had been a zealous Exclusionist, had concurred in the design of insurrection, and had been committed to the Tower, but had succeeded in making his keepers drunk, and in effecting his escape to the Continent. One part of his character deserves notice. It was admitted that everywhere, except on the field of battle, he showed a high degree of courage.

James Scott, Duke of Monmouth was Charles II's illegitimate eldest child and favourite. As a Protestant he was also popular with the people. In exile at the Hague at the time of his father's death, he was unwisely persuaded to make a bid for the Crown. Portrait after Wissing.

In this respect he differed widely from his friend the Duke of Monmouth. Ardent and intrepid on the field of battle, Monmouth was everywhere else effeminate and irresolute. After witnessing the ruin of the party of which he had been the nominal head, he had retired to Holland. The Prince and Princess of Orange had received him most hospitably; for they hoped that, by treating him with kindness, they should establish a claim to the gratitude of his father. The duke had been encouraged to expect that, in a very short time, if he gave no new cause of displeasure, he would be recalled to his native land, and restored to all his high honours and commands. Animated by such expectations, he had carefully avoided all that could give offence in the quarter to which he looked for protection. He saw little of any Whigs, and nothing of those violent men who had been concerned in the worst part of the Whig plot. He was therefore loudly accused, by his old associates, of fickleness and ingratitude.

By none of the exiles was this accusation urged with more vehemence and bitterness than by Robert Ferguson. Violent, malignant, regardless of truth, delighting in intrigue, in tumult, in mischief for its own sake, Ferguson had toiled during many years in the darkest mines of faction. His broad Scotch accent, his tall and lean figure, his lantern jaws, his cheeks inflamed by an eruption, his shoulders deformed by a stoop, and his gait distinguished from that of other men by a peculiar shuffle, made him remarkable wherever he appeared. He had been deeply engaged in the Rye House Plot. There is, indeed, reason to believe that he was the original author of those sanguinary schemes which brought so much discredit on the whole Whig party. When the conspiracy was detected, he escaped to the Continent. As soon as he was in the Low Countries he began to form new projects against the English government, and found among his fellow emigrants men ready to listen to his evil counsels. Monmouth, however, stood obstinately aloof; and, without the help of Monmouth's immense popularity, it was impossible to effect anything.

The unexpected demise of the Crown changed the whole aspect of affairs. Any hope which the proscribed Whigs might have cherished of returning peaceably to their native land was extinguished. Ferguson was in his element. He no longer despaired of being able to seduce Monmouth, who was overwhelmed with misery by the tidings of his father's death and his uncle's accession. During the night which followed the arrival of the news, those who lodged near him could distinctly hear his sobs and his piercing cries. He quitted the Hague the next day, having solemnly pledged his word, both to the Prince and to the Princess of Orange, not to attempt anything against the government of England. He retired to Brussels accompanied by Henrietta Wentworth, Baroness Wentworth of Nettlestede, a damsel of high rank and ample fortune, who loved him passionately, and whom he believed to be his wife in the sight of heaven. Under the soothing influence of female friendship, his lacerated mind healed fast. He seemed to have found happiness in obscurity and repose.

But he was not suffered to remain quiet. Ferguson employed all his powers of temptation. Grey, who was ready for any undertaking, however desperate, lent his aid. No art was spared which could draw Monmouth from retreat; and he was little in the habit of resisting skilful importunity. It is said, too, that he was induced to quit his retirement by the same powerful influence which had made that retirement delightful. Lady Wentworth wished to see him a King.

Duke of Monmouth.

By the English exiles he was joyfully welcomed, and unanimously acknowledged as their head. His soft mind, as usual, took an impress from the society which surrounded him. Ambitious hopes, which had seemed to be extinguished, revived in his bosom. Encouraging messages reached him in quick succession from London. He was assured that the violence and injustice with which the elections had been carried on had driven the nation mad, and that all the great lords who had supported the Exclusion Bill were impatient to rally round him. He consequently became eager for the enterprise from which a few weeks before he had shrunk. The exiles were able to raise, partly from their own resources and partly from the contributions of well wishers in Holland, a sum sufficient for the expedition. Arms, ammunition, and provisions were bought, and several ships which lay at Amsterdam were freighted.

On the morning of the 11th of June, a large ship named the Helderenbergh, accompanied by two smaller vessels, appeared off the port of Lyme. The appearance of the three ships, foreign built and without colours, perplexed the inhabitants. At length seven boats put off from the largest of the strange vessels, and rowed to the shore. From these boats landed about eighty men, well armed and appointed. Among them were Monmouth, Grey, Ferguson, and Anthony Buyse, an officer who had been in the service of the Elector of Brandenburg.

Monmouth commanded silence, kneeled down on the shore, thanked God for having preserved the friends of liberty and pure religion from the perils of the sea, and implored the divine blessing on what was yet to be done by land. He then drew his sword and led his men over the cliffs into the town.

As soon as it was known under what leader and for what purpose the expedition came, the enthusiasm of the populace burst through all restraints. The little town was in an uproar with men running to and fro, and shouting 'A Monmouth! a Monmouth! the Protestant religion!' Meanwhile the ensign of the adventurers, a blue flag, was set up in the market place; and a declaration setting forth the objects of the expedition was read from the Cross.

This declaration, the masterpiece of Ferguson's genius, was a libel of the lowest class, both in sentiment and language. It contained undoubtedly many just charges against the government. But the paper contained other charges of which the whole disgrace falls on those who made them. The Duke of York, it was positively affirmed, had burned down London, had strangled Godfrey, had cut the throat of Essex, and had poisoned the late King. On account of those villainous and unnatural crimes, James was declared a mortal and bloody enemy, a tyrant, a murderer, and an usurper. The sword should not be sheathed till he had been brought to condign punishment as a traitor. Monmouth declared that he could prove himself to have been born in lawful wedlock, and to be, by right of blood, King of England, but that, for the present, he desired to be considered only as the Captain General of the English Protestants who were in arms against tyranny and Popery.

Disgraceful as this manifesto was, it was not unskilfully framed for the purpose of stimulating the passions of the vulgar. The great mass of the population abhorred Popery and adored Monmouth. The turn of fortune which had alienated the gentry from his cause had produced no effect on the common people. To them he was still the good duke, the Protestant duke, the rightful heir whom a vile conspiracy kept out of his own. They came to his standard in crowds. Before he had been twenty-four hours on English ground he was at the head of fifteen hundred men.

The news of the insurrection spread fast. On the evening on which the duke landed, Gregory Alford, Mayor of Lyme, a zealous Tory, took horse for the west. Late at night he stopped at Honiton, and thence despatched a few hurried lines to London with the ill tidings. He then pushed on to Exeter, where he found Christopher Monk, Duke of Albermarle. This nobleman, the son and heir of George Monk, the restorer of the Stuarts, was Lord Lieutenant of Devonshire, and was then holding a muster of militia. Four thousand men of the trainbands were actually assembled under his command. He seems to have thought that, with this force, he should be able at once to crush the rebellion. He therefore marched towards Lyme.

But when, on the afternoon of Monday the 15th of June, he reached Axminster, he found the insurgents drawn up there to encounter him. They presented a resolute front. Albemarle, however, was less alarmed by the preparations of the enemy than by the spirit which appeared in his own ranks. Such was Monmouth's popularity among the common people of Devonshire that, if once the trainbands had caught sight of his well known face and figure, they would probably have gone over to him in a body.

Albermarle, therefore, thought it advisable to retreat. The retreat soon became a rout. Had Monmouth urged the pursuit with vigour, he would probably have taken Exeter without a blow. But he thought it desirable that his recruits should be better trained before they were employed in any hazardous service. He therefore marched towards Taunton, where he arrived on the 18th of June, exactly a week after his landing.

At five in the morning of Saturday the 13th of June, the King had received the letter which the Mayor of Lyme had despatched from Honiton. The Privy Council was instantly called together. Orders were given that the strength of every company of infantry and of every troop of cavalry should be increased. Commissions were issued for the levying of new regiments. The Commons ordered a bill to be brought in for attainting Monmouth of high treason. At the next meeting of the Houses they passed the bill of attainder through all its stages. That bill received the royal assent on the same day; and a reward of five thousand pounds was promised for the apprehension of Monmouth.

While the Parliament was devising sharp laws against Monmouth and his partisans, he found at Taunton a reception which might well encourage him to hope that his enterprise would have a prosperous issue. Every door and window was adorned with wreaths of flowers. No man appeared in the streets without wearing in his hat a green bough, the badge of the popular cause. Damsels of the best families in the town wove colours for the insurgents. But, while Monmouth enjoyed the applause of the multitude, he could not but perceive that the higher classes were, with scarcely an exception, hostile to his undertaking, and that no rising had taken place except in the counties where he had himself appeared. Day labourers, small farmers, shopkeepers, apprentices, dissenting preachers, had flocked to the rebel camp: but not a single peer, baronet, or knight, not a single member of the House of Commons, had joined the invaders. Ferguson, Monmouth's evil angel, had a suggestion ready. The duke had put himself into a false position by declining the royal title. Had he declared himself sovereign of England, his cause would have worn a show of legality. At present it was impossible to reconcile his declaration with the principles of the constitution. None could wonder that men of high rank stood aloof from an enterprise which threatened with destruction that system in the permanence of which they were deeply interested. If the duke would assert his legitimacy and assume the Crown, he would at once remove this objection. The question would cease to be a question between the old constitution and a new constitution. It would be merely a question of hereditary right between two princes.

On such grounds as these Ferguson earnestly pressed the duke to proclaim himself King. Monmouth saw no other way of obtaining the support of any portion of the aristocracy. On the morning of the 20th of June he was proclaimed in the market place of Taunton. His followers repeated his new title with affectionate delight. But, as some confusion might have arisen if he had been called King James II, they commonly used the strange appellation of King Monmouth.

The class which he had hoped to conciliate still stood aloof. The reasons which prevented the great Whig lords and gentlemen from recognising him as their King were at least as strong as those which had prevented them from rallying round him as their captain general. That Monmouth was legitimate, nay, that he thought himself legitimate, intelligent men could not believe. He was therefore not merely an usurper, but an usurper of the worst sort, an imposter. The opinion of almost all the leading Whigs seems to have been that his enterprise could not fail to end in some great disaster to the nation, but that, on the whole, his defeat would be a less disaster than his victory.

On the day following that on which Monmouth had assumed the regal title he marched from Taunton to Bridgewater, one of the few towns which still had some Whig magistrates. He took up his residence in the castle, a building which had been honoured by several royal visits. In the castle field his army was encamped. It now consisted of about six thousand men, and might easily have been increased to double the number, but for the want of arms.

All this time the forces of the government were fast assembling. On the west of the rebel army, Albemarle still kept together a large body of Devonshire militia. On the east, the trainbands of Wiltshire had mustered under the command of Thomas Herbert, Earl of Pembroke. The militia of Sussex began to march westward, under the command of Richard, Lord Lumley. But it was chiefly on the regular troops that the King relied. Churchill had been sent westward with the Blues; and Feversham was following with all the forces that could be spared from the neighbourhood of London.

Monmouth advanced from Bridgewater, harassed through the whole march by Churchill, who appears to have done all that, with a handful of men, it was possible for a brave and skilful officer to effect. The rebel army, much annoyed both by the enemy and by a heavy fall of rain, halted in the evening of the 22nd of June at Glastonbury. From Glastonbury the duke marched to Wells, and from Wells to Shepton Mallet.

Hitherto he seems to have wandered from place to place with no other object than that of collecting troops. It was now necessary for him to form some plan of military operations. Several schemes were discussed. It was suggested that Monmouth might hasten to Gloucester, might cross the

Severn there, might break down the bridge behind him, and, with his right flank protected by the river, might march through Worcestershire into Shropshire and Cheshire. On full consideration, however, it appeared that this plan was impracticable. The rebels were exhausted by toiling, day after day, through deep mud under heavy rain. They could not hope to reach Gloucester without being overtaken by the main body of the royal troops and forced to a general action under every disadvantage.

Then it was proposed to enter Wiltshire. Persons who professed to know that county well assured the duke that he would be joined there by such strong reinforcements as would make it safe for him to give battle.

He took this advice, and turned towards Wiltshire. He first summoned Bath. But Bath was strongly garrisoned for the King; and Feversham was fast approaching. The rebels, therefore, made no attempt on the walls, but hastened to Philip's Norton, where they halted on the evening of the 26th of June.

Feversham followed them thither. Early on the morning of the 27th they were alarmed by tidings that he was close at hand. They got into order, and lined the hedges leading to the town.

The advanced guard of the royal army soon appeared. It consisted of about five hundred men, commanded by the Duke of Grafton. He soon found himself in a deep lane with fences on both sides, from which a galling fire of musketry was kept up. Still he pushed boldly on till he came to the entrance of Philip's Norton. There his way was crossed by a barricade, from which a third fire met him full in front. His men now lost heart, and made the best of their way back. Before they got out of the lane more than a hundred of them had been killed or wounded.

The advanced guard, thus repulsed, fell back on the main body of the royal forces. The two armies were now face to face. Neither side was impatient to come to action. Feversham did not wish to fight till his artillery came up, and fell back to Bradford. Monmouth, as soon as the night closed in, quitted his position, marched southward, and by daybreak arrived at Frome.

The rebel army was in evil case. The march of the preceding night had been wearisome. The rain had fallen in torrents; and the roads had become mere quagmires. It was not now easy to form any plan for a campaign. At this juncture a report reached the camp that the rustics of the marshes near Axbridge had risen in defence of the Protestant religion, had armed themselves with flails, bludgeons, and pitchforks, and were assembling by thousands at Bridgewater. Monmouth determined to return thither, and to strengthen himself with these new allies.

On Thursday, the 2nd of July, Monmouth again entered Bridgewater. The reinforcement which he found there was inconsiderable. The royal army was close upon him. At one moment he thought of fortifying the town; then his mind recurred to the plan of marching into Cheshire. While he was thus wavering between projects equally hopeless, the King's forces came in sight. They consisted of about two thousand five hundred regular troops, and fifteen hundred of the Wiltshire militia. Early on the morning of Sunday, the 5th of July, they left Somerton, and pitched their tents that day about three miles from Bridgewater, on the plain of Sedgemoor.

The steeple of the parish church of Bridgewater is said to be the loftiest in Somersetshire, and commands a wide view over the surrounding country. Monmouth, accompanied by some of his officers, went up to the top of the square tower from which the spire ascends, and observed through a telescope the position of the enemy. Beneath him lay a flat expanse, now rich with cornfields and apple trees, but then, as its name imports, a dreary morass. When Monmouth looked upon Sedgemoor, it had been partially reclaimed by art, and was intersected by many deep and wide trenches which, in that country, are called rhines. In the midst of the moor rose a few villages, of which the names seem to indicate that they once were surrounded by waves. In one of these villages, called Weston Zoyland, the royal cavalry lay; and Feversham had fixed his head quarters there. At a greater distance from Bridgewater, in the village of Middlezoy and its neighbourhood, the Wiltshire militia were quartered. On the open moor, not far from Chedzoy, were encamped several battalions of regular infantry. Monmouth looked gloomily on them. 'I know those men,' he said; 'they will fight. If I had but them, all would go well.'

Yet the aspect of the enemy was not altogether discouraging. The three divisions of the royal army lay apart from one another. There was an appearance of negligence and of relaxed discipline in all their movements. The incapacity of Feversham, who commanded in chief, was notorious. Monmouth conceived that a night attack might be attended with success. He resolved to run the hazard; and preparations were instantly made.

The night was not ill suited for such an enterprise. The marsh fog lay so thick on Sedgemoor that no object could be discerned there at the distance of fifty paces.

The clock struck eleven; and the duke with his body guard rode out of the castle. His army marched by a circuitous path, near six miles in length, towards the royal encampments on Sedgemoor. The foot were led by Monmouth himself. The horse were confided to Grey. Orders were given that strict silence should be preserved, that no drum should be beaten, and no shot fired.

At about one in the morning of Monday the 6th of July, the rebels were on the open moor. But between them and the enemy lay three broad rhines filled with water and soft mud. Two of these, called the Black Ditch and the Langmoor Rhine, Monmouth knew that he must pass. But, strange to say, the existence of a trench, called the Bussex Rhine, which immediately covered the royal encampment, had not been mentioned to him by any of his scouts.

The wains which carried the ammunition remained at the entrance of the moor. The horse and foot, in a long narrow column, passed the Black Ditch by a causeway. There was a similar causeway across the Langmoor Rhine: but the guide, in the fog, missed his way. At length the passage was effected: but, in the confusion, a pistol went off. Some men of the Horse Guards, who were on watch, heard the report, and perceived that a great multitude was advancing through the mist. They fired their carbines, and galloped off in different directions to give the alarm. It was time; for Monmouth was already drawing up his army for action. He ordered Grey to lead the way with the cavalry, and followed himself at the head of the infantry. Grey pushed on till his progress was unexpectedly arrested by the Bussex Rhine. On the opposite side of the ditch the King's foot were hastily forming in order of battle.

'For whom are you?' called out an officer of the Foot Guards. 'For the King,' replied a voice from the ranks of the rebel cavalry. 'For which King?'

The battle of Sedgmoor was fought in early morning darkness in an area of swamp and marshland. The Somersetshire peasantry who had joined Monmouth were no match for the King's troops under Feversham. The ammunition waggoners panicked and fled; and the mounted hacks were cut to pieces by the Life Guards and Blues. This illustration of the battle is from a Dutch book of 1690.

was then demanded. The answer was a shout of 'King Monmouth', mingled with the war cry, which forty years before had been inscribed on the colours of the parliamentary regiments, 'God with us.' The royal troops instantly fired such a volley of musketry as sent the rebel horse flying in all directions. The world agreed to ascribe this ignominious rout to Grey's pusillanimity. Yet it is by no means clear that Churchill would have succeeded better at the head of men who had never before handled arms on horseback, and whose horses were unused, not only to stand fire, but to obey the rein.

A few minutes after the duke's horse had dispersed themselves over the moor, his infantry came up running fast. Monmouth was startled by finding that a broad and profound trench lay between him and the camp which he had hoped to surprise. The insurgents halted on the edge of the rhine, and fired. Part of the royal infantry on the opposite bank returned the fire. During three-quarters of an hour the roar of the musketry was incessant. The Somersetshire peasants behaved themselves as if they had been veteran soldiers, save only that they levelled their pieces too high.

But now the other divisions of the royal army were in motion. The Life Guards and Blues came pricking fast from Weston Zoyland, and scattered in an instant some of Grey's horse, who had attempted to rally. The fugitives spread a panic among their comrades in the rear, who had charge of the ammunition. The waggoners drove off at full speed, and never stopped till they were many miles from the field of battle.

A pictorial description of the Monmouth Rebellion. From a poetical broadside entitled: A Description of the Late Rebellion in the West.

Monmouth was too well acquainted with military affairs not to know that all was over. His men had lost the advantage which surprise and darkness had given them. The King's forces were now united and in good order. The day was about to break. The event of a conflict on an open plain, by broad sunlight, could not be doubtful. Monmouth saw that if he tarried the royal cavalry would soon intercept his retreat. He mounted and rode from the field.

His foot, though deserted, made a gallant stand. But the struggle of the hardy rustics could not last. Their powder and ball were spent. Cries were heard of 'Ammunition! For God's sake ammunition!' But no ammunition was at hand. And now the King's artillery came up. The cannon brought the engagement to a speedy close. The pikes of the rebel battalions began to shake: the ranks broke; the King's cavalry charged again, and bore down everything before them; the King's infantry came pouring across the ditch. The rout was in a few minutes complete. So ended the last fight, deserving the name of battle, that has been fought on English ground.

It was four o'clock: the sun was rising; and the routed army came pouring into the streets of Bridgewater. The uproar, the blood, the gashes, the ghastly figures which sank down and never rose again, spread horror and dismay through the town. The pursuers, too, were close behind. During that day the conquerors continued to chase the fugitives. Before evening five hundred prisoners had been crowded into the parish church of Weston Zoyland. A considerable number were immediately selected for execution. The next day a long line of gibbets appeared on the road leading from Bridgewater to Weston Zoyland. On each gibbet a prisoner was suspended. Four of the sufferers were left to rot in irons.

Meanwhile Monmouth, accompanied by Grey, by Buyse, and by a few other friends, was flying from the field of battle. Before six o'clock he was twenty miles from Sedgemoor. He determined to push for Hampshire, in the hope that he might lurk in the cabins of deerstealers among the oaks of the New Forest, till means of conveyance to the Continent could be procured. He therefore, with Grey and the German, turned to the south east.

They rode on all day, shunning towns and villages. At length, on Cranbourne Chase, the strength of the horses failed. They were turned loose. Monmouth and his friends procured rustic attire, disguised themselves, and proceeded on foot towards the New Forest. They passed the night in the open air: but before morning they were surrounded on every side by toils. Lord Lumley, who lay at Ringwood with a strong body of the Sussex militia, had sent forth parties in every direction. Sir William Portman, with the Somerset militia, had formed a chain of posts from the sea to the northern extremity of Dorset. At five in the morning of the seventh, Grey, who had wandered from his friends, was seized by two of the Sussex scouts. It could hardly be doubted that the chief rebel was not far off. The pursuers redoubled their vigilance and activity. Portman came with a strong body of horse and foot to assist in the search. Attention was soon drawn to a place well fitted to shelter fugitives. It was an extensive tract of land, separated by an enclosure from the open country, and divided by numerous hedges into small fields. In some of these fields the rye, the pease, and the oats were high enough to conceal a man. Others were overgrown with fern and brambles. A poor woman reported that she had seen two strangers lurking in this covert. The outer fence was strictly guarded: the space within was examined with indefatigable diligence; and several dogs of quick scent were turned out among the bushes. The day closed before the work could be completed; but careful watch was kept all night. Thirty times the fugitives ventured to look through the outer hedge; but everywhere they found a sentinel on the alert: once they were seen and fired at; they then separated and concealed themselves in different hiding places.

At sunrise the next morning the search recommenced, and Buyse was found. The corn and copsewood were now beaten with more care than ever. At length a gaunt figure was discovered hidden in a ditch. The pursuers sprang on their prey. Some of them were about to fire: but Portman forbade all violence. The prisoner's dress was that of a shepherd; his beard, prematurely grey, was of several days' growth. He trembled greatly, and was unable to speak. Even those who had often seen him were at first in doubt whether this were truly the brilliant and graceful Monmouth. His pockets were searched by Portman, and in them were found, among some raw pease gathered in the rage of hunger, a watch, a purse of gold, a small treatise on fortification, an album filled with songs, receipts, prayers, and charms, and the George with which, many years before, King Charles II had decorated his favourite son. Messengers were instantly despatched to Whitehall with the good news, and with the George as a token that the news was true. The prisoner was conveyed under a strong guard to Ringwood.

And all was lost; and nothing remained but that he should prepare to meet death as became one who had thought himself not unworthy to wear the Crown of William the Conqueror and of Richard the Lionhearted, of the hero of Cressy and of the hero of Agincourt. But the fortitude of Monmouth was not that highest sort of fortitude which is derived from reflection and from selfrespect. His courage rose and fell with his animal spirits. The spoiled darling of the court and of the populace, accustomed to be loved and worshipped wherever he appeared, was now surrounded by stern gaolers in whose eyes he read his doom. Life seemed worth purchasing by any humiliation; nor could his mind perceive that humiliation must degrade, but could not save him.

As soon as he reached Ringwood he wrote to the King. He professed in vehement terms his remorse for his treason, and begged that he might be admitted to the royal presence. On the following day he despatched letters, imploring the Queen Dowager and the Lord Treasurer to intercede in his behalf.

Monmouth and Grey remained at Ringwood two days. They were then carried up to London, under the guard of a large body of regular troops and militia. The march lasted three days, and terminated at Vauxhall, where a regiment, commanded by George Legge, Lord Dartmouth, was in readiness to receive the prisoners. They were put on board of a State barge, and carried down the river to Whitehall Stairs.

The King cannot be blamed for determining that Monmouth should suffer death. But to see him and not to spare him was an outrage on humanity and decency. This outrage the King resolved to commit. The arms of the prisoner were bound behind him with a silken cord; and, thus secured, he was ushered into the presence of the implacable kinsman whom he had wronged.

Then Monmouth threw himself on the ground, and crawled to the King's feet. He wept. He tried to embrace his uncle's knees with his pinioned arms. He begged for life, only life, life at any price. James gravely replied that he was sorry for the misery which the prisoner had brought on himself, but that the case was not one for lenity. A declaration, filled with atrocious calumnies, had been put forth. The regal title had been assumed. For treasons so aggravated there could be no pardon on this side of the grave. The poor terrified duke vowed that he had never wished to take the Crown, but had been led into that fatal error by others. As to the declaration, he had signed it without looking at it: it was all the work of Ferguson, that bloody villain Ferguson. 'Do you expect me to believe', said James, 'that you set your hand to a paper of such moment without knowing what it contained?' One depth of infamy only remained; and even to that the prisoner descended. He was pre-eminently the champion of the Protestant religion: yet he was not ashamed to hint that he was inclined to be reconciled to the Church of Rome. The King eagerly offered him spiritual assistance, but said nothing of pardon or respite. 'Is there no hope?' asked Monmouth. James turned away in silence. Then Monmouth strove to rally his courage, rose from his knees, and retired with a firmness which he had not shown since his overthrow.

Grey was introduced next. He frankly owned himself guilty, made no excuses, and did not once stoop to ask his life. Both the prisoners were sent to the Tower by water. That same evening two prelates, Turner, Bishop of Ely, and Ken, Bishop of Bath and Wells, arrived at the Tower with a solemn message from the King. It was Monday night. On Wednesday morning Monmouth was to die.

The hour drew near: all hope was over; and Monmouth had passed from pusillanimous fear to the apathy of despair. His children were brought to

Monmouth's declaration, setting forth the objects of his expedition. Macaulay describes it as 'a libel of the lowest class', dictated by Ferguson, Monmouth's evil genius. It undoubtedly spelled the latter's doom when the revolt failed.

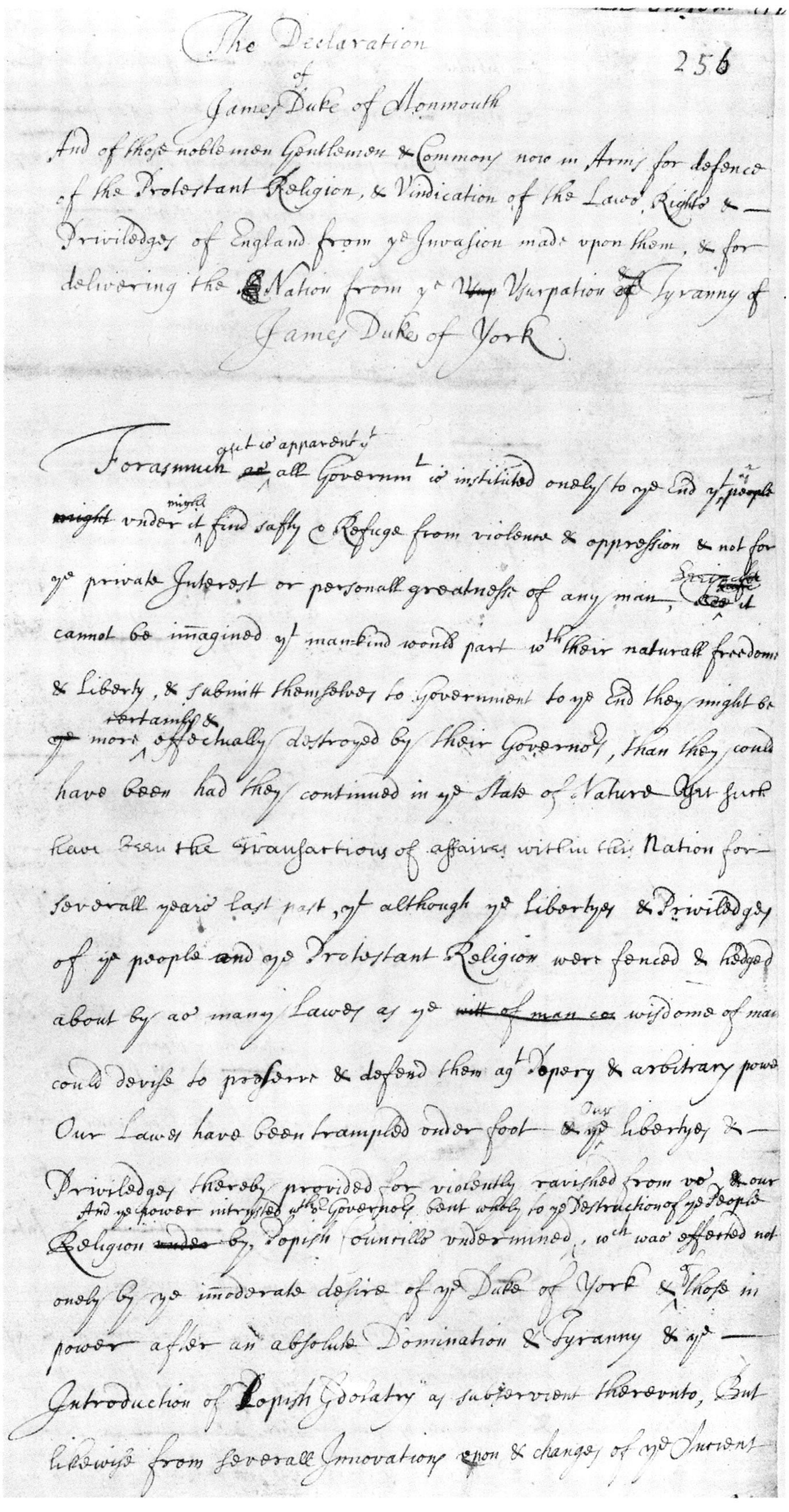

The Declaration
of
James Duke of Monmouth
And of those noblemen Gentlemen & Commons now in Arms for defence of the Protestant Religion, & Vindication of the Laws, Rights & Priviledges of England from ye Invasion made upon them, & for delivering the Nation from ye Usurpation & Tyranny of
James Duke of York

256

Forasmuch as yet it is apparent yt all Governmt is instituted onely to ye End yt ye people might under it find safty & Refuge from violence & oppression & not for ye private Interest or personall greatness of any man, & yt it cannot be imagined yt mankind would part wth their naturall freedom & Liberty, & submitt themselves to Government to ye End they might be ye more certainly & effectually destroyed by their Governors, than they could have been had they continued in ye State of Nature. And such have been the Transactions of affaires within this Nation for severall years last past, yt although ye libertyes & Priviledges of ye people and ye Protestant Religion were fenced & hedged about by as many Lawes as ye wit of man or wisdome of man could devise to preserve & defend them agt Popery & arbitrary power Our Lawes have been trampled under foot & our libertyes & Priviledges thereby provided for violently ravished from us, & our Religion by Popish Councills undermined, And ye power intrusted wth ye Governors bent wholy to ye Destruction of ye People, wch was effected not onely by ye imoderate desire of ye Duke of York & those in power after an absolute Domination & Tyranny & ye Introduction of Popish Idolatry as subservient thereunto, But likewise from severall Innovations upon & changes of ye Ancient

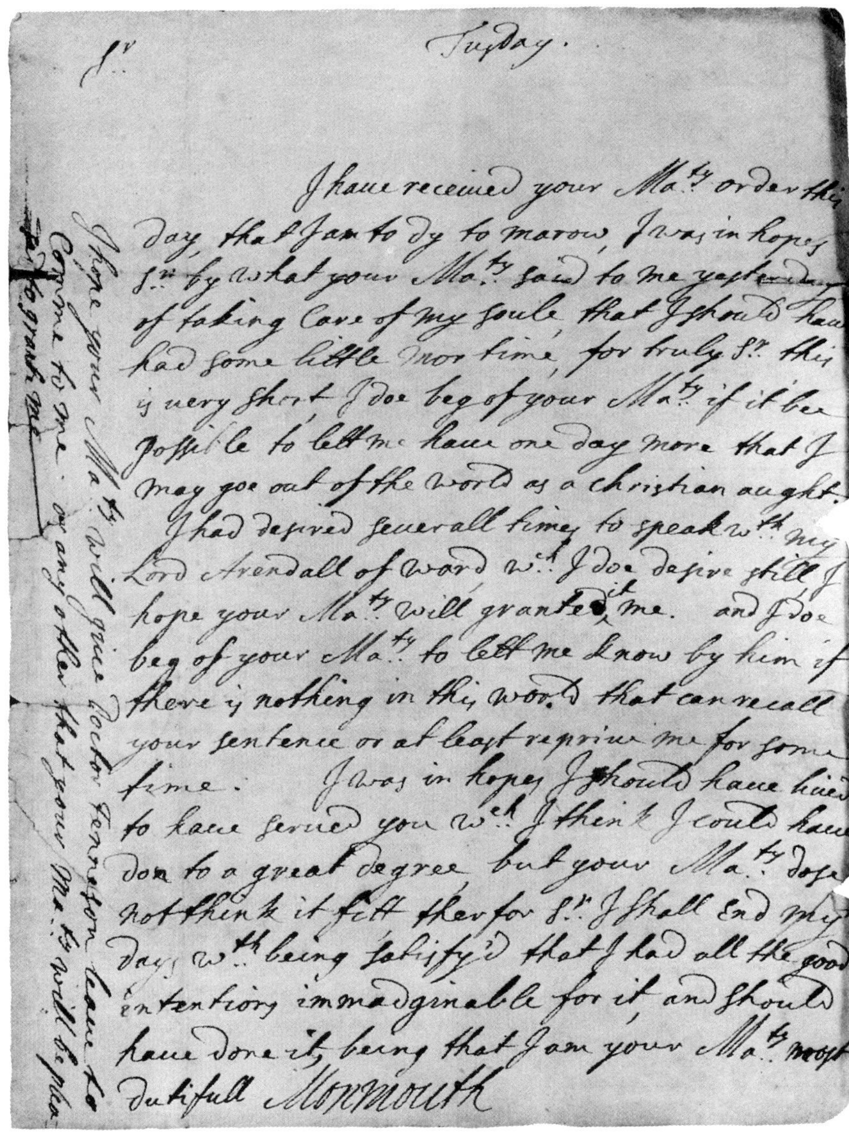

Sr Tusday.

I have received your Maty order this day that I am to dy to marow, I was in hopes Sr by what your Maty said to me yesterday of taking Care of my soule that I should have had some little mor time, for truly Sr this is very short I doe beg of your Maty if it bee possible to lett me have one day more that I may goe out of the world as a christian aught.
I had desired severall times to speak wth my Lord Arendall of word wch I doe desire still I hope your Maty will grante it me. and I doe beg of your Maty to lett me know by him if there is nothing in this world that can recall your sentence or at least reprive me for some time. I was in hopes I should have lived to have served you wch I think I could have don to a great degree but your Maty dose not think it fitt therfor Sr I shall End my days wth being satisfy'd that I had all the good intentions immaginable for it and should have done it, being that I am your Maty most dutifull Monmouth

I hope your Maty will give Doctor Tenison leave to come to me or any other that your Maty will be pleased to grant me

Monmouth's letter to James II on the day before his execution pleading for his life.

his room that he might take leave of them, and were followed by his wife. He spoke to her kindly, but without emotion. Though she was a woman of great strength of mind, and had little cause to love him, her misery was such that none of the bystanders could refrain from weeping. He alone was unmoved.

It was ten o'clock. The coach of the Lieutenant of the Tower was ready. Monmouth requested his spiritual advisers to accompany him to the place of execution. As he passed along the ranks of the guards he saluted them with a smile; and he mounted the scaffold with a firm tread. Tower Hill was covered up to the chimney tops with an innumerable multitude of gazers, who, in awful silence, listened for the last accents of the darling of the people. 'I shall say little', he began. 'I come here, not to speak, but to die. I die a Protestant of the Church of England.' The bishops interrupted him, and told him that, unless he acknowledged resistance to be sinful, he was no member of their Church. He went on to speak of his Henrietta. He loved her to the last, and he could not die without giving utterance to his feelings.

The bishops again interfered, and begged him not to use such language. Their general arguments against resistance had no effect on him. But when they reminded him of the ruin which he had brought on his brave and loving followers, of the souls which had been sent unprepared to the great account, he was touched, and said, in a softened voice, 'I do own that. I am sorry that it ever happened.'

He then accosted John Ketch the executioner. 'Here', said the duke, 'are six guineas for you. Do not hack me as you did my Lord Russell. I have heard that you struck him three or four times. My servant will give you some more gold if you do the work well.' He then undressed, felt the edge of the axe, expressed some fear that it was not sharp enough, and laid his head on the block.

The hangman addressed himself to his office. But he had been disconcerted by what the duke had said. The first blow inflicted only a slight wound. The duke struggled, rose from the block, and looked reproachfully at the executioner. The head sank down once more. The stroke was repeated again and again; but still the neck was not severed, and the body continued to move. Yells of rage and horror rose from the crowd. Ketch flung down the axe with a curse. 'I cannot do it,' he said; 'my heart fails me.' 'Take up the axe, man,' cried the sheriff. At length the axe was taken up. Two more blows extinguished the last remains of life; but a knife was used to separate the head from the shoulders. The crowd was wrought up to such an ecstasy of rage that the executioner was in danger of being torn in pieces, and was conveyed away under a strong guard.

In the meantime many handkerchiefs were dipped in the duke's blood; for by a large part of the multitude he was regarded as a martyr who had died for the Protestant religion. The head and body were placed in a coffin covered with black velvet, and were laid privately under the communion table of Saint Peter's Chapel in the Tower.

The Bloody Assizes: James at the Height of Power

The gaols of Somersetshire and Dorsetshire were filled with thousands of captives: but a rapid and effectual gaol delivery was at hand. Early in September, Jeffreys, accompanied by four other judges, set out on that circuit of which the memory will last as long as our race and language. His ferocious temper needed no spur; yet a spur was applied. The health and spirits of the Lord Keeper had given way. He breathed his last a few days after the judges set out for the west. It was immediately notified to Jeffreys that he might expect the Great Seal as the reward of faithful and vigorous service.

He reached Dorchester, the principal town of the county in which Monmouth had landed; and the judicial massacre began. The court was hung, by order of the Chief Justice, with scarlet. More than three hundred prisoners were to be tried. Jeffreys let it be understood that the only chance of obtaining pardon or respite was to plead guilty. Twenty-nine persons, who put themselves on their country and were convicted, were ordered to be tied up without delay. The remaining prisoners pleaded guilty by scores. Two hundred and ninety-two received sentence of death. The whole number hanged in Dorsetshire amounted to seventy-four.

From Dorchester Jeffreys proceeded to Exeter. Here, comparatively few persons were capitally punished. Somersetshire, the chief seat of the rebellion, had been reserved for the last and most fearful vengeance. In this county two hundred and thirty-three prisoners were in a few days hanged, drawn, and quartered. At every spot where two roads met, on every market place, on the green of every large village which had furnished Monmouth with soldiers, ironed corpses clattering in the wind, or heads and quarters stuck on poles, poisoned the air, and made the traveller sick with horror.

The Chief Justice was all himself. He laughed, shouted, joked, and swore in such a way that many thought him drunk from morning to night. But in him it was not easy to distinguish the madness produced by evil passions from the madness produced by brandy.

He boasted that he had hanged more traitors than all his predecessors together since the Conquest. It is certain that the number of persons whom he put to death in one month, and in one shire, very much exceeded the number of all the political offenders who have been put to death in our island since the Revolution. All the executions of 1715 and 1745 added together will appear to have been few indeed when compared to those which disgraced the Bloody Assizes. The number of rebels whom Jeffreys hanged on this circuit was three hundred and twenty.

The number of prisoners whom he transported was eight hundred and forty-one. These men, more wretched than their associates who suffered death, were distributed into gangs, and bestowed on persons who enjoyed favour at court. The conditions of the gift were that the convicts should be carried beyond sea as slaves, that they should not be emancipated for ten years, and that the place of their banishment should be some West Indian island. It appears that more than one fifth of those who were shipped were flung to the sharks before the end of the voyage. The human cargoes were stowed close in the holds of small vessels. They were never suffered to go on deck. In the dungeon below all was darkness, stench, lamentation, disease and death. Of ninety-nine convicts who were carried out in one vessel, twenty-two died before they reached Jamaica.

No English sovereign has ever given stronger proofs of a cruel nature than James II. Yet his cruelty was not more odious than his mercy. While those who ought to have been spared were slaughtered by hundreds, the few who might with propriety have been left to the utmost rigour of the law were spared. This eccentric clemency may be distinctly traced in every case either to a sordid or to a malignant motive, either to thirst for money or to thirst for blood.

In the case of Grey there was no mitigating circumstance. The rank which he had inherited in the state, and the high command which he had borne in the rebel army, would have pointed him out to a just government as a much fitter object of punishment than any of the hundreds of ignorant peasants whose skulls and quarters were exposed in Somersetshire. But Grey's estate was large and was strictly entailed. If he died, his lands at once devolved on the next heir. If he were pardoned, he would be able to pay a large ransom. He was therefore suffered to redeem himself by giving a bond for forty thousand pounds to the Lord Treasurer, and smaller sums to other courtiers.

How Ferguson escaped was, and still is, a mystery. Of all the enemies of the government he was the most deeply criminal. It was reasonable to expect that a strict search would be made for the archtraitor, as he was often called; and such a search a man of so singular an aspect and dialect could scarcely have eluded. It was confidently reported in the coffee houses of

The notorious Chief Justice Jeffreys, the moving spirit of the Bloody Assizes which followed Monmouth's unsuccessful rebellion. Some three hundred of the rebels were hanged, drawn and quartered; and a further thousand were transported. Portrait attributed to W. Claret.

London that Ferguson was taken. The next thing that was heard of him was that he was safe on the Continent. It was strongly suspected that he had been in constant communication with the government against which he was constantly plotting, that he had, while urging his associates to every excess of rashness, sent to Whitehall just so much information about their proceedings as might suffice to save his own neck, and that therefore orders had been given to let him escape.

And now Jeffreys had done his work, and returned to claim his reward. He was a judge after his master's own heart. James had watched the circuit with interest and delight. At Windsor the Great Seal of England was put into the hands of Jeffreys, and in the next *London Gazette* it was solemnly notified that this honour was the reward of many eminent and faithful services which he had rendered to the Crown.

James was now at the height of power and prosperity. The Whig party seemed extinct. The Parliament was devoted to the King. Eleven-twelfths of the members were either dependents of the court, or zealous Cavaliers from the country. There were few things which such an assembly could pertinaciously refuse to the sovereign; but, happily for the nation, those few things were the very things on which James had set his heart.

One of his objects was to obtain a repeal of the Habeas Corpus Act, which he hated. But the Habeas Corpus Act, though passed during the ascendency of the Whigs, was not more dear to the Whigs than to the Tories. James had yet another design, odious to the party which had set him on the throne and which had upheld him there. He wished to form a great standing army. But the very name of standing army was hateful to the whole nation, and to no part of the nation more hateful than to the Cavalier gentlemen who filled the Lower House.

But both the designs which have been mentioned were subordinate to one great design on which the King's whole soul was bent. His religion was still under proscription. The Test Act excluded from civil and military office all who dissented from the Church of England; and, by a subsequent act, it had been provided that no person should sit in either House of Parliament without solemnly abjuring the doctrine of transubstantiation. That the

Catherine Sedley, who succeeded Arabella Churchill as James's mistress. James seemed to have a predilection for plain women, and his brother Charles observed acidly that he chose ugly women to mortify himself.

King should wish to obtain for the Church to which he belonged a complete toleration was natural and right; nor is there any reason to doubt that, by a little patience, prudence, and justice, such a toleration might have been obtained.

Many members of his Church held commissions in the newly raised regiments. This breach of the law for a time passed uncensured: for men were not disposed to note every irregularity which was committed by a King suddenly called upon to defend his crown and his life against rebels. Yet still James continued to grant commissions to unqualified persons; and speedily it was announced that he was determined to be no longer bound by the Test Act, that he hoped to induce the Parliament to repeal that act, but that, if the Parliament proved refractory, he would not the less have his own way.

Opposition appeared first in the cabinet. Halifax positively refused to promise that he would give his vote in the House of Lords for the repeal either of the Test Act or of the Habeas Corpus Act. The King was peremptory. Halifax was informed that his services were no longer needed, and his name was struck out of the Council Book.

On the 9th of November the Houses met. The Commons were summoned to the bar of the Lords; and the King spoke from the throne. He congratulated his loving subjects on the suppression of the rebellion in the west; but he added that the speed with which that rebellion had risen to a formidable height must convince all men how little dependence could be placed on the militia. He had, therefore, made additions to the regular army. He informed his hearers that he had employed some officers who had not taken the test; but he knew those officers to be fit for public trust. He was determined not to part with servants on whose fidelity he could rely, and whose help he might perhaps soon need.

On the 12th of November the House of Commons resolved itself into a committee on the royal speech. After much debate, it was resolved that a supply should be granted to the Crown; but it was also resolved that a bill should be brought in for making the militia more efficient. This last resolution was tantamount to a declaration against the standing army. Then the expressions which the King had used respecting the test were taken into consideration. It was resolved that an address should be presented to him, reminding him that he could not legally continue to employ officers who refused to qualify, and pressing him to give such directions as might quiet the apprehensions and jealousies of his people.

On the 18th of November the Commons went in procession to Whitehall with the address. The answer of James was a cold and sullen reprimand. He declared himself greatly displeased that the Commons should have profited so little by the admonition which he had given them. 'But,' said he, 'however you may proceed on your part, I will be very steady in all the promises which I have made to you.'

On the following day it became clear that the spirit of opposition had spread from the Commons to the Lords. William Cavendish, Earl of Devonshire, proposed that a day should be fixed for considering the royal speech. Doctor Henry Compton, Bishop of London, spoke strongly for the motion. One of the most remarkable speeches of that day was made by Charles Mordaunt, Viscount Mordaunt, widely renowned, many years later, as Earl of Peterborough. He now addressed the House of Peers, for the first time, with characteristic eloquence, sprightliness, and audacity.

He blamed the Commons for not having taken a bolder line. 'They have been afraid', he said, 'to speak out. They have talked of apprehensions and jealousies. What have apprehension and jealousy to do here? Apprehension and jealousy are the feelings with which we regard future and uncertain evils. The evil which we are considering is neither future nor uncertain. A standing army exists. It is officered by Papists. For what is this force maintained, except for the purpose of subverting our laws, and establishing that arbitrary power which is so justly abhorred by Englishmen?'

The sense of the House was so strongly manifested that, after a closing speech, of great keenness, from Halifax, the courtiers did not venture to divide. An early day was fixed for taking the royal speech into consideration.

On the following morning the King came down, in his robes, to the House of Lords. The Usher of the Black Rod summoned the Commons to the bar; and the Chancellor announced that the Parliament was prorogued.

The prorogation relieved the King from the gentle remonstrances of the Houses: but he had still to listen to remonstrances, similar in effect, though uttered in a tone even more cautious and subdued. Some men who had hitherto served him but too strenuously for their own fame had begun to feel painful misgivings, and occasionally ventured to hint a small part of what they felt. If James could even now be induced to reconsider his course, to let the Houses reassemble, and to comply with their wishes, all might yet be well.

Such were the sentiments of the King's two kinsmen, the Earls of Clarendon and Rochester. The power and favour of these noblemen seemed to be great indeed. The younger brother was Lord Treasurer and prime minister; and the elder, after holding the Privy Seal during some months, had been appointed Lord Lieutenant of Ireland.

But there was at the court a small knot of Roman Catholics who were impatient to climb to the highest honours of the State. One of these was Roger Palmer, Earl of Castelmaine in Ireland, and husband of the Duchess of Cleveland. With him was allied one of the most favoured of his wife's hundred lovers, Henry Jermyn, whom James had lately created a peer by the title of Lord Dover. To the same party belonged an intriguing pushing Irishman named White, who had served the House of Austria as something between an envoy and a spy, and who had been rewarded by that House for his services with the title of Marquess of Albeville.

Soon after the prorogation this reckless faction was strengthened by an important reinforcement. Richard Talbot, Earl of Tyrconnel, arrived at court from Dublin.

Talbot had been introduced to Charles and James when they were exiles in Flanders, as a man fit and ready for the infamous service of assassinating the Protector. He was now no longer young, and was expiating by severe sufferings the dissoluteness of his youth: but age and disease had made no essential change in his character and manners. He still, whenever he opened his mouth, ranted, cursed, and swore with such frantic violence that superficial observers set him down for the wildest of libertines. The multitude was unable to conceive that a man who, even when sober, was more furious and boastful than others when they were drunk, could really be a coldhearted, farsighted, scheming sycophant. Yet such a man was Talbot.

Raised by James to the earldom of Tyrconnel, he had commanded the troops in Ireland during the nine months which elapsed between the termination of the viceroyalty of Ormond and the commencement of the viceroyalty of Clarendon. When the new Lord Lieutenant was about to leave London for Dublin, the general was summoned from Dublin to London. As soon as he was there, he allied himself closely with Castelmaine, Dover and Albeville. These men told their master that he owed it to his religion and to the dignity of his Crown to stand firm against the outcry of heretical demagogues, and exhorted him to let the Parliament see from the first that he would be master in spite of opposition, and that the only effect of opposition would be to make him a hard master.

The obstinate and imperious nature of the King gave great advantages to those who advised him to be firm, to yield nothing, and to make himself feared. One state maxim had taken possession of his small understanding, and was not to be dislodged by reason. 'I will make no concession,' he often repeated; 'my father made concessions, and he was beheaded.'

Another fatal delusion was never dispelled till it had ruined him. He firmly believed that, do what he might, the members of the Church of England would act up to their principles. It had, he knew, been proclaimed from ten thousand pulpits, that even tyranny as frightful as that of the most depraved of the Caesars did not justify subjects in resisting the royal authority; and hence he was weak enough to conclude that the whole body of Tory gentlemen and clergymen would let him plunder, oppress, and insult them, without lifting an arm against him.

In these fatal follies the King was artfully encouraged by a minister who had been an Exclusionist, and who still called himself a Protestant, the Earl of Sunderland. The conduct of this unprincipled politician is to be ascribed to the alternate influence of cupidity and fear on a mind highly susceptible of both those passions. Sunderland wanted more power and more money. More power he could obtain only at Rochester's expense; and the obvious way to obtain power at Rochester's expense was to encourage the dislike which the King felt for Rochester's moderate counsels. Money could be most easily and most largely obtained from the court of Versailles; and Sunderland was eager to sell himself to that court. He therefore betrayed to Barillon all the schemes adverse to France which had been meditated in the English cabinet. The ambassador told his master that six thousand guineas was the smallest gratification that could be offered to so important a minister. Louis consented to go as high as twenty-five thousand crowns, equivalent to about five thousand six hundred pounds sterling. It was agreed that Sunderland should receive this sum yearly, and that he should, in return, exert all his influence to prevent the reassembling of the Parliament.

He was soon appointed to succeed Halifax in the high dignity of Lord President without being required to resign the far more active and lucrative post of Secretary. He felt, however, that he could never hope to obtain paramount influence in the court while he was supposed to belong to the Established Church. All religions were the same to him. He therefore determined to let the King have the delight and glory of effecting a conversion. Some management, however, was necessary. To the world he showed himself as a Protestant. In the royal closet he assumed the character of an earnest enquirer after truth, who was almost persuaded to declare himself a Roman Catholic, and who, while waiting for fuller illumination,

Robert Spencer, Earl of Sunderland, was James's Lord President of the Council. Macaulay observes of Sunderland: 'In this man the political immorality of his age was personified in the most lively manner. Nature had given him a keen understanding, a restless and mischievous temper, a cold heart and an abject spirit.' Despite his repeated deceits however he was one of the great political survivors of the seventeenth century.

was disposed to render every service in his power to the professors of the old faith.

May had been fixed for the meeting of the Houses: but they were again prorogued to November. It was not strange that the King did not wish to meet them: for he had determined to adopt a policy which he knew to be, in the highest degree, odious to them. From his predecessors he had inherited two prerogatives, which, if exerted without any limit, would of themselves have sufficed to overturn the whole polity of the State and of the Church. These were the dispensing power and the ecclesiastical supremacy. By means of the dispensing power, the King purposed to admit Roman Catholics, not merely to civil and military, but to spiritual, offices. By means of the ecclesiastical supremacy, he hoped to make the Anglican clergy his instruments for the destruction of their own religion.

It seemed but too probable that the whole government of the Anglican Church would shortly pass into the hands of her deadliest enemies. Three important sees had lately become vacant, that of York, that of Chester, and that of Oxford. The Bishopric of Oxford was given to Samuel Parker, a parasite, whose religion, if he had any religion, was that of Rome, and who called himself a Protestant only because he was encumbered with a wife. The Bishopric of Chester was bestowed on Thomas Cartwright, a still viler sycophant than Parker. The Archbishopric of York remained several years vacant. As no good reason could be found for leaving so important a place unfilled, men suspected that the nomination was delayed only till the King could venture to place the mitre on the head of an avowed Papist.

The situation of England in the year 1686 cannot be better described than in the words of the French ambassador. 'The discontent', he wrote, 'is great and general: but the fear of incurring still worse evils restrains all who have

The election of 1688 in the Guildhall, Oxford. At the rear of the hall James's messenger orders the election of the King's nominee for alderman. Despotic actions such as this were alienating even those sections of the population who had been his strongest supporters. Painting by Heemskerck.

anything to lose. The King openly expresses his joy at finding himself in a situation to strike bold strokes. He likes to be complimented on this subject. He has talked to me about it, and has assured me that he will not flinch.'

The Prince of Orange

The appellation of Irish was then given exclusively to the Celts and to those families which, though not of Celtic origin, had in the course of ages degenerated into Celtic manners. These people, probably about a million in number, had adhered to the Church of Rome. Among them resided about two hundred thousand colonists, proud of their Saxon blood and of their Protestant faith.

The great preponderance of numbers on one side was more than compensated by a great superiority of intelligence, vigour, and organisation on the other. Between the two populations there was an inequality which legislation had not caused and could not remove. The dominion which one of those populations exercised over the other was the dominion of wealth over poverty, of knowledge over ignorance, of civilised over uncivilised man.

At once an Englishman and a Roman Catholic, James belonged half to the ruling and half to the subject caste, and was therefore peculiarly qualified to be a mediator between them. Unhappily, he became instead the fiercest and most reckless of partisans. Instead of allaying the animosity of the two populations, he inflamed it to a height before unknown. He determined to reverse their relative position, and to put the Protestant colonists under the feet of the Popish Celts. He was not at that time disposed to commit the government wholly to Irish hands. For the present, therefore, he determined to entrust the civil administration to an English and Protestant Lord Lieutenant, and to give the command of the army to an Irish and Roman Catholic general. The Lord Lieutenant was Clarendon: the general was Tyrconnel.

Clarendon was soon informed that it had been resolved to make a complete change in both the civil and the military government of Ireland, and to bring a large number of Roman Catholics instantly into office. The terror of the colonists was extreme. Outnumbered as they were by the native population, their condition would be pitiable indeed if the native population were to be armed against them with the whole power of the state; and nothing less than this was threatened.

The distress and alarm of Clarendon were increased by news which reached him through private channels. Without his knowledge, preparations were making for arming and drilling the whole Celtic population of the country of which he was the nominal governor. Tyrconnel from London directed the design; and the prelates of the Roman Catholic Church were his agents.

In June 1686 Tyrconnel came to Dublin. He brought with him royal instructions touching all parts of the administration, and at once took the real government of the island into his own hands. In a few weeks he had introduced more than two thousand natives into the ranks; and the people about him confidently affirmed that by Christmas day not a man of English race would be left in the whole army.

Clarendon, meanwhile, received letters which informed him that he had incurred the King's serious displeasure. He learned that it had been determined at Whitehall to recall him, and to appoint, as his successor, Tyrconnel. Then for a time the prospect seemed to clear: the King was in better humour; and during a few days Clarendon flattered himself that his brother's intercession had prevailed, and that the crisis was passed.

In truth the crisis was only beginning. While Clarendon was trying to lean on Rochester, Rochester was unable longer to support himself. As in Ireland the elder brother, though retaining the title of Excellency, had really been superseded by the Commander of the Forces, so in England, the younger brother, though holding the white staff, was fast sinking into a mere financial clerk. The real direction of affairs had passed to the cabal which dined with Sunderland on Fridays.

On the evening of the 17th of December, Rochester was called into the royal closet. James was unusually discomposed, and even shed tears. He expressed his regret that his duty made it impossible for him to indulge his private partialities. It was absolutely necessary, he said, that those who had the chief direction of his affairs should partake his opinions and feelings. The office of Lord Treasurer was of such high importance that it could not safely be entrusted by a Roman Catholic King to a person zealous for the Church of England. Rochester saw that all was over.

In his fall he dragged down Clarendon. On the 7th of January 1687, the *Gazette* announced to the people of London that the Treasury was put into commission. On the 8th arrived at Dublin a despatch formally signifying that in a month Tyrconnel would assume the government of Ireland.

The dismission of the two brothers is a great epoch in the reign of James. From that time it was clear that what he really wanted was not liberty of conscience for the members of his own church, but liberty to persecute the members of other churches. Who indeed could hope to stand where the Hydes had fallen? They were the brothers in law of the King, his steady adherents in adversity and peril, his obsequious servants since he had been on the throne. Their sole crime was their religion; and for this crime they had been discarded. In great perturbation men began to look round for help; and soon all eyes were fixed on one whom a rare concurrence both of personal qualities and of fortuitous circumstances pointed out as the deliverer.

William Henry, Prince of Orange Nassau, was now in his thirty-seventh year. But both in body and in mind he was older than other men of the same age. Nature had largely endowed him with the qualities of a great ruler; and education had developed those qualities in no common degree. At eighteen he had sate among the fathers of the commonwealth, grave, discreet, and judicious as the oldest among them. At twenty-one, in a day of gloom and terror, he was placed at the head of the administration. At twenty-three he was renowned throughout Europe as a soldier and a politician. He had put domestic factions under his feet: he was the soul of a mighty coalition; and he had contended with honour in the field against some of the greatest generals of the age.

To a very small circle of intimate friends, he was a different man from the reserved and stoical William whom the multitude supposed to be destitute of human feelings. He was kind, cordial, open, even convivial and jocose, and would bear his full share in festive conversation. Highest in his favour stood a gentleman of his household named Bentinck, who was early pronounced by Temple to be the best and truest servant that ever prince had the good fortune to possess.

Arthur Capel, Earl of Essex, 'a man of solid though not brilliant parts', and once a member of the triumvirate who directed everything for Charles II, was implicated in the Rye House Plot and committed suicide in the Tower. A limewood carving by Grinling Gibbons.

William was not less fortunate in marriage than in friendship. Yet his marriage had not at first promised much domestic happiness. His choice has been determined chiefly by political considerations: nor did it seem likely that any strong affection would grow up between a handsome girl of sixteen, well disposed indeed, and naturally intelligent, but ignorant and simple, and a bridegroom who, though he had not completed his twenty-eighty-year, was in constitution older than her father. For a time William was a negligent husband; and Mary well knew that he was not strictly faithful to her. She, however, bore her injuries with a patience which deserved, and gradually obtained, William's esteem and gratitude. Yet there still remained one cause of estrangement. A time would probably come when the princess would be the chief of a great monarchy, and would hold the balance of Europe, while her lord would find in the British government no place marked out for him, and would hold power only from her bounty and during her pleasure. It is not strange that a man so fond of authority as William, and so conscious of a genius for command, should have strongly felt that jealousy which, during a few hours of royalty, put dissension between Guildford Dudley and the Lady Jane, and which produced a rupture still more tragical between Darnley and the Queen of Scots. The Princess of Orange had not the faintest suspicion of her husband's feelings. Her preceptor, Bishop Compton, had instructed her carefully in religion, but had left her profoundly ignorant of the English constitution and of her own position. She had been nine years married before she discovered the cause of William's discontent; nor would she ever have learned it from himself. At length a complete explanation and reconciliation were brought about by the agency of Gilbert Burnet.

Burnet was at once a historian, an antiquary, a theologian, a preacher, a pamphleteer, a debater, and an active political leader. He had become on conviction a Whig; and he firmly adhered through all vicissitudes to his principles. He had reached the Hague in the summer of 1686, and was received there with kindness and respect. He had many conversations with the princess on politics and religion, and soon became her spiritual director and confidential adviser. The sagacious prince perceived that this pushing talkative divine, who was always babbling secrets, putting impertinent questions, obtruding unasked advice, was nevertheless an upright, courageous and able man, well acquainted with the temper and the views of British sects and factions. He was therefore admitted to as large a share of favour and confidence as was granted to any but those who composed the very small inmost knot of the prince's private friends.

Burnet plainly told the princess what the feeling was which preyed upon her husband's mind. She learned for the first time, with no small astonishment, that, when she became Queen of England, William would not share her throne. She warmly declared that there was no proof of conjugal submission and affection which she was not ready to give. Burnet informed her that the remedy was in her own hands. She might easily, when the Crown devolved on her, induce her Parliament not only to give the regal title to her husband, but even to transfer to him by a legislative act the administration of the government. 'But', he added, 'your Royal Highness ought to consider well before you announce any such resolution.' 'I want no time for consideration,' answered Mary. 'It is enough that I have an opportunity of showing my regard for the prince.' Next day, the decisive interview took place. 'I did not know till yesterday', said Mary, 'that there was such a difference between the laws of England and the laws of God. But I now promise you that you shall always bear rule; and, in return, I ask only this, that, as I shall observe the precept which enjoins wives to obey their husbands, you will observe that which enjoins husbands to love their wives.' Her generous affection completely gained the heart of William. From that time, there was entire friendship and confidence between them.

William long observed the contest between the English factions attentively, but without feeling a strong predilection for either side. Whatever patriotic feeling he had was for Holland. Yet even his affection for the land of his birth was subordinate to another feeling which early became supreme in his soul. That feeling was enmity to France, and to the magnificent King who, in more than one sense, represented France. When William was little more than a boy his country had been attacked by Louis in ostentatious defiance of justice and public law. It was in the agony of that conflict that William had been called to the head of affairs. Hundreds of Calvinistic preachers proclaimed that the same power which had set apart Samson from the womb to be the scourge of the Philistine, had raised up William of Orange to be the champion of all free nations and of all pure Churches; nor was this notion without influence on his own mind. To the confidence which the heroic fatalist placed in his high destiny and in his sacred cause is to be partly attributed his singular indifference to danger. He had a great work to do; and till it was done nothing could harm him.

The feeling with which William regarded France explains the whole of

On 4 January, 1642, the King arrived at the Commons in person to arrest five of the leading members of the Opposition. Having been warned of the King's approach however they had fled into the City of London with its protective train bands. The Speaker, William Lenthall, fell on his knees before the King and said: 'May it please your Majesty, I have neither eyes to see nor tongue to speak in this place but as the House is pleased to direct me, whose servant I am.' A climactic moment in British history had been reached.

After the Battle of Naseby, by John Gilbert. Cromwell's New Model Army inflicted a crushing defeat on the Royalist forces at Naseby in 1645. Though desultory fighting continued for nearly a year, it was effectively the end of the war.

Imaginary reconstruction of the execution of Charles I, by Weesop. The vignette at bottom left shows the King marching to his execution; at bottom right members of the grieving crowd dip their handkerchieves in his blood.

Portrait of Cromwell after Edward Walker.

The Battle of the Boyne was fought on 1 July, 1690, and effectively ended the Jacobite cause. (Painting by Jan Wyck.) Louis XIV would make a further effort two years later to restore James II, but his plans foundered with the sharp defeat of his navy at La Hogue.

The Great Fire of London started near Pudding Lane in the early hours of 2 September, 1666, and eventually burned out an area stretching from the Tower to the Temple and from the Thames to Smithfield. Pepys records that the rubble was still smouldering in January. Jan Wyck's painting shows London at night during the conflagration, with old St. Paul's engulfed by the flames. Wren was to give the city a new skyline.

The burning of the English fleet on the Medway by the Dutch admiral de Ruyter, in June 1667. (Painting by P. C. Van Soest.) This indignity, due to the neglect of the fleet which left the ships as sitting targets at their moorings, was bitterly resented by the people.

Sir John Thornhill's ceiling in the Painted Hall at Greenwich. The centre panel shows William and Mary, and beneath them their plan for the Chapel.

his policy towards England. The chief object of his care was not our island, not even his native Holland, but the great community of nations threatened with subjugation by one too powerful member. It was plain that, when the European crisis came, England would, if James were her master, either remain inactive or act in conjunction with France. And the European crisis was drawing near. The House of Austria had been secured from danger on the side of Turkey, and was no longer under the necessity of submitting patiently to the encroachments and insults of Louis. Accordingly, in July 1686, a treaty was signed at Augsburg by which the princes of the empire bound themselves closely together for the purpose of mutual defence. The name of William did not appear in this instrument: but all men knew that it was his work. Between him and the vassal of France there could, in such circumstances, be no cordial good will. The father in law and the son in law were separated completely and for ever.

At the very time at which the prince was thus estranged from the English court, the causes which had hitherto produced a coolness between him and the two great sections of the English people disappeared. A large portion of the Whigs had favoured the pretensions of Monmouth: but Monmouth was now no more. The Tories, on the other hand, had entertained apprehensions that the interests of the Anglican Church might not be safe under the rule of a man bred among Dutch Presbyterians: but, since that beloved Church had been threatened by far more formidable dangers from a very different quarter, these apprehensions had lost almost all their power. Thus, at the same moment, both the great parties began to fix their hopes on the same leader; and the prince became the unquestioned chief of the whole of that party which was opposed to the government, a party almost coextensive with the nation.

The original purpose of James had been to obtain for the Church of which he was a member, not only complete immunity from all penalties and from all civil disabilities, but also an ample share of ecclesiastical and academical endowments, and at the same time to enforce with rigour the laws against the Puritan sects. Such had been his policy as long as he could cherish any hope that the Church of England would consent to share ascendency with the Church of Rome. But the whole Anglican priesthood, the whole Cavalier gentry, were against him. Dull as was the intellect of James, despotic as was his temper, he felt that he must change his course. He could not safely venture to outrage all his Protestant subjects at once. He could overpower the Anglican Church only by forming against her an extensive coalition, including sects which, though they differed in doctrine and government far more widely from each other than from her, might yet be induced, by their common dread of her intolerance, to suspend their mutual animosities till she was no longer able to oppress them.

On the 18th of March the King informed the Privy Council that he had determined to grant, by his own authority, entire liberty of conscience to all his subjects. On the 4th of April appeared the memorable Declaration of Indulgence.

In this declaration the King avowed that it was his earnest wish to see his people members of that Church to which he himself belonged. But, since that could not be, he announced his intention to protect them in the free exercise of their religion. He proceeded to annul, by his own sole authority, a long series of statutes. He suspended all penal laws against all classes of Nonconformists. He authorised both Roman Catholics and Protestant

Even as Duke of York James had made little attempt to conceal his religious persuasion. Once he was King he went publicly to Mass, and continued to do so throughout his reign. To the apprehension of the people an embassy from the Pope visited the King; they are seen here disembarking at the river stairs of old Somerset House.

Dissenters to perform their worship publicly. He also abrogated all those acts which imposed any religious test as a qualification for any civil or military office.

The Anglican party was in amazement and terror. The House of Stuart leagued with republican and regicide sects against the old Cavaliers of England; Popery leagued with Puritanism against an ecclesiastical system with which the Puritans had no quarrel, except that it had retained too much that was Popish; these were portents which confounded all the calculations of statesmen. The Church was then to be attacked at once on every side; and the attack was to be under the direction of him who, by her constitution, was her head.

When the first agitation produced by the publication of the Indulgence had subsided, it appeared that a breach had taken place in the Puritan party. The minority, headed by a few busy men whose judgment was defective or was biassed by interest, supported the King. But the great body of Protestant Nonconformists, firmly attached to civil liberty, and distrusting the promises of the King, steadily refused to return thanks for a favour, which, it might well be suspected, concealed a snare.

The Anglican body and the Puritan body, so long separated by a mortal enmity, were daily drawing nearer to each other, and every step which they made towards union increased the influence of him who was their common head. William was in all things fitted to be a mediator between these two great sections of the English nation. He could not be said to be a member of either. Yet neither, when in a reasonable mood, could refuse to regard him as a friend. His great object now was to unite in one body the numerous sections of the community which regarded him as their head. In this work he had several able and trusty coadjutors, among whom two were pre-eminently useful, Burnet and Dykvelt.

Of the diplomatists in the service of the United Provinces none was, in dexterity, temper, and manners, superior to Dykvelt. In knowledge of English affairs none seems to have been his equal. A pretence was found for despatching him, early in 1687, to England on a special mission with credentials from the States General. But in truth his embassy was not to the government, but to the opposition; and his conduct was guided by private institutions which had been drawn by Burnet, and approved by William.

The chiefs of all the important sections of the nation had frequent conferences in the presence of the envoy. At these meetings the sense of the Tory party was chiefly spoken by the Earls of Danby and Nottingham. Though more than eight years had elapsed since Danby had fallen from power, his name was still great among the old Cavaliers of England; and he was also highly esteemed at the Hague, where it was never forgotten that he was the person who had induced Charles to bestow the hand of the Lady Mary on her cousin.

Daniel Finch, Earl of Nottingham, was an honourable and virtuous man. Like other zealous churchmen, he had, till recently, been a strenuous supporter of monarchical authority. But to the policy which had been pursued since the suppression of the western insurrection he was bitterly hostile, and not the less so because his younger brother Heneage had been turned out of the office of Solicitor General for refusing to defend the King's dispensing power.

Several eminent Whigs were in constant communication with Dykvelt. From private as well as from public feelings, the Earl of Bedford was adverse to the court: but he was not active in concerting measures against it. His place in the meetings of the malecontents was supplied by his nephew, the celebrated Edward Russell. He was a sailor, had distinguished himself in his profession, and had in the late reign held an office in the palace. But all the ties which bound him to the royal family had been sundered by the death of his cousin William. The daring, unquiet, and vindictive seaman now sate in the councils called by the Dutch envoy as the representative of the boldest and most eager section of the opposition, of those men who, under the names of Roundheads, Exclusionists, and Whigs, had maintained a contest of five and forty years against three successive Kings.

Three men are yet to be mentioned with whom Dykvelt was in confidential communication, and by whose help he hoped to secure the good will of three great professions. Bishop Compton was the agent employed to manage the clergy: Admiral Herbert undertook to exert all his influence over the navy; and an interest was established in the army by the instrumentality of Churchill.

The conduct of Compton and Herbert requires no explanation. They had incurred the royal displeasure by refusing to be employed as tools for the destruction of their own religion. The bishop had by an illegal sentence been suspended from his episcopal functions. The admiral had in one hour been reduced from opulence to penury. The situation of Churchill was widely different. He was now, in his thirty-seventh year, a major general, a peer of Scotland, a peer of England: he commanded a troop of Life Guards; and as yet there was no sign that he had lost any part of the favour to which he owed so much. He was bound to James, as appeared to superficial observers, by the strongest ties of interest. But Churchill himself was no superficial observer. He knew exactly what his interest really was. If his master were once at full liberty to employ Papists, not a single Protestant would be employed. And this man, whose public life, to those who can look steadily through the dazzling blaze of genius and glory, will appear a prodigy of turpitude, believed implicitly in the religion which he had learned as a boy, and shuddered at the thought of formally abjuring it. A terrible alternative was before him; and it soon appeared that there was no guilt and no disgrace which he was not ready to incur, in order to escape from the necessity of parting either with his places or with his religion.

It was not only as a military commander that Churchill was able to render services to the opposition. It was most important to the success of William's plans that his sister in law, who, in the order of succession to the English throne, stood between his wife and himself, should act in cordial union with him. Which side Anne might take depended on the will of others. For she was a willing slave to a nature far more vivacious and imperious than

James's daughters by Anne Hyde. Both were staunch Protestants and were to become Queens of England. The elder girl, Mary, dressed here as Diana, would marry William of Orange. Her younger sister Anne (right) was to be the last of the Stuart Queens. Both portraits by Peter Lely.

her own. The person by whom she was absolutely governed was the wife of Churchill, a woman who afterwards exercised a great influence on the fate of England and of Europe.

The name of this celebrated favourite was Sarah Jennings. She had been brought up from childhood with the Princess Anne, and a close friendship had arisen between the girls. In character they resembled each other very little. Anne was slow and taciturn. To those whom she loved she was meek. The form which her anger assumed was sullenness. She had a strong sense of religion, and was attached even with bigotry to the rites and government of the Church of England. Sarah was lively and voluble, domineered over those whom she regarded with most kindness, and, when she was offended, vented her rage in tears and tempestuous reproaches. To sanctity she made no pretence.

Lady Churchill was loved and even worshipped by Anne. The princess could not live apart from the object of her romantic fondness. She married, and was a faithful wife. But Prince George, a dull man whose chief pleasures were derived from his dinner and his bottle, soon gave himself up with stupid patience to the dominion of the vehement spirit by which his wife was governed. At length the time had arrived when this singular

friendship was to exercise a great influence on public affairs. What part Anne would take in the contest which distracted England was matter of deep anxiety. The influence of the Churchills decided the question; and their patroness became an important member of that extensive league of which the Prince of Orange was the head.

In June 1687 Dykvelt returned to the Hague. He carried with him a packet of letters from the most eminent of those with whom he had conferred during his stay in England. His mission had succeeded so well that a pretence was soon found for sending another agent to continue the work. The new envoy was an illegitimate cousin german of William, and bore a title taken from the lordship of Zulestein. After a short absence, he returned to his country charged with letters and verbal messages not less important than those which had been entrusted to his predecessor. A regular correspondence was from this time established between the prince and the opposition.

The Seven Bishops

Before the end of October 1687 the great news began to be whispered. The Queen was with child.

There was indeed nothing very extraordinary in what had happened. The King had but just completed his fifty-fourth year. The Queen was in the summer of life. She had already borne four children who had died young. As, however, five years had elapsed since her last pregnancy, the people had ceased to entertain any apprehension that she would give an heir to the throne. On the other hand, nothing seemed more natural and probable than that the Jesuits should have contrived a pious fraud. It was certain that they must consider the accession of the Princess of Orange as one of the greatest calamities which could befall their Church. It was equally certain that they would not be very scrupulous about doing whatever might be necessary to save their Church from a great calamity. A suspicion took possession of the public mind. The folly of some Roman Catholics confirmed the vulgar prejudice. They spoke of the auspicious event as strange, as miraculous, as an exertion of the same divine power which had made Sarah proud and happy in Isaac, and had given Samuel to the prayers of Hannah. They foretold with confidence that the unborn infant would be a boy. Their insolent triumph excited the popular indignation. Their predictions strengthened the popular suspicions. From the Prince and Princess of Denmark down to porters and laundresses nobody alluded to the promised birth without a sneer.

On the 27th of April 1688, the King put forth a second Declaration of Indulgence. In this paper he recited at length the declaration of the preceding April. His past life, he said, ought to have convinced his people that he was not a person who could easily be induced to depart from any resolution which he had formed. But, as designing men had attempted to persuade the world that he might be prevailed on to give way in this matter, he thought it necessary to proclaim that his purpose was immutably fixed, that he was resolved to employ those only who were prepared to concur in his design, and that he had, in pursuance of that resolution, dismissed many of his disobedient servants from civil and military employments. He announced that he meant to hold a Parliament in November at the latest; and he exhorted his subjects to choose representatives who would assist him in the great work which he had undertaken.

To the intense dismay of the nation a son was born to James II on 10 June 1688. The people saw the birth as a trick wrought by the Jesuits, it being alleged that the child had been smuggled into the palace in a warming pan, to ensnare them into an unwanted Catholic succession. The son, James Francis Stuart, was to become known to history as the Old Pretender. The incident is illustrated here by an Italian engraving commemorating the birth.

On the 4th of May he made an Order in Council that his declaration of the preceding week should be read, on two successive Sundays, at the time of divine service, by the officiating ministers of all the churches and chapels of the kingdom. In London and in the suburbs the reading was to take place on the 20th and 27th of May, in other parts of England on the 3rd and 10th of June.

When it is considered that the clergy of the Established Chuch regarded the Indulgence as a violation of the laws of the realm, as a breach of the plighted faith of the King, and as a fatal blow levelled at the interest and dignity of their own profession, it will scarcely admit of doubt that the Order in Council was intended to be felt by them as a cruel affront. But, tyrannical and malignant as the mandate was, would the Anglican priesthood refuse to obey? Whoever ventured to resist might in a week be ejected from his parsonage, deprived of his whole income, and left to beg from door to door. If, indeed, the whole body offered an united opposition to the royal will, it was probable that even James would scarcely venture to punish ten thousand delinquents at once. But there was not time to form an extensive combination. The day drew near; and still there was no concert and no formed resolution.

On the 12th of May a grave and learned company was assembled round the table of the Primate at Lambeth. Compton, Bishop of London, Turner, Bishop of Ely, White, Bishop of Peterborough, and Tenison, Rector of Saint Martin's Parish, were among the guests. The great question of which all minds were full was propounded and discussed. The general opinion was that the declaration ought not to be read. Letters were forthwith written to several of the most respectable prelates of the province of Canterbury, entreating them to come up without delay to London. William Lloyd, Bishop of Saint Asaph, hastened to the capital and arrived on the 16th. On the following day came the excellent Ken, Bishop of Bath and Wells, Lake, Bishop of Chichester, and Sir John Trelawney, Bishop of Bristol, a baronet of an old and honourable Cornish family.

On the 18th a meeting of prelates and of other eminent divines was held at Lambeth. After long deliberation, a petition embodying the general sense was written by the archbishop. The King was assured that the Church still was, as she had ever been, faithful to the throne. But Parliament had pronounced that the sovereign was not constitutionally competent to dispense with statutes in matters ecclesiastical. The declaration was therefore illegal; and the petitioners could not be parties to the solemn publishing of an illegal declaration in the house of God.

This paper was signed by the archbishop and by six of his suffragans, Lloyd of Saint Asaph, Turner of Ely, Lake of Chichester, Ken of Bath and Wells, White of Peterborough, and Trelawney of Bristol. The Bishop of London, being under suspension, did not sign.

It was now late on Friday evening; and on Sunday morning the declaration was to be read in the churches of London. It was necessary to put the paper into the King's hands without delay. The six bishops crossed the river to Whitehall. The archbishop, who had long been forbidden the court, did not accompany them.

When the bishops knelt before the King, he graciously told them to rise, took the paper from Lloyd, and said, 'This is my lord of Canterbury's hand.' 'Yes, sir, his own hand,' was the answer. James read the petition: he folded it up; and his countenance grew dark. 'This', he said, 'is a great surprise to me. I did not expect this from your Church, especially from some of you. This is a standard of rebellion.' The bishops broke out into passionate professions of loyalty: but the King, as usual, repeated the same words over and over. 'This is rebellion. This is a standard of rebellion. Did ever a good churchman question the dispensing power before? Have not some of you preached for it and written for it? It is a standard of rebellion. I will have my declaration published.'

The bishops respectfully retired. That very evening the document which they had put into the hands of the King appeared word for word in print, was laid on the tables of all the coffee houses, and was cried about the streets. How the petition got abroad is still a mystery. The prevailing opinion, however, was that some person about the King had been indiscreet or treacherous.

The conduct of the prelates was rapturously extolled by the general voice. The Saturday, however, passed over without any sign of relenting on the part of the government; and the Sunday arrived, a day long remembered.

In the City and Liberties of London were about a hundred parish churches. In only four of these was the Order in Council obeyed. Never

The seven bishops who defied the order of the King that his Declaration of Indulgence should be read from every pulpit in the land on four successive Sundays. The clergy were committed to non-resistance, but this latest instruction proved too much even for them to accept. Top row: *Francis Turner, Bishop of Ely; William Lloyd, Bishop of St Asaph;* Middle Row: *Thomas Ken, Bishop of Bath and Wells; William Sancroft, Archbishop of Canterbury; John Lake, Bishop of Chichester;* Bottom Row: *Jonathon Trelawney, Bishop of Bristol; Thomas White, Bishop of Peterborough. English glass picture c 1688.*

had the Church been so dear to the nation as on the afternoon of that day. The Dutch minister wrote to inform the States General that the Anglican priesthood had risen in the estimation of the public to an incredible degree. The universal cry of the Nonconformists, he said, was that they would rather continue to lie under the penal statutes than separate their cause from that of the prelates.

Another week of anxiety and agitation passed away. Sunday came again. The declaration was read nowhere except at the very few places where it had been read the week before.

Even the King stood aghast for a moment at the violence of the tempest which he had raised. What step was he next to take? He must either advance or recede: and it was impossible to advance without peril, or to recede without humiliation.

On the 27th of May it was notified to the bishops that on the 8th of June they must appear before the King in Council. Perhaps James hoped that some of the offenders, terrified by his displeasure, might submit before the day fixed for the reading of the declaration in their dioceses, and might persuade their clergy to obey his order. If such was his hope it was signally disappointed. Sunday the 3rd of June came; and all parts of England followed the example of the capital.

On the evening of the 8th of June the seven prelates repaired to the palace, and were called into the Council chamber. The Chancellor told them that a criminal information would be exhibited against them in the Court of King's Bench, and called upon them to enter into recognisances. They refused. They were peers of Parliament, they said. No peer could be required to enter into a recognisance in a case of libel; and they should not think themselves justified in relinquishing the privilege of their order. The King was mortified and alarmed. For he had gone so far that, if they persisted, he had no choice left but to send them to prison. They were resolute. A warrant was therefore made out directing the Lieutenant of the Tower to keep them in safe custody, and a barge was manned to convey them down the river.

It was known all over London that the bishops were before the Council. A great multitude filled the courts of Whitehall and all the neighbouring streets. When the seven came forth under a guard, the emotions of the people broke through all restraint. Many dashed into the stream, and, up to their waists in ooze and water, cried to the holy fathers to bless them. All down the river, the royal barge passed between lines of boats, from which arose a shout of 'God bless your lordships.' The very sentinels who were posted at the Traitors' Gate reverently asked for a blessing from the martyrs whom they were to guard.

Scarcely had the gates of the Tower been closed on the prisoners when an event took place which increased the public excitement. It had been announced that the Queen did not expect to be confined till July. But, on the day after the bishops had appeared before the Council, she was carried in a sedan to Saint James's Palace, where apartments had been very hastily fitted up for her reception. There, on the morning of Sunday, the 10th of June, was born the most unfortunate of princes, destined to seventy-seven years of exile and wandering, of vain projects, of honours more galling than insults, and of hopes such as make the heart sick.

Many persons of both sexes were in the royal bedchamber when the child first saw the light; but none of them enjoyed any large measure of public confidence. The cry of the whole nation was that an imposture had been practised. Heated by such suspicions, suspicions unjust, it is true, but not altogether unnatural, men thronged more eagerly than ever to pay their homage to the saintly victims of the tyrant, who, having long foully injured his people, had now filled up the measure of his iniquities by more foully injuring his children.

The bishops remained only a week in custody. On Friday the 15th of June they were brought before the King's Bench. The question whether a peer could be required to enter into recognisances on a charge of libel was argued at great length, and decided by a majority of judges in favour of the Crown. The prisoners then pleaded Not Guilty. That day fortnight, the

29th of June, was fixed for their trial. In the meantime they were allowed to be at large on their own recognisances.

Before the day of trial the agitation had spread to the farthest corners of the island. From Scotland the bishops received letters assuring them of the sympathy of the Presbyterians of that country. The people of Cornwall were greatly moved by the danger of Trelawney. All over the county the peasants chanted a ballad of which the burden is still remembered:

> *'And shall Trelawney die, and shall Trelawney die?*
> *Then thirty thousand Cornish boys will know the reason why.'*

On the 29th of June, Westminster Hall, Old and New Palace Yard, and all the neighbouring streets were thronged with people. Such an auditory had never before been assembled in the Court of King's Bench. Thirty-five temporal peers of the realm were counted in the crowd.

The counsel were by no means fairly matched. The government had required from its law officers services so odious that all the ablest jurists and advocates of the Tory party had, one after another, refused to comply, and had been dismissed from their employments. Sir Thomas Powis, the Attorney General, was scarcely of the third rank in his profession. Sir William Williams, the Solicitor General, had great abilities and dauntless courage: but he wanted discretion; he had no command over his temper; and he was hated by all political parties.

Sawyer and Finch, who, at the time of the accession of James, had been Attorney and Solicitor General, were of counsel for the defendants. With them were joined the two best lawyers that could be found in the Inns of Court, Pemberton and Pollexfen. The junior counsel for the bishops was a young barrister named John Somers. His genius, his industry, his great

The bishops on the way to imprisonment in the Tower. The Thames was alive with wherries pursuing the bishops' barge, their occupants clamouring for a blessing.

and various accomplishments, were well known to a small circle of friends; and his pertinent and lucid mode of arguing had already secured to him the ear of the Court of King's Bench.

The jury was sworn. It consisted of persons of highly respectable station. The foreman was Sir Roger Langley, a baronet of old and honourable family. With him were joined a knight and ten esquires, several of whom are known to have been men of large possessions.

The trial then commenced. The information charged the bishops with having written or published, in the county of Middlesex, a false, malicious, and seditious libel. During three hours the counsel for the petitioners argued with great force in defence of the fundamental principles of the constitution, and proved from the *Journals* of the House of Commons that the bishops had affirmed the truth when they represented to the King that the dispensing power which he claimed had been repeatedly declared illegal by Parliament. Somers rose last. He spoke little more than five minutes: but when he sate down his reputation as an orator and a constitutional lawyer was established. He went through the expressions which were used in the information to describe the offence imputed to the bishops, and showed that every word was altogether inappropriate. False the paper was not; for every fact which it set forth had been shown from the journals of Parliament to be true. Malicious the paper was not; for the defendants had been placed by the government in such a situation that they must either oppose themselves to the royal will, or violate the most sacred obligations of conscience and honour. Seditious the paper was not; for it had not been scattered by the writers among the rabble, but delivered privately into the hands of the King alone; and a libel it was not, but a decent petition such as, by the laws of England, a subject who thinks himself aggrieved may with propriety present to the sovereign.

The Attorney replied shortly and feebly. The Solicitor spoke at great length and with great acrimony, and was often interrupted by the clamours and hisses of the audience. He went so far as to lay it down that no subject or body of subjects, except the Houses of Parliament, had a right to petition the King. The galleries were furious.

It was dark before the jury retired to consider of their verdict. The night was a night of intense anxiety. At six in the morning it was known that the jury were agreed: but what the verdict would be was still a secret.

At ten the court again met. The crowd was greater than ever. The jury appeared in their box; and there was a breathless stillness.

Sir Samuel Astry, Clerk of the Crown, spoke. 'Do you find the defendants, or any of them, guilty of the misdemeanour whereof they are impeached, or not guilty?' Sir Roger Langley answered, 'Not Guilty.' As the words were uttered, Halifax sprang up and waved his hat. At that signal, benches and galleries raised a shout. In a moment ten thousand persons, who crowded the great hall, replied with a still louder shout, which made the old oaken roof crack; and in another moment the innumerable throng without set up a third huzza, which was heard at Temple Bar. As the news spread, streets and squares, market places and coffee houses, broke forth into acclamations. The acquitted prelates took refuge in the nearest chapel from the crowd which implored their blessing. As the noblemen who had attended to support the good cause drove off, they flung from their carriage windows handfuls of money, and bade the crowd drink to the health of the King, the bishops, and the jury.

Lord Dartmouth was in command of the English fleet whose task it was to intercept William's expedition. Though his handling of the pursuit appeared to some to be sluggish and indecisive, he retained the confidence of King James.

William's Expedition

The acquittal of the bishops was not the only event which makes the 30th of June 1688 a great epoch in history. On that day was despatched from London to the Hague an instrument scarcely less important to the liberties of England than the Great Charter.

The prosecution of the bishops, and the birth of the Prince of Wales, had produced a great revolution in the feelings of many Tories. Hitherto they had flattered themselves that the trial to which their loyalty was subjected would, though severe, be temporary, and that their wrongs would shortly be redressed without any violation of the ordinary rule of succession. A very different prospect was now before them. The cradle of the heir apparent of the Crown was surrounded by Jesuits. Deadly hatred of that Church of which he would one day be the head would be studiously instilled into his infant mind, and would be bequeathed by him to his posterity. This vista of calamities had no end. The ablest and most enlightened Tories began to admit that they had overstrained the doctrine of passive obedience.

The Whigs saw that their time was come. In May, Edward Russell had repaired to the Hague. He had strongly represented to the Prince of Orange the state of the public mind, and had advised His Highness to appear in England at the head of a strong body of troops, and to call the people to arms. William knew well that many who talked in high language about sacrificing their lives and fortunes for their country would hesitate when the prospect of another Bloody Circuit was brought close to them. He wanted therefore to have, not vague professions of good will, but distinct invitations and promises of support subscribed by powerful and eminent men. A few signatures would be sufficient, if they were the signatures of statesmen who represented great interests.

With this answer Russell returned to London, where he found the excitement daily increasing. He lost no time in collecting the voices of the chiefs of the opposition. His principal coadjutor in this work was Henry Sidney, brother of Algernon. During June the meetings of those who were in the secret were frequent. At length, on the last day of the month, the decisive step was taken. A formal invitation was despatched to the Hague. The conspirators implored the prince to come among them with as little delay as possible. They pledged their honour that they would join him; and they undertook to secure the cooperation of as large a number of persons as could safely be trusted. This paper was signed in cipher by the seven chiefs of the conspiracy, the Earls of Shrewsbury, Devonshire, and Danby, Lord Lumley, Bishop Compton, Russell, and Sidney. Herbert undertook to be their messenger. He assumed the garb of a common sailor, and in this disguise reached the Dutch coast in safety, on the Friday after the trial of the bishops. He instantly hastened to the prince. Bentinck and Dykvelt were summoned, and several days were passed in deliberation.

Soon it began to be clear that defeat and mortification had only hardened James's heart. Within a fortnight after the trial an order was made, enjoining all chancellors of dioceses and all archdeacons to make a strict inquisition throughout their respective jurisdictions, and to report to the High Commission, within five weeks, the names of all such rectors, vicars, and curates as had omitted to read the declaration. The King anticipated with delight the terror with which the offenders would learn that they were to be cited before a court which would give them no quarter. The number of culprits was little, if at all, short of ten thousand.

It was plain that, if James determined to persist in his designs, he must remodel his army. Yet materials for that purpose he could not find in our island. Hatred of Popery had spread through all classes of his Protestant subjects, and had become the ruling passion even of ploughmen and artisans. But there was another part of his dominions where a very different spirit animated the great body of the population. Already Papists, of Celtic blood and speech, composed almost the whole army of Ireland. Barillon earnestly and repeatedly advised James to bring over that army for the purpose of coercing the English.

James wavered. He wished to be surrounded by troops on whom he could rely: but he dreaded the explosion of national feeling which the appearance of a great Irish force on English ground must produce. At last,

Anti-Jacobite mother-of-pearl plaque of 1688. On the right James II, with the three crowns of England, Scotland and Wales falling off his head, treads on the scales of justice and the scrolls of the law. To the left the sun is rising and shedding its light on an orange tree representing William III. On the left Louis XIV tramples on a cornucopia of plenty whilst holding a fleur-de-lys piercing a bird representing the Pope. The devil plays a harp in the background.

as usually happens when a weak man tries to avoid opposite inconveniences, he took a course which united them all. He brought over Irishmen, not indeed enough to hold down the single city of London, or the single county of York, but more than enough to excite the alarm and rage of the whole kingdom.

Of the many errors which James committed, none was more fatal than this. Not even the arrival of a brigade of Louis's musketeers would have excited such resentment and shame as our ancestors felt when they saw armed columns of Papists, just arrived from Dublin, moving in military pomp along the high roads. The blood of the whole nation boiled.

William determined to make his preparations with all speed. Twenty-four ships of war were fitted out for sea in addition to the ordinary force which the commonwealth maintained. Six thousand sailors were added to the naval establishment. Seven thousand new soldiers were raised. Through the latter part of July and the whole of August the preparations went on rapidly. Meanwhile the intercourse between England and Holland was active. A light bark of marvellous speed constantly ran backward and forward between Schevening and the eastern coast of our island. By this vessel William received a succession of letters from persons of high note in the Church, the State, and the army. Sidney, whose situation in England had become hazardous, passed over to Holland about the middle of August. About the same time Shrewsbury and Russell crossed the German Ocean in a boat which they had hired with great secrecy, and appeared at the Hague. Devonshire, Danby, and Lumley remained in

England, where they undertook to rise in arms as soon as the prince should set foot on the island.

There is reason to believe that, at this conjuncture, William first received assurances of support from a very different quarter. Sunderland had learned that the civil and ecclesiastical polity of England would shortly be vindicated by foreign and domestic arms. Fear bowed down his whole soul, and was so written in his face that all who saw him could read. It could hardly be doubted that, if there were a revolution, the evil counsellors who surrounded the throne would be called to a strict account: and among those counsellors he stood in the foremost rank. There was yet one way in which he might escape, a way more terrible to a noble spirit than a prison or a scaffold. He might still, by a well timed and useful treason, earn his pardon from the foes of the government. A channel of communication was not wanting, a channel worthy of the purpose which it was to serve. The Countess of Sunderland was an artful woman who carried on, with great activity, both amorous and political intrigues. The handsome and dissolute Henry Sidney had long been her favourite lover. Her husband was well pleased to see her thus connected with the court of the Hague. Whenever he wished to transmit a secret message to Holland, he spoke to his wife: she wrote to Sidney; and Sidney communicated her letter to William.

It was impossible that a design so vast as that which had been formed against the King of England should remain during many weeks a secret. Every courier who arrived at Westminster, either from the Hague or from Versailles, brought earnest warnings. But James was under a delusion which appears to have been encouraged by Sunderland. The Prince of Orange, said the cunning minister, would never dare to engage in an expedition beyond sea, leaving Holland defenceless. By such reasoning James was easily lulled into stupid security. The alarm and indignation of Louis increased daily. James was evidently in bad hands. Barillon was cautioned not to repose implicit confidence in the English ministers: but he was cautioned in vain. On him, as on James, Sunderland had cast a spell which no exhortation could break.

Louis bestirred himself vigorously. Bonrepaux, who had always distrusted Sunderland, was despatched to London with an offer of naval assistance. Avaux was ordered to declare to the States General that France had taken James under her protection. A large body of troops was held in readiness to march towards the Dutch frontier.

But James was bent on ruining himself; and every attempt to stop him only made him rush more eagerly to his doom. He was taken with a fit of pride, and determined to assert his independence. He declared that he gave not the least credit to the rumours of a Dutch invasion, and that the conduct of the French government had surprised and annoyed him. His perverse folly naturally excited the indignation of his powerful neighbour. Perhaps provoked by the discourtesy and wrongheadedness of the English government, Louis suddenly withdrew his troops from Flanders, and poured them into Germany.

William smiled inwardly at the misdirected energy of his foe. Louis had indeed, by his promptitude, gained some advantages on the side of Germany: but those advantages would avail little if England should suddenly resume her old rank in Europe. A few weeks would suffice for the enterprise on which the fate of the world depended; and for a few weeks the United Provinces were in security.

The prince had already fixed upon a general well qualified to be second in command. This was indeed no light matter. It was impossible to make choice of any Englishman without giving offence either to the Whigs or to the Tories. On the other hand it was not easy to assign pre-eminence to a foreigner without wounding the national sensibility of the haughty islanders. One man there was, and only one in Europe, to whom no objection could be found, Frederic, Count of Schomberg, a German, generally esteemed the greatest living master of the art of war. He had long passed his seventieth year: but both his mind and his body were still in full vigour. He had been in England, and was much loved and honoured there. He was, with the warm approbation of the chiefs of all the English parties, appointed William's lieutenant.

And now the Hague was crowded with British adventurers of all the various factions which the tyranny of James had united in a strange coalition. Conspicuous in this great assemblage were Charles Gerard, Earl of Macclesfield, an ancient Cavalier who had fought for Charles I; Peregrine Osborne, Lord Dumblane, heir apparent of the Earldom of Danby; and Viscount Mordaunt, exulting in the prospect of adventures irresistibly attractive to his fiery nature.

While these things were passing in Holland, James had at length become sensible of his danger. Intelligence which could not be disregarded came pouring in from various quarters. At length a despatch from Albeville removed all doubts. It is said that, when the King had read it, the blood left his cheeks, and he remained some time speechless. He might, indeed, well be appalled. In a few days he might have to fight, on English ground, for his Crown and for the birthright of his infant son.

The navy and army were far more than sufficient to repel a Dutch invasion. But could the navy, could the army, be trusted? Would not the trainbands flock by thousands to the standard of the deliverer? And where were now those gallant gentlemen who had ever been ready to shed their blood for the Crown? Outraged and insulted, driven from the bench of justice, and deprived of all military command, they saw the peril of their ungrateful sovereign with undisguised delight. The general impatience for the arrival of the Dutch became every day stronger. The gales which at this time blew obstinately from the west, and which at once prevented the prince's armament from sailing and brought fresh Irish regiments from Dublin to Chester, were bitterly cursed by the common people. The weather, it was said, was Popish.

And now it was noised abroad that Sunderland had been dismissed from all his places. There was a strong suspicion among those who watched him closely that, through some channel or other, he was in communication with the enemies of the government. He, with unabashed forehead, imprecated on his own head all evil here and hereafter if he was guilty. At the French embassy his professions still found credit. There he declared that he should remain a few days in London, and show himself at court. He would then retire to his country seat at Althorpe, and try to repair his dilapidated fortunes by economy.

On the 16th of October was held a solemn sitting of the States of Holland. The prince came to bid them farewell. He entreated them to believe that he had always endeavoured to promote the interest of his country. He was now quitting them, perhaps never to return. If he should fall in defence of the reformed religion and of the independence of Europe, he commended his beloved wife to their care.

In the evening he arrived at Helvoetsluys and went on board a frigate called the Brill. His flag was immediately hoisted. It displayed the arms of Nassau quartered with those of England. The motto, embroidered in letters three feet long, was happily chosen. The House of Orange had long used the elliptical device, 'I will maintain'. The ellipsis was now filled up with words of high import, 'The liberties of England and the Protestant religion'.

The prince had not been many hours on board when the wind became fair. On the 19th the armament put out to sea, and traversed about half the distance between the Dutch and English coasts. Then the wind changed, blew hard from the west, and swelled into a violent tempest. The ships, scattered and in great distress, regained the shore of Holland as they best might. The Brill reached Helvoetsluys on the 21st. The prince, though suffering from sea sickness, refused to go on shore. In two or three days the fleet reassembled. One vessel only had been cast away. Not a single soldier or sailor was missing. Some horses had perished: but this loss the prince with great expedition repaired; and, before the *London Gazette* had spread the news of his mishap, he was again ready to sail.

It was on the evening of Thursday the 1st of November that he put to sea the second time. The armament, during twelve hours, held a course towards the northwest. The light vessels sent out by the English admiral for the purpose of obtaining intelligence brought back news which confirmed the prevailing opinion that the enemy would try to land in Yorkshire. All at once, on a signal from the prince's ship, the whole fleet tacked, and made sail for the British Channel. The same breeze which favoured the voyage of the invaders prevented Dartmouth from coming out of the Thames.

At sunset the armament was off Beachy Head. Meanwhile a courier had been riding post from Dover Castle to Whitehall with news that the Dutch had passed the straits and were steering westward. It was necessary to make an immediate change in all the military arrangements. All the forces except those which were necessary to keep the peace of the capital were ordered to move to the west. Salisbury was appointed as the place of rendezvous.

When Sunday the 4th of November dawned, the cliffs of the Isle of Wight were full in view of the Dutch armament. In the afternoon and through the night the fleet held on its course. Torbay was the place where the prince intended to land. But the morning of the 5th was hazy. The pilot of the Brill could not discern the sea marks, and carried the fleet too far to the west. The danger was great. To return in the face of the wind was impossible. There could be little doubt, moreover, that by this time the royal fleet had got out of the Thames and was hastening full sail down the Channel. Russell saw the whole extent of the peril, and exclaimed to Burnet, 'You may go to prayers, doctor. All is over.' At that moment the wind changed: a soft breeze sprang up from the south: the mist dispersed: the sun shone forth; and, under the mild light of an autumnal noon, the fleet turned back, passed round the lofty cape of Berry Head, and rode safe in the harbour of Torbay.

The peasantry of the coast of Devonshire remembered the name of Monmouth with affection, and held Popery in detestation. They therefore crowded down to the seaside with provisions and offers of service. The disembarkation instantly commenced. Sixty boats conveyed the troops to the coast. The prince landed where the quay of Brixham now stands. As soon as he had planted his foot on dry ground he called for horses. Two were procured from the neighbouring village. William and Schomberg mounted and proceeded to examine the country.

The disembarkation had hardly been effected when the wind rose again, and swelled into a fierce gale from the west. The enemy coming in pursuit down the Channel had been stopped by the same change of weather which enabled William to land. During two days the King's fleet lay on an unruffled sea in sight of Beachy Head. At length Dartmouth was able to proceed. He passed the Isle of Wight, and one of his ships came in sight of the Dutch topmasts in Torbay. Just at this moment he was encountered by the tempest, and compelled to take shelter in the harbour of Portsmouth.

On Tuesday, the 6th of November, William's army began to march up the country. Some regiments advanced as far as Newton Abbot. Exeter, in the meantime, was greatly agitated. The magistrates were for the King, the body of the inhabitants for the prince. Everything was in confusion when, on the morning of the 8th, a body of troops, under the command of Mordaunt, appeared before the city. The mayor and aldermen had ordered the gates to be closed, but yielded on the first summons. The deanery was

The trial of the seven bishops, the birth of a male heir, and the arrival of units of the Irish army on English soil were the catalysts finally sealing the fate of James II. A powerful alliance of interests persuaded William of Orange that they looked to him to protect the Protestant religion in England by invasion, and promised support. William duly sailed and landed in England on 5 November 1688. This Dutch engraving represents Britannia welcoming William and Mary while James flees the country.

prepared for the reception of the prince. On the following day he arrived. The magistrates had been pressed to receive him in state at the entrance of the city, but had steadfastly refused. The pomp of that day, however, could well spare them. Such a sight had never been seen in Devonshire.

First rode Macclesfield, at the head of two hundred gentlemen, mostly of English blood, mounted on Flemish war horses. Then, with drawn broadswords, came a squadron of Swedish horsemen in black armour and fur cloaks. Next, surrounded by a goodly company of gentlemen and pages, was borne aloft the prince's banner. On its broad folds the crowd which covered the roofs and filled the windows read with delight that memorable inscription, 'The Protestant religion and the liberties of England'. But the acclamations redoubled when, attended by forty running footmen, the prince himself appeared, armed on back and breast, wearing a white plume and mounted on a white charger. Near to the prince was one who divided with him the gaze of the multitude. That, men said, was the great Count Schomberg, the man whose genius and valour had saved the Portuguese monarchy on the field of Montes Claros, the man who had earned a still higher glory by resigning the truncheon of a Marshal of France for the sake of the true religion. Then came a long column of the whiskered infantry of Switzerland, never till that week seen on English ground. And then marched a succession of bands designated, as was the fashion of that age, after their leaders, Bentinck, Solmes and Ginkell, Talmash and Mackay.

While these things were passing in Devonshire the ferment was great in London. On the whole, however, things as yet looked not unfavourably for James. No rebellion had broken out in the north or the east. No servant of the Crown appeared to have betrayed his trust. The royal army was assembling fast at Salisbury, and, though inferior in discipline to that of William, was superior in numbers.

The prince was undoubtedly surprised by the slackness of those who had invited him to England. By the common people of Devonshire, indeed, he had been received with every sign of good will: but no nobleman, no gentleman of high consideration, had yet repaired to his quarters. The explanation of this singular fact is probably to be found in the circumstance that he had landed in a part of the island where he had not been expected. His friends in the north had made their arrangements for a rising, on the supposition that he would be among them with an army. His friends in the west had made no arrangements at all. At length, on the 12th, a gentleman named Burrington, who resided in the neighbourhood of Crediton, joined the prince's standard, and his example was followed by several of his neighbours.

Men of higher consequence had already set out from different parts of the country for Exeter. But the King had less to fear from those who openly arrayed themselves against his authority, than from the dark conspiracy which had spread its ramifications through his army and his family. Of that conspiracy Churchill must be regarded as the soul. It was not yet time for him to strike the decisive blow. But even thus early he inflicted, by the instrumentality of a subordinate agent, a wound on the royal cause.

Edward Viscount Cornbury, eldest son of the Earl of Clarendon, was a young man of loose principles and violent temper. He had been early taught to consider his relationship to the Princess Anne as the groundwork of his fortunes, and had been exhorted to pay her assiduous court. It had never occurred to his father that the hereditary loyalty of the Hydes could run any risk of contamination in the household of the King's favourite daughter: but in that household the Churchills held absolute sway; and Cornbury became their tool. He commanded one of the regiments of dragoons which had been sent westward. On the 14th of November he was, during a few hours, the senior officer at Salisbury, and all the troops assembled there were subject to his authority.

Suddenly three of the regiments of cavalry were ordered to march westward. Cornbury put himself at their head, and conducted them first to Blandford and thence to Dorchester. From Dorchester they set out for Axminster. Some of the officers began to be uneasy, and demanded an explanation of these strange movements. Cornbury replied that he had instructions to make a night attack on some troops which the Prince of Orange had posted at Honiton. But suspicion was awake. At last Cornbury was pressed to produce his orders. He perceived, not only that it would be impossible for him to carry over all the three regiments, as he had hoped, but that he was himself in a situation of considerable peril. He accordingly stole away with a few followers to the Dutch quarters. Most of his troops returned to Salisbury: but some who had been detached from the main body proceeded to Honiton. There they found themselves in the midst of a large force which was fully prepared to receive them. Resistance was impossible. Their leader pressed them to take service under William. A gratuity of a month's pay was offered to them, and was by most of them accepted.

The news of these events reached London on the 15th. That afternoon, just as the King was sitting down to dinner, arrived an express with the tidings of Cornbury's defection. James turned away from his untasted meal, swallowed a crust of bread and a glass of wine, and retired to his closet. He afterwards learned that, as he was rising from table, several of the lords in whom he reposed the greatest confidence were shaking hands and congratulating each other in the adjoining gallery.

And now the King called together the principal officers who were still in London. Churchill made his appearance with that bland serenity which neither peril nor infamy could ever disturb. The meeting was attended by Henry Fitzroy, Duke of Grafton, colonel of the First Regiment of Foot Guards. He seems to have been at this time completely under Churchill's influence. Two other traitors were in the circle, Kirke and Trelawney, who commanded those two fierce and lawless bands then known as the Tangier Regiments. James addressed the assembly in language worthy of a better man and a better cause. It might be, he said, that some of the officers had conscientious scruples about fighting for him. If so, he was willing to receive back their commissions. But he adjured them as gentlemen and soldiers not to imitate the shameful example of Cornbury. All seemed moved. Churchill was the first to vow that he would shed the last drop of his blood in the service of his gracious master: Grafton was loud and forward in similar protestations; and the example was followed by Kirke and Trelawney.

Deceived by these professions, the King prepared to set out for Salisbury. On the day on which he left London the Prince of Wales was sent to Portsmouth. The fleet commanded by Dartmouth lay close at hand: and it was supposed that, if things went ill, the royal infant would, without difficulty, be conveyed to France.

On the 19th James reached Salisbury, and took up his quarters in the episcopal palace. Evil news was now fast pouring in upon him from all sides. The western counties had at length risen. As soon as the news of Cornbury's desertion was known, many wealthy landowners took heart and hastened to Exeter. While the west was thus rising to confront the King, the north was all in a flame behind him. On the 16th Lord Delamere took arms in Cheshire. The neighbouring counties were violently agitated. Danby seized York, and Devonshire, at the head of a great body of friends and dependents, appeared in arms at Derby. He then proceeded to Nottingham, which soon became the head quarters of the northern insurrection.

All this time the hostile armies in the south were approaching each other. The Prince of Orange, when he learned that the King had arrived at Salisbury, thought it time to leave Exeter. He set out on the 21st, escorted by many of the most considerable gentlemen of the western counties, for Axminster, where he remained several days.

Churchill and some of the principal accomplices were assembled at Salisbury. Kirke and Trelawney had proceeded to Warminster, where their regiments were posted. All was ripe for the execution of the long meditated treason.

Churchill advised the King to visit Warminster, and to inspect the troops stationed there. James assented; and his coach was at the door of the episcopal palace when his nose began to bleed violently. He was forced to postpone his expedition and to put himself under medical treatment. Three days elapsed before the haemorrhage was entirely subdued; and during those three days alarming rumours reached his ears.

Feversham, who held the chief command, reported that there was a bad spirit in the army. It was hinted to the King that some who were near his person were not his friends, and that it would be a wise precaution to send Churchill and Grafton under a guard to Portsmouth. James rejected this counsel. A propensity to suspicion was not among his vices. Nevertheless the reports which he had received of the state of his army disturbed him greatly. On the evening of the 24th he called a council of war. The meeting was attended by those officers against whom he had been most earnestly cautioned. Feversham expressed an opinion that it was desirable to fall back. Churchill argued on the other side. At length the King declared that he had decided for a retreat. Churchill saw or imagined that he was distrusted, and could not conceal his uneasiness. Before the day broke he fled to the prince's quarters, accompanied by Grafton.

Next morning all was confusion in the royal camp. The consternation of James was increased by news which arrived on the same day from Warminster. Kirke had refused to obey orders which he had received from Salisbury. There could no longer be any doubt that he too was in league with the Prince of Orange.

All these things confirmed James in the resolution which he had taken on the preceding evening. Orders were given for an immediate retreat. Salisbury was in an uproar. The camp broke up with the confusion of a flight. No man knew whom to trust or whom to obey. The material strength of the army was little diminished: but its moral strength had been destroyed.

James went that day as far as Andover. On the following morning he set off for London, breathing vengeance against Churchill. That evening he sate in Council with his principal ministers till a late hour. It was determined that he should summon all the lords spiritual and temporal who were then in London to attend him on the following day. Accordingly, on the afternoon of the 27th, the lords met in the dining room of the palace. The assembly consisted of nine prelates and between thirty and forty noblemen, all Protestants. The King himself presided. The traces of severe bodily and mental suffering were discernible in his countenance and deportment. During his absence from London, he said, great changes had taken place. He had observed that his people everywhere seemed anxious that Parliament should meet. He had therefore commanded the attendance of his faithful peers, in order to ask their counsel.

For a time there was silence. Then Rochester declared that he saw no hope for the throne or the country but in a Parliament. He added that it might be advisable to open a negotiation with the Prince of Orange. Jeffreys and Godolphin followed; and both declared that they agreed with Rochester.

Then, with many expressions of sympathy and deference, Halifax declared it to be his opinion that the King must make up his mind to great sacrifices. It was not enough to convoke a Parliament or to open a negotiation with the prince. Some at least of the grievances of which the nation complained should be instantly redressed without waiting till redress was demanded by the Houses or by the captain of the hostile army. Nottingham declared that he agreed with Halifax. The chief concessions which these lords pressed the King to make were three. He ought, they said, forthwith to dismiss all Roman Catholics from office, to separate himself wholly from France, and to grant an unlimited amnesty to those who were in arms against him.

After a long and animated debate the King broke up the meeting. 'My lords,' he said, 'I have made up my mind on one point. I shall call a Parliament. The other suggestions which have been offered are of grave importance; and you will not be surprised that I take a night to reflect on them before I decide.'

The Flight of King James

At first James seemed disposed to make excellent use of the time which he had taken for consideration. The Chancellor was directed to issue writs convoking a Parliament for the 13th of January. Halifax was appointed a commissioner to treat with the Prince of Orange; and with him were joined Nottingham and Godolphin. A proclamation was put forth by which the King not only granted a free pardon to all who were in rebellion against him, but declared them eligible to be members of the approaching Parliament. But these concessions were meant only to blind the lords and the nation to the King's real designs. On the very day on which he issued the proclamation of amnesty, he fully explained his intentions to Barillon. 'This negotiation'; said James, 'is a mere feint. I must send commissioners to my nephew, that I may gain time to ship off my wife and the Prince of Wales. A Parliament would impose on me conditions which I could not endure. As soon, therefore, as the Queen and my child are safe, I will leave England, and take refuge in Ireland, in Scotland, or with your master.'

Already Dover had been sent to Portsmouth with instructions to take charge of the Prince of Wales; and Dartmouth had been ordered to obey Dover's directions in all things concerning the royal infant. The King now sent positive orders that the child should instantly be conveyed to the nearest continental port. But an unexpected impediment compelled him to postpone the execution of his design. His agents at Portsmouth began to entertain scruples. Dover showed signs of hesitation. Dartmouth was still less disposed to comply with the royal wishes. A change of plan was necessary. The child must be brought back to London, and sent thence to France. An interval of some days must elapse before this could be done. During that interval the public mind must be amused by the hope of a Parliament and the semblance of a negotiation. Writs were sent out for the elections. Trumpeters went backward and forward between the capital and the Dutch headquarters. At length passes for the King's commissioners arrived; and the three lords set out on their embassy.

On the morning of Saturday, the 8th of December, they reached Hungerford. The prince's bodyguard was drawn up to receive them with military respect. They were ushered into his bedchamber, where they found him surrounded by a crowd of noblemen and gentlemen. The proposition which the commissioners had been instructed to make was that the points in dispute should be referred to the Parliament, for which the writs were already sealing, and that in the meantime the prince's army would not come within thirty or forty miles of London. Halifax explained that this was the basis on which he and his colleagues were prepared to treat, and retired.

William requested the lords and gentlemen whom he had convoked on this occasion to consult together, unrestrained by his presence, as to the answer which ought to be returned. To himself, however, he reserved the power of deciding in the last resort, after hearing their opinion. He then left them, and retired to Littlecote Hall, a manor house situated about two miles off.

That afternoon the noblemen and gentlemen met in the great room of the principal inn at Hungerford. It soon appeared that the assembly was divided into two parties, a party anxious to come to terms with the King, and a party bent on his destruction. The majority was for rejecting the proposition which the royal commissioners had been instructed to make. The resolution of the assembly was reported to the prince at Littlecote: but he overruled the opinion of his too eager followers, and declared his determination to treat on the basis proposed by the King. On his side he made some demands which even those who were least disposed to commend him allowed to be moderate. He insisted that the existing statutes should be obeyed till they should be altered by competent authority, and that all persons who held offices without a legal qualification should be forthwith dismissed. He thought it reasonable that, since his troops were not to advance within forty miles of London on the west, the King's troops should fall back as far to the east. There would thus be, round the spot where the Houses were to meet, a wide circle of neutral ground.

The propositions of William were framed with a punctilious fairness; and no fault could be found with them by the partisans of the King. To the success of William's vast and profound scheme of policy it was necessary that James should ruin himself by rejecting conditions ostentatiously liberal. The event proved the wisdom of the course which the majority of the Englishmen at Hungerford were inclined to condemn.

On the same day on which the three lords reached Hungerford the Prince of Wales arrived at Westminster. To send him and the Queen out of the country without delay was now the first object of James. But who could be trusted to manage the escape? James bethought him of a French nobleman who then resided in London, Antonine, Count of Lauzun. He had courage and a sense of honour, had been accustomed to eccentric adventures, and had a strong propensity to knight errantry. He eagerly accepted the high trust which was offered to him; and the arrangements for the flight were promptly made.

On the morning of Monday, the 10th of December, the King learned that his wife and son had begun their voyage. About the same time a courier arrived at the palace with despatches from Hungerford. Had James been a little more discerning, those despatches would have induced him to reconsider all his plans. But it soon appeared that William, in offering those terms which the Whigs at Hungerford had censured as too indulgent, had risked nothing. Already James had entrusted his most valuable movables to the care of several foreign ambassadors. But before the flight there was still something to be done. The tyrant pleased himself with the thought that he might avenge himself on a people who had been impatient of his despotism by inflicting on them at parting all the evils of anarchy. He ordered the Great Seal and the writs for the new Parliament to be brought to his apartment. The writs he threw into the fire. To Feversham he wrote a letter which could be understood only as a command to disband the army. Still, however, he concealed, even from his chief ministers, his intention of absconding. Just before he retired he directed Jeffreys to be in the closet early on the morrow. Everybody withdrew except the Duke of Northumberland. This young man, a natural son of Charles II by the Duchess of Cleveland, commanded a troop of Life Guards, and was a Lord of the Bedchamber. It seems to have been then the custom of the court that, in the Queen's absence, a Lord of the Bedchamber should sleep on a pallet in the King's room; and it was Northumberland's turn to perform this duty.

At three in the morning of Tuesday the 11th of December, James rose, took the Great Seal in his hand, laid his commands on Northumberland not to open the door of the bedchamber till the usual hour, and disappeared through a secret passage. Sir Edward Hales was in attendance with a hackney coach. James was conveyed to Millbank, where he crossed the Thames in a small wherry. As he passed Lambeth he flung the Great Seal into the midst of the stream, where, after many months, it was accidentally caught by a fishing net and dragged up.

At Vauxhall he landed. A carriage and horses had been stationed there for him; and he immediately took the road towards Sheerness, where a hoy belonging to the Custom House had been ordered to await his arrival.

Northumberland did not open the door of the royal apartment till it was broad day. The antechamber was filled with courtiers who came to make their morning bow and with lords who had been summoned to Council. The news of James's flight passed in an instant from the galleries to the streets; and the whole capital was in commotion.

It was a terrible moment. The King was gone. The prince had not arrived. No regency had been appointed. The Great Seal, essential to the administration of ordinary justice, had disappeared. It was soon known that Feversham had, on receipt of the royal order, instantly disbanded his forces. The populace of London had, during some weeks, shown a strong disposition to turbulence and rapine. The urgency of the crisis united for a short time all who had any interest in the peace of society. Rochester saw that there was only one way of averting general confusion. 'Muster your

The Lord Chancellor taken disguis'd in Wapping
Brother Petars what doest thou say —
Remember ye West
Remember ye Bishops
Knock his brains out
Remember mr Conesh
Tear me to peeces.
Remember Maudlin College

troop of Guards,' he said to Northumberland; 'and declare for the Prince of Orange.'

It was necessary to the public safety that there should be a provisional government; and the eyes of men naturally turned to the magnates of the realm. Most of the peers who were in the capital repaired to Guildhall, and were received there with all honour by the magistracy of the City. Sancroft took the chair; and, under his presidency, the lords drew up, subscribed, and published a declaration. By this instrument they declared that they had determined to join with the Prince of Orange, in order that the freedom of the nation might be vindicated, and that the Protestant interest throughout the world might be strengthened. Till His Highness should arrive, they were prepared to take on themselves the responsibility of giving such directions as might be necessary for the preservation of order. A deputation was sent to lay this declaration before the prince, and to inform him that he was impatiently expected in London.

Never, within the memory of man, had there been so near an approach to entire concord among all intelligent Englishmen as at this conjuncture; and never had concord been more needed. All those evil passions which it is the office of government to restrain, were on a sudden emancipated from control; avarice, licentiousness, revenge, the hatred of sect to sect, the hatred of nation to nation. When the night approached, forth came, from every den of vice, thousands of housebreakers and highwaymen, cutpurses and ringdroppers. With these were mingled thousands of idle apprentices, who wished merely for the excitement of a riot.

The morning of the 12th of December rose on a ghastly sight. The capital in many places presented the aspect of a city taken by storm. The lords met at Whitehall, and exerted themselves to restore tranquillity. The trainbands were ordered under arms. In spite, however, of the efforts of the provisional government, the agitation grew hourly more formidable. It was heightened by an event which can hardly be related without a feeling of vindictive pleasure. A scrivener who lived at Wapping, and whose trade was to furnish the seafaring men there with money at high interest, had some time before lent a sum on bottomry. The debtor applied to equity for relief against his own bond; and the case came before Jeffreys. The counsel for the borrower, having little else to say, said that the lender was a Trimmer. The Chancellor instantly fired. 'A Trimmer! where is he? I have heard of that kind of monster. What is it made like?' The unfortunate creditor was forced to stand forth. The Chancellor glared fiercely on him, stormed at him, and sent him away half dead with fright. 'While I live', the poor man said, 'I shall never forget that terrible countenance.' And now the day of retribution had arrived. The Trimmer was walking through Wapping, when he saw a well known face looking out of the window of an alehouse. The eyebrows, indeed, had been shaved away. The dress was that of a common sailor from Newcastle, and was black with coal dust; but there was no mistaking the savage eye and mouth of Jeffreys. The alarm was given. In a moment the house was surrounded by hundreds of people shaking bludgeons and bellowing curses. The fugitive's life was saved by a company of the trainbands; and he was carried before the Lord Mayor. The throng without was constantly becoming more numerous and more savage. Jeffreys begged to be sent to prison. An order to that effect was procured from the lords who were sitting at Whitehall; and he was conveyed in a carriage to the Tower. Two regiments of militia were drawn out

With the flight of James his closest associates were left unprotected. A scrivener who had once appeared before the terrible Judge Jeffreys to be terrified out of his wits, spied his unforgettable features peering out of a Wapping alehouse. He raised the alarm, but Jeffreys was rescued from an enraged mob by a company of the train bands. This contemporary engraving shows his capture.

to escort him, and found the duty a difficult one. The thousands who were disappointed of their revenge pursued the coach, with howls of rage, to the gate of the Tower. The wretched man meantime was in convulsions of terror. He wrung his hands: he looked wildly out, sometimes at one window, sometimes at the other, and was heard even above the tumult, crying 'Keep them off, gentlemen! For God's sake keep them off!' At length he was safely lodged in the fortress where some of his most illustrious victims had passed their last days, and where his own life was destined to close in unspeakable ignominy and horror.

On the following morning the people of London were surprised by a rumour that the King had been detained, and was still in the island. The report was fully confirmed before the evening.

James had travelled with relays of coach horses along the southern shore of the Thames, and on the morning of the 12th had reached Emley Ferry near the island of Sheppey. There lay the hoy in which he was to sail. He went on board: but the wind blew fresh; and the master would not venture to put to sea without more ballast. A tide was thus lost. Midnight was approaching before the vessel began to float. By that time the news that the King had disappeared, and that London was in confusion, had travelled fast down the Thames. The rude fishermen of the Kentish coast eyed the hoy with suspicion and with cupidity. It was whispered that some persons in the garb of gentlemen had gone on board of her in great haste. Perhaps they were Jesuits; perhaps they were rich. Fifty or sixty boatmen boarded the hoy just as she was about to make sail. The King's appearance excited suspicion. He was rudely pulled and pushed about. His money and watch were taken from him. He had about him his coronation ring, and some other trinkets of great value; but these escaped the search of the robbers, who indeed were so ignorant of jewellery that they took his diamond buckles for bits of glass.

At length the prisoners were put on shore and carried to an inn. A crowd had assembled there to see them; and James, though disguised by a wig of different shape and colour from that which he usually wore, was at once recognised. For a moment the rabble seemed to be overawed; but the exhortations of their chiefs revived their courage. They assured the King that they would not hurt him: but they refused to let him depart.

From the moment when it was known that the King was still in England, Sancroft absented himself from the sittings of the peers. Halifax, who had just returned from the Dutch headquarters, was placed in the chair. His sentiments had undergone a great change in a few hours. He had been deceived, and had been used as an instrument for deceiving the nation. His mission to Hungerford had been a fool's errand. His judgment and his resentment alike induced him to relinquish the schemes of reconciliation on which he had hitherto been intent, and to place himself at the head of those who were bent on raising William to the throne.

The business of the day was nearly over, and Halifax was about to rise, when he was informed that a messenger from Sheerness was in attendance. The man told his story with many tears, and produced a letter in the King's hand, and addressed to no particular person, but imploring the aid of all good Englishmen.

Such an appeal it was hardly possible to disregard. The lords ordered Feversham to hasten with a troop of the Life Guards to the place where the King was detained, and to set His Majesty at liberty.

James's first attempt at escape failed when he was inadvertently detained by a group of fishermen. He was allowed by William to escape a second time. Once in France he was generously treated by Louis XIV. The illustration shows James on the left being greeted by the French King at Saint Germains-en-Laye, which Louis had placed at the disposal of the exiled court; in the background Mary of Modena awaits her husband.

Feversham soon arrived. He had left his troop at Sittingbourne: but there was no occasion to use force. The King was suffered to depart without opposition, and was removed by his friends to Rochester. He was in a pitiable state. The rough corporal usage which he had now, for the first time, undergone, seems to have discomposed him more than any other event of his chequered life. Yet, had he possessed an ordinary measure of good sense, he would have seen that those who had detained him had unintentionally done him a great service. He had another chance, a last chance. Great as his offences had been, to dethrone him, while he remained in his kingdom and offered to assent to such conditions as a free Parliament might impose, would have been almost impossible.

During a short time he seemed disposed to remain. He sent Feversham from Rochester with a letter to William. The substance of the letter was that His Majesty was on his way back to Whitehall, that he wished to have a personal conference with the prince, and that Saint James's Palace should be fitted up for His Highness.

William was now at Windsor. He had learned with deep mortification of the events which had taken place on the coast of Kent. No course was open to him which was altogether free from objections, no course which would place him in a situation so advantageous as that which he had occupied a few hours before. Yet something might be done. The King's first attempt to escape had failed. What was now most to be desired was that he should make a second attempt with better success. It might not be impossible, without either using or threatening violence, to make so weak a man uneasy about his personal safety. He would soon be eager to fly. All facilities for flight must then be placed within his reach; and care must be taken that he should not again be stopped by any officious blunderer.

William soon had an excellent opportunity of commencing his system of intimidation. Feversham arrived at Windsor with James's letter. He was asked for his safe conduct. He had none. William refused to see him, and ordered him to be put under arrest. Zulestein was instantly despatched to inform James that the prince declined the proposed conference, and desired that His Majesty would remain at Rochester.

But it was too late. James was already in London. He arrived there on the afternoon of Sunday the 16th of December. He had been apprehensive that the common people would offer him some affront: but the very violence of the recent outbreak had produced a remission. In no quarter was any disposition shown to insult the King. Some cheers were raised as his coach passed through the City, and a few bonfires were lighted in honour of his return. His feeble mind was extravagantly elated by these unexpected signs of popular goodwill. But scarcely had he entered his palace when Zulestein was announced. William's cold and stern message was delivered. Zulestein retired; and soon a gentleman entered the bedchamber with the news that Feversham had been put under arrest. James was greatly disturbed.

His fate, meanwhile, was the subject of grave deliberation at Windsor. The court of William was now crowded with eminent men of all parties. Several of the lords who had, during the anarchy of the preceding week, taken upon themselves to act as a provisional government, had, as soon as the King returned, quitted London for the Dutch headquarters. One of these was Halifax.

On the 17th, all the peers who were at Windsor were summoned to a consultation at the castle. The subject proposed for deliberation was what should be done with the King. On one point they were agreed. He could not be suffered to remain where he was. That one prince should fortify himself in Whitehall, and the other in Saint James's, was universally felt to be inexpedient. The lords, therefore, thought it advisable that James should be sent out of London. Ham, regarded as the most luxurious of villas, was proposed as a convenient retreat. A short message to the King was drawn up; and William appointed Halifax, Shrewsbury, and Delamere to be the messengers.

A little after midnight the three lords arrived at Whitehall. The King was awakened; and they were ushered into his bedchamber. They delivered into his hand the letter with which they had been entrusted, and informed him that the prince would be at Westminster in a few hours, and that His Majesty would do well to set out for Ham before ten in the morning. James made some difficulties. He did not like Ham: he would greatly prefer Rochester. The lords answered that they had not authority to accede to His Majesty's wish, but that they would send off an express to the prince, who was to lodge that night at Sion House. A courier started immediately, and returned before daybreak with William's consent.

On the morning of the 18th of December, a rainy and stormy morning, the royal barge was early at Whitehall stairs: and round it were eight or ten boats filled with Dutch soldiers. Several noblemen and gentlemen attended the King to the waterside. It is said, and may well be believed, that many tears were shed. While the barge was slowly working its way on rough waves down the river, brigade after brigade of the prince's troops marched into London from the west. In defiance of the weather a great multitude assembled between Albemarle House and Saint James's Palace, to greet the prince. Every hat, every cane, was adorned with an orange riband. William, however, who had no taste for crowds and shouting, took the road through the park. Before nightfall he arrived at Saint James's in a light carriage, accompanied by Schomberg. In a short time all the rooms and staircases in the palace were thronged by those who came to pay their court.

Though the acclamations were loud, William felt that the difficulties of his enterprise were but beginning. It was now necessary that he should exchange the character of a general for that of a magistrate; and this was no easy task. It was impossible to take any step without offending prejudices and rousing angry passions. He therefore determined to leave to the legislature the office of settling the government. Authority strictly parliamentary there was none in the State: but it was possible to bring together, in a few hours, an assembly which would be regarded by the nation with a large portion of the respect due to a Parliament. The peers were summoned to Saint James's on the 21st of December. About seventy attended. The prince requested them to consider the state of the country, and to lay before him the result of their deliberations. Shortly after appeared a notice inviting all gentlemen who had sate in the House of Commons during the reign of Charles II to attend His Highness on the morning of the 26th.

A strong party among the peers still cherished the hope that the constitution and religion of England might be secured without the deposition of the King. Several messengers were sent to Rochester with letters for him. He was assured that his interests would be strenuously defended, if only he could, at the last moment, make up his mind to renounce designs abhorred by his people. The advice was good; but James was in no condition to take it. To the earnest entreaties of the agents whom his friends had sent to Rochester, he had only one answer. His head was in danger. Fright overpowered every other feeling. He determined to depart; and it was easy for him to do so.

The arrangements were expeditiously made. On the evening of the 22nd the King assured some of the gentlemen who had been sent to him from London that he would see them again in the morning. He went to bed, rose at dead of night, stole out at a back door, and went through the garden to the shore of the Medway. A small skiff was in waiting. Soon after dawn the fugitive was on board of a smack which was running down the Thames.

That afternoon the tidings of the flight reached London. The King's adherents were confounded. The good news encouraged the prince to take a bold and important step. He was informed that communications were passing between the French embassy and the party hostile to him. He was a general: and, as such, he was not bound to tolerate, within the territory of which he had taken military occupation, the presence of one whom he regarded as a spy. Before that day closed Barillon was informed that he must leave England within twenty-four hours.

On Monday the 24th the lords met again, and resolved that two addresses should be presented to William. One requested him to take on himself provisionally the administration of the government; the other recommended that he should invite all the constituent bodies of the kingdom to send up representatives to Westminster.

The commoners who had been summoned met in Saint Stephen's Chapel, and formed a numerous assembly. Addresses were proposed and adopted similar to those which the lords had already presented. The resolutions of the meeting were communicated to the prince. He forthwith announced his determination to comply with the joint request of the two Chambers which he had called together, to issue letters summoning a Convention of the Estates of the Realm, and, till the convention should meet, to take on himself the executive administration.

PART 4

The Reign of William and Mary

The Glorious Revolution

William addressed himself with vigour to the work of restoring order. He published a proclamation by which all magistrates were continued in office, and another containing orders for the collection of the revenue. A way was found of employing the thousands of Irish soldiers whom James had brought into England. It was determined that they should be conveyed to the Continent, where they might, under the banners of the House of Austria, render effectual service to the cause of the Protestant religion. Dartmouth was removed from his command; and the navy was conciliated by assurances that every sailor should speedily receive his due. In a very few days the confusion which the invasion, the insurrection, the flight of James, and the suspension of all regular government had produced, was at an end, and the kingdom wore again its accustomed aspect.

The King of France, meanwhile, saw with peculiar emotion the calamities of the House of Stuart. His heart was naturally compassionate;

Broadsheet reflecting the tremendous fears felt in England in the 1670s concerning the Roman Church and the Pope. The country was in a ferment of excitement and suspicion over the alleged Popish Plot; and over the possibility of the Duke of York succeeding to the throne.

Woodcut from a contemporary broadsheet showing the Pope persuading Catholics to betray the country.

and this was an occasion which could not fail to call forth all his compassion. As soon as the news that the Queen of England was on the French coast had been brought to Versailles, a palace was prepared for her reception. Louis went forth in state to receive the exiled Queen. Before the procession had gone far it was announced that Mary was approaching. Louis alighted and advanced on foot to meet her. The cavalcade then turned towards Saint Germains.

At Saint Germains, on the brow of a hill which looks down on the windings of the Seine, Francis I had built a castle, and Henry IV had constructed a noble terrace. Of the residences of the French kings none stood in a more salubrious air or commanded a fairer prospect. Saint Germains had now been selected to be the abode of the royal family of England.

On the following day James arrived. Louis embraced him with brotherly tenderness. The two Kings then entered the Queen's room. 'Here is a gentleman', said Louis to Mary, 'whom you will be glad to see.' In a few hours the royal pair were informed that, as long as they would do the King of France the favour to accept of his hospitality, forty-five thousand pounds sterling a year would be paid them from his treasury.

In England, the elections went on rapidly and smoothly. There was scarcely a county in which the gentry and yeomanry had not, many months before, fixed upon candidates, good Protestants, whom no exertions must be spared to carry, in defiance of the King; and these candidates were now generally returned without opposition.

At break of day, on the 22nd of January, the House of Commons was crowded with knights and burgesses. On the benches appeared many faces which had been well known in that place during the reign of Charles II, but had not been seen there under his successor. But the veterans who now, after a long seclusion, returned to public life, were all speedily thrown into the shade by two younger Whigs who, on this great day, took their seats for the first time, Charles Montague and John Somers.

On the 28th the Commons resolved themselves into a committee of the whole House. Richard Hampden, son of the illustrious leader of the Roundheads, was placed in the chair, and the great debate began.

It was soon evident that an overwhelming majority considered James as no longer King. But the majority was made up of two classes. One class consisted of eager and vehement Whigs, who, if they had been able to take their own course, would have given to the proceedings of the convention a decidedly revolutionary character. The other class admitted that a revolution was necessary, but regarded it as a necessary evil, and wished to disguise it under the show of legitimacy. It was not easy to draw up any form of words which would please all whose assent it was important to obtain; but at length, out of many suggestions offered from different quarters, a resolution was framed which gave general satisfaction. It was moved that King James II, having endeavoured to subvert the constitution

William of Orange and Princess Mary by Van Dyck. Mary was the eldest sister of James II and the mother of William III.

of the Kingdom by breaking the original contract between King and people, and, by the advice of Jesuits and other wicked persons, having violated the fundamental laws, and having withdrawn himself out of the kingdom, had abdicated the government, and that the throne had thereby become vacant. The motion was adopted without a division.

On the following morning the Lords assembled early. Hampden appeared at the bar, and put the resolution of the Commons into the hands of Halifax. The Upper House then resolved itself into a committee; and Danby took the chair.

The Tories insisted that their plan should be discussed before the vote of the Commons which declared the throne vacant was considered. This was conceded to them; and the question was put whether a Regency, exercising kingly power during the life of James, in his name, would be the best expedient for preserving the laws and liberties of the nation?

The contest was long and animated. The chief speakers in favour of a Regency were Rochester and Nottingham. Halifax and Danby led the other side. So numerous were the Tories in the Upper House that, notwithstanding the weakness of their case, they very nearly carried the day. A hundred lords divided. Forty-nine voted for a Regency, fifty-one against it.

Up to this moment the small body of peers which was under the guidance of Danby had acted in union with Halifax and the Whigs. The proposition that James had ceased to be King had been the rallying point of the two parties which had made up the majority. But from that point their path diverged. The next question to be decided was whether the throne was vacant; and this was a question of grave practical importance. If the throne was vacant, the estates of the realm might place William in it. If it was not vacant, he could succeed to it only after his wife, after Anne, and after Anne's posterity.

It was, according to the followers of Danby, an established maxim that our country could not be, even for a moment, without a rightful prince. If, these politicians said, we once admit that the throne is vacant, we admit that it is elective. The sovereign whom we may place on it will be a sovereign, not after the English, but after the Polish, fashion. This danger we avoid if we logically follow out the principles of the constitution to their consequences. There has been a demise of the Crown. At the instant of the demise the next heir became our lawful sovereign. We consider the Princess of Orange as next heir; and we hold that she ought, without any delay, to be proclaimed, what she already is, our Queen.

The Whigs answered that it was idle to apply ordinary rules to a country in a state of revolution. The truth was that the laws of England had made full provision for the succession when the power of a sovereign and his natural life terminated together, but had made no provision for the very rare cases in which his power terminated before the close of his natural life; and with one of those very rare cases the convention had now to deal. That James no longer filled the throne both Houses had pronounced. Neither common law nor statute law designated any person as entitled to fill the throne between his demise and his decease. It followed that the throne was vacant, and that the Houses might invite the Prince of Orange to fill it.

Many attempts were made to prevent an open breach between the party of the prince and the party of the princess. A great meeting was held at the Earl of Devonshire's house, and the dispute was warm. Halifax was the chief speaker for William, Danby for Mary. Of the mind of Mary Danby knew nothing. She had been some time expected in London, but had been detained in Holland by strong westerly winds. Had she arrived earlier the dispute would probably have been at once quieted. Halifax on the other side had no authority to say anything in William's name. The prince had maintained an impenetrable reserve, and had not suffered any word, look, or gesture, indicative either of satisfaction or of displeasure, to escape him.

At length Danby received from Mary an earnest, and almost angry, reprimand. She was, she wrote, the prince's wife; she had no other wish than to be subject to him: the most cruel injury that could be done to her would be to set her up as his competitor; and she never could regard any person who took such a course as her true friend.

And now William thought that the time had come when he ought to explain himself. He accordingly sent for Halifax, Danby, Shrewsbury, and some other political leaders of great note, and addressed to them a few deeply meditated words.

He had hitherto, he said, remained silent: but a crisis had now arrived at which it was necessary for him to declare his intentions. He did not desire to take any part in English affairs; but, if he did consent to take a part, there was one part only which he could usefully or honourably take. If the estates offered him the Crown for life, he would accept it. If not, he should, without repining, return to his native country.

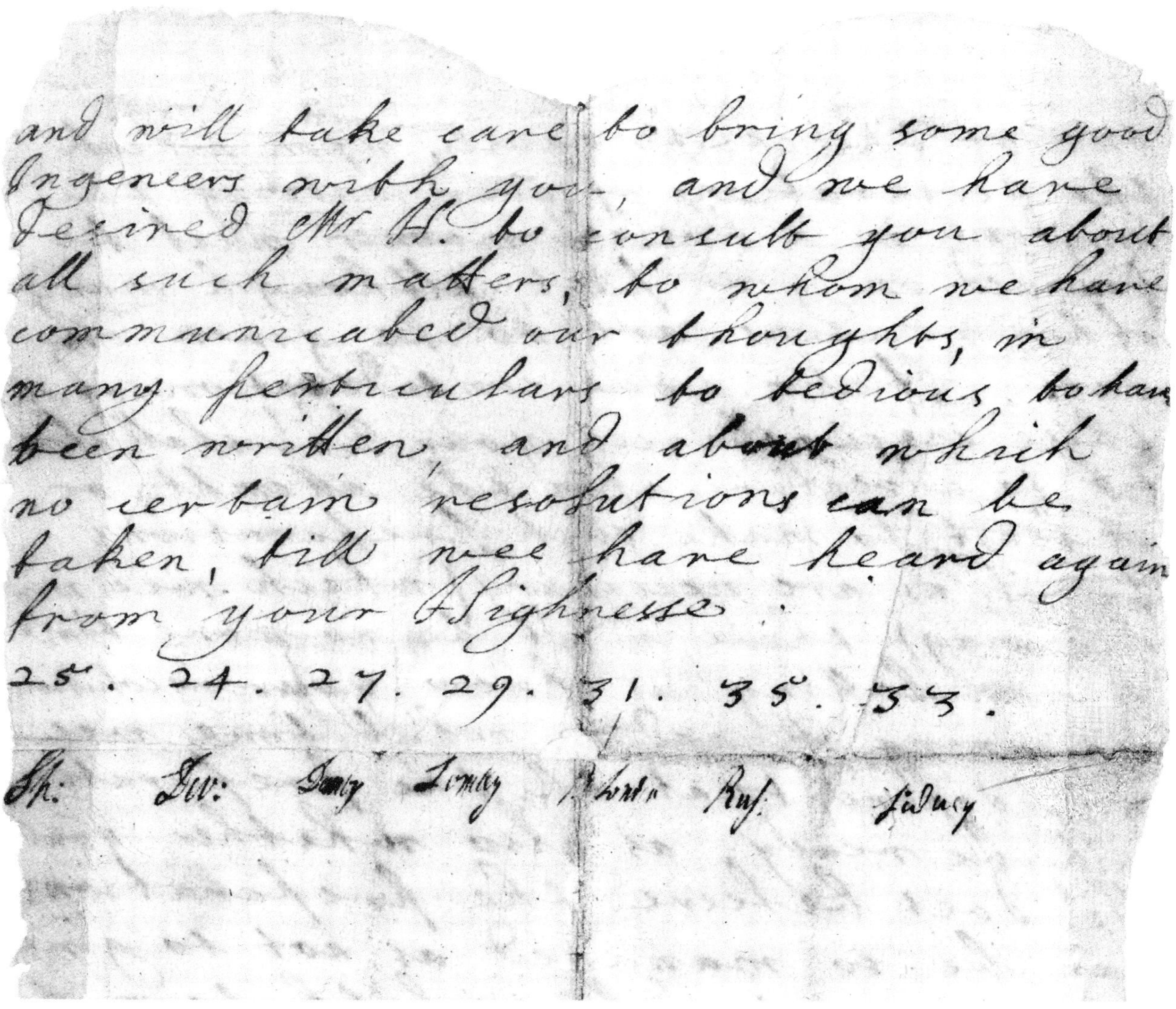
and will take care to bring some good Ingeneers with you, and wee have desired Mr H. to consult you about all such matters, to whom wee have communicated our thoughts, in many perticulars to tedious to have been written, and about which no certain resolutions can be taken, till wee have heard again from your Highnesse.

25. 24. 27. 29. 31. 35. 33.

Sh: Dev: Danby Lumley [illegible] Rus: Sidney

The final page of the letter of 'invitation' sent to William. The signatories identified themselves by number. They were: The Earl of Devonshire; Edward Russell, the Earl of Shrewsbury, the Earl of Danby, Lord Lumley, Henry Sidney and Dr Henry Compton.

Vertrek van zyn Koninglyke Hoogheid van Hellevoetsluis na Engeland.

William and Mary with attendants at Helvoetsluys prior to his departure in 1688.

What he had said was in a few hours known all over London. That he must be King was now clear. The only question was whether he should hold the regal dignity alone or conjointly with the princess. The general feeling was that Mary had given an unprecedented proof of conjugal submission and affection, and that the very least return that could be made to her would be to bestow on her the dignity of Queen Regnant. All those who considered James as no longer King were agreed as to the way in which the throne must be filled. William and Mary must be King and Queen. The heads of both must appear together on the coin: writs must run in the names of both: but the administration, which could not be safely divided, must belong to William alone.

The Commons determined to postpone all reforms till the ancient constitution of the kingdom should have been restored in all its parts, and forthwith to fill the throne without imposing on William and Mary any other obligation than that of governing according to the existing laws of England. In order that the questions which had been in dispute between the Stuarts and the nation might never again be stirred, it was determined that the instrument by which the Prince and Princess of Orange were called to the throne should set forth, in the most distinct and solemn manner, the fundamental principles of the constitution. This instrument, known by the name of the Declaration of Right, was prepared by a committee, of which Somers was chairman.

By this time the wind had ceased to blow from the west. The ship in which the Princess of Orange had embarked lay off Margate on the 11th of February, and, on the following morning, anchored at Greenwich.

On the morning of Wednesday, the 13th of February, the court of Whitehall and all the neighbouring streets were filled with gazers. The magnificent Banqueting House had been prepared for a great ceremony. The walls were lined by the yeomen of the guard. Near the northern door, on the right hand, a large number of peers had assembled. On the left were the Commons. The southern door opened: and the Prince and Princess of Orange, side by side, entered, and took their place under the canopy of State.

Both Houses approached bowing low. William and Mary advanced a few steps. Halifax, as Speaker of the House of Lords, stood forth. The convention, he said, had agreed to a resolution which he prayed Their Highnesses to hear. They signified their assent; and the clerk of the House of Lords read, in a loud voice, the Declaration of Right. When he had concluded, Halifax, in the name of all the estates of the realm, requested the prince and princess to accept the Crown.

William, in his own name and in that of his wife, answered that the Crown was, in their estimation, the more valuable because it was presented to them as a token of the confidence of the nation. 'We thankfully accept', he said, 'what you have offered us.' Then, for himself, he assured them that the laws of England should be the rules of his conduct, that it should be his study to promote the welfare of the kingdom, and that, as to the means of doing so, he should constantly recur to the advice of the Houses. These words were received with a shout of joy which was heard in the streets below, and was instantly answered by huzzas from many thousands of voices. The Lords and Commons then reverently retired from the Banqueting House and went in procession to the great gate of Whitehall. The kettle drums struck up: the trumpets pealed; and Garter

Manot's impression of the departure of William's fleet from Helvoetsluys in November 1688. His flag displayed the motto three feet long, 'I will maintain the Liberties of England and the Protestant religion'.

King at Arms, in a loud voice, proclaimed the Prince and Princess of Orange King and Queen of England, charged all Englishmen to bear true allegiance to the new sovereigns, and besought God to bless William and Mary with a long and happy reign.

Thus was consummated the English Revolution. To superficial observers it might well seem that William was, at this time, one of the most enviable of human beings. He was in truth one of the most anxious and unhappy. He well knew that the difficulties of his task were only beginning. Already that dawn which had lately been so bright was overcast; and many signs portended a dark and stormy day. The truce between the two great parties was at an end. They had been, during a few months, united by a common danger. But the danger was over: the union was dissolved; and the old animosity broke forth again in all its strength.

The internal government of England could be carried on only by the advice and agency of English ministers. Those ministers William selected in such a manner as showed that he was determined not to proscribe any set of men who were willing to support his throne. On the day after the Crown had been presented to him in the Banqueting House, the Privy Council was sworn in. Most of the councillors were Whigs: but the names of several eminent Tories appeared in the list. The four highest offices in the State were assigned to four noblemen, the representatives of four classes of politicians.

In practical ability and official experience Danby had no superior among his contemporaries. To the gratitude of the new sovereigns he had a strong claim; for it was by his dexterity that their marriage had been brought about. The enmity which he had always borne to France was a scarcely less powerful recommendation. Yet the Whigs regarded him with unconquerable distrust and aversion. Even in becoming a rebel, he had not ceased to be a Tory. The Whigs were of opinion that he ought to think himself amply

The disembarkation of the Prince of Orange at Brixham; a nineteenth-century redrawing of a contemporary copperplate engraving. The Brill *and her escorting fleet were lucky to make the right landfall, but a contrary wind changed and they made harbour safely. 'Well, doctor, what do you think of predestination now?' William is reported to have said to Dr Burnet.*

Christmas, 1688. William of Orange enters London to a tumultuous welcome: engraving by de Hooghe. 'Every hat, every cane, was adorned with an orange riband.'

rewarded for his recent merits by being suffered to escape the punishment of those offences for which he had been impeached ten years before. He, on the other hand, thought himself entitled to the great place of Lord High Treasurer, which he had formerly held. But he was disappointed. William, on principle, thought it desirable to divide the power of the Treasury among several commissioners. Danby was offered his choice between the Presidency of the Council and a Secretaryship of State. He sullenly accepted the Presidency, and hardly attempted to conceal his anger at not having been placed higher.

Halifax, the most illustrious man of that small party which boasted that it kept the balance even between Whigs and Tories, took charge of the Privy Seal, and continued to be Speaker of the House of Lords.

The vexation with which the Whigs saw Danby presiding in the Council, and Halifax bearing the Privy Seal, was not diminished by the news that Nottingham was appointed Secretary of State. Some of those zealous churchmen who had never ceased to profess the doctrine of nonresistance, who had voted for a Regency, and who had to the last maintained that the English throne could never be one moment vacant, yet conceived it to be their duty to submit to the decision of the convention. They had not, they said, rebelled against James. They had not elected William. But, now that they saw on the throne a sovereign whom they never would have placed there, they were of opinion that no law, divine or human, bound them to carry the contest further. One of the most eminent politicians of this school was Nottingham. William doubtless hoped that his appointment would be considered by the clergy and the Tory country gentlemen as a sufficient guarantee that no evil was meditated against the Church.

The other Secretary was Charles Talbot, Earl of Shrewsbury. No man so young had within living memory occupied so high a post in the government. He had but just completed his twenty-eighth year. Nobody, however, thought his youth an objection to his promotion. He had already secured for himself a place in history by the conspicuous part which he had taken in the deliverance of his country. By the Whigs he was almost adored. None suspected that, with many great and many amiable qualities, he had such faults both of head and of heart as would make the rest of his life burdensome to himself and almost useless to his country.

The naval administration and the financial administration were confided to boards. Herbert was First Commissioner of the Admiralty. Mordaunt, one of the most vehement of the Whigs, was placed at the head of the Treasury.

In the royal household were placed some of those Dutch nobles who stood highest in the favour of the King. Bentinck had the great office of Groom of the Stole. Zulestein took charge of the robes. The Master of the Horse was Auverquerque, a gallant soldier, who had, on the bloody day of Saint Dennis, saved the life of William.

On the fifth day after he had been proclaimed, the King went with royal state to the House of Lords, and took his seat on the throne. The Commons were called in; and he, with many gracious expressions, reminded his hearers of the perilous situation of the country, and exhorted them to take such steps as might prevent unnecessary delay in the transaction of public business. As soon as he had retired, a bill declaring the convention a Parliament was laid on the table of the Lords. The bill passed rapidly, and received the royal assent on the tenth day after the accession of William and Mary.

The year 1689 is a not less important epoch in the ecclesiastical than in the civil history of England. In that year began the long struggle between two great parties of conformists. Those parties indeed had, under various forms, existed within the Anglican communion ever since the Reformation; but till after the Revolution they did not appear marshalled in regular order of battle against each other, and were therefore not known by established names. Some time after the accession of William they began to be called the High Church party and the Low Church party; and, long before the end of his reign, these appellations were in common use.

The head of the Low Church party was the King. A few days after his accession, he took a step which indicated, in a manner not to be mistaken, his sentiments touching ecclesiastical polity and public worship. He found only one see unprovided with a bishop. Seth Ward, who had during many years had charge of the diocese of Salisbury, had died. The choice of a successor was no light matter. That choice would be considered by the country as a prognostic of the highest import. The preference was given to Burnet, who was popularly regarded as the personification of the Latitudinarian spirit.

When Burnet took his seat in the House of Lords, he found that assembly busied in legislation of grave importance. The ancient oaths of allegiance and supremacy contained some expressions which had always been

Peter Hoadley's portrait of William and Mary.

The Thames at Whitehall. The graceful shape of Inigo Jones's Banqueting House dominates the extended huddle of the adjacent Tudor palace. During the time of Charles II Whitehall was the focus of political intrigue and of fashionable gaiety.

Earl Godolphin holding the white wand of office as Lord Treasurer: portrait by Godfrey Kneller. A hard-working courtier, Godolphin served Charles II, James II, William III and Anne. 'Sidney Godolphin,' said Charles, 'is never in the way and never out of the way.'

disliked by the Whigs, and other expressions which Tories, honestly attached to the new settlement, thought inapplicable to princes who had not the hereditary right. The convention had therefore, while the throne was still vacant, framed those oaths of allegiance and supremacy by which we still testify our loyalty to our sovereign. By the act which turned the convention into a Parliament, the members of both Houses were required to take the new oaths. As to other persons in public trust, it was hard to say how the law stood. One form of words was enjoined by statutes, regularly passed, and not yet regularly abrogated. A different form was enjoined by the Declaration of Right, an instrument which might well be thought equal in authority to any statute. It was therefore felt to be necessary that the legislature should, without delay, pass an act abolishing the old oaths, and determining when and by whom the new oaths should be taken.

The bill which settled this important question originated in the Upper House. It was unanimously agreed that no person should, at any future time, be admitted to any office, civil, military, ecclesiastical, or academical, without taking the oaths to William and Mary. It was also unanimously agreed that every person who already held any civil or military office should be ejected from it, unless he took the oaths on or before the 1st of

The Prince and Princess of Orange crowned King and Queen of England. Contemporary etching by Romeyn de Hooghe, published as an illustration in a broadside. The Convention which met following the flight of James had as its main task the settlement of the Crown. After discussing a number of alternatives, the members decided that the only feasible course was to offer the Crown jointly to William and Mary.

August 1689. But the strongest passions of both parties were excited by the question whether persons who already possessed ecclesiastical or academical offices should be required to swear fealty to the King and Queen on pain of deprivation. The Primate and some of the most eminent bishops had already absented themselves from Parliament, and would doubtless relinquish their palaces and revenues, rather than acknowledge the new sovereigns. The example of these great prelates might be followed by a multitude of divines of humbler rank, by hundreds of canons, prebendaries, and fellows of colleges, by thousands of parish priests. To such an event no Tory could look forward without the most painful emotions of compassion for the sufferers and of anxiety for the Church.

The bill for settling the oaths came down from the Lords framed in a manner favourable to the clergy. All lay functionaries were required to swear fealty to the King and Queen on pain of expulsion from office. But it was provided that every divine who already held a benefice might continue to hold it without swearing, unless the government should see reason to call on him specially for an assurance of his loyalty. In the Lower House, however, the feeling against the Jacobite priests was irresistibly strong. A clause was proposed and carried which required every person who held

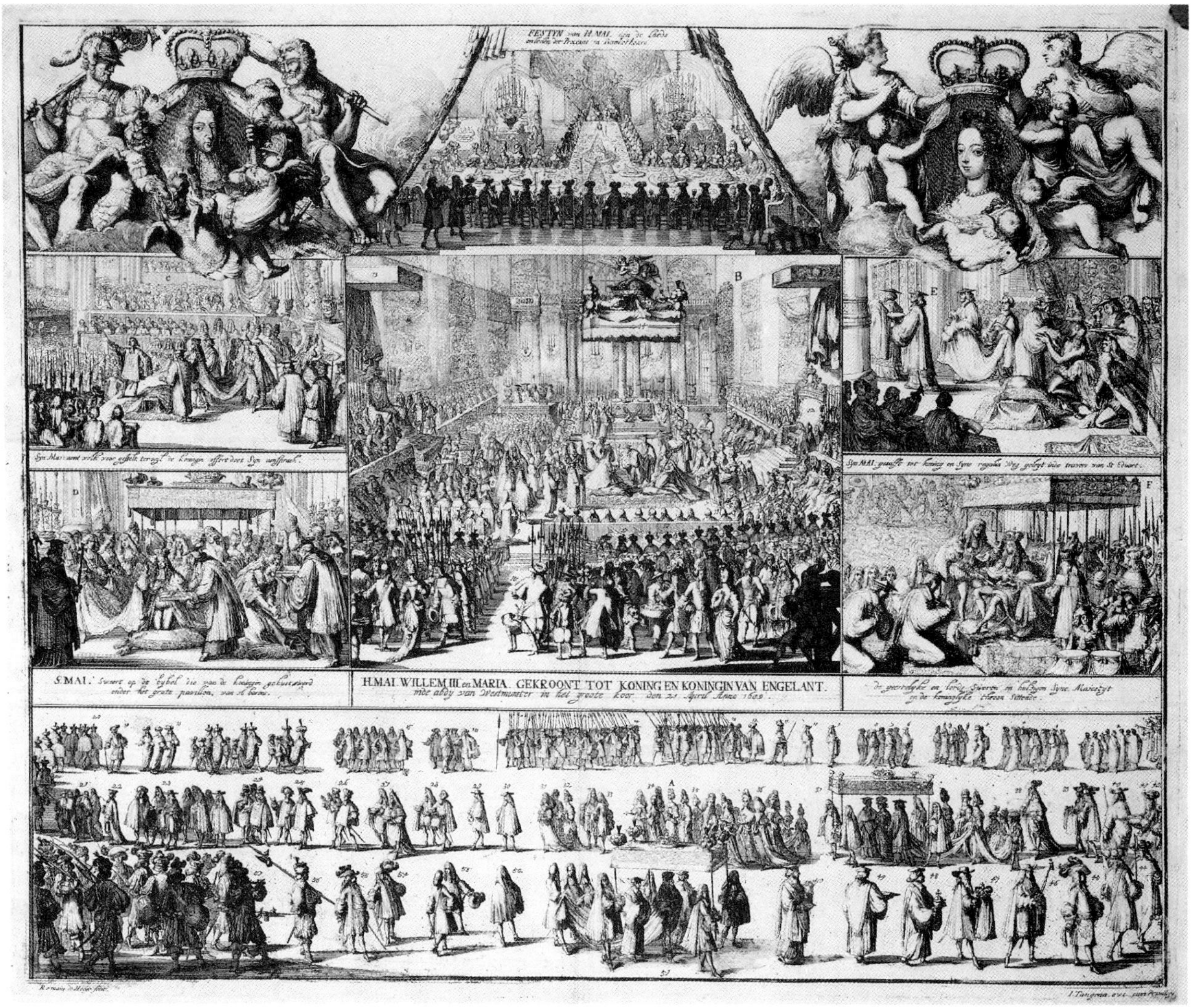

The Coronation of William and Mary: an engraving by de Hooghe illustrating different aspects of the ceremony.

any ecclesiastical or academical preferment to take the oaths by the 1st of August 1689, on pain of suspension. Six months were allowed to the nonjuror for reconsideration. If, on the 1st of February 1690, he still continued obstinate, he was to be finally deprived.

The bill, thus amended, was sent back to the Lords. The Lords adhered to their original resolution. But the Commons were firm: time pressed: the unsettled state of the law caused inconvenience in every department of the public service; and the Peers very reluctantly gave way.

These debates were interrupted by the solemnities and festivities of the coronation, which took place on the 11th of April. In some things it differed from ordinary coronations. Mary, being not merely Queen Consort, but also Queen Regnant, was inaugurated in all things like a King, was girt with the sword, lifted up into the throne, and presented with the Bible, the spurs, and the orb. The Primate did not make his appearance; and his place was supplied by Compton. Burnet, the junior prelate, preached with all his wonted ability, and more than his wonted taste and judgment. On the whole, the ceremony went off well, and produced something like a revival of the enthusiasm of the preceding December. Honours were, as usual,

Political satire of 1690: The Protestant Grindstone. William Sancroft the Archbishop of Canterbury, and Henry Compton, the Bishop of London, turn the stone grinding the Pope's nose, while William and Mary look on. To the left stand Jesuit priests, to the right William's Dutch followers led by Count Schomberg.

liberally bestowed at this festive season. Several eminent men took new appellations by which they must henceforth be designated. Danby became Marquess of Caermarthen, Churchill Earl of Marlbourgh, and Bentinck Earl of Portland. Mordaunt was made Earl of Monmouth, not without some murmuring on the part of old Exclusionists, who still remembered with fondness their Protestant Duke, and who had hoped that his attainder would be reversed, and that his title would be borne by his descendants.

Meanwhile questions of external policy were every day becoming more and more important. The work at which William had toiled during many anxious years was at length accomplished. The great coalition was formed. It was plain that a desperate conflict was at hand. The oppressor of Europe would have to defend himself against England allied with Charles II, King of Spain, with the Emperor Leopold, and with the Germanic and Batavian federations. As the season for military operations approached, the solemn appeals of injured nations to the God of battles came forth in rapid succession. The manifesto of the Germanic body appeared in February; that of the States General in March; that of the House of Brandenburg in April; and that of Spain in May.

Here, as soon as the ceremony of the coronation was over, the House of Commons determined to take into consideration the late proceedings of the French King. A committee, consisting chiefly of ardent Whigs, was appointed to prepare an address. William's attention was called to the wrongs which France had done to him and to his kingdom; and he was assured that, whenever he should resort to arms for the redress of those wrongs, he should be heartily supported by his people. He thanked the Commons warmly. Ambition, he said, should never induce him to draw the sword: but he had no choice: France had already attacked England; and it was necessary to exercise the right of self-defence. A few days later war was proclaimed.

Of the grounds of the quarrel alleged by the Commons in their address, and by the King in his manifesto, the most serious was the interference of Louis in the affairs of Ireland. In that country great events had, during several months, followed one another in rapid succession. Of those events it is now time to relate the history.

The Troubles in Ireland

William had assumed, together with the title of King of England, the title of King of Ireland. For all our jurists then regarded Ireland as a mere colony, bound to pay allegiance to the sovereign whom the mother country had called to the throne.

In fact, however, the Revolution found Ireland emancipated from the domination of the English colony. The civil power had, in the space of a few months, been transferred from the Saxon to the Celtic population. The transfer of the military power had been not less complete. The highest offices in the state, in the army, and in the Courts of Justice, were, with scarcely an exception, filled by Papists. Such was the state of Ireland when the Prince of Orange landed at Torbay. From that time every packet which arrived at Dublin brought tidings, such as could not but increase the mutual fear and loathing of the hostile races.

During some weeks there were outrages, insults, evil reports, violent panics, the natural preludes of the terrible conflict which was at hand. Ever since the recall of Clarendon there had been a large emigration of timid and quiet people from the Irish ports to England. That emigration now went on faster than ever. The English who remained began to draw close together. Every large country house became a fortress. Great numbers of gentlemen and yeomen quitted the open country, and repaired to those towns which had been founded for the purpose of bridling the native population. A considerable body of armed colonists mustered at Sligo, another at Charleville, a third at Mallow, a fourth at Bandon. But the principal strongholds of the Englishry during this evil time were Enniskillen and Londonderry.

Enniskillen, though the capital of the county of Fermanagh, was then merely a village. The other great fastness of Protestantism was a place of more importance. Eighty years before, during the troubles caused by the last struggle of the houses of O'Neil and O'Donnel against the authority of James I, the ancient city of Derry had been surprised by one of the native chiefs: the inhabitants had been slaughtered, and the houses reduced to ashes. The insurgents were speedily put down and punished: the government resolved to restore the ruined town: the Lord Mayor, aldermen, and Common Council of London were invited to assist in the work; and a new city soon arose which, on account of its connection with the capital of the empire, was called Londonderry. The buildings covered the summit and slope of a hill which overlooked the broad stream of the Foyle, then whitened by vast flocks of wild swans. The dwellings were encompassed by a wall of which the whole circumference was little less than a mile. The inhabitants were Protestants of Anglo-Saxon blood.

While the Prince of Orange was marching unopposed to London, and the result of the negotiations which were pending in England was uncertain, Tyrconnel could not venture to take a bloody revenge on the refractory Protestants of Ireland. He therefore thought it expedient to affect for a time a clemency and moderation which were by no means congenial to his disposition. The task of quieting the Englishry of Ulster was entrusted to William Stewart, Viscount Mountjoy, one of the very few members of the Established Church who still held office in Ireland. He was Master of the Ordnance in that kingdom, and was colonel of a regiment in which an uncommonly large proportion of the Englishry had been suffered to remain. He hastened with his regiment to Londonderry, and was well received there. The citizens readily permitted him to leave within their

Richard Talbot, Earl of Tyrconnel: portrait attributed to H. Rigaud. 'Dick' Talbot, a close friend of James II since the 1650s, had been appointed by him Lord Lieutenant of Ireland in succession to Clarendon. When William invaded England, Tyrconnel controlled Ireland.

walls a small garrison exclusively composed of Protestants, under the command of his lieutenant colonel, Robert Lundy, who took the title of governor.

By this time the Prince of Orange had arrived at Westminster in triumph, and had taken on himself the administration of the realm. Perceiving that, till the government of England was settled, it would not be in his power to interfere effectually by arms in the affairs of Ireland, he determined to try what effect negotiation would produce.

No British statesman had then so high a reputation throughout Europe as Sir William Temple. There was no height of power to which he might not have risen, if he would have consented to lend his assistance to the new government. But power had less attraction for his Epicurean temper than ease and security. With some hesitation, however, he consented to let his eldest son John enter into the service of William. On subjects connected with Ireland, John Temple's opinion had great weight. The young politician flattered himself that he had secured the services of an agent eminently qualified to bring the negotiation with Tyrconnel to a prosperous issue.

Anne as a young woman just before her marriage to Prince George of Denmark: portrait by Wissing and Van der Vaart. Macaulay describes her as slow and taciturn. 'To those whom she loved she was meek. The form which her anger took was sullenness.'

Richard Hamilton was one of a remarkable family which had sprung from a noble Scottish stock, but which had long been settled in Ireland, and which professed the Roman Catholic religion. Having gained, in foreign service, some military experience, he had returned to his native country, and had been appointed Brigadier General in the Irish army. When the Dutch invasion was expected, he came across Saint George's Channel with the troops which Tyrconnel sent to reinforce the royal army. After the flight of James, those troops submitted to the Prince of Orange. Richard Hamilton not only made his own peace with what was now the ruling power, but declared himself confident that, if he were sent to Dublin, he could conduct the negotiation which had been opened there to a happy close. John Temple declared that he would answer for his friend Richard as for himself; and Hamilton set out for Ireland proclaiming that he would soon bring Tyrconnel to reason.

It is not impossible that Hamilton may have really meant to keep his promise. But when he arrived at Dublin he found that he had undertaken a

Prince George of Denmark, represented in semi-classical costume and wearing the ribbon of the garter: portrait by John Riley, c 1687. A dull and rather stupid man, Charles II once remarked of him: 'I've tried him drunk, and I've tried him sober but there's nothing in him.'

task which he could not perform. The hesitation of Tyrconnel was at an end. He had found that he had no longer a choice. He had with little difficulty stimulated the ignorant and susceptible Irish to fury. To calm them was beyond his skill. It was necessary for him to protest that he had never harboured any thought of submission, and that he had pretended to negotiate only for the purpose of gaining time. Yet, before he openly declared against the English settlers, and against England herself, what must be a war to the death, he wished to rid himself of Mountjoy. It was a sacred duty, Tyrconnel said, to avert the calamities which seemed to be impending. King James himself would not wish his Irish friends to engage in an enterprise which must be fatal to them and useless to him. If any man of weight would repair to Saint Germains and explain the state of things, His Majesty would easily be convinced. Tyrconnel insisted that Mountjoy should go as the representative of the loyal members of the Established Church, and should be accompanied by Chief Baron Rice, a Roman Catholic high in the royal favour. The two ambassadors departed together, but with very different commissions. Rice was charged to tell James that Mountjoy was a traitor at heart, and had been sent to France only that the Protestants of Ireland might be deprived of a favourite leader. The King was to be assured that he was impatiently expected in Ireland, and that, if he would show himself there with a French force, he might speedily retrieve his fallen fortunes.

As soon as the two envoys had departed, Tyrconnel set himself to prepare for the conflict which had become inevitable; and he was strenuously assisted by the faithless Hamilton. The Irish nation was called to arms; and the call was obeyed with strange promptitude and enthusiasm. It seems probable that, at the end of February, at least a hundred thousand Irishmen were in arms. Near fifty thousand of them were soldiers. The rest were banditti, whose violence and licentiousness the government affected to disapprove, but did not really exert itself to suppress.

In Leinster, Munster, and Connaught, it was utterly impossible for the English settlers to offer any effectual resistance to this terrible outbreak of the aboriginal population. The country seats which the Protestant landowners had recently fortified in the three southern provinces could no longer be defended. Many families submitted, delivered up their arms, and thought themselves happy in escaping with life. But many resolute gentlemen and yeomen were determined to perish rather than yield. They packed up such valuable property as could easily be carried away, burned whatever they could not remove, and set out for those spots in Ulster which were the strongholds of their race and of their faith. The flower of the Protestant population of Munster and Connaught found shelter at Enniskillen. Whatever was bravest and most truehearted in Leinster took the road to Londonderry.

To reduce the Protestants of Ulster to submission before aid could arrive from England was now the chief object of Tyrconnel. A great force was ordered to move northward, under the command of Richard Hamilton. At the fame of his approach, the colonists burned their furniture, pulled down their houses, and retreated northward. All Lisburn fled to Antrim; and, as the foes drew nearer, all Lisburn and Antrim together came pouring into Londonderry. Thirty thousand Protestants were crowded behind the bulwarks of the City of Refuge. There, at length, on the verge of the ocean, hunted to the last asylum, and baited into a mood in which men may be destroyed, but will not easily be subjected, the imperial race turned desperately to bay.

Meanwhile Mountjoy and Rice had arrived in France. Mountjoy was instantly put under arrest and thrown into the Bastille. James determined to comply with the invitation which Rice had brought and applied to Louis for the help of a French army. But Louis was unwilling to send a large body of troops to Ireland. He saw that France would have to maintain a long war on the Continent against a formidable coalition: her expenditure must be immense; and he felt it to be important that nothing should be wasted. An army was therefore for the present refused: but everything else was granted. The Brest fleet was ordered to be in readiness to sail. Arms for ten thousand men and great quantities of ammunition were put on board. About four hundred captains, lieutenants, cadets, and gunners were selected for the important service of organising and disciplining the Irish levies. The chief command was held by a veteran warrior, the Count of Rosen. What Frenchman should attend the King of England in the

Sarah Churchill, Duchess of Marlborough, after Kneller. Sarah was loved and even worshipped by Anne. Through the influence of the Churchills Anne was drawn into the extensive network in England working in favour of William's intervention.

character of ambassador was the subject of grave deliberation at Versailles. The Count of Avaux, whose sagacity had detected all the plans of William, was the man on whom the choice of Louis fell.

James arrived at Brest on the 5th of March, embarked there on board of a man of war called the Saint Michael, and sailed within forty-eight hours. On the afternoon of the 12th, he landed in the harbour of Kinsale. By the Roman Catholic population he was received with shouts of unfeigned transport. Horses sufficient to carry a few travellers were with some difficulty procured; and, on the 14th, James proceeded to Cork.

On the 24th he entered Dublin. The next morning he held a Privy Council, and issued a proclamation convoking a Parliament to meet on the 7th of May.

John Churchill, Duke of Marlborough, after Kneller. Though acknowledging his brilliant genius, Macaulay nevertheless considered him 'a prodigy of turpitude' for the part he played during the decisive days of 1688.

The first question to be decided was whether James should remain at Dublin, or should put himself at the head of his army in Ulster. The point really in issue was whether the King should be in Irish or in British hands. If he remained at Dublin, he would be forced to plunder, perhaps to attaint, innocent Protestant gentlemen and clergymen by hundreds; and he would thus do irreparable mischief to his cause on the other side of Saint George's Channel. If he repaired to Ulster, he would be within a few hours' sail of Great Britain. As soon as Londonderry had fallen, he might cross the sea with part of his forces, and land in Scotland. When he was once on British ground, it would no longer be in the power of the Irish to extort his consent to their schemes of spoliation and revenge.

Tyrconnel, who had just been created a duke, advised his master to stay at Dublin; but James, whose personal inclinations were naturally on the

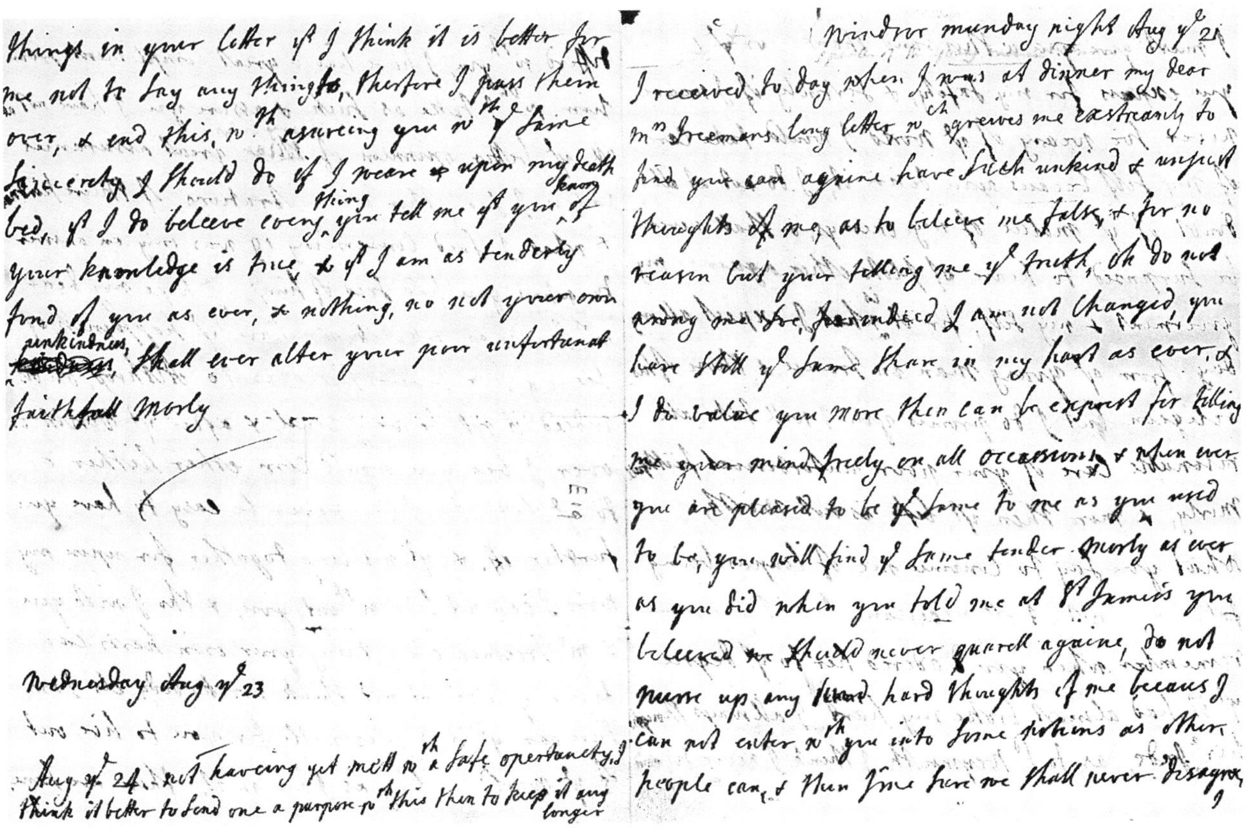

things in your letter yt I think it is better for me not to say any things, therfore I pass them over, & end this wth assureing you wth ye same sincerety I should do if I weare upon my death bed, yt I do believe every thing you tell me yt you know of your knowledge is true, & yt I am as tenderly fond of you as ever, & nothing, no not your own unkindness, shall ever alter your poor unfortunat faithfull Morly

Wednesday Aug ye 23

Aug ye 24. not haveing yet mett wth a safe opertunety, I think it better to send one a purpose wth this then to keep it any longer

Windsor munday night Aug ye 21

I received to day when I was at dinner my dear Mrs Freemans long letter wch greeves me eastreamly to find you can agine have such unkind & unjust thoughts of me as to believe me falss & for no reason but your telling me ye truth, oh do not wrong me soe, for indeed I am not changed, you have still ye same share in my hart as ever, & I do believe you more then can be exprest for telling me your mind freely on all occasions & when ever you are pleased to be ye same to me as you used to be, you will find ye same tender Morly as ever as you did when you told me at St James's you believed we should never quarell againe, do not nurse up any hard thoughts of me becaus I can not enter wth you into some notions as other people can, & then since here we shall never disagree

So painful was it for Princess Anne to be constricted by formalities when it came to communicating with her beloved friend Sarah that they adopted the names of Mrs Morly and Mrs Freeman. Their correspondence under these names continued for twenty years. In this letter Anne signs herself 'your poor unfortunat faithfull Morly'.

British side of the question, determined to go northward. The royal party set out, leaving Tyrconnel in charge at Dublin, and hastened towards Londonderry. James found his army concentrated a few miles south of the city. The French generals who had sailed with him from Brest were in his train; and two of them, Rosen and Maumont, were placed over the head of Richard Hamilton.

In the camp it was generally expected that Londonderry would fall without a blow. The assailants were sure of one important ally within the walls. Lundy, the governor, professed the Protestant religion; but he was in secret communication with the enemies of his Church. He seems to have thought resistance hopeless; and in truth, to a military eye, the defences of Londonderry appeared contemptible. The fortifications consisted of a simple wall overgrown with grass and weeds. Even if the place should be able to repel a large army, hunger must soon bring the contest to an end. The stock of provisions was small; and the population had been swollen to seven or eight times the ordinary number.

Just at this moment a glimpse of hope appeared. On the 14th of April ships from England anchored in the bay. They had on board two regiments which had been sent, under the command of a colonel named Cunningham, to reinforce the garrison. Cunningham and several of his officers went on shore and conferred with Lundy. Lundy dissuaded them from landing their men. The place, he said, could not hold out. The best thing that the two regiments could do would be to sail back to England. Cunningham and his companions could scarcely venture to oppose their opinion to that of a person whose local knowledge was necessarily far superior to theirs, and whom they were by their instructions directed to obey. They returned to the ships, and made preparations for departing.

But the spirit of the soldiers and citizens swelled up high and fierce against the perfidious chief who had betrayed them. Many of his own officers declared that they no longer thought themselves bound to obey him. Meanwhile it was rumoured that the persons most in Lundy's confidence were stealing out of the town one by one. Long after dusk on the evening of the 17th it was found that the gates were open and that the keys had disappeared. The officers who made the discovery took on themselves to change the passwords and to double the guards. The night, however, passed over without any assault. After some anxious hours the day broke. A tumultuous council of the chief inhabitants was called. Some of them vehemently reproached the governor to his face with his treachery. While the altercation was at the height, the sentinels who paced the ramparts announced that the vanguard of the hostile army was in sight. Two gallant soldiers, Major Henry Baker and Captain Adam Murray, called the people to arms. They were assisted by the eloquence of an aged clergyman, George Walker, rector of the parish of Donaghmore. Soldiers, gentlemen, yeomen, artisans, rushed to the walls and manned the guns. James, who had approached within a hundred yards of the southern gate, was received with a shout of 'No surrender', and with a fire from the nearest bastion. An officer of his staff fell dead by his side. The King and his attendants made haste to get out of reach of the cannon balls. Lundy hid himself in an inner chamber. There he lay during the day, and, with the generous and politic connivance of Murray and Walker, made his escape at night in the disguise of a porter.

And now Londonderry was left destitute of all military and of all civil government. Betrayed, deserted, disorganised, unprovided with resources, begirt with enemies, the noble city was still no easy conquest. The number of men capable of bearing arms within the walls was seven thousand; and the whole world could not have furnished seven thousand men better qualified to meet a terrible emergency with clear judgment, dauntless valour, and stubborn patience. Two governors were elected, Baker and Walker. Baker took the chief military command. Walker's especial business was to preserve internal tranquillity, and to dole out supplies from the magazines. The inhabitants capable of bearing arms were distributed into eight regiments. In a few hours every man knew his post, and was ready to repair to it as soon as the beat of the drum was heard.

On the evening of the 19th of April, a trumpeter came to the southern gate, and asked whether the engagements into which the governor had entered would be fulfilled. The answer was that the men who guarded these walls had nothing to do with the governor's engagements, and were determined to resist to the last.

James had fully expected that the city would yield as soon as it was known that he was before the walls. Finding himself mistaken, he determined to return instantly to Dublin. Rosen accompanied the King. The direction of the siege was entrusted to Maumont.

The operations now commenced in earnest. The besiegers began by battering the town. It was soon on fire in several places. But the spirit of the people rose so high that their chiefs thought it safe to act on the offensive. On the 21st of April a sally was made under the command of Murray. The

Sir William Temple, painting by Gaspar Netscher. The English resident at Brussels and author of the Triple Alliance, Temple was one of the most expert diplomats of the age. He formed a high opinion of William, and William in turn trusted him and valued his judgement.

Irish stood their ground resolutely; and a furious and bloody contest took place. Maumont was struck in the head by a musket ball, and fell a corpse. The besiegers lost several other officers, and about two hundred men, before the colonists could be driven in. In consequence of the death of Maumont, Richard Hamilton was once more commander of the Irish army. His exploits in that post did not raise his reputation. He was a fine gentleman and a brave soldier; but he had no pretensions to the character of a great general, and had never, in his life, seen a siege.

May passed away: June arrived; and still Londonderry held out. Nothing was left but to try the effect of hunger. All the avenues leading to the city by land were closely guarded. The river was fringed with forts and batteries, which no vessel could pass without great peril. After some time it was determined to make the security still more complete by throwing a barricade across the stream, about a mile and a half below the city. Several boats full of stones were sunk. A row of stakes was driven into the bottom of the river. Large pieces of fir wood, strongly bound together, formed a boom which was more than a quarter of a mile in length, and which was firmly fastened to both shores by cables a foot thick. Within the walls the distress became extreme. So early as the 8th of June horseflesh was almost the only meat which could be purchased; and of horseflesh the supply was scanty.

On the 15th of June a gleam of hope appeared. The sentinels on the top of the cathedral saw sails nine miles off in the bay of Lough Foyle. Thirty vessels of different sizes were counted. A messenger from the fleet eluded the Irish sentinels, dived under the boom, and informed the garrison that Kirke had arrived from England with troops, arms, ammunition, and provisions to relieve the city.

A few hours of feverish joy were followed by weeks of misery. Kirke thought it unsafe to make any attempt on the lines of the besiegers, and retired to the entrance of Lough Foyle, where, during several weeks, he lay inactive.

And now the pressure of famine became every day more severe. Pestilence began, as usual, to make its appearance in the train of hunger. Fifteen officers died of fever in one day. The Governor Baker was among those who sank under the disease. His place was supplied by Colonel John Mitchelbourne.

July was far advanced; and the state of the city was, hour by hour, becoming more frightful. The number of the inhabitants had been thinned more by famine and disease than by the fire of the enemy. The fighting men of the garrison were so much exhausted that they could scarcely keep their legs. A very small quantity of grain remained, and was doled out by mouthfuls. Dogs, fattened on the blood of the slain who lay unburied round the town, were luxuries which few could afford to purchase. There was scarcely a cellar in which some corpse was not decaying. Such was the extremity of distress that the rats who came to feast in those hideous dens were eagerly hunted and greedily devoured.

It was no slight aggravation of the sufferings of the garrison that all this time the English ships were seen far off in Lough Foyle. Communication between the fleet and the city was almost impossible. On the 13th of July, however, a piece of paper sewed up in a cloth button came to Walker's hands. It was a letter from Kirke, and contained assurances of speedy relief. But more than a fortnight of intense misery had since elapsed; and the hearts of the most sanguine were sick with deferred hope. By no art could the provisions which were left be made to hold out two days more.

Just at this time Kirke received from England a despatch, which contained positive orders that Londonderry should be relieved. He accordingly determined to make an attempt which, as far as appears, he might have made six weeks earlier.

Among the merchant ships which had come to Lough Foyle under his convoy was one called the *Mountjoy*. The master, Micaiah Browning, a native of Londonderry, had brought from England a large cargo of provisions. He now eagerly volunteered to take the first risk of succouring his fellow citizens; and his offer was accepted. Andrew Douglas, master of the *Phoenix*, who had on board a great quantity of meal from Scotland, was willing to share the danger and the honour. The two merchantmen were to be escorted by the *Dartmouth*, a frigate of thirty-six guns, commanded by Captain John Leake, afterwards an admiral of great fame.

It was the 28th of July. The sun had just set: the evening sermon in the cathedral was over; and the heartbroken congregation had separated, when the sentinels on the tower saw the sails of three vessels coming up the Foyle. The ships were in extreme peril: for the river was low; and the only navigable channel ran very near to the left bank, where the head quarters of the enemy had been fixed, and where the batteries were most numerous. Leake performed his duty with a skill and spirit worthy of his noble profession, exposed his frigate to cover the merchantmen, and used his guns with great effect. At length the little squadron came to the place of peril. Then the *Mountjoy* took the lead, and went right at the boom. The huge barricade cracked and gave way: but the shock was such that the *Mountjoy* rebounded, and stuck in the mud. A yell of triumph rose from the banks: the Irish rushed to their boats, and were preparing to board: but the *Dartmouth* poured on them a well directed broadside, which threw them into disorder. Just then the *Phoenix* dashed at the breach which the *Mountjoy* had made, and was in a moment within the fence. Meanwhile the tide was rising fast. The *Mountjoy* began to move, and soon passed safe through the broken stakes and floating spars. But her brave master was no more. A shot from one of the batteries had struck him; and he died by the most enviable of all deaths, in sight of the city which was his birthplace, which was his home, and which had just been saved by his courage and self-devotion from the most frightful form of destruction.

It was ten o'clock before the ships arrived at the quay. The whole population was there to welcome them. A screen made of casks filled with earth

The siege of Londonderry, from a contemporary Dutch engraving. When William invaded England in 1688 Tyrconnel controlled Ireland. In 1689 the Protestant community contracted itself into enclaves at Londonderry and Enniskillen. The siege of Londonderry with its 30,000 inhabitants, conducted by James, lasted 105 days before it was lifted; and the Enniskilleners scored a victory at Newtown Butler. Ulster was saved for the Protestants, but the stubborn Jacobite resistance was to deny the Williamites victory for some time.

was hastily thrown up to protect the landing place from the batteries on the other side of the river; and then the work of unloading began. First were rolled on shore barrels containing six thousand bushels of meal. Then came great cheeses, casks of beef, flitches of bacon, kegs of butter, sacks of pease and biscuit, ankers of brandy. It is easy to imagine with what tears grace was said over the suppers of that evening. There was little sleep on either side of the wall. The Irish guns continued to roar all night; and all night the bells of the rescued city made answer with a peal of joyous defiance. Through the three following days the batteries of the enemy continued to play. But, on the third night, flames were seen arising from the camp; and, when the 1st of August dawned, a line of smoking ruins marked the site lately occupied by the huts of the besiegers; and the citizens saw far off the long column of pikes and standards retreating up the left bank of the Foyle towards Strabane.

So ended this great siege, the most memorable in the annals of the British isles. It had lasted a hundred and five days. The garrison had been reduced from about seven thousand effective men to about three thousand. The loss of the besiegers cannot be precisely ascertained. Walker estimated it at eight thousand men. The means both of attack and of defence had undoubtedly been such as would have moved the great warriors of the Continent to laughter; and this is the very circumstance which gives so peculiar an interest to the history of the contest. It was a contest, not between engineers, but between nations; and the victory remained with the nation which, though inferior in number, was superior in civilisation, in capacity for self-government, and in stubbornness of resolution.

Scottish Affairs

The violence of revolutions is generally proportioned to the degree of maladministration which has produced them. It is therefore not strange that the government of Scotland, having been during many years far more oppressive and corrupt than the government of England, should have fallen with a far heavier ruin.

William saw that he must not think of paying to the laws of Scotland that scrupulous respect which he had wisely paid to the laws of England. It was absolutely necessary that he should determine by his own authority how that convention which was to meet at Edinburgh should be chosen, and that he should assume the power of annulling some judgments and some statutes. He accordingly summoned to the Parliament House several lords who had been deprived of their honours by sentences which the general voice loudly condemned as unjust; and he took on himself to dispense with the act which deprived Presbyterians of the elective franchise.

The consequence was that the choice of almost all the shires and burghs fell on Whig candidates. Nor was it only at the elections that the popular feeling, so long and so severely compressed, exploded with violence. Throughout a large part of Scotland the clergy of the Established Church were, to use the phrase then common, rabbled. The morning of Christmas day was fixed for the commencement of these outrages. For nothing disgusted the rigid Covenanter more than the reverence paid by the prelatist to the ancient holidays of the Church. On Christmas day, therefore, the Covenanters held armed musters by concert in many parts of the western shires. Each band marched to the nearest manse, and sacked the cellar and larder of the minister. The priest of Baal was reviled and insulted, sometimes beaten, sometimes ducked. He was then carried to the market place, and exposed during some time as a malefactor. His gown was torn to shreds over his head; and he was dismissed with a charge, never, as he valued his life, to officiate in the parish again.

The disorder spread fast. Covenanters from the west, who had done all that was to be done in the way of pelting and hustling the curates of their own neighbourhood, came dropping into Edinburgh, by tens and twenties, for the purpose of protection, or, if need should be, of overawing the Convention. They showed themselves little in any public place: but it was known that every cellar was filled with them; and it might well be apprehended that, at the first signal, they could pour forth from their caverns, and appear armed round the Parliament House.

James had entrusted the conduct of his affairs in Scotland to John Graham of Claverhouse, now Viscount Dundee, and Colin Lindsay, Earl of Balcarras. They had some hope that they might be at the head of a majority in the Convention, and therefore exerted themselves vigorously to animate their party. They had, however, received from Saint Germains full powers to adjourn the Convention to Stirling if things went ill at Edinburgh.

The 14th of March, the day fixed for the meeting of the Estates, arrived, and the Parliament House was crowded. The first matter to be decided was the choice of a president. The Duke of Hamilton was supported by the Whigs, the Marquess of Athol by the Jacobites. When the votes were counted, it appeared that Hamilton had a majority of forty.

The population of Edinburgh was in an excited state. Dundee's old soldiers were known to be gathering round him; and it might well be apprehended that he would make some desperate attempt. He, on the other hand, had been informed that the western Covenanters who filled the cellars of the city had vowed vengeance on him: and, in truth, when we consider that their temper was singularly savage and implacable, and that they had been taught to regard the slaying of a persecutor as a duty, we may well wonder that a man who had shed the blood of the saints like water should have been able to walk the High Street in safety during a single day.

On the 15th of March Dundee received information that some of the Covenanters had bound themselves together to slay him and Sir George Mackenzie, whose eloquence and learning, long prostituted to the service of tyranny, had made him more odious to the Presbyterians than any other man of the gown. Dundee applied to Hamilton for protection; and Hamilton advised him to bring the matter under the consideration of the Convention at the next sitting.

When the Convention reassembled on the morning of Saturday the 16th of March, it was proposed that measures should be taken for the personal security of the members. It was alleged that the life of Dundee had been threatened; and Mackenzie complained that he too was in danger. But the matter was lightly treated by the majority: and the Convention passed on to other business.

There was to be no other meeting till Monday morning. The Jacobite leaders held a consultation, and came to the conclusion that Dundee and Balcarras must use the powers with which they had been entrusted. The minority must forthwith leave Edinburgh and assemble at Stirling. Athol assented, and undertook to bring a great body of his clansmen from the

Highlands to protect the deliberations of the Royalist Convention. Everything was arranged for the secession; but, in a few hours, the tardiness of one man and the haste of another ruined the whole plan.

The Monday came. The Jacobite lords and gentlemen were actually taking horse for Stirling, when Athol asked for a delay of twenty-four hours. The members of his party, unwilling to separate from him, consented to the postponement which he requested, and repaired once more to the Parliament House. Dundee alone refused to stay a moment longer. His life was in danger. He would not remain to be a mark for the pistols and daggers of murderers. Brave as he undoubtedly was, he seems, like many other brave men, to have been less proof against the danger of assassination than against any other form of danger. His old troopers, who had shared his crimes, and who now shared his perils, were ready to be the companions of his flight.

Meanwhile the Convention had assembled. Mackenzie was on his legs, pathetically lamenting the hard condition of the Estates, when he was interrupted by some sentinels who came running from the posts near the castle. They had seen Dundee at the head of fifty horse on the Stirling road. Up to that moment the hatred with which the Presbyterian members of the assembly regarded the merciless persecutor of their brethren in the faith had been restrained by the decorous forms of parliamentary deliberation. But now the explosion was terrible. Hamilton himself was the fiercest man in the hall. 'It is high time', he cried, 'that we should look to ourselves. The enemies of our religion and of our civil freedom are mustering all around us; and we may well suspect that they have accomplices even here. Lock the doors. Let nobody go out but those whom we shall appoint to call the citizens to arms.' The assembly raised a general cry of assent. The Jacobites, silent and unresisting, became prisoners. Lord Leven went forth and ordered the drums to beat. The Covenanters of Lanarkshire and Ayrshire promptly obeyed the signal. The force thus assembled was amply sufficient to overawe the adherents of the House of Stuart. From Dundee nothing was to be hoped or feared; for he had already galloped westward. Hamilton now ordered the doors to be opened. The suspected members were at liberty to depart. Humbled and broken-spirited, they stole forth through the crowd of stern fanatics which filled the High Street. All thought of secession was at an end.

Soon the Estates had a guard on which they could rely more firmly than on the undisciplined Covenanters of the west. A squadron of English men of war from the Thames had arrived in the Firth of Forth. On board were the three Scottish regiments which had accompanied William from Holland. This little force was commanded by Hugh Mackay, a Highlander of noble descent, who had long served on the Continent, and who was distinguished by courage of the truest temper, and by a piety such as is seldom found in soldiers of fortune. The Convention passed a resolution appointing Mackay general of their forces.

The arrival of Mackay's troops quelled the spirit of the Jacobites. Only five members voted against the resolution which pronounced that James had forfeited his right to the allegiance of his subjects. The Convention then went forth in procession to the High Street. Several great nobles ascended the octagon tower from which rose the city cross surmounted by the unicorn of Scotland. Hamilton read the vote of the Convention; and a King at Arms proclaimed the new sovereigns with sound of trumpet. On the same day the Estates issued an order that the parochial clergy should, on pain of deprivation, publish from their pulpits the proclamation which had just been read at the city cross, and should pray for King William and Queen Mary.

Before the end of the interregnum, a formidable enemy had set up the standard of civil war in a region about which the politicians of Westminster, and indeed most of the politicians of Edinburgh, knew no more than about Abyssinia or Japan.

The explanation of the readiness with which a large part of the population of the Highlands, twice in the seventeenth century, drew the sword for the Stuarts is to be found in the internal quarrels which divided the commonwealth of clans. At different times different races had risen to an authority which had produced general fear and envy. The Macdonalds had once possessed, in the Hebrides and throughout the mountain country of Argyleshire and Invernessshire, an ascendency similar to that which the House of Austria had once possessed in Christendom. But the ascendency of the Macdonalds had, like the ascendency of the House of Austria, passed away; and the Campbells, the children of Diarmid, had become in the Highlands what the Bourbons had become in Europe. Some tribes had been expelled from their territory, some compelled to pay tribute, some incorporated with the conquerors. At length the number of fighting men who bore the name of Campbell was sufficient to meet in the field of battle the combined forces of all the other western clans. It was during those civil troubles which commenced in 1638 that the power of this aspiring family reached the zenith. Of all the Highland princes whose history is well known to us, the Marquess of Argyle, who, as chief of the tribe of Campbell, was known by the proud name of Mac Callum More, was the greatest and most dreaded. It was while his neighbours were watching the increase of his power with hatred which fear could scarcely keep down that Montrose called them to arms. A powerful coalition of clans waged war, nominally for King Charles, but really against Mac Callum More.

The feelings which had produced the coalition against the Marquess of Argyle retained their force long after his death. His son, Earl Archibald, inherited, with the ascendency of his ancestors, the unpopularity which such ascendency could scarcely fail to produce. There was great joy from sea to sea when, in 1681, he was arraigned on a futile charge, condemned to death, driven into exile, and deprived of his dignities: there was great alarm when, in 1685, he returned from his banishment, and sent forth the fiery cross to summon his kinsmen to his standard; and there was again great joy when his enterprise had failed, when his head had been fixed on the Tolbooth of Edinburgh, and when those chiefs who had regarded him as an oppressor had obtained from the Crown, on easy terms, remissions of old debts and grants of new titles.

On a sudden all was changed. The Revolution came. The heir of Argyle returned in triumph. The sentence which had deprived him of his estate and of his honours was treated by the majority of the Convention as a nullity. There was terror and agitation in the castles of twenty petty kings. The uneasiness was great among the Stewarts of Appin, whose territory was close pressed by the sea on one side, and by the race of Diarmid on the other. A similar spirit animated the Camerons. Their ruler, Sir Ewan Cameron, of Lochiel, surnamed the Black, was in personal qualities unrivalled among the Celtic princes. He was a gracious master, a trusty ally, a terrible enemy. His countenance and bearing were singularly noble. In agility and skill at his weapons he had few equals among the inhabitants of the hills. He was eminently wise in council, eloquent in debate, and skilful in managing the minds of men. He held a large territory peopled by a race which reverenced no lord, no king but himself. For that territory, however, he owed homage to the House of Argyle; and he was deeply in debt to his feudal superiors in rent. Scarcely any chief in Invernessshire had gained more than he by the downfall of the House of Argyle, or had more reason than he to dread the restoration of that house.

But of all the Highlanders who looked on the recent turn of fortune with painful apprehension, the fiercest and the most powerful were the Macdonalds. Since the downfall of the House of Argyle, the Macdonalds, if they had not regained their ancient superiority, might at least boast that they had now no superiors. Relieved from the fear of their mighty enemy in the west, they had turned their arms against weaker enemies in the east, against the clan of Mackintosh and against the town of Inverness.

Inverness was a Saxon colony among the Celts, a solitary outpost of civilisation in a region of barbarians. Common enmities and common apprehensions had produced a good understanding between the town and the clan of Mackintosh. The foe most dreaded by both was Colin Macdonald of Keppoch. If Keppoch had ever stood in any awe of the government, he was completely relieved from that feeling by the general anarchy which followed the Revolution. He wasted the lands of the Mackintoshes, advanced to Inverness, and threatened the town with destruction. Sunday the 28th of April was a day of alarm and confusion. The savages went round and round the small colony of Saxons like famished wolves round a sheepfold. The day closed without an assault: the Monday and the Tuesday passed away in intense anxiety; and then an unexpected mediator made his appearance.

Dundee, after his flight from Edinburgh, had retired to his country seat in that valley through which the Glamis descends to the ancient castle of Macbeth. Some of his old troopers formed a garrison sufficient to protect his house against the Presbyterians of the neighbourhood. Here he might possibly have remained unharmed and harmless, had not an event for which he was not answerable made his enemies implacable, and made him desperate.

An emissary of James had crossed from Ireland to Scotland with letters addressed to Dundee and Balcarras. The messenger was arrested, interrogated, and searched; and the letters were found. Hamilton ordered Balcarras and Dundee to be arrested. Balcarras was taken, and was confined in the Tolbooth of Edinburgh. But to seize Dundee was not so easy an enterprise. He betook himself to the hill country, pushed northward through Strathdon and Strathbogie, crossed the Spey, and, on the morning of the 1st of May, arrived with a small band of horsemen at the camp of Keppoch before Inverness.

The new situation in which Dundee was now placed, the new view of society which was presented to him, naturally suggested new projects to his inventive spirit. The hundreds of athletic Celts whom he saw in their national order of battle were evidently not allies to be despised. If he could form a great coalition of clans, if he could muster under one banner ten or twelve thousand of those hardy warriors, if he could induce them to submit to the restraints of discipline, what a career might be before him!

Keppoch hated the Campbells with all the hatred of a Macdonald, and promptly gave in his adhesion to the cause of the House of Stuart. Dundee undertook to settle the dispute between Keppoch and Inverness. The town agreed to pay two thousand dollars, a sum which probably exceeded any treasure that had ever been carried into the wilds of Coryarrick. Half the sum was raised by the inhabitants; and Dundee is said to have passed his word for the remainder.

He next tried to reconcile the Macdonalds with the Mackintoshes; but he soon found that it was no light matter to take up a Highland feud. What Argyle was to Keppoch, Keppoch was to the Mackintoshes. The Mackintoshes therefore remained neutral. Those chiefs, on the other hand, to whom the name of Campbell had long been hateful, greeted Dundee eagerly, and promised to meet him at the head of their followers on the 18th of May. The fiery crosses wandered from hamlet to hamlet over all the heaths and mountains thirty miles round Ben Nevis; and when Dundee reached the trysting place in Lochaber he found that the gathering had begun. The head quarters were fixed close to Lochiel's house, a large pile built entirely of fir wood. Lochiel, surrounded by more than six hundred broadswords, was there to receive his guests. Macnaghten of Macnaghten and Stewart of Appin were at the muster with their little clans. Macdonald of Keppoch led his warriors. Macdonald of Glengarry rode on horseback before his four hundred plaided clansmen in a steel cuirass and a coat embroidered with gold lace. Another Macdonald, destined to a lamentable and horrible end, led a band of hardy freebooters from the dreary pass of Glencoe.

Mackay, meanwhile, wasted some weeks in marching, in countermarching, and in indecisive skirmishing. It was difficult in such a country to track the enemy. It was impossible to drive him to bay. The general found that he had tired his men and their horses almost to death, and yet had effected nothing. An experience of little more than a month satisfied him that there was only one way in which the Highlands could be subdued. A chain of fortresses must be built in the most important situations, and must be well garrisoned.

While Mackay was representing in his letters to the council at Edinburgh the necessity of adopting this plan, Dundee was contending with difficulties which all his energy and dexterity could not completely overcome.

A tribe of Celts was easily turned into a battalion of soldiers. All that was necessary was that the military organisation should be conformed to the patriarchal organisation. The chief must be colonel: his uncle or his brother must be major: the tacksmen must be the captains: the company of each captain must consist of those peasants who lived on his land: the hereditary piper and his sons formed the band; and the clan became at once a regiment. In such a regiment was found from the first moment that exact order and prompt obedience in which the strength of regular armies consists. Every man looked up to his immediate superior; and all looked up to the common head. But with the chief this chain of subordination ended. He knew only how to govern, and had never learned to obey. Of his brother chiefs, some were his enemies and some his rivals. All his followers sympathised with all his animosities, considered his honour as their own, and were ready at his whistle to array themselves round him in arms against the commander in chief.

What Dundee saw of his Celtic allies must have made him desirous to have in his army some troops who would not, at a signal from their colonel, turn their arms against their general and their King. He accordingly, during the months of May and June, sent to Dublin a succession of letters imploring assistance. He received such answers as encouraged him to hope that a large and well appointed force would soon be sent from Ulster to join him. He did not wish to try the chance of a battle before these succours arrived. Mackay, on the other hand, was weary of marching to and fro in a desert. His men were exhausted and out of heart. He thought it desirable that they should withdraw from the hill country; and William was of the same opinion.

In June therefore the civil war was completely suspended. Dundee remained in Lochaber, awaiting the arrival of troops and supplies from Ireland. The clans went back to their own glens, having promised to reassemble on the first summons.

Since the splendour of the House of Argyle had been eclipsed, no Gaelic chief could vie in power with the Marquess of Athol. The men who followed his banner were, in strength and courage, inferior to no tribe in the mountains. But the clan had been made insignificant by the insignificance of the chief. The Marquess was the falsest, the most pusillanimous, of mankind. Already, in the space of six months, he had been several times a Jacobite, and several times a Williamite. After repeatedly vowing fidelity to both parties, and repeatedly betraying both, he began to think that he should best provide for his safety by quitting the country to which he was bound by every tie of duty and honour at the very crisis of her fate. He stole away to England, settled himself at Bath, and pretended to drink the waters. His principality, left without a head, was divided against itself. One word from the marquess would have sent two thousand claymores to the Jacobite side. But that word he would not speak; and the consequence was, that the conduct of his followers was as irresolute and inconsistent as his own.

While they were waiting for some indication of his wishes, they were called to arms at once by two leaders, either of whom might claim to be the representative of the absent chief. Lord Murray, the marquess's eldest son, declared for King William. Stewart of Ballenach, the marquess's confidential agent, declared for King James. The people knew not which summons to obey.

The most important military post in Athol was Blair Castle. About five miles south of this stronghold, the valley of the Garry contracts itself into the celebrated glen of Killiecrankie. In the days of William III, Killiecrankie was deemed the most perilous of all those dark ravines through which the marauders of the hills were wont to sally forth. The only path was narrow and rugged; and, in some places, the way ran so close by the precipice that the traveller had great need of a steady eye and foot. The country which lay just above this pass was now the theatre of a war such as the Highlands had not often witnessed. Ballenach, at the head of a body of vassals who considered him as the representative of the marquess, occupied Blair Castle. Murray, with twelve hundred followers, appeared before the walls, and demanded to be admitted into the mansion of his family. The garrison refused to open the gates. Messages were sent off by the besiegers to Edinburgh, and by the besieged to Lochaber. Mackay and Dundee agreed in thinking that the crisis required prompt and strenuous exertion. Mackay hastened northward, and ordered his troops to assemble in the low country of Perthshire. He soon had with him the three Scotch regiments which had served in Holland, and which bore the names of their colonels, Mackay himself, Balfour, and Ramsay. There was also a gallant regiment of infantry from England, called Hastings's. With these old troops were joined two regiments newly levied in the Lowlands. One of them was commanded by Lord Kenmore, the other by Lord Leven. Two troops of horse, Lord Annandale's and Lord Belhaven's, probably made up the army to the number of above three thousand men.

Dundee, meanwhile, had summoned all the clans which acknowledged his commission to assemble for an expedition into Athol. But the call was so unexpected, and the time allowed was so short, that the muster was not a very full one. The whole number of broadswords seems to have been under three thousand. With this force Dundee set forth. On his march he was joined by succours which had just arrived from Ulster. They consisted of little more than three hundred Irish foot, ill armed, ill clothed, and ill disciplined. Their commander was an officer named Cannon.

While Mackay from one side, and Dundee from the other, were advancing towards Blair Castle, important events had taken place there. Murray's adherents soon began to waver in their fidelity to him. They saw arrayed against them a large number of their kinsmen, commanded by a gentleman who was supposed to possess the confidence of the marquess. The besieging army melted rapidly away. Murray's force dwindled to three or four hundred men: even in those men he could put little trust; and the Macdonalds and Camerons were advancing fast. He therefore raised the siege, and retired with a few followers into the defile of Killiecrankie. There he was soon joined by a detachment of two hundred fusileers whom Mackay had sent forward to secure the pass.

Early in the morning of Saturday the 27th of July, Dundee arrived at Blair Castle. There he learned that Mackay's troops were already in the ravine of Killiecrankie. A council of war was held: Dundee determined to fight; and the confederated clans in high spirits set forward to encounter the enemy.

The enemy meanwhile had made his way up the pass. The ascent had been long and toilsome: for even the foot had to climb by twos and threes; and the baggage horses, twelve hundred in number, could mount only one at a time. At length the passage was effected; and the troops found themselves in a valley of no great extent. Their right was flanked by a rising ground, their left by the Garry. Wearied with the morning's work, they threw themselves on the grass to take some rest and refreshment.

Early in the afternoon, they were roused by an alarm that the Highlanders were approaching. Regiment after regiment started up and got into order. In a little while the summit of the ascent which was about a musket shot before them was covered with bonnets and plaids. Dundee drew up his men with as much skill as their peculiar character permitted him to exert. Each tribe, large or small, formed a column separated from the next column by a wide interval.

Meanwhile a fire of musketry was kept up on both sides. The space between the armies was one cloud of smoke. Not a few Highlanders dropped; and the clans grew impatient. The sun however was low in the west before Dundee gave the order to prepare for action. His men raised a great shout. The enemy, probably exhausted by the toil of the day, returned a feeble and wavering cheer. 'We shall do it now,' said Lochiel: 'that is not the cry of men who are going to win.'

It was past seven o'clock. Dundee gave the word; and the whole line advanced firing. When only a small space was left between the armies, the Highlanders suddenly flung away their firelocks, drew their broadswords, and rushed forward with a fearful yell. The Lowlanders prepared to receive the shock: but the soldiers were still fumbling with the muzzles of their guns and the handles of their bayonets when the whole flood of Macleans, Macdonalds, and Camerons came down. In two minutes the battle was lost and won. The ranks of Balfour's regiment broke. Ramsay's men turned their backs and dropped their arms. Mackay's own foot were swept away by the furious onset of the Camerons. Mackay called on the horse: but Belhaven's troopers, appalled by the rout of the infantry, galloped off in disorder: Annandale's men followed: all was over; and the mingled torrent of redcoats and tartans went raving down the valley to the gorge of Killiecrankie.

Mackay spurred bravely through the thickest of the claymores and targets, and reached a point from which he had a view of the field. His whole army had disappeared, with the exception of some Borderers whom Leven had kept together, and of Hastings's regiment, which still kept unbroken order. All the men that could be collected were only a few hundreds. The general made haste to lead them across the Garry, and, having put the river between them and the enemy, paused for a moment to meditate on his situation.

He could hardly understand how the conquerors could be so unwise as to allow him even that moment for deliberation. But the energy of the Celtic warriors had spent itself in one furious rush and one short struggle. The pass was choked by the twelve hundred beasts of burden which carried the provisions and baggage of the vanquished army. Such a booty was irresistibly tempting to men who were impelled to war quite as much by the desire of rapine as by the desire of glory. Dundee himself might have been unable to persuade his followers to quit the heaps of spoil, and to complete the great work of the day; and Dundee was no more.

At the beginning of the action he had taken his place in front of his little band of cavalry. He bade them follow him, and rode forward. But the horse hesitated. Dundee turned round, stood up in his stirrups, and, waving his hat, invited them to come on. As he lifted his arm, his cuirass rose, and exposed the lower part of his left side. A musket ball struck him: his horse sprang forward and plunged into a cloud of smoke and dust, which hid from both armies the fall of the victorious general. A person named Johnstone was near him, and caught him as he sank down from the saddle. 'How goes the day?' said Dundee. 'Well for King James,' answered Johnstone: 'but I am sorry for your lordship.' 'If it is well for him,' answered the dying man, 'it matters the less for me.' He never spoke again. The body, wrapped in two plaids, was carried to the Castle of Blair.

Mackay, who was ignorant of Dundee's fate, expected to be hotly pursued, and had very little expectation of being able to save the remains of the vanquished army. He resolved to push across the mountains towards the valley of the Tay. By the help of a pocket map, he was able to find his way. He marched all night; and at length the weary fugitives came in sight of Weems Castle. The proprietor of the mansion was a friend to the new government, and extended to them such hospitality as was in his power. Refreshed, they again set forth, and marched all day over bog, moor, and mountain. Late at night they reached Castle Drummond, which was held for King William by a small garrison; and, on the following day, they proceeded with less difficulty to Stirling.

From the pass of Killiecrankie the Highlanders had retired, proud of their victory, and laden with spoil, to the Castle of Blair. But they had bought their victory dear. A hundred and twenty Camerons had been slain: the loss of the Macdonalds had been still greater; and several gentlemen of note had fallen.

As far as the great interests of the State were concerned, it mattered not at all whether the battle of Killiecrankie were lost or won. It is very improbable that even Dundee, if he had survived the most glorious day of his life, could have surmounted those difficulties which sprang from the peculiar nature of his army. It is certain that his successor was altogether unequal to the task.

Cannon called a council of war to consider what course it would be advisable to take. Lochiel was for advancing, for marching towards Mackay wherever Mackay might be, and for giving battle again. But he was overruled. His pride was severely wounded. He had been willing to be the right hand of Dundee: but he would not be ordered about by Cannon. He quitted the camp, and retired to Lochaber.

Mackay's arrangements were by this time complete; and he had little doubt that, if the rebels came down to attack him, the regular army would retrieve the honour which had been lost at Killiecrankie. His chief difficulties arose from the unwise interference of the ministers of the Crown at Edinburgh with matters which ought to have been left to his direction. The Cameronian regiment, composed of soldiers who were all rigid Puritans, was sent to garrison Dunkeld. Of this arrangement Mackay altogether disapproved. He knew that at Dunkeld these troops would be near the enemy; that they would be far from all assistance; that they would be surrounded by a hostile population; and that in all probability some great effort would be made to destroy them.

It soon appeared that his forebodings were just. The inhabitants of the country round Dunkeld furnished Cannon with intelligence, and urged him to make a bold push. On the morning of the 21st of August, all the hills round Dunkeld were alive with bonnets and plaids. The Highlanders, estimated by those who saw them at from four to five thousand men, came furiously on. The outposts of the Cameronians were speedily driven in. But the greater part of the regiment made its stand behind a wall which surrounded a house belonging to the Marquess of Athol. The struggle lasted four hours. By that time the Cameronians were reduced nearly to their last flask of powder; but their spirit never flagged. The Highlanders began to fall back: disorder visibly spread among them; and whole bands began to march off to the hills. It was in vain that their general ordered them to return to the attack. Perseverance was not one of their military virtues; and in a short time the whole Gaelic army was in full retreat towards Blair. The victorious Puritans threw their caps into the air, raised a psalm of triumph and thanksgiving, and waved their colours.

The Cameronians had good reason to be joyful; for they had finished the war. In the rebel camp all was discord and dejection. The Highlanders blamed Cannon: Cannon blamed the Highlanders; and the host which had been the terror of Scotland melted fast away. On the 24th of August, exactly four weeks after the Gaelic army had won the battle of Killiecrankie, that army ceased to exist. All the fruits of victory were gathered by the vanquished. The Castle of Blair opened its gates to Mackay; and a chain of military posts, extending northwards as far as Inverness, protected the cultivators of the plains against the predatory inroads of the mountaineers.

King William in Ireland

Twenty-four hours before the war in Scotland was brought to a close by the discomfiture of the Celtic army at Dunkeld, the Parliament broke up at Westminster. The House had sate ever since January without recess. The most exciting question of this long session was, what punishment should be inflicted on those men who had, during the interval between the dissolution of the Oxford Parliament and the Revolution, been the advisers or the tools of Charles and James. Among the many offenders was one who stood alone and unapproached in guilt and infamy.

On that terrible day which was succeeded by the Irish Night, the roar of a great city disappointed of its revenge had followed Jeffreys to the drawbridge of the Tower. His imprisonment was not strictly legal: but he at first accepted with thanks and blessings the protection which those dark walls afforded him against the fury of the multitude. Soon, however, he became sensible that his life was still in peril. Whether the legal guilt of murder could be brought home to him may be doubted. But he was morally guilty of so many murders that, if there had been no other way of reaching his life, a retrospective Act of Attainder would have been demanded by the whole nation. The rage of his enemies was such that, in language seldom heard in England, they proclaimed their wish that he might go to the place of wailing and gnashing of teeth, to the worm that never dies, to the fire that is never quenched. His spirit sank down under the load of public abhorrence. His constitution, originally bad, and much impaired by intemperance, was completely broken by distress and anxiety. He was tormented by a cruel internal disease, which the most skilful surgeons of that age were seldom able to relieve. One solace was left to him, brandy.

Disease, assisted by strong drink and by misery, did its work fast. The patient's stomach rejected all nourishment. He dwindled in a few weeks from a portly man to a skeleton. On the 18th of April he died, in the forty-first year of his age. He had been Chief Justice of the King's Bench at thirty-five, and Lord Chancellor at thirty-seven. In the whole history of the English bar there is no other instance of so rapid an elevation, or of so terrible a fall. The emaciated corpse was laid, with all privacy, next to the corpse of Monmouth in the chapel of the Tower.

On the 20th of August the Parliament broke up for a short recess. The same *Gazette* which announced that the Houses had ceased to sit announced that Schomberg had landed in Ireland.

The general to whom the direction of the expedition against Ireland was confided had wonderfully succeeded in obtaining the affection of the English nation. He had been made a Duke, a Knight of the Garter, and Master of the Ordnance: and yet his elevation excited none of the jealousy which showed itself as often as any mark of royal favour was bestowed on Bentinck, on Zulestein, or on Auverquerque. Schomberg landed in the north of Ulster. The force which he had brought with him did not exceed ten thousand men: but the coffee-house politicians of London fully expected that such a general with such an army would speedily reconquer the island.

He marched first to Carrickfergus. That town was held for James by two

A contemporary tapestry portrait of William III. Though of frail health and physique, he was possessed of indomitable courage. On his departure for the Irish campaign he confided to Burnet: 'I am sure I am fitter to conduct a campaign than to manage your Houses of Lords and Commons.'

regiments of infantry. Schomberg battered the walls; and the Irish, after holding out a week, capitulated. Schomberg proceeded to Lisburn, and thence, through towns left without an inhabitant, to Loughbrickland. While he was advancing, the Irish forces were rapidly assembled from every quarter. On the 10th of September the royal standard of James was unfurled on the tower of Drogheda; and beneath it were soon collected twenty thousand fighting men. By this time Schomberg had reached Dundalk. The distance between the two armies was not more than a long day's march. It was therefore generally expected that the fate of the island would speedily be decided by a pitched battle.

In a few days, however, it became clear that Schomberg had determined not to fight. His reasons were weighty. He had some good Dutch and French troops: but the bulk of his army consisted of English peasants who had just left their cottages. These inexperienced recruits were for the most part commanded by officers as inexperienced as themselves. Schomberg made up his mind to stand on the defensive till his men had been disciplined, and till reinforcements and supplies should arrive.

He entrenched himself near Dundalk in such a manner that he could not be forced to fight against his will. During some weeks he remained secure within his defences, while the Irish lay a few miles off. He set himself assiduously to drill the new levies. He ordered the musketeers to be constantly exercised in firing, sometimes at marks, and sometimes by platoons; and, from the way in which they at first acquitted themselves, it plainly appeared that he had judged wisely in not leading them out to battle. It was found that not one in four of the English soldiers could manage his piece at all; and whoever succeeded in discharging it, no matter in what direction, thought that he had performed a great feat.

The autumnal rains of Ireland are usually heavy; and this year they were heavier than usual. The whole country was deluged; and the duke's camp became a marsh. The peasants of Yorkshire and Derbyshire had neither constitutions prepared to resist the pernicious influence, nor skill to protect themselves against it. They sickened and died by hundreds. In the midst of difficulties hourly multiplying, the great qualities of Schomberg appeared hourly more and more conspicuous. The effective men under his command did not now exceed five thousand. Nevertheless so masterly were the old man's dispositions that with this small force he faced during several weeks twenty thousand troops who were accompanied by a multitude of armed banditti. At length early in November the Irish dispersed, and went to winter quarters. The duke then broke up his camp and retired into Ulster.

The Church was, at this time, in a distracted state. The 1st of August had been fixed as the day before the close of which all beneficed clergymen and all persons holding academical offices must, on pain of suspension, swear allegiance to William and Mary. During the earlier part of the summer, the Jacobites had hoped that the number of nonjurors would be so considerable as to alarm and embarrass the government. But this hope was disappointed. Above twenty-nine thirtieths of the profession submitted to the law. In general the compliance was tardy, sad, and sullen. Many, no doubt, deliberately violated what they believed to be their duty. Conscience told them that they were committing a sin. But they had not fortitude to resign the parsonage, the garden, the glebe, and to go forth without knowing where to find a meal or a roof for themselves and their little ones. Even of those whose understandings were fully convinced that obedience was due to the existing government, very few kissed the book with the heartiness with which they had formerly plighted their faith to Charles and James. Still the thing was done. Ten thousand clergymen had solemnly called heaven to attest their promise that they would be true liegemen to William; and this promise had at least deprived them of a great part of their power to injure him.

Those clergymen and members of the universities who incurred the penalties of the law were about four hundred in number. Foremost in rank stood the Primate and six of his suffragans, Turner of Ely, Lloyd of Norwich, Frampton of Gloucester, Lake of Chichester, White of Peterborough, and Ken of Bath and Wells.

The Parliament met again on the 19th of October. On the day of meeting an important change struck every eye. Halifax was no longer on the woolsack. Sick of public life, he had begun to pine for the silence and solitude of his seat in Nottinghamshire, an old Cistercian Abbey buried deep among woods. Early in October it was known that he would no longer preside in the Upper House. It was at the same time whispered as a great secret that he meant to retire altogether from business, and that he retained the Privy Seal only till a successor should be named.

Meanwhile the King was weary of his Crown. He had tried to do justice to both the contending parties; but justice would satisfy neither. The Tories hated him for protecting the Dissenters. The Whigs hated him for protecting the Tories. The last campaign in Ireland had been disastrous. It might well be that the next campaign would be more disastrous still. Every part of the administration was thoroughly disorganised; and the people were surprised and angry because a foreigner, newly come among them, had not, in a year, put the whole machine of government to rights. The King felt that he could not, while thus situated, render any service to that great cause to which his soul was devoted. But he would endure his splendid slavery no longer. He would return to his native country. He would content himself with being the first citizen of a commonwealth to which the name of Orange was dear. As for the turbulent and ungrateful islanders, Mary must try what she could do with them. If she had little knowledge of politics and war, she had what might be more useful, feminine grace and tact, a sweet temper, a smile and a kind word for everybody. Holland, under his government, and England, under hers, might act cordially together against the common enemy.

He called together a few of his chief counsellors, and told them his purpose. The ministers were thunderstruck. For once all quarrels were suspended. The Tory Caermarthen on one side, the Whig Shrewsbury on the other, expostulated and implored with a pathetic vehemence rare in the conferences of statesmen. At length the King was induced to give up his design of abdicating the government. But he announced another design which he was fully determined not to give up. Since he was still to remain at the head of the English administration, he would go himself to Ireland.

That he had seriously meditated a retreat to Holland long continued to be a secret. That he had resolved to take the command of his army in Ireland was soon rumoured all over London. It was known that his camp furniture was making, and that Sir Christopher Wren was busied in constructing a house of wood which was to travel about, packed in two waggons, and to be set up wherever His Majesty might fix his quarters. His resolution, he told his friends, was unalterably fixed. Everything was at stake; and go he must, even though the Parliament should present an address imploring him to stay.

He soon learned that such an address would be immediately moved in both Houses and supported by the whole strength of the Whig party. This intelligence satisfied him that it was time to take a decisive step. He would not discard the Whigs: but he would give them a lesson of which they stood much in need. He would not let them have the exclusive possession of power.

On the 27th of January, Black Rod knocked at the door of the Commons. The Speaker and the members repaired to the House of Lords. The King was on the throne. He announced his intention of going to Ireland, and prorogued the Parliament. None could doubt that a dissolution would speedily follow. As the concluding words, 'I have thought it convenient now to put an end to this session,' were uttered, the Tories, both above and below the bar, broke forth into a shout of joy. The King meanwhile surveyed his audience with that bright eagle eye which nothing escaped. 'I saw', he wrote to Portland the next day, 'faces an ell long. I saw some of those men change colour with vexation twenty times while I was speaking.'

All the acts of William, at this time, indicated his determination to restrain the violence of the Whigs, and to conciliate the good will of the Tories. Within a week after the prorogation, the 1st of February came, the day on which those ecclesiastics who refused to take the oaths were to be finally deprived. The Primate and five of his suffragans were still inflexible. They consequently forfeited their bishoprics: but Sancroft was informed that the King had not yet relinquished the hope of being able to make some arrangement which might avert the necessity of appointing successors, and that the nonjuring prelates might continue for the present to reside in their palaces.

And now appeared a proclamation dissolving the Parliament. The writs for a general election went out; and soon every part of the kingdom was in a ferment. Public feeling had undergone a great change during the year which had elapsed since the Convention had met; and it was soon plain that the Tories would have a majority in the new House of Commons.

The King meanwhile was making, in almost every department of the executive government, a change corresponding to the change which the general election was making in the composition of the legislature. Caermarthen was now the chief adviser of the Crown on all matters relating to the internal administration and to the management of the two Houses of Parliament. The white staff, and the immense power which accompanied the white staff, William was still determined never to entrust to any subject. Caermarthen therefore continued to be Lord President; but he took possession of a suite of apartments in Saint James's Palace which was considered as peculiarly belonging to the prime minister. Sir John Lowther became First Lord of the Treasury, and was the person on whom Caermarthen chiefly relied for the conduct of the ostensible business of the House of Commons.

A new Commission of Admiralty was issued. At the head of the naval administration was placed Thomas Herbert, Earl of Pembroke. Nothing was omitted which could reconcile Torrington to this change. For, though he had been found an incapable administrator, he still stood so high in general estimation as a seaman that the government was unwilling to lose his services. He was assured that no slight was intended to him; and, in an evil hour for England, he consented to remain at the head of the naval force on which the safety of her coasts depended.

On the 20th of March, the new Parliament met. On the 20th of May, the King informed the Houses that his visit to Ireland could no longer be delayed, that he had therefore determined to prorogue them, and that he should not call them again from their homes till the next winter. 'Then,' he said, 'I hope, by the blessing of God, we shall have a happy meeting.'

The activity with which William had personally urged forward the preparations for the next campaign had produced an extraordinary effect. Abundant supplies of food, clothing, and medicine were sent across Saint George's Channel. Great numbers of recruits were sent to fill the chasms which pestilence had made in the English ranks. Fresh regiments from Scotland, Cheshire, Lancashire, and Cumberland had landed in the Bay of Belfast. Before the end of May the English force in Ulster amounted to thirty thousand fighting men.

Louis proposed to take into his own service, and to form by the best discipline then known in the world, four Irish regiments. In return for these troops, who were in number not quite four thousand, he undertook to send to Ireland between seven and eight thousand excellent French infantry, who were likely in a day of battle to be of more use than all the kernes of Leinster, Munster, and Connaught together.

One great error he committed. The army which he was sending to assist James was destined for a service on which the fate of Europe might depend, and ought therefore to have been commanded by a general of eminent abilities. There was no want of such generals in the French service. But James begged hard for Lauzun, and carried this point against the strong representations of Avaux, and against the judgment of Louis himself.

In order that one man might fill a post for which he was unfit, it was necessary to remove two men from posts for which they were eminently fit. Rosen was a skilful captain, and Avaux was a skilful politician. It would have been an affront to the old general to put him under the orders of Lauzun; and between the ambassador and Lauzun there was such an enmity that they could not be expected to act cordially together. Both Rosen and Avaux, therefore, were recalled to France. They sailed from Cork early in the spring by the fleet which had conveyed Lauzun thither. At Dublin Lauzun was appointed Commander in Chief of the Irish army, and took up his residence in the castle.

William meanwhile was busied in making arrangements for the government and defence of England during his absence. Mary would be in constant need of wise counsel; and where was such counsel to be found? If the interior cabinet were composed exclusively either of Whigs or of Tories, half the nation would be disgusted. Yet, if Whigs and Tories were mixed, it was certain that there would be constant dissension. He finally selected nine privy councillors, by whose advice he enjoined Mary to be guided. Four of these, Devonshire, Dorset, Monmouth, and Edward Russell, were Whigs. The other five, Caermarthen, Pembroke, Nottingham, Marlborough, and Lowther, were Tories.

On the 4th of June the King set out for Ireland. In four days he arrived at Chester, where a fleet of transports was awaiting the signal for sailing. He embarked on the 11th of June, and was convoyed across Saint George's Channel by a squadron of men of war under the command of Sir Cloudesley Shovel.

Scarcely had William set out from London when a great French fleet commanded by the Count of Tourville left the port of Brest and entered the British Channel. Tourville was the ablest maritime commander that his country then possessed. He now stood over to the English shore, and proceeded slowly along the coast of Devonshire and Dorsetshire.

The Queen and her Council hastened to take measures for the defence of the country. Torrington took the command of the English fleet which lay in the Downs, and sailed to Saint Helen's. He was there joined by a Dutch squadron under the command of Evertsen. It seemed that the cliffs of the Isle of Wight would witness one of the greatest naval conflicts recorded in history. On the east of the huge precipice of Black Gang Chine were collected the maritime forces of England and Holland. On the west, stretching to that white cape where the waves roar among the Needles, lay the armament of France.

It was on the 26th of June that the hostile fleets took up these positions.

The Queen and the interior Council of Nine had now to consider a question of the gravest importance. What orders were to be sent to Torrington? The safety of the State might depend on his judgment and presence of mind; and some of Mary's advisers apprehended that he would not be found equal to the occasion. Their anxiety increased when news came that he had abandoned the coast of the Isle of Wight to the French, and was retreating before them towards the Straits of Dover. Russell proposed to send to the admiral a reprimand couched in terms so severe that the Queen did not like to sign it. The language was much softened: but, in the main, Russell's advice was followed. Torrington was positively ordered to retreat no further, and to give battle immediately.

The despatch reached him when he was off Beachy Head. He read it, and was in a great strait. Not to give battle was to be guilty of direct disobedience. To give battle was, in his judgment, to incur serious risk of defeat. He succeeded in finding out a middle way which united all the inconveniences which he wished to avoid. Some of his ships should skirmish with the enemy: but the great body of his fleet should not be risked. There is but too good reason to believe that he was base enough to lay his plans in such a manner that the loss might fall almost exclusively to the share of the Dutch.

It was on the 29th of June that the admiral received the order to fight. The next day, at four in the morning, he bore down on the French fleet, and formed his vessels in order of battle. He placed the Dutch in the van and gave them the signal to engage. That signal was promptly obeyed. During many hours the van maintained the unequal contest with very little assistance from any other part of the fleet. At length the Dutch admiral drew off, leaving one shattered and dismasted hull to the enemy. To keep the sea against the French after this disastrous action was impossible. The Dutch ships which had come out of the fight were in lamentable condition. Torrington ordered some of them to be destroyed: the rest he took in tow: he then fled along the coast of Kent, and sought a refuge in the Thames. As soon as he was in the river, he ordered all the buoys to be pulled up, and thus made the navigation so dangerous that the pursuers could not venture to follow him.

During the three days which followed the arrival of the tidings from Beachy Head the aspect of London was gloomy and agitated. But on the fourth day all was changed. Bells were pealing: flags were flying: men were eagerly shaking hands with each other in the streets. A courier had that morning arrived at Whitehall with great news from Ireland.

William had landed at Carrickfergus on the afternoon of the 14th of June. As soon as he was on dry ground he mounted and set off for Belfast. On the road he was met by Schomberg.

Belfast was then a small English settlement of about three hundred houses. William was welcomed at the North Gate by the magistrates and burgesses in their robes of office. The multitude pressed on his carriage with shouts of 'God save the Protestant King'. Before midnight all the heights of Antrim and Down were blazing with bonfires. The light was seen across the bays of Carlingford and Dundalk, and gave notice to the outposts of the enemy that the decisive hour was at hand. Within forty-eight hours after William had landed, James set out from Dublin for the Irish camp, which was pitched near the northern frontier of Leinster.

Loughbrickland was the place appointed by William for the rendezvous of the scattered divisions of his army. While his troops were assembling, he exerted himself indefatigably to improve their discipline and to provide for their subsistence. It was strange to see how rapidly this man, so unpopular at Westminster, obtained a complete mastery over the hearts of his brethren in arms. They observed with delight that, infirm as he was, he took his share of every hardship which they underwent; that he thought more of their comfort than of his own; that he never once, from the day on which he took the field, lodged in a house, but slept in his small travelling hut of wood.

On the 24th of June he marched southwards with all his forces. He was fully determined to take the first opportunity of fighting. On the 30th of June, his army reached the summit of a rising ground near the southern frontier of the county of Louth. Beneath lay a valley, now so rich and so cheerful that the Englishman who gazes on it may imagine himself to be in one of the most highly favoured parts of his own highly favoured country. Fields of wheat, woodlands, meadows bright with daisies and clover, slope gently down to the edge of the Boyne. That bright and tranquil stream, the boundary of Louth and Meath, is here about to mingle with the sea. Two miles to the east of the place from where William looked down on the river, a cloud of smoke from factories and steam vessels overhangs the busy town and port of Drogheda. On the Meath side of the Boyne, the ground, still all corn, grass, flowers, and foliage, rises with a gentle swell to an eminence surmounted by a conspicuous tuft of ash trees which overshades the ruined church and desolate graveyard of Dunore.

In the seventeenth century the landscape presented a very different aspect. Drogheda was a small knot of narrow, crooked, and filthy lanes, encircled by a ditch and a mound. Without the walls of the town, scarcely a dwelling was to be seen except at a place called Oldbridge. At Oldbridge the river was fordable; and on the south of the ford were a few mud cabins, and a single house built of more solid materials.

When William caught sight of the valley of the Boyne, he could not suppress an exclamation and gesture of delight. It was plain that the contest would be sharp and short. The pavilion of James was pitched on the eminence of Dunore. All the southern bank of the river was lined by the camp and batteries of the hostile army. 'I am glad to see you, gentlemen,' said the King, as his keen eye surveyed the Irish lines. 'If you escape me now, the fault will be mine.'

Each of the contending princes had some advantages over his rival. James, standing on the defensive behind entrenchments, with a river before him, had the stronger position: but his troops were inferior both in number and in quality to those which were opposed to him. He probably had thirty thousand men. About a third part of this force consisted of excellent French infantry and excellent Irish cavalry. But the rest of his army was the scoff of all Europe. The Irish dragoons were bad; the Irish foot worse.

William had under his command near thirty-six thousand men, born in many lands, and speaking many tongues. About half the troops were natives of England. The Scotch footguards marched under the command of their countryman James Douglas. Conspicuous among the Dutch troops were Portland's and Ginkell's Horse, and Solmes's Blue regiment. Germany had sent to the field some warriors sprung from her noblest houses.

Victorieus gevegt van Koning William. tegens den gewesen Koning Iacobus in Irland. den 8 July 1690.

The Battle of the Boyne, 1 July 1690: contemporary English print. The Boyne was hailed in England and Europe as a great victory; and, indeed, the importance of the battle was enormous – James had been driven out of Ireland for good. But there was much hard fighting still ahead at Limerick and Athlone before the Jacobite forces were finally defeated.

Prince George of Hesse Darmstadt, a gallant youth, rode near the King. A strong brigade of Danish mercenaries was commanded by Duke Charles Frederic of Wurtemberg. But in that great array, so variously composed, were two bodies of men animated by a spirit peculiarly fierce and implacable, the Huguenots of France thirsting for the blood of the French, and the Englishry of Ireland impatient to trample down the Irish.

It was still early in the day. The King rode slowly along the northern bank of the river, and closely examined the position of the Irish, from whom he was sometimes separated by an interval of little more than two hundred feet. He was accompanied by Schomberg, Sidney, Solmes, Prince George of Hesse, and others. At length he alighted at a spot nearly opposite to Oldbridge, sate down on the turf to rest himself, and called for breakfast. The sumpter horses were unloaded: the canteens were opened; and a tablecloth was spread on the grass.

The chiefs of the Irish army soon discovered that the person who, surrounded by a splendid circle, was breakfasting on the opposite bank, was the Prince of Orange. They sent for artillery. Two field pieces, screened from view by a troop of cavalry, were brought down almost to the brink of the river, and placed behind a hedge. William, who had just risen from his meal, and was again in the saddle, was the mark of both guns. The first shot struck one of the holsters of Prince George of Hesse, and brought his horse to the ground. 'Ah!' cried the King; 'the poor prince is killed.' As the words passed his lips, he was himself hit by a second ball, a six-pounder. It merely tore his coat, grazed his shoulder, and drew two or three ounces of blood. Both armies saw that the shot had taken effect; for the King sank down for a moment on his horse's neck. A yell of exultation rose from the Irish camp. But William's deportment soon reassured his friends. 'There is no harm done,' he said: 'but the bullet came quite near enough.' A surgeon was sent for: a plaster was applied; and the King, as soon as the dressing was finished, rode round all the posts of his army amidst loud acclamations. Such was the energy of his spirit that, in spite of his feeble health, in spite of his recent hurt, he was that day nineteen hours on horseback.

A cannonade was kept up on both sides till the evening. Long after sunset William made a final inspection of his forces by torchlight, and gave orders that everything should be ready for forcing a passage across the river on the morrow. Every soldier was to put a green bough in his hat. The word was Westminster.

The King's resolution to attack the Irish was not approved by all his lieutenants. Schomberg, in particular, pronounced the experiment too hazardous, and retired to his tent in no very good humour.

The 1st of July dawned. Soon after four both armies were in motion. William ordered his right wing, under the command of Meinhart Schomberg, one of the duke's sons, to march to the bridge of Slane, some miles up the river, to cross there, and to turn the left flank of the Irish army. This move made Lauzun uneasy. What if the English right wing should get into the rear of the army of James? About four miles south of the Boyne was a place called Duleek, where the road to Dublin was so narrow that two cars could not pass each other. If Meinhart Schomberg should occupy this spot, it would be impossible for the Irish to retreat. Disturbed by this apprehension, the French general marched with his countrymen and with Sarsfield's horse in the direction of Slane Bridge. Thus the fords near Oldbridge were left to be defended by the Irish alone.

It was now near ten o'clock. William put himself at the head of his left wing, which was composed exclusively of cavalry, and prepared to pass the river not far above Drogheda. The centre of his army, which consisted almost exclusively of foot, was entrusted to the command of Schomberg, and was marshalled opposite to Oldbridge. At Oldbridge had been collected the whole Irish army, foot, dragoons, and horse, Sarsfield's regiment alone excepted. A fortification had been made by French engineers out of the hedges and buildings; and a breastwork had been thrown up close to the water side. Tyrconnel was there; and under him were Richard Hamilton and the Earl of Antrim.

Schomberg gave the word. Solmes's Blues, ten abreast, descended into the water. Next plunged Londonderry and Enniskillen. A little to the left of them, Caillemot crossed, at the head of a long column of French refugees. A little to the left of Caillemot, the main body of the English infantry struggled through the river. Still further down the stream the Danes found another ford. In a few minutes the Boyne, for a quarter of a mile, was alive with muskets and green boughs.

A wild shout of defiance rose from the whole shore: during one moment the event seemed doubtful: but the Protestants pressed resolutely forward; and in another moment the whole Irish line gave way. Tyrconnel looked on in helpless despair, as whole regiments flung away arms, colours, and cloaks, and scampered off to the hills without striking a blow or firing a shot.

Richard Hamilton put himself at the head of the cavalry, and, under his command, they made a gallant attempt to retrieve the day. They maintained a desperate fight in the bed of the river with Solmes's Blues. They drove the Danish brigade back into the stream. They fell impetuously on the Huguenot regiments, which, not being provided with pikes, began to give ground. Caillemot received a mortal wound in the thigh. Four of his men carried him back across the ford to his tent. Schomberg, who had remained on the northern bank, and who had thence watched the progress of his troops with the eye of a general, now thought that the emergency required from him the personal exertion of a soldier. Without defensive armour he rode through the river, and rallied the refugees whom the fall of Caillemot had dismayed. 'Come on,' he cried in French, pointing to the Popish squadrons: 'come on, gentlemen: there are your persecutors.' Those were his last words. As he spoke, a band of Irish horsemen rushed upon him and encircled him for a moment. When they retired, he was on the ground. His friends raised him: but he was already a corpse.

During near half an hour the battle continued to rage along the southern shore of the river. All was smoke, dust, and din. But, just at this conjuncture, William came up with the left wing. He had found much difficulty in crossing. His charger had been forced to swim, and had been almost lost in the mud. As soon as the King was on firm ground he took his sword in his left hand – for his right arm was stiff with his wound and his bandage – and led his men to the place where the fight was hottest. One ball struck the cap of his pistol: another carried off the heel of his jackboot: but his lieutenants in vain implored him to retire to some station from which he could give his orders without exposing a life so valuable to Europe. His troops, animated by his example, gained ground fast. The Irish cavalry made their last stand at a house called Plottin Castle, about a mile and a half south of Oldbridge. There the Enniskilleners were repelled with the loss of fifty men, and were hotly pursued, till William rallied them and turned the chase back. In this encounter Richard Hamilton was severely wounded, taken prisoner, and instantly brought before the prince whom he had foully wronged. On no occasion did the character of William show itself in a more striking manner. 'Is this business over?' he said; 'or will your horse make more fight?' 'On my honour, sir,' answered Hamilton, 'I believe that they will.' 'Your honour!' muttered William: 'your honour!' That half suppressed exclamation was the only revenge which he condescended to take for an injury for which many sovereigns would have exacted a terrible retribution. Then, restraining himself, he ordered his own surgeon to look to the hurts of the captive.

And now the battle was over. Hamilton was mistaken in thinking that his horse would continue to fight. Whole troops had been cut to pieces. It was enough that these gallant soldiers had disputed the field till they were left without support, or hope, or guidance, till their bravest leader was a captive, and till their King had fled.

James had watched, from a safe distance, the beginning of the battle on which his fate and the fate of his race depended. When it became clear that the day was going against Ireland, he was seized with an apprehension that his flight might be intercepted, and galloped towards Dublin. The French auxiliaries, who had been employed the whole morning in keeping William's right wing in check, covered the flight of the beaten army. The retreat was effected with less loss than might have been expected; for William did not show in the pursuit the energy which he had shown in the battle.

The slaughter had been less than on any battle field of equal importance and celebrity. Of the Irish only about fifteen hundred had fallen: but they

Marshal Schomberg, veteran of a series of great actions and William's senior commander, fell during the Battle of the Boyne and was buried at Dublin.

were almost all cavalry, the flower of the army, whose place could not easily be supplied. The loss of the conquerors did not exceed five hundred men: but among them was the first captain in Europe. It was announced that the brave veteran would have a public funeral at Westminster. In the meantime his corpse was embalmed with such skill as could be found in the camp, and was deposited in a leaden coffin.

The victorious army advanced that day to Duleek, and passed the warm summer night there under the open sky. On the following day, Drogheda surrendered without a blow, and the garrison, thirteen hundred strong, marched out unarmed.

Meanwhile Dublin had been in violent commotion. From daybreak on the 1st of July the streets were filled with persons eagerly asking and telling news. Towards five in the afternoon, a few runaways on tired horses came straggling in with evil tidings. By six it was known that all was lost. Soon after sunset, James, escorted by two hundred cavalry, rode into the castle.

And now the tide of fugitives came in fast. Till midnight all the northern avenues of the capital were choked by trains of cars and by bands of dragoons. At two in the morning Dublin was still: but, before the early dawn of midsummer, the horse came pouring through the streets, with ranks fearfully thinned, yet preserving, even in that extremity, some show of military order. Two hours later Lauzun's drums were heard; and the French regiments, in unbroken array, marched into the city.

Before six o'clock, the Lord Mayor and some of the principal Roman Catholic citizens were summoned in haste to the castle. James took leave of them with a speech which did him little honour. He had often, he said, been warned that Irishmen would never acquit themselves well on a field of battle; and he had now found that the warning was but too true. 'I will never command an Irish army again. I must shift for myself; and so must you.' He took his departure, crossed the Wicklow hills with all speed, and never stopped till he was fifty miles from Dublin. At sunrise on the 3rd of July he reached the harbour of Waterford. Thence he went by sea to Kinsale, where he embarked on board of a French frigate, and sailed for Brest.

After his departure the confusion in Dublin increased hourly. Guards were posted at the gates: the castle was occupied by a strong body of troops; and it was generally supposed that the enemy would not be admitted without a struggle. But towards the evening Tyrconnel and Lauzun collected all their forces, and marched out of the city. Instantly the face of things in Dublin was changed. The Protestants everywhere came forth from their hiding places. At eight that evening a troop of English dragoons arrived. They were met by the whole Protestant population on College Green. Hundreds embraced the soldiers, hung fondly about the necks of the horses, and ran wildly about, shaking hands with each other. On the morrow a large body of cavalry arrived; and soon from every side came news of the effects which the victory of the Boyne had produced. Within twenty-five miles of the capital there was not a Papist in arms.

William fixed his head quarters at Finglass, about two miles from Dublin. Thence, on the morning of Sunday the 6th of July, he rode in great state to the cathedral, and there, with the Crown on his head, returned public thanks to God. There the remains of Schomberg were deposited, as it was then thought, only for a time; and there they still remain.

William meanwhile received from Mary a letter requesting him to decide an important question on which the Council of Nine was divided. Marlborough was of opinion that all danger of invasion was over for that year. The sea, he said, was open: for the French ships had returned into port, and were refitting. Now was the time to send an English fleet, with five thousand troops on board, to the southern extremity of Ireland. Such a force might easily reduce Cork and Kinsale, two of the most important strongholds still occupied by the forces of James. William highly approved of the plan, and gave orders that it should be executed by the general who had formed it.

William was now advancing towards Limerick. In that city the army which he had put to rout at the Boyne had taken refuge. He would not have had the trouble of besieging the place, if the advice of Lauzun and of Lauzun's countrymen had been followed. They laughed at the thought of defending such fortifications, and indeed would not admit that the name of fortifications could properly be given to heaps of dirt. Lauzun therefore gave his voice for evacuating Limerick. The truth is, that the judgment of the adventurous Frenchman was biassed by his inclinations. He and his companions were sick of Ireland. The dull, squalid, barbarous life, which they had now been leading during several months, was more than they could bear.

Very different was the feeling of the children of the soil. On the day of the Boyne the courage of the ill trained and ill commanded kernes had ebbed to the lowest point. When they had rallied at Limerick, their blood was up. With one voice officers and men insisted that the city should be defended to the last. At the head of those who were for resisting was the brave Colonel Patrick Sarsfield; and his exhortations diffused through all ranks a spirit resembling his own.

Tyrconnel was altogether incompetent to decide the question on which the French and the Irish differed. He would probably, had his temper been as hot as in the old days, have voted for running any risk however desperate. But age, pain, and sickness had left little of the ranting, bullying, fighting Dick Talbot of the Restoration. He had sunk into deep despondency. His wife was already in France with the little which remained of his once ample fortune: his own wish was to follow her thither; his voice was therefore given for abandoning the city.

At last a compromise was made. Lauzun and Tyrconnel, with the French troops, retired to Galway. The great body of the native army, about twenty thousand strong, remained at Limerick.

Lauzun and Tyrconnel had scarcely departed when the advanced guard of William's army came in sight. Soon the King himself, accompanied by Auverquerque and Ginkell, rode forward to examine the fortifications. The general expectation in the English camp was that the city would be an easy conquest. Nor was that expectation unreasonable: for even Sarsfield desponded. One chance, in his opinion, there still was. William had brought with him none but small guns. Several large pieces of ordnance were slowly following from Cashel. If the guns and gunpowder could be intercepted and destroyed, there might be some hope.

A few hours, therefore, after the English tents had been pitched before Limerick, Sarsfield set forth, under cover of the night, with a strong body of horse and dragoons. During the day he lurked with his band in a wild mountain tract named from the silver mines which it contains. In this desolate region Sarsfield found no lack of guides: for all the peasantry of Munster were zealous on his side. He learned in the evening that the detachment which guarded the English artillery had halted for the night, seven miles from William's camp. When it was dark the Irish horsemen were conducted to the spot where the escort lay sleeping round the guns. The surprise was complete. Some of the English sprang to their arms and made an attempt to resist, but in vain. About sixty fell. One only was taken alive. The rest fled. The victorious Irish made a huge pile of waggons and pieces of cannon. Every gun was stuffed with powder, and fixed with its mouth in the ground; and the whole mass was blown up.

Sarsfield had long been the favourite of his countrymen; and this most seasonable exploit raised him still higher in their estimation. Their spirits rose; and the besiegers began to lose heart. William did his best to repair his loss. Batteries were constructed of small field pieces, which made some impression on the feeble defences of Limerick. But soon the autumnal rain began to fall. Cases of fever had already occurred; and there was reason to fear that the roads, already deep in mud, would soon be in such a state that

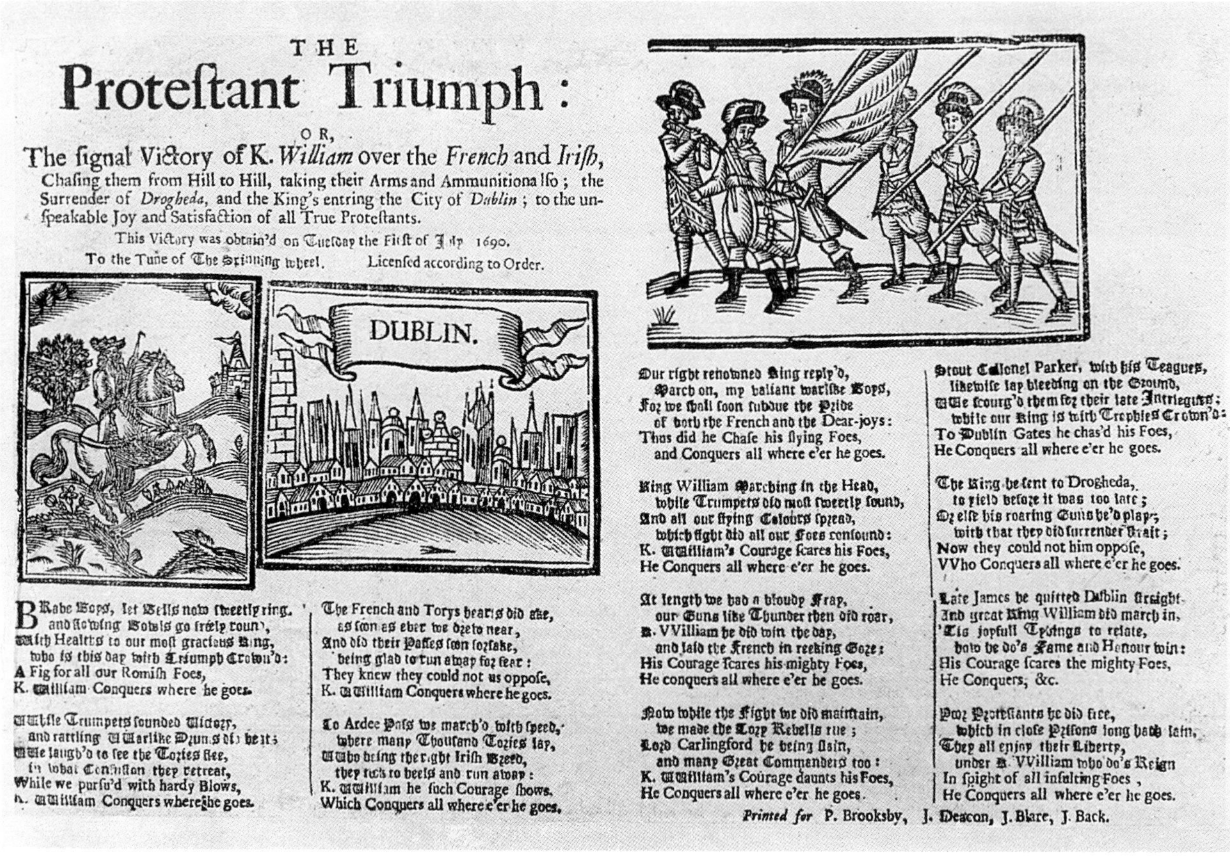

THE

Proteſtant Triumph:

OR,

The ſignal Victory of K. *William* over the *French* and *Iriſh*,

Chaſing them from Hill to Hill, taking their Arms and Ammunition a lſo; the Surrender of *Drogheda*, and the King's entring the City of *Dublin*; to the unſpeakable Joy and Satisfaction of all True Proteſtants.

This Victory was obtain'd on Tueſday the Firſt of July 1690.

To the Tune of The Spinning Wheel. Licenſed according to Order.

Brave Boys, let Bells now ſweetly ring,
and flowing Bowls go freely round,
With Healths to our moſt gracious King,
who is this day with Triumph Crown'd:
A Fig for all our Romiſh Foes,
K. William Conquers where he goes.

While Trumpets ſounded Victory,
and rattling Warlike Drums did beat;
We laugh'd to ſee the Tories flee,
in what Confuſion they retreat,
While we purſu'd with hardy Blows,
K. William Conquers where he goes.

The French and Torys hearts did ake,
as ſoon as ever we drew near,
And did their Paſſes ſoon forſake,
being glad to run away for fear:
They knew they could not us oppoſe,
K. William Conquers where he goes.

To Ardee Paſs we march'd with ſpeed,
where many Thouſand Tories lay,
Who being the right Iriſh Breed,
they took to heels and run away:
K. William he ſuch Courage ſhows,
Which Conquers all where e'er he goes.

Our right renowned King reply'd,
March on, my valiant warlike Boys,
For we ſhall ſoon ſubdue the Pride
of both the French and the Dear-joys:
Thus did he Chaſe his flying Foes,
and Conquers all where e'er he goes.

King William Marching in the Head,
while Trumpets did moſt ſweetly ſound,
And all our flying Colours ſpread,
which ſight did all our Foes confound:
K. William's Courage ſcares his Foes,
He Conquers all where e'er he goes.

At length we had a bloudy Fray,
our Guns like Thunder then did roar,
K. VVilliam he did win the day,
and laid the French in reeking Gore:
His Courage ſcares his mighty Foes,
He conquers all where e'er he goes.

Now while the Fight we did maintain,
we made the Tory Rebells rue;
Lord Carlingford he being ſlain,
and many Great Commenders too:
K. William's Courage daunts his Foes,
He Conquers all where e'er he goes.

Stout Collonel Parker, with his Teagues,
likewiſe lay bleeding on the Ground,
We ſcourg'd them for their late Intrigues;
while our King is with Trophies Crown'd:
To Dublin Gates he chas'd his Foes,
He Conquers all where e'er he goes.

The King he ſent to Drogheda,
to yield before it was too late;
Or elſe his roaring Guns he'd play;
with that they did ſurrender ſtrait;
Now they could not him oppoſe,
VVho Conquers all where e'er he goes.

Late James he quitted Dublin ſtraight
And great King William did march in,
'Tis joyfull Tydings to relate,
how he do's Fame and Honour win:
His Courage ſcares the mighty Foes,
He Conquers, &c.

Poor Proteſtants he did free,
which in cloſe Priſons long hath lain,
They all enjoy their Liberty,
under K. VVilliam who do's Reign
In ſpight of all inſulting Foes,
He Conquers all where e'er he goes.

Printed for P. Brooksby, J. Deacon, J. Blare, J. Back.

Broadsheet celebrating the victory of William at the Boyne and his triumphant entry into Dublin.

no wheeled carriage could be dragged through them. The King determined to raise the siege, and to move his troops to a healthier region.

It was with no pleasurable emotions that Lauzun and Tyrconnel learned at Galway the fortunate issue of the conflict in which they had refused to take part. They were weary of Ireland: they were apprehensive that their conduct might be unfavourably represented in France: they therefore determined to be beforehand with their accusers, and took ship together for the Continent.

William meanwhile proceeded to Waterford, and sailed thence for England. When he arrived in London, the expedition destined for Cork was ready to sail from Portsmouth; and Marlborough had been some time on board waiting for a fair wind. He was accompanied by Grafton. On the 18th of September the fleet stood out to sea, and, on the 21st, appeared before the harbour of Cork. The troops landed, and were speedily joined by the Duke of Wurtemberg, with several regiments detached from the army which had lately besieged Limerick.

Cork was vigorously attacked; and in forty-eight hours all was over. Through a bog known by the name of the Rape Marsh, four English regiments, up to their shoulders in water, advanced to the assault. Grafton, ever foremost in danger, was struck by a shot from the ramparts, and was carried back dying. The close fighting was just about to begin when a parley was beaten. Articles of capitulation were speedily adjusted; and the garrison, between four and five thousand men, became prisoners.

No commander has ever understood better than Marlborough how to improve a victory. A few hours after Cork had fallen, his cavalry were on the road to Kinsale. A trumpeter was sent to summon the place. The Irish set fire to the town, and retired into two forts called the Old and the New. The English horse arrived just in time to extinguish the flames. Marlborough speedily followed with his infantry. The Old Fort was scaled; and four hundred and fifty men who defended it were killed or taken. The New Fort it was necessary to attack in a more methodical way. Batteries were planted: trenches were opened: mines were sprung: in a few days the besiegers were masters of the counterscarp; and all was ready for storming, when the governor offered to capitulate. The garrison, twelve hundred strong, was suffered to retire to Limerick; but the conquerors took possession of the stores.

Marlborough's success had been complete and rapid. He presented himself at Kensington only five weeks after he had sailed from Portsmouth, and was most graciously received. 'No officer living,' said William, 'who has seen so little service as my Lord Marlborough, is so fit for great commands.'

The End of the Irish War

The nonjuring bishops had, during the year which followed their deprivation, continued to reside in the official mansions which had once been their own. Burnet had, at Mary's request, laboured to effect a compromise. Sancroft and his brethren were informed that, if they would consent to perform their spiritual duty, a bill should be brought into Parliament to excuse them from taking the oaths. The offer was imprudently liberal: but those to whom it was made could not consistently accept it. For in almost every service of the Church, William and Mary were designated as King and Queen. The only promise that could be obtained from the deprived prelates was that they would live quietly; and even this promise they had not all kept. It was now evident that William's forbearance had only emboldened the adversaries whom he had hoped to conciliate. Even Caermarthen, even Nottingham, declared that it was high time to fill the vacant sees.

John Tillotson was nominated to the archbishopric, and was consecrated on Whitsunday, in the Church of Saint Mary Le Bow. The crowd which lined the streets greeted the new Primate warmly. For he had, during many years, preached in the City; and his eloquence, his probity, and the gentleness of his temper and manners, had made him the favourite of the Londoners. But the applause of his friends could not drown the roar of execration which the Jacobites set up. According to them, he was a thief who had not entered by the door, but had climbed over the fences. The storm of obloquy which he had to face for the first time at more than sixty years of age was too much for him. His spirits declined: his health gave way: yet he neither flinched from his duty nor attempted to revenge himself on his persecutors. After his death a bundle of the savage lampoons which the nonjurors had circulated against him was found among his papers with this indorsement: 'I pray God forgive them: I do.'

In May 1691 William set out for the Continent, where the regular campaign was about to open. The military operations in Flanders commenced early in June and terminated at the close of September. No important action took place. The two armies marched and countermarched, drew near and receded. Languid as the campaign was, it is on one account remarkable. During more than a century our country had sent no great force to make war by land out of the British isles. In 1691, for the first time since Henry VIII laid siege to Boulogne, an English army appeared on the Continent under the command of an English king.

While the hostile armies watched each other in Flanders, hostilities were carried on with somewhat more vigour in other parts of Europe. But nowhere were the events of the summer so important as in Ireland.

From October 1690 till May 1691, no military operation on a large scale was attempted in that kingdom. The area of the island was not unequally divided between the contending races. The whole of Ulster, the greater part of Leinster, and about one third of Munster had submitted to the English. The whole of Connaught, the greater part of Munster, and two or three counties of Leinster were held by the Irish.

On the English side of the pale there was a rude and imperfect order. Two Lords Justices, assisted by a Privy Council, represented King William at Dublin Castle. The colonists had been formed into a strong militia, under the command of officers who had commissions from the Crown. Trade and industry had begun to revive. The fugitives who had taken refuge in England came back in multitudes; and, by their intelligence, diligence, and thrift, the devastation caused by two years of confusion and robbery was soon in part repaired.

In that part of Ireland, meanwhile, which still acknowledged James as King, there could hardly be said to be any law, any property, or any government. The Roman Catholics of Ulster and Leinster had fled westward by tens of thousands, driving before them a large part of the cattle which had escaped the havoc of two terrible years. The influx of food into the Celtic region, however, was far from keeping pace with the influx of consumers. An incessant predatory war raged along the line which separated the domain of William from that of James. Every day companies of freebooters stole into the English territory, burned, sacked, pillaged, and hastened back to their own ground. To guard against these incursions was not easy; for the peasantry of the plundered country had a strong fellow feeling with the plunderers.

Early in the spring Tyrconnel returned, and was received at Limerick, even by his enemies, with decent respect. He had been authorised to announce that he should soon be followed by several ships, laden with provisions and military stores. This announcement was most welcome to the troops, who had long been without bread, and who had nothing stronger than water to drink.

During some weeks the supplies were impatiently expected. Even the beef and mutton, which, half raw, half burned, had hitherto supported the army, had been scarce; and the common men were on rations of horseflesh when the promised sails were seen in the mouth of the Shannon.

A distinguished French general, named Saint Ruth, was on board with his staff. He brought a commission which appointed him commander in chief of the Irish army, and was assisted by another general officer named D'Usson. The French ships brought some arms, some ammunition, and a plentiful supply of corn and flour. The spirits of the Irish rose; and the Te Deum was chaunted with fervent devotion in the cathedral of Limerick.

On the other side of the Pale, all was ready for action. The greater part of the English force was collected, before the close of May, in the neighbourhood of Mullingar. Ginkell commanded in chief. He had under him the two best officers, after Marlborough, of whom our island could then boast,

Talmash and Mackay. The Marquess of Ruvigny, the hereditary chief of the refugees, and elder brother of that brave Caillemot who had fallen at the Boyne, had joined the army with the rank of major general.

On the 6th of June Ginkell moved his head quarters from Mullingar. On the 7th he reached Ballymore. At Ballymore stood an ancient fortress, which was defended by above a thousand men. The English guns were instantly planted. In a few hours the besiegers had the satisfaction of seeing the besieged running like rabbits from one shelter to another. The governor begged piteously for quarter, and obtained it. The whole garrison was marched off to Dublin.

Ginkell passed some days in reconstructing the defences of Ballymore. This work had scarcely been performed when he was joined by the Danish auxiliaries under the command of the Duke of Wurtemberg. The whole army then moved westward, and, on the 19th of June, appeared before the walls of Athlone.

Athlone was perhaps, in a military point of view, the most important place in the island. The town, which was surrounded by ramparts of earth, lay partly in Leinster and partly in Connaught. The English quarter, which was in Leinster, had once consisted of new and handsome houses, but had been burned by the Irish some months before, and now lay in heaps of ruin. The Celtic quarter, which was in Connaught, was old and meanly built. The Shannon, which is the boundary of the two provinces, rushed through Athlone in a deep and rapid stream, and turned two large mills which rose on the arches of a stone bridge. Above the bridge, on the Connaught side, a castle towered to the height of seventy feet, and extended two hundred feet along the river. Fifty or sixty yards below the bridge was a narrow ford.

During the night of the 19th the English placed their cannon. On the morning of the 20th the firing began. At five in the afternoon an assault was made. The Irish gave way and ran towards the bridge; and in a few hours Ginkell had made himself master of the English quarter of Athlone.

But his work was only begun. Between him and the Irish town the Shannon ran fiercely. The bridge was so narrow that a few resolute men might keep it against an army. The mills which stood on it were strongly guarded; and it was commanded by the guns of the castle.

On the 21st the English were busied in flinging up batteries along the Leinster bank. On the 22nd, soon after dawn, the cannonade began. The firing continued all that day and the following night. When morning broke again, one whole side of the castle had been beaten down. Still however the Irish defended the bridge resolutely. During several days there was sharp fighting hand to hand in the strait passage. The courage of the garrison was sustained by the hope of speedy succour. Saint Ruth had completed his preparations; and the tidings that Athlone was in danger had induced him to take the field in haste at the head of an army. He seems to have thought that the bridge and the ford might easily be defended till the autumnal rains, and the pestilence which ordinarily accompanied them, should compel the enemy to retire. He therefore contented himself with sending successive detachments to reinforce the garrison. The immediate conduct of the defence he entrusted to his second in command, D'Usson, and fixed his own head quarters two or three miles from the town.

On the 30th of June Ginkell called a council of war. The difficulty of effecting a passage over the bridge seemed almost insuperable. It was

proposed to try the ford. The Duke of Wurtemberg, Talmash, and Ruvigny gave their voices in favour of this plan; and Ginkell consented.

It was determined that the attempt should be made that very afternoon. The Irish, fancying that the English were about to retreat, kept guard carelessly. Meanwhile, fifteen hundred grenadiers, each wearing in his hat a green bough, were mustered on the Leinster bank of the Shannon. Mackay commanded. He did not approve of the plan: but he executed it as zealously as if he had himself been the author of it.

It was six o'clock. A peal from the steeple of the church gave the signal. The grenadiers, with a great shout, plunged twenty abreast up to their cravats in water. In a few minutes the head of the column reached dry land. The Irish, taken unprepared, fired one confused volley and fled. The conquerors clambered up the bank over the remains of walls shattered by a cannonade of ten days. Planks were placed on the broken arches of the bridge, and pontoons laid on the river, without any opposition on the part of the terrified garrison. With the loss of twelve men killed and about thirty wounded the English had forced their way into Connaught.

At the first alarm D'Usson hastened towards the river; but he was met, swept away, trampled down, and almost killed by the torrent of fugitives. He was carried to the camp in such a state that it was necessary to bleed him. 'Taken!' cried Saint Ruth, in dismay. 'It cannot be. A town taken, and I close by with an army to relieve it!' Cruelly mortified, he struck his tents under cover of the night, and retreated in the direction of Galway. He pitched his camp about thirty miles from Athlone, near the ruined castle of Aghrim, and determined to await the approach of the English army.

The spot on which he had determined to bring the fate of Ireland to issue seems to have been chosen with great judgment. His army was drawn up on the slope of a hill, which was almost surrounded by red bog. In front, near the edge of the morass, were some fences out of which a breastwork was without difficulty constructed.

On the 11th of July, Ginkell fixed his head quarters at Ballinasloe, about four miles from Aghrim, and rode forward to take a view of the Irish position. On his return, he gave orders that early on the morrow every man should be under arms without beat of drum. Two regiments were to remain in charge of the camp: the rest were to march against the enemy.

Soon after six, the next morning, the English were on the way to Aghrim. But some delay was occasioned by a thick fog which hung till noon over the moist valley of the Suck; and the afternoon was far advanced when the two armies at length confronted each other with nothing but the bog and the breastwork between them. The English and their allies were under twenty thousand; the Irish above twenty-five thousand.

At five the battle began. The English foot made their way, sinking deep in mud at every step, to the Irish works. Again and again the assailants were driven back. Again and again they returned to the struggle. The fight had lasted two hours: the evening was closing in; and still the advantage was on the side of the Irish. But Mackay and Ruvigny, with the English and Huguenot cavalry, had succeeded in passing the bog at a place where two horsemen could scarcely ride abreast. Saint Ruth at first laughed when he saw the Blues, in single file, struggling through the morass under a fire which every moment laid some gallant hat and feather on the earth. But soon he saw them laying hurdles on the quagmire. A broader and safer path was formed: squadron after squadron reached firm ground: the flank

William Bentinck, first Earl of Portland, was the closest friend and confidant of the seemingly cold-blooded William. As a young man he had nursed the Prince through a severe attack of smallpox, an episode never forgotten by William.

of the Irish army was speedily turned. The French general was hastening to the rescue when a cannon ball carried off his head. Till the fight was over neither army was aware that he was no more. The crisis of the battle had arrived; and there was none to give direction. Mackay and Ruvigny with their horse charged the Irish in flank. Talmash and his foot returned to the attack in front with dogged determination. The breastwork was carried. The Irish, still fighting, retreated from enclosure to enclosure. At length they broke and fled.

The beaten army had now lost all the appearance of an army. One great stream of fugitives ran towards Galway, another towards Limerick. The conquerors marched first against Galway. D'Usson was there, and had under him seven regiments, thinned by the slaughter of Aghrim and utterly disheartened. He soon saw that resistance was impossible, and made haste to capitulate. The garrison was suffered to retire to Limerick with the honours of war.

The infantry assembled at Limerick were about fifteen thousand men. The Irish horse and dragoons, three or four thousand in number, were encamped on the Clare side of the Shannon. The communication between their camp and the city was maintained by means of a bridge called the Thomond Bridge, which was protected by a fort. These means of defence were not contemptible. But the fall of Athlone and the slaughter of Aghrim had broken the spirit of the army. Tyrconnel himself was convinced that all was lost. His only hope was that he might be able to prolong the struggle till he could receive from Saint Germains permission to treat. He wrote to request that permission, and prevailed on his countrymen to bind themselves by an oath not to capitulate till an answer from James should arrive.

A few days after the oath had been administered, Tyrconnel was no more. On the 11th of August he dined with D'Usson. The party was gay. The Lord Lieutenant seemed to have thrown off the load which had bowed down his body and mind. Soon after he had risen from table, an apoplectic stroke deprived him of speech and sensation. On the 14th be breathed his last.

On the day on which Tyrconnel died, the advanced guard of the English army came within sight of Limerick. Ginkell encamped on the same ground which William had occupied twelve months before. The batteries played day and night; and soon roofs were blazing and walls crashing in every part of the city.

Ginkell was bent on cutting off all communication between Limerick and the county of Clare. He attacked the fort which protected the Thomond Bridge. The soldiers who had garrisoned it fled to the city. The town major, a French officer, who commanded at the Thomond Gate, afraid that the pursuers would enter with the fugitives, ordered that part of the bridge which was nearest to the city to be drawn up. Many of the Irish went headlong into the stream and perished there. Others cried for quarter, and held up handkerchiefs in token of submission. But the conquerors were mad with rage; and no prisoners were made till the heaps of corpses rose above the parapets.

This disaster seemed likely to produce a general mutiny in the besieged city. The cry for capitulation became so loud and importunate that the generals could not resist it. On the evening of the following day, the drums of Limerick beat a parley; and Ginkell willingly consented to an armistice. A negotiation was therefore opened with a sincere desire on both sides to put an end to the contest. It was agreed that there should be a cessation of arms, and that a fleet of French transports should be suffered to come up the Shannon in peace and to depart in peace. The signing of the treaty was deferred till the Lords Justices, who represented William at Dublin, should arrive at Ginkell's quarters.

On the 1st of October they arrived. On the 2nd the articles of capitulation were definitively settled. On the 3rd they were signed. It was agreed that such Irish officers and soldiers as should declare that they wished to go to France should be conveyed thither, and should, in the meantime, remain under the command of their own generals. Part of Limerick was to be immediately delivered up to the English. But the island on which the cathedral and the castle stand was to remain in the keeping of the Irish.

Soon the exiles departed, to learn in foreign camps that discipline without which natural courage is of small avail, and to retrieve on distant fields of battle the honour which had been lost by a long series of defeats at home. In Ireland there was peace. The domination of the colonists was absolute. The native population was tranquil with the ghastly tranquillity of exhaustion and of despair.

The Battle of La Hogue

On the 6th of March 1692, William set out for the Continent, leaving the Queen his vicegerent in England. He would perhaps have postponed his departure if he had been aware that the French government had, during some time, been making great preparations for a descent on our island.

Louis had yielded to the importunity of James. It was resolved that a camp should be formed on the coast of Normandy, and that in this camp all the Irish regiments which were in the French service should be assembled under their countryman Sarsfield. With them were to be joined about ten thousand French troops. The whole army was to be commanded by Marshal Bellefonds. Four and forty men of war, some of which were among the finest that had ever been built, were assembled in the harbour of Brest under Tourville. Three hundred transports were collected near the spot where the troops were to embark. It was hoped that all would be ready early in the spring, before the English ships were half rigged or half manned, and before a single Dutch man of war was in the Channel.

James was on the point of setting out for the place of embarkation before the English government was at all aware of the danger which was impending. It had been long known indeed that many thousands of Irish were assembled in Normandy: but it was supposed that they had been assembled merely that they might be mustered and drilled before they were sent to Flanders, Piedmont, and Catalonia. Now, however, intelligence, arriving from many quarters, left no doubt that an invasion would be almost immediately attempted. Vigorous preparations for defence were made. Before the end of April the English fleet was ready to sail. William had been hastening the maritime preparations of the United Provinces; and his exertions had been successful. The whole force of the confederate powers was assembled at Saint Helen's in the second week of May, more than ninety sail of the line, manned by between thirty and forty thousand of the finest seamen of the two great maritime nations. Russell had the chief command. He was assisted by Sir Ralph Delaval, Sir John Ashby, Sir Cloudesley Shovel, Rear Admiral Carter, and Rear Admiral Rooke. Of the Dutch officers Van Almonde was highest in rank.

On the 15th of May the masts of Tourville's squadron were seen from the cliffs of Portland. One messenger galloped with the news from Weymouth to London. Another took the coast road, and carried the intelligence to Russell. All was ready; and on the morning of the 17th the allied fleet stood out to sea.

Tourville had received positive orders to protect the descent on England, and not to decline a battle. Though these orders had been given before it was known at Versailles that the Dutch and English fleets had joined, he was not disposed to take on himself the responsibility of disobedience. He sailed from Brest, steered first towards the north east, came in sight of the coast of Dorsetshire, and then struck across the Channel towards La Hogue, where the army which he was to convoy to England had already begun to embark on board of the transports. He was within a few leagues of Barfleur when, before sunrise, on the morning of the 19th of May, he saw the great armament of the allies stretching along the eastern horizon. He determined to bear down on them. By eight the two lines of battle were formed; but it was eleven before the firing began.

Carter was the first who broke the French line. He was struck by a splinter of one of his own yardarms, and fell dying on the deck. He would not be carried below. He would not let go his sword. 'Fight the ship,' were his last words: 'fight the ship as long as she can swim.' The battle lasted till four in the afternoon. During the earlier part of the day the wind was favourable to the French: they were opposed to only half of the allied fleet; and against that half they maintained the conflict with their usual courage and with more than their usual seamanship. After a hard and doubtful fight of five hours, Tourville thought that enough had been done to maintain the honour of the white flag, and began to draw off. But by this time the wind had veered, and was with the allies. They were now able to avail themselves of their great superiority of force. They came on fast. The retreat of the French became a flight. Tourville fought his own ship desperately. She was named, in allusion to Louis's favourite emblem, the *Royal Sun*, and was widely renowned as the finest vessel in the world. Surrounded by enemies, she lay like a great fortress on the sea, scattering death on every side from her hundred and four portholes. Long after sunset, she got clear of her assailants, and, with all her scuppers spouting blood, made for the coast of Normandy. She had suffered so much that Tourville removed his flag to a ship of ninety guns which was named the *Ambitious*. By this time his fleet was scattered far over the sea. About twenty of his smallest ships made their escape by a road which was too perilous for any courage but the courage of despair. In the double darkness of night and of a thick sea fog, they ran, with all their sails spread, through the boiling waves and treacherous rocks of the Race of Alderney, and, by a strange good fortune, arrived without a single disaster at Saint Maloes.

Those French vessels which were too bulky to venture into the Race of Alderney fled to the havens of the Cotentin. The *Royal Sun* and two other three-deckers reached Cherburg in safety. The *Ambitious*, with twelve other ships, took refuge in the Bay of La Hogue.

The three ships which had fled to Cherburg were closely chased by an English squadron under the command of Delaval. He found them hauled up into shoal water where no large man of war could get at them. He therefore determined to attack them with his fireships and boats. In a short time the *Royal Sun* and her two consorts were burned to ashes. Part of the crews escaped to the shore; and part fell into the hands of the English.

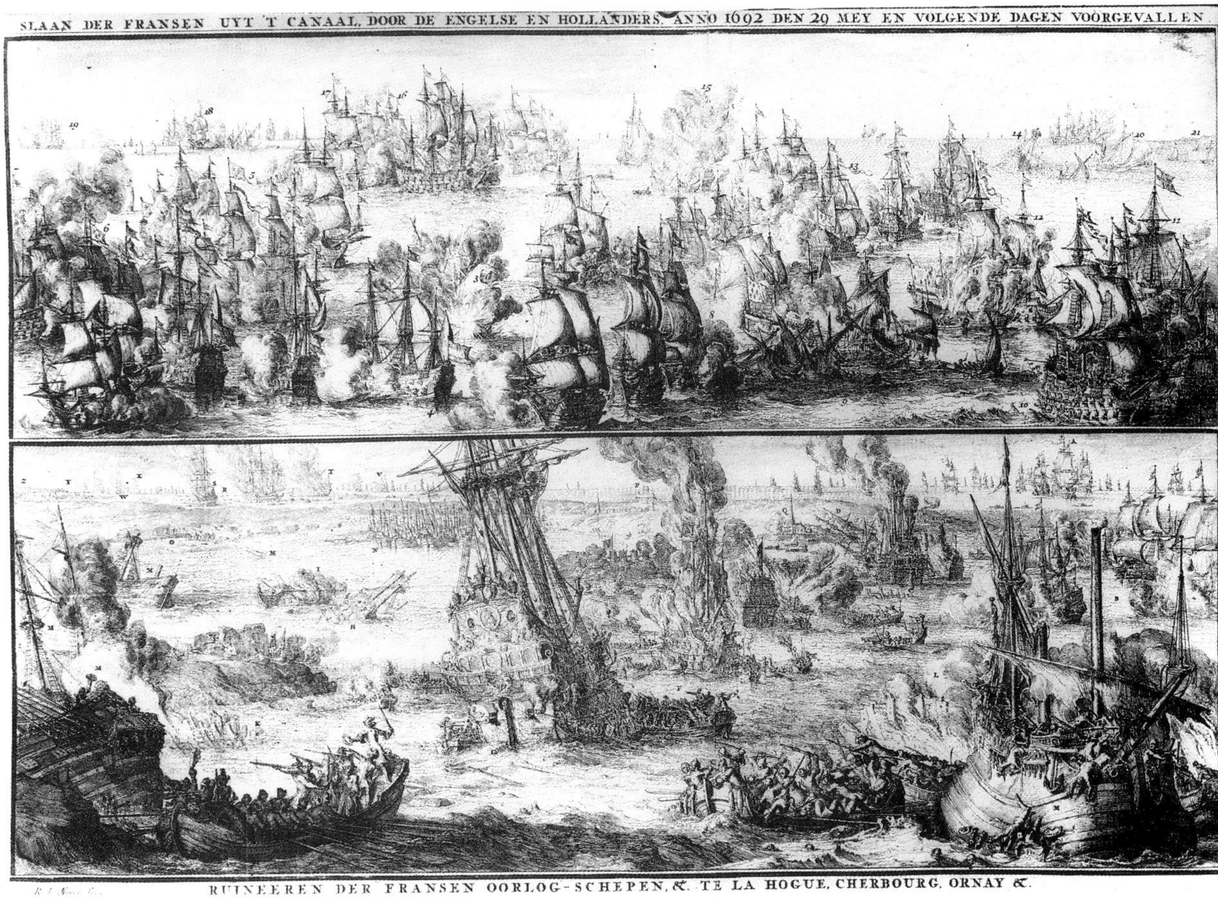

SLAAN DER FRANSEN UYT 'T CANAAL, DOOR DE ENGELSE EN HOLLANDERS. ANNO 1692 DEN 29 MEY EN VOLGENDE DAGEN VOORGEVALLEN.
RUINEEREN DER FRANSEN OORLOG-SCHEPEN, &c. TE LA HOGUE, CHERBOURG, ORNAY &c.

The total defeat of the French Fleet by the British and Dutch at La Hogue: a contemporary Dutch print. Macaulay records that 'this was the first great check that had ever been given to the arms of Louis XIV, and the first great victory that the English had gained over the French since the day of Agincourt'.

Meanwhile Russell with the greater part of his fleet had blockaded the Bay of La Hogue. Here, as at Cherburg, the French men of war had been drawn up into shallow water. They were close to the camp of the army which was destined for the invasion of England. Six of them were moored under a fort named Lisset. The rest lay under the guns of another fort named Saint Vaast, where James had fixed his headquarters.

Russell prepared for an attack. On the afternoon of the 23rd of May all was ready. A flotilla consisting of sloops, of fireships, and of two hundred boats, was entrusted to the command of Rooke. The rowers pulled manfully and with loud huzzas towards the six huge wooden castles which lay close to Fort Lisset. Tourville ordered his sailors to man their boats, and would have led them to encounter the enemy in the bay. But his example and his exhortations were vain. His boats turned round and fled in confusion. The English boarded the men of war, set them on fire, and having performed this great service without the loss of a single life, retreated at a late hour with the retreating tide.

At eight the next morning the tide came back strong; and with the tide came back Rooke and his two hundred boats. The enemy made a faint attempt to defend the vessels which were near Fort Saint Vaast: but the struggle was soon over. The French poured fast out of their ships on one side: the English poured in as fast on the other, and, with loud shouts, turned the captured guns against the shore. James, Bellefonds, and Tourville looked on in helpless despondency while the second conflagration proceeded. The conquerors, leaving the ships of war in flames, made their way into an inner basin where many transports lay. Eight of these vessels were set on fire. Several were taken in tow; and the victorious flotilla slowly retired, insulting the hostile camp with a thundering chant of 'God save the King'.

Thus ended, at noon on the 24th of May, the great conflict which had raged during five days over a wide extent of sea and shore. One English fireship had perished in its calling. Sixteen French men of war had been sunk or burned down to the water-edge. The battle is called, from the place where it terminated, the battle of La Hogue.

This was the first great check that had ever been given to the arms of Louis XIV, and the first great victory that the English had gained over the French since the day of Agincourt. The stain left on our fame by the shameful defeat of Beachy Head was effaced. This time the glory was all our own. The Dutch had indeed done their duty: but the English had borne the brunt of the fight. Russell who commanded in chief was an Englishman. Delaval who directed the attack on Cherburg was an Englishman. Rooke who led the flotilla into the Bay of La Hogue was an Englishman. Yet the pleasure with which the good news was received here must not be ascribed solely or chiefly to national pride. The island was safe. The pleasant pastures, cornfields and commons of Hampshire and Surrey would not be the seat of war. Whigs and Tories joined in thanking God for this great deliverance; and the most respectable nonjurors could not but be glad at heart that the rightful King was not to be brought back by an army of foreigners.

Acknowledgements

The pictures on pages 57, 69, 71, 72 right, 156, 157, 195 below and 203 are reproduced by gracious permission of Her Majesty The Queen. All other photographs and illustrations are supplied by, or reproduced by kind permission of, the following:

BBC Hulton Picture Library 34, 36, 37, 135, 148 left, 181, 230, 245
D.E. Bower Collection, Chiddingstone Castle, Kent 140, 167
British Library 12
British Museum 9, 15 left, 29, 30, 32, 49, 65, 66, 67, 68, 73 right, 78, 90 below, 94, 99, 120, 124, 126, 139, 163, 171, 178, 185, 186, 190 below, 193
City Museum and Art Gallery, Birmingham 51
Commissioners of the Royal Hospital, Chelsea 144
Courtauld Institute of Art 73 left, 76, 80, 123
Crown Copyright. Royal Library, Windsor 19, 190 above, 197
Mary Evans Picture Library 43, 50, 54–5
Guildhall Museum 154
Mansell Collection 93, 98, 136, 159, 192, 211, 236
His Grace the Duke of Marlborough 207
National Army Museum 45
National Gallery of Scotland 116, 121, 202
National Maritime Museum 23, 86
National Monuments Record 75
National Portrait Gallery 18, 35, 39, 82, 83, 88, 118, 129, 143, 165, 196, 201, 205, 206, 209, 233, 240
Oxford City Council 148 below
Pepys Library, Magdalene College, Oxford 90 above
Public Record Office 8, 189
Rijksmuseum, Amsterdam 85, 187, 195 above, 198
Royal Academy of Arts 151
Earl Spencer 72 left
Mrs P.A. Tritto, Parham Park 161
Victoria and Albert Museum 63, 223
Walker Art Gallery, Liverpool 15 right
Warwick Castle 21
Weidenfeld and Nicolson Archives 6, 10, 13, 24, 26, 40, 41, 61, 87, 109, 115, 117, 125, 199

Endpapers: 'The Procession of Charles II' by Dick Stoop (Private Collection/The Bridgeman Art Library